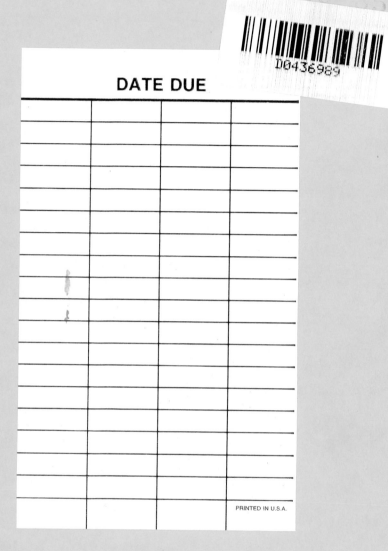

DATE DUE

PRINTED IN U.S.A.

Asian
Power
and
Politics

ASIAN POWER AND POLITICS

The Cultural
Dimensions
of Authority

Lucian W. Pye
With Mary W. Pye

THE BELKNAP PRESS OF
HARVARD UNIVERSITY PRESS
Cambridge, Massachusetts
and London, England 1985

LIBRARY OF CONGRESS CATALOGING IN PUBLICATION DATA

Pye, Lucian W., 1921–
     Asian power and politics.

     Bibliography: p.
     Includes index.
     1. Asia—Politics and government.
2. Asia—Social conditions.
3. Authority.
4. Legitimacy of governments—Asia.
5. Paternalism—Asia.
I. Pye, Mary W.
II. Title.
JQ36.P94   1985   306′.2′095   85-2581
ISBN 0-674-04978-0 (alk. paper)

Designed by Gwen Frankfeldt

Contents

Preface

THROUGHOUT ASIA TODAY the drama of politics is being played out by leaders and followers whose roles are largely prescribed by culturally determined concepts about the nature of power. From India and Southeast Asia to China and Japan, government officials—whether they are civil servants, politicians, or men in uniform—are all experiencing tensions between inherited ideals of authority and imported ideas of what political power can accomplish. The East is thus in the process of extensive change, but it is also pursuing paths different from those the West followed in achieving modernization. Largely because Asian cultures have spawned quite different concepts about what the nature and limits of political power should be, the story of their transformation is unique in the contemporary world.

Briefly put, my thesis is that political power is extraordinarily sensitive to cultural nuances, and that, therefore, cultural variations are decisive in determining the course of political development. More particularly, Asian cultures have historically had a rich variety of concepts of power. They share, however, the common denominator of idealizing benevolent, paternalistic leadership and of legitimizing dependency. Thus, although Europe did succeed in imposing on Asia its legalistic concept of the nation-state, the Asian response has been a new, and powerful, form of nationalism based on paternalistic authority.

Because these paternalistic forms of power answer deep psychological cravings for the security of dependency, peculiarly close ties between leaders and followers have tended to develop and become the critical element in the creation of political power. This process contrasts with political development in the West, where the growth of individual autonomy has taken precedence over the perpetuation of dependency. Thus in the West it seemed natural and inevitable to have persistent conflicts in the political realm between demands for greater popular participation and assertions of sovereign authority. In Asia the masses of the people are more respectful of authority. Their leaders are concerned about questions of dignity, the need to uphold national pride, and other highly symbolic matters. Those in power want above all to be seen as protecting the prestige of the collectivity, which they are inclined to place above the goal of efficiency or of advancing specific interests in concrete ways.

By focusing on the role of power in the political development of Asia, I have sought to return to the fundamentals of modern political science— but with one very important difference. Whereas modern political theorists, from Charles Merriam and Harold Lasswell through Robert Dahl and Samuel P. Huntington, have conceived of power as a universal phenomenon—operating under the same laws whether in ancient Greece or in the contemporary international system of states, in parliaments or in city halls—and moreover have sought to identify its properties scientifically, I have treated power as something that differs profoundly from culture to culture. My argument is that in different times and places people have thought of power in very different ways, and it is precisely these differences that are the governing factors in determining the diverse paths of political development. In my view theories which seek to specify general propositions about power miss the point entirely. Of all social phenomena power is one of the most sensitive to cultural nuances; its potentialities and its limitations are always constrained by time and place.

It is safe to assume that societies have reasonably coherent views about such fundamental political concepts as authority and power, for these are matters that always bulk large in the collective experiences of political cultures and in the personal lives of individuals. Out of the long years of infancy and childhood people develop profound emotional sentiments, and extraordinary fantasies, about how power operates, and in the process they learn ways of managing and manipulating the games basic to superior-subordinate relationships. These early socialization patterns are reinforced by the ways in which religious beliefs about divine powers instruct people in understanding what is involved in a culture's rules about the relationships between guardian leaders and loyal followers.

Given the richness of human ingenuity in playing the roles of superiors and subordinates it might seem that there should be an infinite variety of styles and techniques when it comes to the operations of power. Fortunately for the political scientist, societies tend to cluster the acceptable uses of power into quite limited, but culturally distinctive, patterns. Proof that such nuances of political cultures are important is easily available. Note, for example, that probably no other skill is as sensitive to the parochialism of culture as that of the politician. Politicians simply do not travel well; it is usually a safe bet that the hero in one constituency would have trouble getting elected in another. Could a Boston "pol" make it in Charleston, South Carolina, to say nothing of Tokyo? And is there any American congressional district in which the typical French or Italian prime minister could easily win election? Intellectuals can readily cross national boundaries and win acclaim, but the successful transplanted politician is rare indeed.

In addition to highlighting the subtle cultural differences that shape the modernization of the various Asian countries, it is necessary to trace historical changes in Asian views about power. In ancient times power was generaly associated with beliefs about the role of authority in upholding the cosmic order. Later, with the advance of more secular ideas, power was usually identified with social status. Not until modern times, and so far only to a limited extent in any Asian country, has power been seen as primarily utilitarian, useful for tasks more precise than just sustaining the social order.

It is therefore important in comparing Asia and the West to explore the consequences of treating power as status—with all the accompanying demands for dignity and deference—rather than as decision-making, as setting agendas and determining courses of action. What a society expects of power determines in large degree what it gets from its political system. Should power be used to give a people pride and self-respect, or should it be used to solve detailed practical problems involving competing interests and trade-offs between them?

In comparing the approaches to modernization that result from different cultural ways of defining power and authority I shall not try to rank countries according to their relative "success" in achieving modernization. Athough I shall note how certain approaches to power have created problems while others have facilitated advances, my basic assumption is that all the countries of Asia are undergoing change. If at any one time some may seem to have raced ahead, this does not mean that some other country may not in time "catch up" and go "ahead." My interest in comparison is only to isolate the factors which may help to explain different patterns of development.

From earliest childhood I had to confront the mysteries of cultural differences, but it was only with my first intensive fieldwork experience in Malaya that I gained scientific insights into such differences. In the early 1950s I spent nearly a year interviewing Malayan Chinese who had gone into the jungle to fight under the banner of Marxism–Leninism–Mao Zedong Thought. As I worked on this companion study to Gabriel A. Almond's *Appeals of Communism,* which was based on interviews with former Communists in four Western countries, I was struck by how different my Chinese interviewees were from his American, British, French, and Italian respondents. Whereas the Westerners either demonstrated, or at least rationalized, a craving for autonomy and individual identity, and wanted to be masters of their own fate, my Malayan Chinese wanted above all to achieve a sense of belonging, to be able to submerge their individualism in some larger group and to believe that no matter who led them, he would be in contact with almost magical sources of power.

My eyes were further opened to the value Asians set on dependency when my researches took me to Burma to interview politicians and administrators who were grappling with the problems of nation-building. Again I was to learn that self-evident concepts of Western politics were not applicable because the Burmese had quite different ideas about the nature and the uses of power. Later, fieldwork in Hong Kong and several countries in Southeast Asia and visits to India reinforced my awareness that different cultures emphasize very different views as to what authority should be like or should actually do.

Yet, out of all these experiences I found a common underlying theme. This was that for most Asians the acceptance of authority is not inherently bad but rather is an acceptable key to finding personal security. For most Asians the happiest times in their lives are inevitably their childhood years, when they are the most dependent, whereas autonomy and self-identity usually bring loneliness and the sadness of independence. In addition, the stern demands of filial piety and the imperative to express awe of parental authority generally work to repress oedipal reactions and thus to heighten the earlier implanted narcissistic cravings. I could not escape the conclusion that the search for autonomy and for individual identity has been a distinctly Western quest. For Asians the search for identity means finding a group to belong to—that is, locating an appropriate paternalistic form of authority.

In selecting my plane of analysis I rejected the increasingly narrow, but highly sophisticated, focus of the separate social science disciplines and have sought instead an approach which will exploit the best of several different academic fields. I have done this because of a conviction that political analysis without historical perspective is as flat and as lacking in human vividness as is sociological theorizing without the benefits of the insights of depth psychology. By focusing on political culture one becomes, in fact, obligated to explore all aspects of behavior, making use of whatever advantages are offered by all the relevant disciplines.

In this study "Asia" does not include Soviet Asia, Mongolia, or Southwest Asia, which is really more a part of the Middle East. The focus is instead on the major Confucian, Buddhist, Hindu, and Islamic cultures (excluding Sri Lanka because that violence-torn society raises themes not dealt with here). Although the fashion of the day in scholarship is specialization to the point of producing only single-country studies, I make no apology for dealing with so many of the countries of Asia. My reasoning is that it is conventional in the study of political development and modernization to deal with all of the Third World, the developing world, in general terms; hence to limit the focus to Asia is as much an act of modesty as one of hubris. At the same time I feel humbled by, and respectful of, the outstanding scholarship being practiced by specialists on the various countries of Asia. I regret not being better able to integrate all their findings into this book.

The study will start with a brief justification for even theorizing about political modernization, for this endeavor went out of favor in the academic turmoil of the late sixties. It will then proceed in ever narrowing concentric circles as it moves from a general overview of the historic patterns of changing concepts of power in most of Asia to, first, variations between broad cultural areas—the Confucian East Asian societies, the Southeast Asian cultures, and the Hindu (and also Muslim) patterns of South Asia—and then to differences within these cultural areas. This is important because the differences among, say, the main Confucian societies are just as important as the differences between the Confucian cultures and the South and Southeast Asian cultures. Moreover, I need to accentuate these cultural differences by identifying what is common in most Asian cultures in order to legitimize my conclusion. Only then is it possible to grasp the true dimensions of paternalistic authority and the ways in which Asians have mastered dependency and turned it into a psychologically liberating force that manifests its true qualities in the deepest meanings of loyalty. Asian forms of nationalism, racial identity, and company loyalty constitute new forms of authoritarianism. They are new in the sense that they are built out of the complex personal bonding ties of superiors and subordinates, of patrons and clients—ties in which it is often obscure who is manipulating whom, and for what purpose.

Over the last three decades I have, in addition to doing fieldwork in Asia, had many occasions to visit Asian countries; but a sabbatical leave and a most appreciated grant from the Rockefeller Brothers Fund gave me an opportunity to travel through most of the countries of Asia, staying long enough in each one to get a sense of the conditions there, and eventually to arrive at a feeling for where they all stand at a common point in history. While this experience provided the baseline for this work, it would not have been possible to undertake such a broad comparative study had not excellent monographic research been produced on each of the Asian countries. I am, therefore, heavily indebted to several generations of scholars who have worked the various vineyards of Asian studies.

It is easy to explain why power and culture are the two central concepts of this book. At the time I began my formal training in political science there was optimism that the discipline was about to make giant strides in becoming an accumulative science because of the discovery that power was the essence of politics. At the same time American intellectuals were excited by the promise of new revelations from the theories of culture and personality that were being enthusiastically propagated by the anthropologists Clyde Kluckhohn, Margaret Mead, and Ruth Benedict. My thinking about political psychology was later stimulated and expanded by the experience of jointly preparing and teaching seminars at M.I.T. with both Nathan Leites and Harold Lasswell, and by working with Erik Erikson in an M.I.T. faculty group when he was codifying the theories that came out of his Luther study and beginning his study of Gandhi. It goes without saying that my understanding of the theories of political development owes much to participating in the work of the Committee on Comparative Politics of the Social Science Research Council, but I welcome this opportunity to acknowledge again my great intellectual and personal indebtedness to Gabriel Almond.

Over the years at M.I.T. I have been extremely fortunate in having had a number of outstanding students whose researches on Asian political cultures have turned out to be learning experiences for me. Thus, while formally I was the mentor and they the students, in fact my understanding of Asia was broadened by their research and fieldwork. It is with pleasure that I acknowledge now my debt to the following scholars. On Japan, there were Richard Samuels, Lewis Austin, Takashi Inoguchi; on China, Richard Solomon, Susan Shirk, Alan P. L. Liu, Dorothy Grouse Fontana, Paul Hiniker, Talbott Huey, John Frankenstein, and Sophia Lu-tao Wang; on the Philippines, Jean Grossholtz, Aprodicia Laquian, and Loretta Sicat. On Vietnam, there were Samuel Popkin, Jane Pratt, and Paul Berman; on Indonesia, Karl Jackson, David Denoon, and Yahya Muhaimin; on Singapore and Malaysia, William Parker, Vincent Lowe, Russell Betts, Colin MacAndrews, and Zakaria Haji Ahmed; on Thailand, Herbert Rubin and Charles Murray; on India and Pakistan, Stanley Heginbotham, Mary Fainsod Katzenstein, Albert Cantril, and Ahmed Rehman. Thomas Berger provided helpful research assistance for this book.

I am most appreciative of the careful and thoughtful reading of drafts of the manuscript by Gabriel Almond, Karl Jackson, Richard Samuels, Robert Scalapino, and Myron Weiner, each of whom did his best to save me from errors. Lola Klein cheerfully and diligently transformed my nearly illegible handwriting into neatly typed pages. Charles Lockman helped by putting some of the chapters on his word processor. My thanks also to Charles Ellis for administrative assistance. Dorothy Whitney was masterful in editing the final draft, combining subtlety and rigor in an uncommonly skillful way.

Mary Pye's involvement in the project has been so complete and her assistance so critical to its completion that she is quite properly recognized as my collaborator.

In the light of all this help, for which I am indeed most appreciative, it is clear that any failings are entirely my own responsibility.

L. W. P.

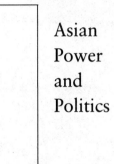

Asian
Power
and
Politics

1 Asia and Theories of Development

O N THE FACE OF IT, the mere idea of treating Asia as a single entity is absurd. Knowledgeable people realize that "Asia" is only a geographical expression, that the continent abounds in diversities, and that the peoples there should never be confused with one another. Only relics of the nineteenth century and the hopelessly uninformed would lump Asians together and speak of "Orientals," or of "Eastern thought." Asia certainly is as rich in its differences as is Europe.

Yet, we do speak of Europe as though, hidden behind its diversity, there lies some common, shared quality which justifies our thinking of Europe as a single entity. We agree that to say that something is "European" has meaning. But a similar generalization in regard to Asia is quickly ruled out as unjustifiable. Few will question that there is a European civilization; and although the French, English, Germans, Italians, and the rest may speak their separate tongues, they do share the legacies of Greece and Rome, of a common Christendom, and all that makes up the Judeo-Christian tradition. Behind the manifest variations of Asia, however, lies not one civilization but different root civilizations, the Sinic and the Hindu, and also the Muslim and the Buddhist traditions. Asia has a more varied past than Europe and therefore has not the same sense of a common descent.

Conventional wisdom, holding that at times it is appropriate to minimize Europe's diversities and concentrate on its common heritage, judges Asia's differences to be unmanageable. Comparisons within Europe are thus considered justifiable, while attempts to compare Asian countries are like "comparing apples and oranges."

Yet, with all this acknowledged, the pull of comparison in Asia persists. People do want to know how India and China are doing compared with each other. We find it natural to ask whether the "Japanese model," and now more recently the "South Korean–Singapore model," will be relevant for other parts of Asia. The "Chinese revolution" and then the successes of Hanoi led some people to talk of a general pattern of "Asian peasant rebellions." Others have found significance, and barely suppressed satisfaction, in contrasting the "hard" cultures of Confucian East Asia with the "soft" cultures of Hindu India and Buddhist Southeast Asia.

If we reflect on those comparisons within Asia which come most naturally, it soon becomes apparent that they share one quality: it is not that they are variations on a common past, as with the countries of Europe, but rather that they share similar hopes for the future. The common element in Asia is that it is a continent in pursuit of economic growth, national power, and all that can be lumped together under the general label of modernization. The unity of Europe lies in its history; the unity of Asia is in the more subtle, but no less real, shared consciousness of the desirability of change and of making a future different from the past.

Furthermore, in varying degrees, Asia's desire for change, largely a concern of the elite, came from a single source—Western technological civilization. Although the West came to Asia in a number of guises, creating different colonial traditions and different perceptions of danger and opportunity, the extraordinary historical fact is that, in spite of the trauma of that interlude of variegated Western challenges, enlightened Asians have been able to penetrate the Western masquerade of diversity and grasp at some of the most unifying features of Western secular civilization. In the process Asians have moved beyond the phase of seeking to become Westernized and have come to the stage of striving for modernization. Japan, as the pacesetter, in its "low posture" style, has slipped past the stage of self-conscious concern about becoming Westernized and has quietly joined the ranks of the most modernized, so much a part of the West that it has become conventional to dispense with the phrase "the West and Japan" and to speak instead of the "advanced industrial societies," by which everyone understands that Japan is to be classed with Europe and North America. Other rapidly changing Asian countries are not far behind Japan, and consequently the very idea of becoming Westernized will lose meaning as we think of the more generalized concept of a world culture.[1]

In Defense of Development Theory

The objection may be raised that in identifying the unity of Asia by its common pursuit of modernization we have done little more than to say that Asia's diversity is encompassed by the larger category of societies variously called the "Third World," the "developing" or "emerging" nations, or simply the "LDCs," which presumably share this same concern for achieving modernization. After all, if the criterion is "modernization," how does Asia differ from Africa and Latin America? Moreover, isn't the concept of modernization, which was popular in the 1950s and 1960s, now somewhat tarnished, if not discredited, and hardly worthy of being the central concept of a serious study?

These are two valid questions which call for sober answers, particularly since both questions are in a sense awkwardly related. It is true that the development or modernization theories created in the 1950s and 1960s did lump together Asia, Africa, and Latin America. Yet it is also true that an important reason for dissatisfaction with those theories was precisely the fact that they were stretched too thin by being applied to all three continents. From the vantage point of the 1980s it is evident that in essence the earlier modernization theories had a close empirical fit with the experiences of Asia but not with those of either Africa or Latin America. It is apparent now that the postcolonial African political systems generally lacked the blend of nationalism and earnest commitment to modernization that was characteristic of Asia. As for Latin America, it is an inappropriate stretching of the imagination to classify that continent's well-established countries as "newly emerging" states, as though they were just breaking away from colonial rule. South and Central American countries have had long histories of independence and have, over time, molded their own distinctive political and social systems. They are not at all comparable to those Asian states whose terminal phases of colonialism pointed them in the direction of elite-guided social and economic change which was intensified by the drive of newfound nationalism.[2] Nor are they comparable to China or Japan, which from the moment they were exposed to the dangers of Western colonial domination sought to gain national strength and economic security by adopting modernizing technologies.[3]

Indeed, reflection on the problems raised by Latin America helps to clarify some of the inappropriate criticisms of modernization theories, at least as applied to Asia. First of all, Latin America was subsumed under general discussions of development partly in response to policy concerns rather than intellectual ones. Specifically, the Kennedy administration's decision to oppose the spread of Castroism by initiating the Alliance for

Progress expressed Washington's belief that Latin America should be ready for the reforms that might put it on the road to progress and modernization. But it was soon apparent that most of Latin America was not committed to such objectives. Furthermore, the policy incentives of the Latin Americans, even when directed toward change, revealed assumptions and desires quite different from those of the modernizing Asians. For example, Raul Prebisch, and then increasingly the United Nations Economic Commission for Latin America, called for "trade, not aid," an appeal which sounded to Asian ears downright antidevelopment, if not reactionary. From India to South Korea, Asian leaders counted heavily on Western, and especially United States, aid and downplayed the importance of trade, even though, paradoxically, trade would turn out in the end to be vital for their development. The issue for the Asians was only that they wanted no strings tied to their aid.

The differences between Asia and Latin America became even more manifest when certain Latin American intellectuals revived, in a distorted form, the old Leninist theory about the "colonies and semi-colonies," and called it *dependencia,* or "dependency theory." The enthusiasm of Latin Americans for that theory and the rejection of it by Asian intellectuals illustrate the difference between the two continents with respect to development. Whatever the merits of dependency theory relating to Latin America—and we can leave it to others to explain why some Latin American intellectuals embrace such a demeaning and despairing theory—it is unmistakably clear that the theory is not only irrelevant but wrong with respect to Asia. All of the dramatically successful economies of Asia have grown as the result of their close involvement with what the dependency school chooses to call the "world economy." Today, newly industrializing states, including the People's Republic of China, compete vigorously in wooing multinational corporations, and none has lost control over its own destiny. By contrast, the stagnation and impotence which the theory associates with "dependency" are to be found in Asia only in those countries that, at least for a time, have sought "autonomy" and isolation from the world economy. The Chinese during the Cultural Revolution period paid a high price to learn this fact; and, as a new convert to the benefits of dealing with multinationals, the Deng Xiaoping regime has declared, in the words of the *Beijing Review* of March 1982, "Not a single country in the world, no matter what its political system, has ever modernized with a closed-door policy."

Instead of fearing what the dependency theorists call the workings of "monopoly capitalism," the five governments of the Association of Southeast Asian Nations (ASEAN) energetically strive to outdo one another in attracting foreign capital and technology so as to provide more interesting and remunerative jobs for their people and more revenues for themselves—a competition which led Deputy Prime Minister Goh Keng Swee of Singapore to say that the three abominations his country would not tolerate were "hippies, long-haired boys, and critics of multinational corporations," and while he may have had tongue in cheek about the first two, he was certainly deadly serious about the last. Sri Lanka, after two decades of stagnation, began in the late 1970s to try to follow the ASEAN lead, and in 1980 the Chinese Communists went to the extraordinary length of establishing "special economic zones" for foreign enterprises. Even India, long suspicious of foreign firms and committed to import-substitution policies, began in the early 1980s to open, albeit haltingly, its economy a bit—in part because Indian firms had reached the point of wanting to become multinationals and hence New Delhi had to be more reciprocating, and in part because it wanted to follow the successfully developing Asians in their export promotion tactic.

By contrast, Burma, which has resolutely shielded itself from the reach of the world economy, has stagnated, and its people have suffered a decline in their standard of living as the government has stubbornly followed the "Burmese path to socialism." Nevertheless, by the early 1980s the "black market" had grown to such proportions and was so successful in providing consumer goods that the Burmese peasants once again became interested in producing for the market, and consequently the country had a surprising 6 percent a year growth in GNP.

Thus, ironically, at the very time when there was widespread criticism of and disillusionment with earlier theories of political and economic development, events in Asia were suggesting that possibly those theories had been too cautious. During the twenty years of the sixties and seventies, the peoples of East and Southeast Asia were living through the longest period of rapidly rising economic growth ever experienced in human history. Aside from Japan, which had average growth rates of 9.8 percent and 6 percent, respectively, for the two decades, the so-called gang of four—South Korea, Taiwan, Singapore, and Hong Kong—performed at 9.3 percent, and the ASEAN countries all had rates of over 8 percent.[4]

Although the problems of poverty remained, sectors of India's economy were growing at almost comparable rates. The "green revolution" in the Punjab and elsewhere made the country for a time more than self-sufficient in grain. In terms of human capital, India developed the third largest pool of engineers in the world, and it began vigorously to export engineering equipment and machine tools. Sri Lanka by 1980 was beginning to follow the ASEAN example of opening its economy for investment, and even the "basket case," Bangladesh, did better than merely survive.

Ironically, while these advances were taking place, public attention in the United States was caught up with the drama of China's announced Four Modernizations program, and the impression was created that this newly opening country was making even more rapid progress than the rest of Asia. Although China still has tremendous problems and progress will be slow in a country of one billion people, it is significant that after decades of experimentation with more radical approaches the Chinese leadership has finally come to the conclusion that development calls for technically sounder methods. China is thus trying, to some degree, to fall in line with the rest of Asia.[5]

The misfortune that the disillusionment with political theory coincided with a remarkable period of Asian development may be compounded by the possibility that by the time scholars are ready once more to examine seriously Asian events, the problems of Asian countries will have been lifted to a higher and more difficult plane. This is because in the year 2000 the already mushrooming number of Asian babies will have reached employment age; and this means, according to the calculations of Myron Weiner, that there will be some eighty million Asians a year seeking jobs. And, of course, improvements in education will mean that they will want significant careers rather than just to follow ancient pursuits.

The American public, understandably, sometimes has problems separating rhetoric from facts about that still distant continent, and hence it is not so surprising that, according to polls, a majority of Americans in 1980 believed that China had a higher standard of living than Singapore, South Korea, or Taiwan. The public's problem of getting a clear picture of the condition of Asia has been extensively documented by pollsters who have systematically questioned Americans about their knowledge of Asian countries. In a 1980 Gallup poll done for Potomac Associates and reported by William Watts, a national sample of Americans found it most appropriate to characterize "Asia" with the four adjectives or phrases "crowded with too many people," "underdeveloped," "political unrest," and "dirty, with poor sanitation"; and only 4 percent saw Asians as "peace loving" while only 3 percent said they were "well dressed"—and this at a time when the scruffy look was de rigueur on American campuses. Understandably, Vietnam and North Korea were the two most "disliked" countries in Asia, and Japan was the most "liked," ranking internationally with West Germany and New Zealand, while India was less liked than either China or Taiwan, thus confirming Harold Isaacs's earlier finding that Americans prefer Chinese to Indians by a wide margin. More significant was the amount of ignorance about Asia unearthed by the pollsters. For example, more than a third of the sample did not know that the Philippines had once been an American colony; most thought that Russians were more "hard working" than either South Koreans or Taiwanese, that the PRC was more politically stable than Singapore, and that Vietnam was the most unstable country in Asia. Most people admitted that their knowledge came largely from television, both news and special feature programs, including such situation comedies as $M^*A^*S^*H$. At the same time, however, the survey showed that traditional stereotypes about Asia are still vivid in the American mind. That news reports have contradicted these stereotypes has not created any particular tensions or problems of cognitive dissonance for Americans, apparently because few feel the need to get the picture of Asia straight. Therefore in the 1980s Asia remains slightly mysterious and in many respects still confusing to Americans.[6]

Western Theories and Asian Facts

The suggestion that Asian developments, blurred as they have been in American perceptions, provide substantial support for earlier theories of modernization and development is itself ironic because in the past Western social science theories have generally not stood up well to Asian evidence. It is worth noting at the outset of this study of Asia that all manner of convincing theories developed to explain Western experiences, and judged to encapsulate universal truths, have been repeatedly confounded by Asian facts. Indeed, there is no more humbling, but also challenging, way to begin a study of Asian developments than to take note of the fate of such theories in the East.

For example, even as Karl Marx was constructing his grand theories about social transformations according to his laws of historical materialism, he sensed that they would not hold up with respect to the East. As Myron Weiner, following the analysis of Shlomo Avineri, has pointed out, Marx himself was more sensitive to the uniqueness of Asia than most subsequent "Marxists" have been. "Thus, Marxists speak of feudalism in India, when Marx asserted that feudalism did not exist in the Asiatic mode of production; Marxists condemn imperialism, while Marx himself was concerned with the 'regenerating' as well as 'destructive' elements of the British role in India; and while Marxists seek to show how the distribution of economic wealth determines the distribution of political power, Marx himself emphasized the autonomous character of state power and the ways in which political power affected cultural, social structures and economic relations . . ." in Asia.[7]

Marx's understanding of the East stemmed in part from other European thinkers who had earlier recognized some of the distinctive characteristics of Asian societies. Montesquieu, for example, in *The Spirit of Laws,* presented "Oriental despotism" as an ideal type that had as its key value fear, in which there was no secure private property, the ruler relied upon religion rather than law, and the entire system was essentially static because of the dominant role of custom and taboos.[8] His version of Oriental despotism also, paradoxically, led to a high degree of equality in that everyone was vulnerable to the whims of the despot. Interestingly, it was Adam Smith, and subsequently John S. Mill, who, before Marx, identified the key role that irrigation played in Asian imperial systems.[9] Marx, as Wittfogel so vigorously elaborated, took up the idea that Oriental despotism was a product of "hydraulic societies," arguing that the need to maintain irrigation arrangements involving total river systems required a centralized authority which could manage the total system, keep up the dykes between village communities, and allocate water among all claimants—a requirement that encouraged a form of absolutist state.[10]

The distinctive characteristics of Asia were particularly troublesome for Marx because he had set for himself the task of finding a universal theory of history, based on a unilinear concept of progress. Asia defied his theory because, except for Japan, feudalism was not the basic historical arrangement before the beginnings of capitalism. Recognizing the problem, Marx evolved the concept of an "Asiatic mode of production."[11] At different points Marx gave somewhat different emphases to this concept.[12] Sometimes he advanced the proposition that Asia was distinctive because in theory the state owned the land (something factually incorrect in most of Chinese history), and therefore the state stressed agriculture over industry and devoted attention to public works, which helped to centralize authority (a somewhat more correct understanding). At other times Marx said the distinctive character of the Asiatic mode of production was economies built around "self-sustaining villages" which retarded the development of true divisions of labor, and thus marginal advantages were not realized. As fuzzy as the concept is, and as inconsistent with Asian realities, Marx at least recognized the limits of his prime theories when it came to Asia. In his frustration he tended to denounce Asia, saying that China was "vegetating in the teeth of history" and that the "Indian country has no history at all," for India had no movement toward progress until, as Marx saw it, the positive consequences of British colonial rule became evident.[13]

In contrast to Marx's recognition of the theoretical problems raised by Asia, later social scientists have generally been unaware of how Asian facts might limit the validity of theories based only on Western experience. Coming out of an intellectual tradition which was built largely upon European and early Greek and Roman experiences, even the most contemporary social scientists have usually acted as though universal laws of human behavior could be based on an analysis of Western experience alone. Evidence to the contrary produced by anthropologists could be dismissed as applying to the uncivilized. Yet, to ignore Asian experiences in the light of current Asian achievements is truly troublesome, for it could be interpreted as a manifestation of a continued Eurocentric point of view associated with the era of colonialism.

The ignoring of Asia is especially disturbing when theories advanced to explain differences in Western experiences could otherwise be checked by noting whether the interpretations stand up when Asian developments are considered. An excellent example of this is Louis Hartz's theory about "liberal America," which is possibly the most widely accepted thesis, since Turner's theory of the "frontier," for explaining the sources of America's distinctive character.[14]

According to Hartz's argument, America, as a "new society," was spared the abiding internal tensions which a preceding era of feudalism had left in a class-divided Europe. Presumably the prior existence of feudal, hierarchical distinctions in Europe ensured a continuing battle of classes, and therefore a natural distrust of labor and capital toward each other, which in turn encouraged the growth of both Marxist and socialist ideologies, on the one hand, and embittered conservative reactionaries, on the other. Lacking such a heritage of feudal divisions, America moved readily toward becoming a consensual society. Those who have sought to preach class warfare in America have only been able to attract limited followings because there has been no historical tradition for such distrust.

The theory seems eminently plausible, supported as it is by two reasonable lines of logic. First, feudalism was based on sharp hierarchical distinctions, and hence societies which emerge from feudalism should provide fertile grounds for class warfare politics and the appeals of Marxism and conservatism; while, second, a society without such a tradition, starting "anew" with few class differences, might logically come to stress the equalitarian ideals of liberalism and operate on the basis of a national consensus.

Yet when the theory is transported to Asia and applied to Japan, it crumbles. Japan, like Europe, was a feudal society before modernization, and it had hierarchical and class distinctions as sharp as, if not sharper than, those in Europe. The relation of samurai to commoner, whether peasant or *chonin,* that is, merchant, was in many respects more severe than that of knight and nobleman to the European commoner and merchant, and the role of Emperor was a less moderating influence than that of the Church in Europe. Yet with modernization the hierarchically divided Japanese society has emerged as a homogeneous and possibly an even more consensual society than the United States. There has been even less indigenous radicalism, or appeal to class, in Japan than in America with its populist traditions, which are accounted for in Hartz's theory. Many of the distinctive qualities of American politics which Hartz attributes directly to our lack of a feudal tradition, such as the commitment to the legitimacy of the majority while tolerating minority views, are equally to be found in Japan, which has a strong feudal tradition.

The point of departure in this study is thus the assertion that Asia supports modernization and development theories more than the critics of those theories are inclined to acknowledge, even though Asian facts have frequently challenged Western theories that pretend to be universal. Asia is modernizing, but in ways that are different from the Western experience. The challenge is to identify those differences.

Some Points of Theory Clarified

First, however, in view of what many critics of the earlier theories of political development have written, we need to clear up some misunderstandings and confusions about the concepts used in those formulations. We do this not in order to revive old debates, although distortions in the writing of intellectual history should be corrected, but rather to tidy up assumptions and concepts so as to prevent further misunderstandings.[15]

As a first step it is necessary to note that political development and modernization theories have generally been heuristic theories, not systematic causal theories. The focus of the theories has been to spell out concepts and to identify factors and processes so as better to guide empirical work. By providing a preliminary basis for classification and typology-building, the theories set the stage for case studies with comparative dimensions. Opinions will differ as to whether heuristic theories or formal, causal, or deductive theories are the more interesting and useful. The overwhelming majority of scholars of comparative politics have, however, shown a decided preference for heuristic theories over convoluted ways of elucidating the obvious by mathematical formulas.[16]

The power, and also the charm, of heuristic theories is that they can provoke the imagination well beyond the simple alternatives of truth and falsification. As with Max Weber's provocative use of ideal types or Ruth Benedict's and other anthropologists' descriptions of modal personality types, heuristic theories strive to capture the essential elements of a phenomenon; and consequently, should any such theory match in all respects the specific realities of a particular situation, it would lose its scientific dimension of stimulating comparison by becoming only a description of the singular case. Useful heuristic theories thus have, in a sense, the potency of caricature.

In addition to stimulating comparative insights, the heuristic theories of the fifties and sixties provided architectonic matrices which suggested priorities for research and provided central themes for coherent analyses. The study of political development had focus in terms of both the examination of change and the presumption of critical variables, functions, and impending problems. Although not a prisoner of nineteenth century concepts of easy progress, the approach still embodied an appreciation of what people tend to value, seek to achieve, and often envy in others. In the wake of disillusionment with "political development" as a field of study came a congeries of ad hoc problems and topics—military rule, multinational corporations, peasant revolts, religious revivalism, and other topics of the day's news—without any effort to suggest priorities of significance.

A second and less precise criticism of political development theory is that it was overly optimistic and held out the promise that the newly emerging countries were likely soon to become effective, modernized nation-states. In part, this problem was one of time scale, the theorists having not specified the amounts of time covered by their projections of change, while their critics were often reacting to the day's headlines. Authors were generally not explicit as to whether they were writing in terms of decades or centuries. Only people who have not read the literature carefully would, however, characterize the early writings on political development as unqualifiedly optimistic. Much of the early empirical work was directed precisely toward explaining why certain ex-colonial countries were having difficulties and were unlikely to make much progress.[17] Samuel P. Huntington's discussion of political "decay" did make more explicit the "breakdown" of modernization, but his call for a "change to change," that is, for talking about political change rather than development, went too far, and in his subsequent work he acknowledged a general historical trend involving problems of mobilization and greater participation.[18] Development theorists, like Marxists, were trying to point the direction of history, not necessarily calibrate its pace.

The problem of direction raises a third source of confusion, that of the dichotomous scheme which contrasts sharply "traditional" and "modern" modes of behavior. Formulated during a century of reflection on social change, by an impressive line of social theorists, including Henry

Maine, Ferdinand Toennies, and Emile Durkheim, to say nothing of Karl Marx and Max Weber, the concepts sought to encapsulate the essential differences between pre-industrial-revolution and post-industrial-revolution societies. Revisionist critics have sought to dismiss the utility of the contrasts, which were summarized in Talcott Parsons's five pattern variables, by citing examples of "traditional" behavior in "modern" societies, and vice versa. In doing so they have missed the point which Gabriel Almond made at the beginning of political-development theorizing when he explained that *all political cultures are mixed.*[19] The reason why political, as contrasted with social, systems must have a dual character is that political systems are held together by a sense of collective identity and thus are based upon sentiments of loyalty which evoke parochial attachments to unique historical experiences. Politics always sets limits on universalisms as it defines "we's" and "they's," citizens and foreigners. All governments must evoke some traditions in order to preserve the collectivity and to elicit commitments from their subjects.

Precisely because of this need for some elements of historical continuity, political development theory did not, as some of its critics have suggested, assert the prospect of a convergence of all political systems. National cultures are much too distinctive, even in long-industrialized countries, to justify the fear of a single, homogenized modern culture enveloping all of mankind. This, however, is not to say that there is not a diffusion of science and technology which, when blended with a form of secular and rational thought, constitutes the world culture, to distinguish it from the earlier phenomena of Westernization. Thus, in every society there is a combining of degrees of the world culture and of local customs. That Japan, for example, has many unique elements in its modernization does not make it an exception to the general theory, for its preservation and utilization of traditional sentiments has not negated, but rather has strengthened, the essential fact that Japan, for all of its group orientation, is a meritocracy of the highest degree and thus manifests the essence of the world culture. The degree to which the Japanese people value belonging to a group and being members of the team should not make Americans, who also excel at team sports, believe that Japanese do not strive to the utmost to be the best as individuals.

Questions about the role of culture have led to another major misunderstanding about development theories. This is the charge that only certain cultural values can produce positive development—such as Protestantism for economic development and Anglo-American values for democracy—and that any identification of cultural variables means that an attempt is being made to explain everything psychologically. As David Gellner has succinctly pointed out, the common fallacies in interpreting

Max Weber's *The Protestant Ethic and the Spirit of Capitalism* have arisen from the tendency to argue that because Weber identified the Protestant ethic as critical in explaining why modern capitalism emerged in Europe, he believed that such an ethic was a necessary and sufficient factor for producing economic growth.[20] Robert Bellah has, of course, shown that Japanese culture possessed the functional equivalents of Weber's Protestant ethos, but neither Weber nor Bellah would argue that: (1) a culture of a different type cannot, as a latecomer, achieve economic development, or (2) any culture that has the same elements is destined to have economic development. The point is that different cultures will produce different styles of modernization, and that some cultural traits can facilitate, while others will impede, development. To point out the influence of culture on historical developments is not, as critics seem at times to be saying, the same as to hold that everything is determined by psychology.

In part this problem of explanation is related to two peculiar and related tendencies in the social sciences. The first is a problem Nathan Leites identified in the first issue of *World Politics:* "It is a frequent fallacy in the human sciences to believe that, if somebody at a certain moment talks about the importance of Factor A, he is running down the importance of factors B, C . . ."[21] This tendency is particularly strong when cultural and psychological considerations are introduced, and it leads to the second peculiar practice of trying to make an issue of the relative importance of structure as against culture, of cognitive factors as against subjective influences, and of power calculations as against policy preferences, when of course it is well known that probably the greatest weakness of social scientists is their general inability to weigh the relative importance of causal factors. There is no scientific answer to most questions about relative importance, and, therefore, merely to raise the issue is to appeal to bias and prejudice.[22]

On another point, revisionist critics have claimed that development theories underplayed the importance of the international system, and particularly the influences of the "world economic system," in determining the patterns of change in the underdeveloped areas. Although the early theories uniformly spoke of the "Western impact," the "legacies of colonialism," "nationalist responses to imperialism," and the role of "foreign aid," and thus did not entirely ignore international considerations, there was a tendency to treat system developments, as far as possible, as autonomous processes. The accent was in part on the uniqueness of the separate systems, but at the same time interest was focused on building typologies reflecting stages or degrees of development.

In no small measure this tendency to try to conceptualize autonomous political systems stemmed from a desire to emulate developments in the discipline of economics by creating macro-system models comparable to those of Keynesian macroeconomics. Much of the earlier work on power relationships and on "who gets what, when, and how" can be seen as similar to microeconomics with its stress on utility functions and market exchanges. The introduction of systems analysis, with its input and output functions, was in a sense modeled after the national income flows of macroeconomics. And, just as Keynes's *General Theory* left out issues of balance of payments and treated national economies as autonomous, closed systems, so, for much the same reasons, did the systems theorists in political science. In this respect the criticism of development theorists for downplaying the international system has the same lack of validity as F. A. Hayek's well-known attack on Keynesianism.

In addition, the inclination to view development in terms of autonomous countries also reflected an unfortunate division within political science between the subfields of comparative politics and international relations. The extraordinary vitality of comparative politics in the 1950s and 1960s stemmed largely from the excitement of treating in a more comparative fashion variations in the experiences of a host of separate countries, an approach which offered the promise of being more "scientific," especially since the door was opened to more quantitative forms of analysis. This possibility arose because the end of Western colonialism dramatically increased the number of so-called nation-states so as to open the way to statistically significant comparisons. At the same time the study of international relations also sought to become more "scientific," but by following a different route—that of formal modeling of different international power systems or "regimes"—and by rigorous analysis of the military-strategic balance of East and West. It is ironic, in light of the charge made in the late 1970s that development theory was a mask for advancing United States national interests, to note that the vitality of comparative politics during the earlier period sprang in part from trying to overlook the Cold War and ideological debates, even to the extent of omitting from most studies analyses of the developing Communist countries.[23] The two different approaches to becoming more "scientific" pulled the two subfields in different directions, with the result that each spoke a different technical language, and therefore each tended to show scholarly deference to the other and not impinge upon the other's domain.

Even if there had been greater sensitivity to the importance of international factors, work in comparative politics and development theory at that time probably would not have followed the line desired by revisionist critics. These critics have generally treated foreign aid, technical assistance, cultural exchanges, and the operations of multinational corporations as pernicious operations through which those at the "center" of the "world economy" persist in controlling the "periphery." Development theorists have generally taken a more positive view of these efforts at furthering development in the Third World. In recent years this debate has declined as the leaders of the more successfully developing countries have not only called for more foreign aid but in some cases have become more competitive in attracting investment by multinational corporations.

These issues concerning the world economy and the role of multinational corporations are a part of the explicitly ideological criticism of development theories which has asserted that those theories were biased in favor of order and stability and opposed to revolution and popular participation. Much of this criticism was fueled by the passions generated by the Vietnam War and by a glorification of Mao's Cultural Revolution. Now that the world knows more about the disastrous consequences of the Cultural Revolution—Deng Xiaoping has said that one hundred million people "suffered severely"—it is less easy to romanticize the virtues of "spontaneous political participation." Also after Pol Pot it is necessary to become more discriminating in idealizing "peasant revolutionaries." Finally, with Havana and Hanoi pleading for "normalized" relations with the "world capitalist system," only diehard ideologues equate that system with "imperialism."[24]

New Theoretical Directions Needed

In short, the world has changed. Change has come not only since the development theorists initiated their work but also in the context within which the critics were most vocal. The formation of OPEC and the ensuing oil crisis, debates within the Group of 77, and the problem of Third World country indebtedness to private banks all make it clear that the task of understanding the problems of development is more complex than the critics of development theories supposed.

Certain aspects of those theories also need to be extended, for the changes in the developing world over the last two decades call for a new evaluation of the concepts and theories of the earlier development theorists. Events have proved that the early literature reflected an undue sensitivity to the potential fragility of the new states. Except for Pakistan they have all survived nearly intact, thanks not only to their own capabilities but also to the impotence of their neighbors, and even more to the protective shelter of an international system which has been more benign and protecting than the dependency theorists ever imagined.

Democracy has had rough going, but the successes of insurgencies have been rarer. Authoritarian regimes have endured with fewer difficulties than the theorists predicted; and often they have allowed more participation, at least at the local levels, and have been more responsive to popular sentiments than theories of authoritarianism suggested would be possible. The revival of some forms of religious passion, such as Islamic fundamentalism, pose still unanswered questions. Are there limits to the penetrations of secular values? Are we seeing in the revivals, especially of Islam, a swing of the pendulum? Or is this a last gasp of clerics claiming temporal authority? Above all, the early literature underestimated the problems of political succession, of the difficulties even the authoritarian systems are having in arranging for the passing of the baton.

Some of these problems, which need now to be faced, were close to the top of the agenda when work on development theory went out of fashion. In the present stage of revival of interest in development theory, Harry Eckstein has again, as he has on occasions in the past, provided intellectual leadership by clarifying concepts that others have been using too loosely, placing them in the context of Western intellectual history, and pointing out the direction for forward movement. Specifically, Eckstein argues that development theory ran into problems because it had been "historically myopic," uninformed about the role of "developmental thought" in Western philosophy and social theory, and that it failed to answer fundamental questions about "the long passage from primal to highly advanced politics." What, for example, was the "essential nature of a polity in its 'primitive' and 'simple' forms?" What "forces make the 'advancement' of primal politics toward 'higher' forms?" What are the "stages" and the "forces" that "move politics from stage to stage?" And finally, what are the implications of the answers to these questions for the "present less developed, and for 'advanced,' modern politics?"[25] In searching for the basics of what should be the focus of political development, Eckstein does not credit contemporary theorists with as strong a grounding in classical Western thought as I believe they have had. The fact that they did not usually deal with the nineteenth century theorists with Eckstein's thoroughness does not mean that they were uninfluenced by that tradition. The heavy demands of trying to combine the collection of current data, usually in the form of fieldwork, with theoretical formulations often meant that for the sake of economy in exposition the most recent summary and integration of classical social theory was used. Thus Parsons's role theory and pattern variables became code words for referring to a whole body of classical theory.

At the same time it is probably true that scholars working on development problems often carelessly discarded earlier concepts and failed to appreciate the full implications of the original formulations. Scholars would dip into the classical literature and grasp concepts which they then applied willy-nilly, thereby debasing their value. An obvious example is the way in which Max Weber's concepts, such as "rational-legal," "charismatic," and "patrimonialism," were indiscriminately applied, to the point that rational-legal became essentially irrational administration. Any leader manifesting even the slightest charm was said to have charisma, and any relationship of patron and client or of leader and longtime associate was classed as an example of patrimonialism.[26] These practices were probably manifestations, not of ignorance, but of the "iron law of the vulgarization of concepts," which holds that any concept which in its original formulation and context seems to be robust, vivid, and precise will be instantly latched onto by social scientists and stretched to a point of diffuse fuzziness by being used indiscriminately in unrelated contexts.[27] Note how Erikson's concept of "identity" has been applied to almost any group psychology problem, or how Marx's concepts of class and class conflict have been vulgarized. Chalmers Johnson has observed that the Maoists in China enthusiastically identified some sixty specific "classes" in their society, which were used to justify splendid amounts of conflict.[28]

Eckstein's central point is well taken, however, for undoubtedly the concept of political development takes on more meaning when viewed in historical and cultural contexts that extend back to the beginning of polities, and thus it involves tracing the progression of change down to the present. An explanation for the exaggerated focus on the current scene, which has produced somewhat ahistorical studies, is, in my judgment, not so much that historical patterns were considered irrelevant, as the interesting fact that political scientists in the sixties found it easier to work with economists, psychologists, and sociologists than with historians.[29]

In short, one reason for the ahistorical quality of political development studies was that in the 1950s and 1960s comparative politics became strongly interdisciplinary, and therefore the search for perfection, and for density in analysis, took the form of incorporating the insights and findings of such related fields as sociology, anthropology, psychology, and economics. In a sense there had to be a trade-off in forms of scholarship: while the historically oriented writers could complain of a failure to appreciate the importance of historical perspective, the more interdisciplinary observers could respond by faulting historical studies for being unsophisticated in their treatment of culture and psychology. Political scientists are caught in a tradition which requires them to take into account the work of all the surrounding disciplines.

Yet, a price had to be paid for becoming interdisciplinary. Specifically, concentration was diverted from the essentials of the political realm. The fact that politics has a highly parochial dimension and is therefore firmly set in specific historical contexts was often overlooked in the search for more generalized formulations about broad categories of political systems, such as "transitional," "non-Western," "developing." In trying to fit into a single picture all that was known about people experiencing profound social change, political scientists achieved a peculiar kind of abstract "thick description," one which delineated categories but was not so culturally or situationally specific as to explain the actual state of the political realm in particular cases. Political development studies, as Eckstein suggests, undoubtedly lost something by giving up the long historical perspective that extends from the earliest primitive forms of politics to the contemporary world. Such a perspective would also have protected political development theorists from the criticism that the effort had been a failure because "progress" in the developing world was not instantly visible. Everywhere mankind has come a long way—and there is still a long way to go.

Power, Authority, and Legitimacy

As we reexamine the political development of Asian states, it would seem, in the light of this review of debates about political development theories, that the first priority should be to find a theoretical lens that will ensure both a vivid focus on the political domain and a long historical perspective. The concept of the political system, while invaluable as a means of identifying all the varieties of activities which contribute to shaping the political process, needs to be supplemented by concepts that concentrate more specifically upon the actual dynamics of politics in particular situations and that also identify changes over time.

This requirement suggests that the most plausible candidate for such a key concept might be the concept of power. There certainly is widespread agreement among political scientists that power lies at the heart of politics, especially when that concept is related to the associated concepts of authority and legitimacy.

It is peculiar that the importance of the concept of power was not more explicitly acknowledged in early development theories, particularly since the standard definition of political culture, originated by Almond, focused attention on power. He said that "every political system is embedded in a particular pattern of orientation to political action," meaning that political cultures are based on attitudes about power.[30] Furthermore, the failure to concentrate on power was strange because in the late 1940s and early 1950s the concept of power was near the center of political science, and many felt at that time that it might even provide the discipline with a breakthrough, playing the role that money does in economic theory.

There are several plausible reasons why power did not serve as a central concept in the early work on political development. For our purposes, however, the important consideration is that the theorists on power were searching for a universal concept and a set of principles which would be valid in all human societies. Starting with Charles E. Merriam and Bertrand Russell and going on to Harold Lasswell and those in international relations who were interested in balance of power concepts and geopolitics,[31] the overwhelming concern of the theorists of power was to treat all manifestations of power as a single basic phenomenon which operated according to universal principles, regardless of time, place, or culture. Even when the nature of power was being examined in local communities, the search was still for universal properties, whether the study was done in a pluralist spirit,[32] or according to elitist theories.[33]

It is our contention in this book that the attempt of power theorists to treat the phenomenon of power as a universal concept has been unfortunate for the study of comparative politics in general and for comparative political development in particular. Indeed, it is the central argument of this study that people at different times and in different places have had quite different understandings of the concept of power, and that it is precisely these differences which form identifiable patterns along which can be traced the paths of political development. Instead of glossing over differences about how power, for example, becomes authority, as is done in a search for general "scientific" principles, we shall want to accentuate these differences. Our argument is that changes in people's subjective understanding of the nature of power, changes in their expectations about authority, and changes in their interpretations of what constitutes legitimacy are the key determinants of political development. We shall also seek to demonstrate that while there have been many cultural traditions of power, there is also a persistent general direction of those changes, which, not surprisingly, is consistent with the main outlines of development theory.

In Defense of Political Culture

It should be unnecessary to make even a token defense of the use of culture as the foundation stone of our comparative analysis, but regrettably, scholars whose preferences lie with structural analysis and rational choice models have felt it necessary to disparage political culture studies. Given the limitations of all the social sciences, it is rather like the pot calling the kettle black when one approach attacks another. Without in any way minimizing other approaches we will briefly cite some of the merits of the political culture approach.

Since culture deals with the human imagination, and the imagination is the starting point of all significant actions, it is reasonable, when assessing why different societies have taken different paths to modernization, to examine the role of culture as one factor. Culture is unquestionably significant, in some undetermined degree, in shaping the aspirations and fears, the preferences and prejudices, the priorities and expectations of a people as they confront the challenges of social and political change. Culture is not a matter of the rule of the irrational as opposed to objective, rational behavior, for the very character of rational judgment varies with time and place. Common sense exists in all cultures, but it is not the same from culture to culture. Sentiments about change, judgments about utility, expectations as to what different forms of power can and cannot accomplish are all influenced by cultural predispositions.

Culture also is a remarkably durable and persistent factor in human affairs. It is the dynamic vessel that holds and revitalizes the collective memories of a people by giving emotional life to traditions. Culture has this vital quality because it resides in the personality of everyone who has been socialized to it. People cling to their cultural ways not because of some vague feeling for their historical legacies and traditions, but because their culture is part and parcel of their personalities—and we know from psychoanalysis how hard (and expensive) it is to change a personality. Cultural change therefore involves true trauma.

Political culture has been criticized from two completely contradictory points of view. It is said by some that the concept opens the way to fuzzy thinking and sloppy explanations, but others denounce it for being too deterministic. The problem in most cases is one of incorrect expectations as to what should be derived from a political culture analysis. One way to suggest the virtue of examining culture in order to understand politics is to consider the analogous role of culture in the realm of music. There are clearly quite distinct traditions of music, and for anyone brought up in any particular tradition it is usually easy to pick up melodies and to hum along with completely new songs in that tradition, while at the same time being confused by music of a different tradition. One can of course rationally identify the music of different traditions, but generally one feels more at home if the music is of one's own culture. This is the case, moreover, not just because of the individual's sense of familiarity, but even more because there is an inner "structure" or "logic" to each musical tradition. In each tradition the characteristics of music, from melody and rhythm to dissonance and chords, have their inherent "fit," which helps to explain why people acquainted with a particular tradition can so readily respond to, and even join in playing or singing, completely new pieces. Thus while change and innovation are possible—but impossible to predict—the results of such novelty may be readily understood in the light of the tradition.

Finally, culture is helpful in mapping different routes of political development because it treats seriously the nuances in behavior patterns which may seem only trivial but which actually are critical in distinguishing between successes and failures. In the subtleties of cultures are to be found both the values a people seek and the obstacles that must be overcome if their goal is to be reached. By beginning with culture, therefore, we are allowing the different Asian peoples to define for themselves what they want with respect to modernization.

Previews of Culturally Different Concepts of Power

Partly to illuminate the contention that there are significant differences in concepts of power and that these differences stand out in comparing Asia and the West, and partly to challenge the way in which certain Western, and especially American, concepts of power have been inappropriately treated as universal scientific concepts, we shall risk getting ahead of our story by spelling out some of these differences in understanding what constitutes power.

To begin with, Harold Lasswell's definition of power as "participation in the making of significant decisions" rings true in American culture, as witnessed by the instinctive demands of students in the rebellious sixties to "participate in the decisions that affect our lives." At that time legitimacy seemed to require that power be shared, and thus students were called upon to participate in various forms of decision-making. As rational as all this may seem to Americans, in no traditional Asian culture would such a definition of power have been acceptable. In most of Asia the concept of power was exactly the opposite: to have power was to be spared the chore of decision-making. In such Asian cultures the aspiration that impelled people up the ladder of power was that they might eventually rise above the need to trouble themselves with decisions. Decisions are what vex the minds of the weak and make life troublesome. In Asia, achieving power meant becoming free of care and having subordinates who themselves were taxed with the problems of decision-making. Rulers had followers who were classed as officials but who were expected, like servants, to look after all the problems of the "household." If their behavior was exemplary, there was no need ever to give them a command. If decisions had to be made, then it was appropriate to call in technicians—astrologers in the past, economists today.

Whereas Americans feel that it is exhilarating to make decisions and that being denied a choice is depressing, the calculus of pleasure and pain is reversed in some Asian societies. Making decisions means taking risks, while security lies in having no choices to make. It is the unfortunate weak who have to confront alternatives and make trade-offs, and thus become vulnerable to mistakes, while the powerful need merely act according to prescribed rules. Thus, the more powerful the figure the more constrained the life; kings and emperors were totally bound by rituals, customs, and sumptuary laws which governed every aspect of their conduct and limited their choices.

When power is seen as unrelated to choice, politics becomes a way of trying to freeze society into its existing mold. The legitimacy of the social order is premised upon principles that are somewhat insensitive to the public performance of the supreme figure. Consequently, in terms of the contemporary American notion of power as decision-making, there is a perverse reversal of priorities: rulers are not held accountable for the policies of their governments, but they can be criticized for their private behavior.

In these cultures people tend to see power as status, a tendency which is still widespread in much of Asia and which even today many Asian rulers nostalgically wish to preserve. For when power implies the security of status there can be no political process. Contention and strife cease. All are expected to devote themselves to displaying the proper respect and honor for others, according to their station. Any criticism of leaders becomes an attack upon the social system. Hence to criticize is to display bad taste, to be less than worthy.

At other times in Asian history, power has been seen in highly personal terms. Political elitehood was associated with such considerations as wealth, birth, wisdom, education, religiosity, skills, or simply features of personality. The particular basis of elitehood makes considerable difference in the way power is perceived and in the style of political action. In general, birth has played a smaller role in Asian history than in Europe, with only Japan having a form of feudalism comparable to the Western variety. But, of course, India had the caste system. On the other hand, where Asian societies have opened the door for some degree of competition, the consequences have generally not been meritocracies according to standards of efficiency in governmental performance. Rather, Asian cultures have tended to seek gradations according to virtue, producing what Susan Shirk has called, with respect to Maoist China, "virtuocra-cies."[34] Rulers supposedly are more virtuous than others and thus they deserve more status and power. In China, of course, virtue was associated with the doctrines of Confucianism; in parts of Southeast Asia virtue was related to religious performance. The result in all cases was a form of rule by example which inevitably became highly personalized.

Today, in most of Asia, power is seen as residing in the person of high officials and not in their offices or in institutions. Leaders capture insti-tutions and change them for their own purposes.[35] The degree to which power is still personalized and not institutionalized in constitutionally defined offices can be seen from the fact that in every Asian country except Japan there are or will be succession crises. The passing of Deng Xiaoping, Ferdinand Marcos, General Suharto, Lee Kuan Yew will cer-tainly bring significant change in the politics of each leader's country, as has happened in India with the assassination of Indira Gandhi.

Once power is personalized, legitimacy becomes linked to private be-havior; and thus personal morality becomes a public matter. Hence the nearly universal theme of Asian politics continues to be charges and countercharges of corruption. The usual characterization of corrupt be-havior is not so much that officials have used public office for private gain (which to a degree is generally acceptable), but rather that in their private lives leaders have not behaved in an exemplary fashion.

The distinctive nuances in attitudes about power in the various coun-tries have, of course, been shaped by a blend of responses to immediate realities and memories of past experiences. Since much of the historical record can be traced in the available literature, it is understandable that scholars, especially foreign ones, seeking to investigate political cultures have tended generally to give prime importance to those "realities" which have been dominant in the respective histories. How much weight should be given to interpretations based on such public histories is hard to judge, but it seems certain that traditional scholarship has tended to exaggerate the significance of such "objective" historical influences, important as they certainly are. Scholars feel on surer ground when they restrict them-selves to the conventions of historical interpretation of tradition and avoid as much as possible the probably more significant subjective realm of a people's collective cultural memories. Seeking to understand how a cul-ture at any particular moment succeeds in blending memories and present perceptions becomes, too often, a problem that is conveniently ignored.

This is likely because, next to religion, politics probably offers people the greatest scope for fantasies about cause and effect. There seem to be no easily established bounds to a people's sense of the possible, or their expectations about the probable—particularly when they are speculating about the workings of power. Notions about what those seen as powerful can or should be able to do are easily magnified for at least two reasons.

First, the very nature of political authority, regardless of its distinctive dimensions, is that those possessing it have to command more influence and accomplish more things than ordinary people. People also want to believe that their leaders are capable of doing great things because in this way they become personally associated with a potentially successful collectivity. The individual's self-esteem is thus inflated in proportion to his capacity to imagine greatness in his acknowledged leader.

A more important reason, however, for the tendency to believe that the powerful have almost magical capabilities is that everybody has experienced in infancy and childhood the "reality" that parents and adults do seem to have unlimited power and can, if they wish, perform deeds that to the child seem miraculous. Young children know that parents can make everything all right for them, and when things aren't right it seems as though parents are willfully withholding their magical powers. Thus superiors who are strong should clearly have the ability to benefit or harm one, but the way they will choose to act is what is hard to predict. These early private experiences usually are expanded into community patterns as people share with their peers their early fantasies of what "superiors" can, almost effortlessly, do. It is not unnatural for people to generalize from their parents' behavior to that of other authority figures.[36]

There is thus a general predisposition to expect that authority figures can perform great feats which will affect one's well-being, if only they are inclined to do so. The dividing lines between the possible, the plausible, and the desirable are thus peculiarly vague when people build up their expectations about the scope of efficacy of the politically powerful. Consequently, when political leaders fail to deliver what is wanted, it is natural to suspect their motivations, not their capabilities. Coming of age means in all cultures that to some degree the earliest fantasies of omnipotence get suppressed to some degree, but the limits of the reality of social power always remain vague.

Thus the combination of unfettered imaginations, fueled by the earliest individual experiences, the constraints of sharing those fantasies, and finally the qualified limitations of the community's historic memories (which, however, have their own exaggerations) all add up to images of power that are unique to each culture and are not firmly bounded by reality. Furthermore, the sentiments associated with such images cover a wide range, running from fear, and even terror, to awe and deference, and including above all the comforts of dependency, of feeling that one is being protected, nurtured, and guided by a wonderfully superior force.

The very extremes underline the key fact that there is ambivalence in all feelings about authority.

Political Culture and Modernization

Our review of Asian experiences will reveal that some of these cultural patterns have been surprisingly helpful for modernization, while others have created apparent problems. It would be tempting to try to isolate the constructive patterns and to suggest that they should be widely adopted. Unfortunately, however, cultural traits are not so easily shared, a fact which is usually overlooked by those who call for cross-cultural learning—whether it be Asians taking up Western ways or Americans employing Japanese management practices.[37] Glib discussions of "technology transfer" encourage the idea that what works well in one society can be easily adopted by another, when in fact the processes of cultural diffusion have throughout history operated slowly and usually at considerable social cost.

This is particularly true with respect to any arrangement involving superior-subordinate relations, such as political and social power relationships, organizational forms, and management practices. The reason for this is that, along with learning about the magical powers of parents and adults, all individuals also develop preferred defense mechanisms for reducing the sense of threat from the powerful and for maximizing positive responses from them. People tend to learn very early how best to deal with power and authority, and they even develop patterns of behavior which they expect will help them effectively manipulate the powerful. Indeed, not only do cultural concepts about power involve expectations about what power holders can or should do, but they also include notions as to how best to deal with power so as to reduce dangers and gain advantages. Private and deeply held psychological adoptions of such defense mechanisms also tend to become peer patterns as children learn from one another what works and what does not in dealing with parents and authority figures. What is learned eventually reinforces cultural norms. Hence attempts to change them are likely to trigger hostile reactions.

For these reasons, along with others that do not need stating, the conviction behind this study is that there are many different Asian paths toward modernization, and therefore we shall be generally unsympathetic to the suggestion that what has been effective in one country should necessarily be tried in another. We shall point out, for example, the limits of the "Korean model," or of Japanese institutions; and we shall stress the different mixes of policies and practices among even the countries that are often treated as being similar, such as the "gang of four" of Korea, Taiwan, Hong Kong, and Singapore.

We do not, however, want to suggest that, as significant as differences in nuances about power are, there may not exist at a more general level certain Asian concepts of power, which in all likelihood separated Asian approaches toward modernization from the Western experience. The fact that most Asians were latecomers and had to react to the impact of the West gave a common dimension to Asian problems of modernization. Moreover, there do seem to be some features of Asian civilizations that have set them apart from Western civilization. Probably the most significant of these is the Asian tendency to place more value on the collectivity and to be less sensitive than the West to the values of individualism.[38]

In all societies views about power encompass a continuum which extends from concern for the well-being of the individual to protecting the interests of the whole community. Thus Asian societies are not without norms about how the individual should be treated by the powerful, and in the West there have similarly been concerns about the strength of the social fabric and not just the protection of individual rights. Yet, while recognizing the need for such qualifications, it is still possible to note the existence in general of such a distinction and to suggest that it is likely to be significant in making Asian modernization different from Western modernization.

Thus, the Western belief that progress should result in ever greater scope for individual autonomy is not taken as self-evident by most Asians, who are more inclined to believe that greater happiness comes from suppressing self-interest in favor of group solidarity. The success of the Japanese, and now of the Koreans, Taiwanese, and Singaporeans, in building modern institutions through strong group loyalties suggests that individualism does not have to be either a prerequisite or a consequence of economic development. Although in recent years there has been greater appreciation of this fact with respect to industrial management practices, there has been almost no recognition that it can also produce quite different patterns of political development. Instead we find, paradoxically, that while Americans seem almost envious of Asian feelings of group solidarity when it comes to economic organization, they continue to classify the same behavior in the political realm as a form of authoritarianism. Many Asian regimes have unquestionably been obnoxiously authoritarian. Yet a reverence for individualism can blind Westerners to the fact that Asians can find satisfaction and security in knowing that their social fabric is firm and that they have the blessings of belonging to some larger and coherent community. The pluralism which seems so desirable to Westerners was rejected in those Asian cultures in which there were only the two alternatives of consensus: loyalty and conformity, or selfishness and opportunistic scheming. Thus, before passing judgment, it is necessary to acknowledge the importance of both individual freedom and society's needs, and to recognize that Westerners are likely to be more sensitive to the first issue and Asians to the second.[39]

The Asian orientation toward the group, rather than stressing the individual, affects not only basic political values but a wide range of ordinary political behavior. It elevates tests of loyalty and commitment, for example, to matters of utmost political importance, while downplaying the legitimacy of using politics to advance special interests. In the East Asian societies which were once infused with Confucian values political associations are themselves seen as being properly modeled after the family and the clan, and hence participants are expected to act as though they were banded together in a blood relationship. This importance of belonging and of suppressing personal preferences in favor of the group's interests has other, secondary consequences. The divide between friend and foe becomes exceedingly vivid and is not amenable to change. Conflicts take on the long range and uncompromising perspectives of family feuds. There cannot be the kaleidoscopic realignments typical of the coalition politics of interest-oriented political systems. Changes of loyalty are distrusted by all concerned, for the reward of participation is assumed to be mainly the benefit of having a sense of belonging and not the hope of payoffs from any policies that may be realized. Individuals are expected to stick to their group loyalties or stay out of politics altogether: anything else is pure opportunism. But naturally there are variations on this theme among the East Asian societies.

The patterns in South and Southeast Asia, while not so explicitly modeled on the family, are also strongly group-oriented, but according more to the ties of patron-client relationships. In South Asia, and especially India, this has meant that the politics of patronage generally prevails over the politics of policy implementation. In Southeast Asia the politics of entourages and cliques, of personal networks and associations, are critical for the building of coherent national power structures. Thus, even such hierarchical institutions as national bureaucracies and military establishments tend to be facades for pyramids of informal, but enduring, patron-client groupings.

Above all, Asian stress on group associations encourages a leadership style which often strikes Westerners as being highly paternalistic. Among Asians, however, the concept of paternalism does not have the stigma it does in the West. In most Asian cultures leaders are expected to be nurturing, benevolent, kind, sympathetic figures who inspire commitment and dedication. The Western concept of the leader as being the commanding executive, firm in decision-making and vulnerable to second-guessing, is less appreciated in Asia. The relationship of power to the responsibilities of office accountability rests upon quite different concepts of power and authority.

As our analysis proceeds, it will become apparent that the general trend in Asia has been from views about power which stress status and hierarchy, divine order and ethical propriety, toward views that power should be useful in achieving practical goals. The ideal of development and modernization might therefore seem to be a utilitarian concept of power, a concept that would be very Western. Yet instinctively we pause before accepting such a conclusion because several generations of Americans, taught by the texts of Margaret Mead and Ruth Benedict, know that it is wrong to be ethnocentric. Indeed, Americans are probably the only people in the world who know the anxieties of saying something inconsistent with cultural relativism.

So it should be emphasized here that there are limits to utilitarian views of power. Exceeding these brings about the completion of the circle, in that it makes "modern" man stand on the same ground as "traditional" man. In other words, people can come to believe that the holders of power, that is, government and "the authorities," can solve all problems *if they only want to do so*. This assumption of the potential omnipotence of public policy in a highly rationalistic polity is exactly the same as the view of traditional man, who believed in the magical powers of demigod kings and medicine men. Both the ancient believers in the mystical power of the traditional upholders of the cosmic order, such as the Son of Heaven, and those "modern" people who are convinced that governments, if they only want to, can take care of all problems share the idea that they live in a world in which power is such that nothing needs to be accidental.

The irony of evolving concepts of power is that the power of modern science and technology has brought us right back to the views of ancient man: even death should not be a matter of chance or accident but should result from the will, or rather lack of will and skill, of somebody. The doctor who is sued for malpractice and the medicine man who is cursed are both believed to have *caused* evil things to happen because each is supposed to have the power to prevent evil.[40]

This peculiar return to origins is the outcome of the evolution of the concept of power in the West. The same thing need not happen in Asia, where the struggle to break from such an omnipotent and willful vision of power is of fresher memory, and therefore the virtues of living in a more probabilistic world are likely to be more appreciated.[41] Asians in the 1980s and 1990s will probably be like the Americans of the 1940s and 1950s who routinely took risks because they accepted probabilities rather than expecting certainties.

In any case, it is certain that in the past the Asian pattern of evolving concepts of power differed greatly from that of Western history. The overview of the evolution of Asian concepts of power in the next chapter shows that people in those cultures have positive feelings about dependency and have usually regarded a craving for autonomy as quixotic and unbecoming in civil relations. Before turning to that overview, however, three final comments are in order.

The first deals with the relationship between the distinctive political cultures of each Asian society and the policy choices of their respective leaders in seeking modernization. On this matter there are two diametrically opposed views: one holds that the policies of governments tend in the main to reflect the characteristics and predispositions of their cultures; the other is that leaders can be either wise or foolish in using features of their nation's culture in their strategies of modernization. The first view is highly deterministic and presupposes that policy choices are essentially dictated by cultural predispositions, while the second suggests that there is scope for rational choice, and room for accidents, and therefore the test of governance is how skillful leaders are in taking advantage of, and avoiding the obstacles inherent in, the basic characteristics of their national cultures. On balance this study will be tilted toward the second view, with the proviso that the predisposition of leaders in determining what they understand as the scope of their decision-making is largely set by constraints inherent in their own identification with their country's political culture.

The second comment is in fact a warning that in exploring the views about power in the various Asian societies we are going to find repeatedly that logically coherent views do not necessarily prevail and that people, in their collective moods and inclinations, are quite capable of adhering to contradictory positions. Thus, we may be forced repeatedly to generalize that in some political cultures there is a proclivity along certain lines, but there also may be an exactly contrary tendency. The fact that a political culture can enduringly hold to contradictory propensities has to be accepted as a fact and not as a sign of equivocation or fuzzy analysis; it is testimony only to the richness of cultural patterns, invented out of the limitless resources of the human psyche, which in many cultures have not been disciplined to accept the confines of logical consistency.

Finally, a comment on the structure of our analysis. Claude Lévi-Strauss once distinguished two approaches to comparative analysis.[42] The first, which he labeled "Aristotelian," works toward building a systematic typology by clustering similar facts in the same categories and striving toward ever more comprehensive generalizations. Such an approach has an elegant orderliness, especially if the categories can become the boxes of a fourfold table or matrix. The other approach, which he called "Galilean," involves examining all the cases in search of similarities and variations and then asking what might account for what is found while holding intact the particularities of the individual cases.

Our approach will be Galilean in that, starting with the general overview of all the appropriate Asian systems, we shall arrive at three clusterings of countries: the East Asian Confucian cultures of China, Japan, Korea, and Vietnam; the Southeast Asian patron-client systems of Burma, Thailand, Indonesia, and the Philippines; and finally the South Asian Hindu and British-colonial systems. Rather than treating these as Aristotelian categories, we shall continue the Galilean approach in the next three chapters by looking for the explanations of the variations among those in each grouping. Finally, we shall focus on each of the main countries in the remaining chapters in order to capture its distinctive features. By this method of ever more detailed analysis we will preserve and respect the individuality of each country even while suggesting that at varying degrees of abstraction they share some common Asian attitudes toward power.

The question of how detailed to make our analysis has been troublesome. Separate monographs could be, and indeed in some cases have been, written on the attitudes toward power and authority in each of the countries. The intellectual life of the social sciences presents a pattern in which the preferred explanations swing like a pendulum from the extreme of craving elegance in theoretical formulation and the ruthless application of Occam's razor to the other extreme of only being satisfied with "thick description." Theories which start off with all the beauty of simplicity— such as those of Marx, Keynes, or Freud—constantly accumulate qualifications and elaboration to the point of losing their power of abstract elegance in their richness of detail. But after a time "thick description" can also lose its charm as scholars long for purity of theory. In the area of political development the swing from the clarity of early structural-functionalism or even dependency theories has been going on for some time, but it does seem that at last there is some retreat from wanting "all the details." In this book we fall between the extremes: for some readers we shall be cluttering up our analysis with too many details, while for others there will not be enough, especially if they can think of exceptions to our generalizations.

2 | The Evolution of Asian Concepts of Power

A T ANY PARTICULAR TIME diverse concepts of power have been in contention in all Asian cultures. There have also been constant fluctuations in the interpretations of the nature of legitimacy. Indeed, day-to-day politics has often been filled with debates over the effectiveness of different strategies for testing the power of particular leaders, and much political talk has focused on whether power was being properly used for acceptable purposes. Yet, viewed from a longer historical perspective, it is possible to discern broad trends and to identify stages in the evolution of attitudes toward power and authority and in the myths that have upheld legitimacy in each of the Asian cultures. The process seems to have been one of accretion since new concepts have not necessarily replaced the old. Instead, a blending has usually occurred, or, possibly, distinct and even contradictory themes have coexisted. Over time, however, the accumulated effects of changes in attitudes and behavior have produced discernible new bases of political life.

Our purpose in this chapter is not to detail the evolution of concepts of power and legitimacy in Asian cultures, but only to note certain general patterns which were significant in setting the stage for the twentieth century problem of achieving the kinds of power essential for the tasks of governing the modernization process. We shall then be able to see how the different evolutionary patterns have contributed to both the general Asian approaches to modernization and the more particular situation in each country of Asia. In this chapter we will trace the outline of the "woods" rather than look at the "trees,"[1] reserving our more precise historical judgments for subsequent chapters.

It may seem that we are using the terms power, authority, and legitimacy very loosely. Certainly our basic theoretical approach denies us the right to impose our own culturally limited definitions. Having it as our purpose to determine how the different Asian cultures conceived of power, authority, and legitimacy, we cannot begin by suggesting, for example, that legitimacy and authority are considered, respectively, to be legally and morally sanctioned power, as has been customary in Western political thought.[2] As we shall see, the Asian societies did have ways of trying to tame and inflate power simultaneously.

According to their concepts of authority and legitimacy, the Asians wanted to control and inhibit their rulers, while at the same time recognizing the society's need to dictate general behavior that would extend beyond the ability of any individual to use force. Not surprisingly, by inventing the "myths" that make possible the extended grandeur of authority and legitimacy, Asians fell back upon many of the same themes that run through other societies: identification with the supernatural; definitions of model moral behavior; beliefs in the importance of birth, wealth, age, and learning; and the obligations to respect goodness and gentleness and to show deference for the aged, awe of theatrical splendor, and astonishment at the bold authoritative act.[3] Yet there are significant differences in the mix and in their nuances, and in dealing with appreciations of power it is precisely these nuances which make for dramatic differences from society to society.

In seeking to chart in general terms the evolution of concepts of power we are not trying to record the changing strategies and tactics in the use of force or coercion, but rather we are interested in the changing political concepts that help to define the evolving images of authority and beliefs about legitimacy. Thus we can set aside most of what would make up histories of warfare and the evolution of military technologies and strategies. We want to capture instead the sentiments and attitudes that have made the existence of government possible and that have determined the acceptable limits and obligations of ruling authorities. Thus our concern is with power as defined by the political culture of particular times and places.

As a start we need only identify what we shall call "primitive power," that is, the crude, brutal use of force to intimidate. It is the power associated with brigandage, piracy, and pillage that takes over when there is no effective civil authority. Such primitive power amounts to pure aggression; it is to be contrasted with force which can be used in a cold, calculating way, completely devoid of aggressive sentiments. We start with the notion that the most basic function of government is to manage those manifestations of aggression which are basic to human nature.[4] Substantial authority can arise only when primitive power has been superseded. The beginning (and the end) of government coincides with the ending (or the beginning) of the reign of primitive power; and the sense of horror this power can evoke has an ambiguous relationship to all forms of legitimate authority. The fears it inspires can concentrate the collective mind and make preferable legitimate authority, even when that authority is considerably less than ideal. Thus harsh authority becomes acceptable because the alternative is seen as ultimate brutality. Nevertheless, the very capacity to imagine the horrors of primitive power can also lead people to fancy that their government may be approaching the borderline.

Our concern will not be with the historical incidences of primitive power or with identifying the moments when it might have prevailed in Asian history. Rather, we shall ask how the thought of primitive power has shaped and colored the changing concepts of legitimacy and of the proper use of power in the various Asian cultures. In all cultures there must be collective fantasies about the dangers inherent in primitive power for all except the lawless few. Does the culture tend to conceive of primitive power as a scourge that existed before the advent of civilization, something that belonged to a distant past? Or is primitive power a continuing, lurking danger, ready to surface with any faltering of established authority? Is it something that ominously lies ahead as society slowly becomes more degenerate and as rulers leave the ways of righteousness? Is it a cyclical phenomenon, experienced frequently in the past and likely to be experienced in the future? Did it destroy an idyllic community that was supposedly the beginning of history, the idealization of which has subsequently been behind much of the strife and conflicts of history, and which in turn will be eliminated by the arrival of another, and final, idyllic age (as in Christianity or Marxism)?

In the West the ideal of progressive modernization, until very recent times, has held that the problem of authority was how to inhibit it so as to allow spontaneous forces to achieve creative goals. Power thus has tended to be taken as a given, which needs to be constantly worked against if there is to be freedom and justice. In Asian societies the problem of modernization is generally seen as being one of building up enough power to carry out effective programs. In part, this difference can be traced to differences in perceptions about the danger of primitive power and the origins of the state.

Locating the Dangers of Primitive Power

In contrast to the West, traditional Asian cultures, with the notable exception of Japan, have generally not located primitive power in the distant past but have thought of it more as an ever-lurking danger in the future. The modern West has placed great value on progress, and hence the Western imagery of history has been one of a steady retreat from primitive power toward ever more refined and delineated forms of authority—to the point that some would say modern democracies are in danger of losing the capacity to rule.[5] In contrast, in much of Asia, again excepting Japan, the dominant view has been that idealized authority existed at the dawn of history and that the main danger of primitive power lies ahead, when there may be a breakdown of established authority.

Consistent with this view is the general acceptance by Asians of idealized authority even while they may dislike the practices of those currently in power. The greater Asian acknowledgment of the need for, and indeed the desirability of, authority contrasts sharply with the Western enthusiasm for limiting authority, which is unaccompanied by any fear that the result could be the revival of primitive power. Most Asians respect authority too much to share the Western distrust of authority and power, which was summarized in an editorial in the *Economist* in 1984: "the point about power is not who has it, but that nobody should have too much of it, because power is a bad thing."

In modern Western political philosophy it has been taken as self-evident that the correct starting point for speculative theory should be the question of the "origins" of the state, and it has generally been argued, most forcefully by Hobbes, that what existed before the state was a condition of primitive power, of brutish anarchy.[6] There has also been, of course, the counter-theme of an idyllic primitive community, a Garden of Eden or at least a primitive communism, but this has not been the dominant Western view of the origin of the state.

Furthermore, as it happened, the modern European state system emerged out of the prolonged strife and conflict of the late Middle Ages. Thus the widespread acceptance of the principles of Absolutism was facilitated in no small measure by memories of the horrors of pillage and ceaseless violence which Barbara Tuchman has so vividly brought to life in her description of the fourteenth century.[7] Absolutism answered a deeply felt need for order, but it also opened the way in Europe for authority to be used for novel purposes, that is, for guiding change, and not just for freezing the status quo. As Samuel Huntington has shrewdly pointed out, the doctrine of the Divine Right of Kings legitimized the possibility of temporal authority changing the laws, thereby allowing governments to design rational policies based on a sense of utility.[8] Previously the paramount idea had been that the laws of God and Nature were immutable and should prevail. Thereafter Western state-building proceeded in the spirit of quest and constant innovation.[9] It is true, of course, as Keith Thomas has pointed out, that Europe was not entirely without models for its state-building because it always had memories of Greece and Rome and of the Old Testament Kingdoms.[10] Yet, in a comparative perspective, the emerging European definitions of legitimacy were based less on idealizations of the past and more on the newfound considerations and doctrines of church-state relations.

Thus, in very general terms, it can be said that in the West the primacy of primitive power is largely associated with the past, either in the distant era before civilization, or during the reign of the barbarians after Rome, or with the violence which preceded the establishment of the state system under the rule of Absolutism. The modern era in the West has been largely devoid of instinctive fears of the revival of primitive power and has been free to concentrate on the desirability of whittling away at the power of the state, a reaction to the lingering effects of Absolutism.

By contrast, in Asia—where there have been speculative political philosophies, as in China, or religiously inspired myths about the origins of society, as in some Southeast Asian cultures and in the Hindu sacred texts—the dominant theme has been that, at the beginning, idealized forms of power existed, even though at times they were in contention with the forces of evil. Thus in China, even before Confucius, there was the notion of model emperors who had given all the elements of civilization to the Chinese people: Emperor Pan Gu had separated heaven from earth, Emperor Yu Chao had taught how to build houses, Emperor Sui Ren had shown how to start fires, Emperor Fu Xi had invented fish nets, Emperor Shen Nong had taught the people agriculture, and so on. In the terms of our analysis it is significant that the Chinese imagination came up with the idea of emperors, that is, political rulers, for the achievement of things which in the West were traditionally associated with divine or mythical powers.

In Southeast Asia, and more particularly in the Javanese, Burmese, and Thai cultures, the contending forces of good and evil, of light and darkness, of sea and mountains were mystical spirits believed to have been present before mankind existed. Consequently the concept of the origin of each society generally took the form of people needing to organize their community in order to protect themselves from the supernatural, which they believed they could do by adhering to strict taboos and following precise standards of conduct. The taboos were usually especially strict for the leaders, who had the major responsibility for protecting the entire community. As with the Chinese, the threat of primitive power was always present, and it would be released if men in authority failed to adhere to exemplary standards.[11]

Modern history in Southeast Asia has reinforced the sense that the violence of primitive power is a real possibility in the future. The racial riots that tore Malaysia apart in 1972 have left an anxious population aware of their constant need for civil authority. Lawlessness and banditry, at times under a barely disguised cloak of political insurgency, have been endemic throughout the region from Burma to the Philippines.

Attitudes toward authority in Hindu culture are more complicated and ambiguous, largely because modern Indian thought is divided over innumerable issues relating to early Indian history. The debate over the origins of the caste system reveals considerable uncertainty as to the nature of Hindu society at the dawn of history. Furthermore, the extended periods of foreign rule reinforced a tendency to depict the substantive core of Hindu culture as being without a political dimension, and authority as being differentiated according to caste and religious standards. By the nineteenth century, when Indian thinkers were writing about the origins of the Hindu state, their views had been heavily influenced by exposure to Western concepts and values. Many Westernized Indians, including Gandhi and Nehru, who disliked the concept of caste, suggested that originally the system had been little more than a division of labor in an ideal community but had become rigid and deterministic during the "dark centuries" of the Indian "Middle Ages." Other, more orthodox Indians felt that Mogul and British rule had corrupted Hindu society, and they argued that after independence there should be a revival of ancient Hindu standards.[12]

The ancient Hindu texts, however, give a picture of Indian history as a gradual process of corruption and decline from a golden age. The *Vana Parvan* speaks of the purity which men once enjoyed when unhappiness did not exist and every wish was fulfilled. Men were then equal to the gods. Decay set in, however, and the *Santi Parvan* tells of the horrors of a life without kings, laws, or social restrictions: "But then error crept in, virtue declined, lust and greed and jealousy appeared, there was no distinction between right and wrong, the Vedas disappeared and finally virtue ceased to exist." Thereafter the very concept of kingship was based on the need to prevent such a state of anarchy from coming into being. The doctrine of *Matsyanyaya* depicted the state of anarchy as analogous to big fish devouring little fish, and hence became a doctrine in defense of property. As noted in the *Santi Parvan:* "Nobody thus, with reference to any article in his possession, would be able to say, 'this is mine.' Wives, sons, food, and other kinds of property would not then exist. Ruin would overtake everything if the king did not exercise the duty of protection . . . If the king did not protect, everything would be exterminated prematurely, and every part of the country would be overcome by robbers and everything would fall into a terrible hell."[13]

Clearly, at one time the Hindu view of the origin of the state was sensitive to the dangers of anarchy. On the other hand, the ideals of Hindu religion contain doctrines suggesting that state authority should be of more marginal importance and that people should have inner standards of conduct. Consequently it is possible for present-day Indians to debate the question of primitive power in their cultural history, especially because of the complications introduced by the psychological issues of nativism, Westernization, and national identity. Nonetheless, when the problem of modernization arose, most Indians responded that, whatever might have happened in the past, they were in agreement that any serious erosion of authority would unleash the devastating effects of primitive power—a conclusion made vivid by memories of the carnage associated with partition and the breakdown of authority at that time.[14] Indeed, the frequency of not just religious riots but other forms of spontaneous mass violence calling for harsh police responses has been a constant reminder that anarchy is always a possibility in India. The bloodshed in the wake of Prime Minister Indira Gandhi's assassination revived the specter. And in Pakistan and Bangladesh the grip of civil authority has never been secure.

The one outstanding exception to the general Asian pattern is Japan, whose approach to primitive power was closer to the European experience. Japan too, before the emergence of the state system, passed through its Age of Troubles, some two hundred years of constant violence, feuding, and treachery, a period of primitive power run rampant. The final emergence of the Tokugawa system and the reassertion of the Shogunate as the effective power in maintaining order produced a form of centralized feudalism more like European arrangements than anything known in Asia.[15]

Before its era of internal disorders Japan had known legitimate stability and had been inspired by Confucian and Buddhist ideals of government and civil relations in much the same way as Europe had found inspiration in the epics of Greece and Rome. Thus once again Japan, as yet untouched by Western culture, had on its own achieved an historical evolution which paralleled the European experience.

What was most distinctive about Japan's attainment of control over primitive power and of the order upon which the modern state was built was that the Japanese, like the Europeans, but completely different from most other Asians, were able to find order while still giving scope to competition. The blending of order and competitiveness was made institutionally possible by a form of centralized feudalism in which daimyos still competed in various ways even while the supreme Shogun maintained general order. In terms of both political and economic history, the root of the "miracle" of Japan is precisely the unique elements of the culture which have made it possible for the Japanese to be highly disciplined and group-oriented and at the same time to remain extremely competitive, always striving to excel over one another and over all out-groups. Later we shall try to explain this quality of Japanese culture and to account for the difficulties the other Asian cultures have had in simultaneously maintaining competitiveness and order.

In summary, the collective fantasy about the danger of primitive power in most of Asia has held that the threat is omnipresent and lurks in the future, and that therefore any significant erosion of authority is always dangerous—a view that inclines Asians toward accepting what for the Western mind would appear to be authoritarianism. By contrast, in the West and to some degree in Japan, the dangers from primitive power seem long past, and therefore constraining authority can be accepted with equanimity. These are apparently deeply held fantasies, for they have been little affected by events.

The fantasy of the imminent danger of anarchy seems to suggest that socialization in such cultures has left people with suppressed rage, which they feel they can barely control, or perhaps which they must totally control if they are to prevent horrendous consequences. This hypothesis will be elucidated as we come to the various patterns of first experiences with discipline. Is exaggerated passivity toward parental authority a deliberate attempt to prove that one has no hostility toward one's parents? This question suggests a clue to Asian fears of a breakdown of authority.

There is a further contradiction between Asia and the West, particularly America, which has a paradoxical twist: although Asians have traditionally tended to crave stronger authority, their politics until recent times has not been directed toward policy choices and implementation. They want authority, but they have less interest in policies. In contrast, the West has had a long history of politics focused on policy issues, coupled with an enthusiasm for checking authority—an equilibrium which, at least in the United States, has at times ensured that there will be insufficient power to carry out the preferred policies.

The reason the Asians are more sensitive to the values of authority than to the values of applying power for policy purposes lies in the history of their concepts of power, which evolved from the unambiguous violence of primitive power into culturally distinct conceptions of governmental power.

Power as Ritual: Gaining Access to the Supernatural

In the history of governmental practices in Asia, the first and earliest theme deserving notice is the extent to which nearly all of the Asian cultures treated power as some form of ritual; that is, they developed early the idea that the correct performance of ritual produced the highest type of power. Those allowed to participate in the prescribed rituals were by definition the most powerful people of the community. The symbolic connections between acts of ritual and ruling are to be found in archeological sites from China to Southeast Asia, from the Indus River to the Japanese islands.

Although from early times Chinese culture was centered on this-worldly matters, the emperor's power to rule stemmed from his duty to perform the rituals that made him the Son of Heaven. In Southeast Asia the Hinduized states were ruled by god-kings whose elaborate rituals, carried out with sacred paraphernalia, presumably ensured that their structure of government matched at all points the design of the forces that ruled the cosmos. Hence as god-kings they were, through their rituals, a part of the cosmic order. Oddly, in India, the most otherworldly of Asian cultures, there was less need for the ruler to carry out rituals for the well-being of the entire society. Everyone in the society was individually absorbed in his own effort to influence the supernatural, following the rules of his caste, that is, his dharma, so as to improve the prospects of his karma in the next incarnation. Also, the rulers were not of the Brahmin or priestly caste. Yet, this qualification aside, the power of Indian rulers resided in no small measure in the ceremonial rituals they regularly performed.

In relating power to ritual, Asian cultures were implying that infinite powers lay external to the exceedingly finite powers at the command of any individual. The Chinese emperor, as the Son of Heaven, had to conduct himself in an exemplary way in order that society as a whole might benefit from the omnipotent goodness of Heaven and be protected from the incalculably bad consequences of Heaven's wrath. The events of man were seen as governed not by men alone but by such external forces as Heaven, the Tao, the Way, or more simply, by luck, fortune, and happenstance. Because the controlling forces of life and of history were believed to exceed the power of any one actor, the essence of Chinese political strategy was carefully to design ways to ensure that one was on the side of the controlling forces and that one's opponents would be defeated by such forces of fate without the need to expend any of one's own limited power. The Chinese notion of power emphasized the importance of timing, of selecting the propitious moment, of understanding when best to act—considerations which do not appear in the standard lists of the elements of power drawn up by Western theorists.[16]

By seeing the main forces of history as external to the actors and only marginally influenced by rituals, most Asian cultures disassociated two concepts which in the West were usually intimately linked: the concepts of power and responsibility.[17] Power that is generated by the performance of correct rituals lacks any precision of purpose. The person who carries out the rituals can be held accountable only for the general state of affairs which follows as a consequence of the ceremonies. The connection between cause and effect is not close enough to make it possible to criticize the precise ways in which power has been used.[18] Indeed, there is no way even to think about power as being in the service of policies guided by rational choice.

Even the rituals associated with ruling became in a sense talismans which presumably protected the community from all forms of evil and were believed to bring good luck. High officials acted out their ritual roles for the good of all, and at the common level there was the added insurance provided by the shamans.[19] Specific dangers and benefits had their different rituals, but in the main, ritualized power was a very blunt tool of rule.

Indeed, the indiscriminate quality of ritualized power meant that it could not be easily directed to favor the few and to harm the interests of the many. When the ruler behaved correctly, everyone benefited. Some might have more need than others to be protected, and some might have little hope even if good fortune did smile on the community as a whole. Yet ritualized power was not a form of power which could readily "set the agenda" for the community or deny the emergence of issues. It was common practice, especially in Southeast Asia but also often in China, for those who had problems to seek out the authorities in order to gain the blessings that might change their fortunes.[20] Rulers were expected to be responsive to the concerns of the people.

Historically there were two general bases for legitimizing power by ritual, both of which stressed the dominance of external, unseen forces. One was the Sinic approach, which asserted an ethical-moral sociopolitical order; the other, used in many of the Southeast Asian cultures, conceived of ritualized power in relation to a cosmic order ruled ultimately by otherworldly forces.

Power in an Ethical-Moral Social Order

Historically the Chinese have been unique among civilizations because they early came to see government in predominantly secular terms. Although the Chinese ruler was thought to be the Son of Heaven and was expected to perform what in other cultures would have been called priestly duties, the basic rationalizations upon which the myths of legitimacy were based were essentially this-worldly. In place of a divine source of authority, the Chinese, with their Confucianism, created an elaborate intellectual structure of an ethical order which all enlightened peoples were expected to acknowledge and respect. The political order was seen as essentially coterminous with the social order, and everything depended upon correct conduct in fulfilling personal roles, especially in seeking a harmonious family life.

In the Confucian tradition the Chinese adopted the taboo that it was inadmissible to speak of power except in moralistic terms. The realities of power and the overt use of force had to be disguised and transformed into matters of morality. At the same time, and somewhat paradoxically, the Chinese committed themselves to seeing relations always in hierarchical terms and attributing almost unlimited potential to those at the top. Rulers were accordingly limited to having only moral authority, though they were also expected to be able to relieve everyone's distresses.[21]

The concept of rule by example was premised on the notion that all people could be educated to appreciate virtue and to show deference to those who were their superiors in virtue. Needless to say, the Chinese also recognized that some people were bad and hence deserved punishment.[22] In a peculiar way the very acknowledgment that rule by example should be enough to create civil order legitimized extremely severe punishments, for if people have it in their nature to respond properly to good examples, then those who do not do so are truly evil, deserving of harsh, even vicious, treatment. Hence, because the concept of a moral order was also tainted with fear, imperial edicts couched in high moral tones would end with the standard admonition: "Tremble and obey."

These sentiments are well expressed in two quotations used by Arthur Wright in introducing papers on the Confucian "persuasion." The first is from the sixth century scholar-official Yen Chih-t'ui: "Influence for moral betterment proceeds from those above to those below; it extends from the elder generation to the younger. This is why, when the father is not kind, the son is not filial; when the elder brother is not friendly, the younger is not respectful; when the husband is unjust, the wife is not obedient. When the father is kind and the son refractory; when the elder brother is friendly and the younger is rude; when the husband is just and the wife is insolent, then these are people who are naturally evil, and they must be subjected to punishment, since they are not to be changed by counsel and guidance . . . The gentleness tempered with severity used in governing the household is indeed like that which is required in governing the state."[23]

The second quotation is from a seventeenth century official: "When the people are at peace, they are governed and live according to the rules of conduct (li), but when troubles arise, punishments must be used. When these penalties are not sufficient to control the people, the sanctions of religion must be employed, for men are frightened of spiritual forces which they cannot see or hear. We know that Buddha lived in ancient times, and we may employ his teaching, with that of Lao Tzi, even though we do not use their names, to reinforce the doctrines of Confucianism."[24]

The acknowledged need to be severe in administering punishments provided an outlet for aggression, which otherwise was supposed to be completely repressed in the Confucian model of authority. The ideal was that governing would be possible if rulers were arrayed in a hierarchy of ascending virtue which would awe the masses into correct conduct, except in the cases where punishment was needed. The rituals of government told everyone that those in authority were certifiably superior men, officials in what Susan Shirk has called a "virtuocracy."[25] Power so conceived was the very antithesis of the kind of power appropriate for the give-and-take of a competitive political process.

Indeed, the very essence of rule by moral example was anti-politics; that is, it precluded the kinds of activities associated with using power competitively in support of different values. Instead, rule by moral example favored the ideal of a static, conformist social order. Everyone was expected to know what the moral standards were that had to be shared by the entire community in order to achieve the passive state essential for such a style of governance. Those who were safely included in the elite could engage in debates about alternative definitions of virtue, but for the society as a whole there should be conformity and consensus. Yet, precisely because the norm of stylized rule allowed no concessions to the realities of contention, the counternorms of officialdom had to allow scope for devious tactics, intrigue, subtle ploys, and ingenious dissimulation among those certified as the most virtuous. The life of officialdom was thus built upon the foundations of hypocrisy. On the one hand, those within the mandarinate had to uphold with every written and spoken word the highest moral tenets of their Confucian ideology; on the other hand, the reality of the bureaucratic hierarchy called for constant scheming and calculated strategies for winning favors and hurting enemies.

Rule by ritual that was also based upon doctrines of an ethical-moral social order had to be limited government. Not only was such a form of power too diffuse and clumsy to implement discreet and subtle politics, but even more important, such power could easily evaporate if it was put too often to the test of trying to do too much. Their very pretensions of omnipotence meant that rulers had to be extraordinarily circumspect in admitting to a desire to accomplish any substantive policy, for if the objective lay beyond their capacities they would be discredited. As with devoutly religious people who are taught not to pray to God for worldly things for fear of showing up His limited powers in answering prayers, so emperors set severe limits on their policy ambitions. Ray Huang has explained how the Ming emperors and their ministers confined government to performing rituals while avoiding policy programs that would be certain to fail. To rule over such a vast and diverse country it was wisest to limit government as much as possible and to prove the excellence of the elite by attending primarily to ritual matters.[26]

Power as Ritual in Support of the Cosmic Order

Clifford Geertz has described the Hinduized Balinese state as a model of government by ritual, in which power was associated with ensuring that man and society were in proper relation to the cosmic order.[27] The blending of the powers of this world with those of the other world of spirits was so perfect that no part of government was really of the mundane world. Elsewhere in Southeast Asia the diffusion of the Indian idea of god-kings and of authority devoted solely to carrying out the rituals believed essential for the orderly relations of man, nature, and the sphere of the spirits helped to create for the first time political systems of historical significance: Pagan in Burma, Angkor in Cambodia, and Srivijaya in Sumatra.

The ideal of rule by a god-king meant that power had a sacred quality and therefore could not be debased and used for mere utilitarian purposes. The consensus was that those who ruled should devote all their time and energies to performing acts which would ward off evil spirits and help good spirits to triumph. Everyone should cooperate in supporting the rituals because the community as a whole, and not just the elite, had a stake in the cosmic order.[28]

Power as ritual endured in large part because it harmonized with a view of the social order in which every person had his or her ordained role. Although the version of Hinduism which spread to Southeast Asia was stripped of the concept of caste, and the more egalitarian doctrines of Buddhism eventually proved to be still more attractive to the indigenous cultures of the region, Southeast Asians responded positively to reincarnation, the basic idea of Indian religion, and to the principle that each individual occupied the station he deserved. Kings were superior to nobles, and nobles to commoners, as in European feudalism. But whereas in European feudalism competitive power was legitimately mobilized in rivalries among the lords, in Southeast Asia land was not so scarce as to make the owning of estates the basis for status differences. Rather, it was lineage that counted. From birth, allegiances were owed and protection provided in complex systems of mutual obligations. People kept to their stations because they believed that by so doing they were helping to preserve the cosmic order and thereby protecting themselves from greater misfortunes. The elite naturally could mobilize resources, but their rationale for doing so was that they would use what they collected for ritual purposes, thereby supporting the cosmic order.

Although the ideal of governmental power as theater and ritual reached its height in Bali, Pagan in Burma was in some respects a more telling example of nonutilitarian power. The greatness of Pagan lay in its dedication to religiously inspired construction; this civilization built some seven thousand monumental pagodas before it became exhausted and collapsed. In Europe the lasting greatness of the Middle Ages was also due to the grandeur of its religiously inspired architecture, its great cathedrals, but European society had other dimensions as well as other objectives for authority. In the case of Pagan the single-minded goal of government was to mobilize resources for, in worldly terms, a purposeless activity, since the only value of pagodas was to give their builders merit in the next world. The kingdoms which emerged subsequently in Burma took on more mundane dimensions, including particularly the practice of warfare. But still, some of the fiercest fighting, such as the Burmese conquests of the Mon kingdom, which depopulated much of the lower delta, was inspired by the wish to capture sacred Buddhist texts. The long history of Burma's victories over the Thai kingdom, and of Thai victories over the Cambodian kingdoms, had surprisingly little impact on the concepts of authority in the region. Warfare took the form mainly of raids in which the vanquished became slaves, as in the case of the Cambodians who were forced to dig the canals of Bangkok; but such military adventures did not evoke in the victors a martial tradition of authority.[29]

The experience of periodic raids and warfare did, however, have one lasting consequence for mainland Southeast Asian cultures. It instilled in all of them a deep distrust of foreigners and a suspicion that the presence of outsiders would endanger the entire community. Warfare did not teach the various kingdoms how to improve their capacity to raise forces and project power more effectively, but instead it made them more xenophobic. This was quite different from the function of warfare in Europe, where both experience with, and threats of, war forced governments to improve their capabilities, particularly in organizing their people and extracting resources from them.[30] In Southeast Asia the only internal effect of victory was the reaffirmation that everyone should adhere to his or her proper station in the natural order of things. Defeat, on the other hand, brought a general collapse of the system.

The Southeast Asian belief that kingly powers and the supernatural were blended did not take the essentially utilitarian form of asking for divine support for mundane activities. Southeast Asians did not just pray for victories in their wars, as most peoples have, but they saw all governmental activities as dedicated to achieving harmony with the supernatural—a belief that at times required them to fight against others. In short, this-worldly purposes could not be furthered by asking for the help of other-worldly power. Rather it was the other way around, in that this-worldly activities might be directed toward achieving other-worldly goals.

Enduring Consequences of Ritual Politics

The Chinese and the Southeast Asian versions of ritualized power produced two lasting effects. They left their respective cultures with, first, a deep sense that the locus of power was external to any particular actor, and, second, an awareness that cause and effect in political affairs could be extremely complex and might involve much that was invisible.

Whether the rituals were presumed to be efficacious for a moral order or for a cosmic one, the first consequence was to believe that there were massive forces, beyond the direct command of individuals, that controlled the destinies of rulers and of whole societies. Included in the Chinese tradition was the Taoist belief in the all-powerful Tao or Way that controlled the universe, as well as the Confucian belief that by practicing moral virtue rulers could tap omnipotent forces which would give order to the entire country. In Southeast Asia the external forces were explicitly supernatural powers in the form of particular spirits, such as the nats in Burma or the more impersonal forces of nature found in the Javanese cultures. In both cases all actors were perceived as inherently weak, and leaders sensed their own vulnerability as they judged events to be governed by forces ranging from the earlier version of Heaven, spirits, or nature to the later more secular concepts of fortune, luck, or even history.

Instead of conceiving of the political power of leaders as that quantum of power which was the sum of the elements of power in the possession of each actor, these Asian cultures operated as though decisive force was somehow beyond the total command of anyone. Therefore, it was impossible for their political leaders to calculate rationally the relative power at the disposal of the others involved in political relations, for it was always possible for some apparently weaker participant to be more successful in benefiting from the vagaries of the external forces.

In China this led to the development of the doctrine of rule by "non-effort," or wu-wei. Even militarily the calculus of power was not limited to the raising of material forces, but stratagems, deception, and winning with minimum effort were also emphasized. In Southeast Asia decision-making hung on the words of astrologers and mystics whose calculations were hardly objective.

The second major consequence of treating power as ritual was that both cultures developed extraordinarily convoluted interpretations of political cause and effect. Explanations of events did not have to be limited to observable facts. The logic of cause and effect also included the activities of the invisible, supernatural world, which provided rich possibilities for justifying, blaming, and explaining what had happened. Planning, too, had to be based on many considerations other than the merely physical. Fantasies about spirits, ghosts, and other supernatural forces enriched Southeast Asian political cultures with highly imaginative theories of causation in history. As a result, all manner of acts and events took on significance as explanations of political developments. Southeast Asians who considered themselves wise in the workings of power could find connections between apparently quite separate developments. To this day they tend to leave no room for coincidences and accidents, and Western diplomats must constantly try to convince them that there is nothing to the elaborate theories with which they try to link random developments.

Ritual and Status as Substitutes for Power

Although the history of India may be clouded with ambiguities and contradictory explanations, the character of Hinduism in shaping Indian society and culture is unambiguously clear. The elaboration of rituals which set apart the more than two thousand *jati* that make up what

Westerners have called the caste system came to provide a powerful basis for the orderly structuring of society, with a minimum role being assigned to governmental authority. The classifying of the *jati* into the four varna (or colors) of Brahman (priest), Kshatriya (warrior), Vaisya (merchant), and Sudra (laborer) meant that ritual had become status.

In a fundamental sense, temporal authority was not essential in Hindu society because the rituals and the taboos of pollution required that everyone adhere to his assigned social status. Each caste could handle its own problems of discipline through its respective panchayat, or council of elders.

The caste structure of the Hindu social order reduced the trauma that might have resulted from the long history of foreign conquests of India. The invaders simply became another grouping with its own rules of conduct. The Indians themselves could ignore most of the activities of the invaders because they were more concerned with their own rituals and rules of status.

It is paradoxical that, whereas Hinduism gives high status to the priestly role and to religious sensitivity, it also allows for a sharp separation between religion and government. Government can therefore be largely amoral. Hindu statecraft reflected the specialized knowledge of a small group of rulers, in a sense a caste, and was not a concern of the population as a whole. Yet the powerful disciplining role of ritual and status in Hinduism prevented the emergence of a view of politics as contention over the use of power to further different values in the form of precise policies.

The Politics of Status and the Value of Dignity

The next step in the evolution of the concept of power in Asia was the secularization of the magical concepts of moral and cosmic forces so that power became identified with the legitimacy of the existing social order. Power became nothing more than social status, and to exercise power was simply to perform high-status roles. In some respects power became even less utilitarian since it could only be used properly in adhering to the norms of established roles. To use power for practical purposes, particularly to advance one's own interests, could compromise the legitimacy of one's status and thereby turn the whole society against the taboo violator.

In this phase, the politics of status, the differences between the Confucian and Southeast Asian societies were less striking. In the world of status politics the participants were concerned above all with dignity, deference, and evoking awe. The power of Chinese mandarins came from their status, and as their status improved they were seen as deserving greater deference and were thought to command greater power. Those who were perceived as overly ambitious manipulators in maximizing power lost respect and hence lost power.

To the extent that people with status could exploit their positions explicitly, they were expected to do so in ways that would benefit those of lower status who were in need of help. In Southeast Asian cultures this process produced the various systems of patron-client relations. Such an exchange relationship included a form of dependency in which, in return for manifesting deference and awe, inferiors could expect security and understanding.

In Asia the politics of status refined the people's sensitivity to the essence of personal relations and also produced elaborate calculations of mutual obligations. Because the notion of relationships is inherent in the concept of status, the politics of status became in practice a highly personal form of politics. The imperative that people should above all recognize their personal obligations and their ties of acquaintanceship meant that any attempt by powerful officials to advance impersonal public policies was usually seen as a way of avoiding personal obligations and duties. In the Chinese context, in which the family was the prime unit of social identity, officials were expected to place their lineage obligations above any abstract notion of public policy; in Southeast Asia a broader network of personal obligations had recognized priority. In both situations it would have been considered a scandal for officials to avoid such personal obligations by using the excuse of having to adhere to more universalistic norms or to treat people only according to merit.

Paradoxically, in the politics of status the issue of corruption is always present. Whenever officials were attacked it was not that their programs were faulty, for they rarely had programs, or that their policies were ill conceived, but rather that they were personally corrupt and lacking in moral sensitivity. There was, however, always a fine line between being truly corrupt and only doing the right thing for those to whom one owed personal obligations. People of high status had a duty to help those dependent upon them, and hence many particularistic activities were not seen as corruption. Corruption was associated with the violation of personal morality, the seeking of material benefits for the self alone.[31] Or, more often, corruption was associated with failing to adhere to the standards attached to one's status or role.

Status politics was personalized politics in which those with power were circumscribed by elaborate rules of conduct that inhibited their effectiveness in commanding others for a larger public purpose. Status rested upon ceremonial behavior, that is, on careful observance of ritualized practices. Chinese history is filled with accounts of the frustrations of emperors who were virtual prisoners of the mandarins, who diligently saw to it that they carried out all the prescribed rituals of government. Freud in *Totem and Taboo* vividly describes the powerlessness of traditional rulers who were entangled in so much ceremony that they could do nothing that would damage their subjects, who, for their part, kept coming up with new "traditions" to further inhibit the actions of those who were supposed to rule over them.

Corruption was thus universally understood to be, above all, the violation of these norms of constraint upon those of high status. Improper conduct, and not necessarily or even usually the use of status for private material benefit, was what suggested that the power holder might be shamelessly violating the taboos of his status.

In all Asian societies, including Japan, there has been ambivalence about the relationship between wealth and power. The general view was usually one in which wealth should not properly lead to power. In China, merchants were assigned low social status, hence denied power; and they could only improve the status of their heirs by educating them as scholar-officials. In Southeast Asia to this day the very wealth of the Chinese has been enough to legitimize their exclusion from the circle of the particularly powerful, while in India, of course, sharp caste differences separated the Vaisyas as merchants from the Kshatriyas and Rajputs as rulers. Yet throughout Asia it has also been considered natural for wealthy people to have high status and hence power. Particularly in Southeast Asia the cultures have provided for more than just an acceptance of a world divided between the rich and the rest; indeed, wealthy people are required as the necessary patrons of others. Those who are wealthy and hence have power are automatically expected to act in ways that are helpful to those who are dependent upon them. This obligation of charity could in many cases be discharged by little more than a symbolic money donation, but it had to be met.

When power was seen as properly associated with status, the thrust of political behavior was always in the direction of stability and order for the total system as well as dignity for the individuals at every station in society. For kings and emperors this meant that grandeur and splendor were prime objectives. Officials commanded awe simply by their presence. At the same time, however, lesser figures also had their right to dignity. In the Confucian system of hierarchy the peasant was formally ranked just below the leading scholar-official, and whereas in actuality rural people were rarely so honored, they still had their rights of respectability. In the Hindu-Buddhist cultures the concept of dharma allocated to each of the recognized roles of society a special ethic and hence a claim to a proper degree of dignity.

The secularizing of power that occurred when the rituals of either the cosmic or the ethical order were elaborated toward a more vivid recognition of status caused most Asians to distrust politics. They regarded it as a competition between collective values and the desires of special interests. The result was a well-established attitude of anti-politics. The ideal of a competitive political process could hardly emerge in cultures that treated leaders as objects of reverence. Constructive criticism of leaders could only take the form of asking that they adhere more closely to the passive postures that evoked dignity. To do other than extol the established norms was to challenge the entire system, that is, to become a rebel and hence a legitimized target for the release of the suppressed aggressions of everybody in the society.

Indeed, criticism was not generally seen as the advancing of alternative policies and values, but rather as bad taste and a lack of civility. Those who overtly disrupted the political order became outcasts, unworthy of membership in the community.

Consequently politics became the articulation of consensus. The Chinese Confucian order was built on the iron principles of orthodoxy. In every Southeast Asian culture there have also been explicit rules for consensus decision-making. In Indonesia the ideal of *gotong-rojang* is an elaborate version of collective decision-making in which everyone can advance his views but in the end the senior figure declares what the consensus is.

The stifling of contention in deference to the value of orderly status relations produced an effect in most Asian societies which suggests the idea of authoritarianism to the Western mind. Yet because these societies had a very different concept of power, it is only partially correct to see the relationship of superior and inferior as authoritarian. The intolerance of criticism and the pressure for conformity do justify the charge of authoritarianism, and at times even of despotism. Yet precisely because the Asian view of power was not one of command and decision-making, the hierarchical status relations were in fact not imbued with the spirit of domination inherent in true authoritarianism. The effect of this difference was to encourage the development of forms of paternalistic authority, and the suppression of criticism in paternalistic authoritarianism is quite a different matter from the denial of criticism where power is associated with the advance of policies and programs. In that Western view of power, authority and participation are seen as contending forces, with authority striving to stifle participation. By contrast, paternalism is meaningless without participation, for there can be no father without children. In Asian politics patrons and clients seek each other out for different but equally compelling reasons, and the spirit of mutual dependency is quite different from the Western expectation that the bonds which tie superiors and inferiors are likely only to allow the former to manipulate the latter for their own interests.

Colonial Rule: The Politics of Law and Order

The Western impact produced paradoxical consequences in Asia: in the countries which escaped foreign colonialization, such as China and Japan, the possibility of it was enough to provoke some leaders into perceiving that power might be put to new, and essentially Western, goals; while in those countries that did fall to colonial rule, traditional views of power as status and a source of dignity continued to predominate. Western domination opened some minds to ask what might be the source of the West's superior power; while for others the reality of foreign rule reinforced dependency attitudes and the idea that government was the sanctioning of the social hierarchy.

In both China and Japan advocates of learning from the West challenged those who called for the reinforcement of traditional values and practices. In China the issue became one of Confucian values versus Western technology.[32] To cope with the manifest superiority of Western military power, Chinese intellectuals concentrated on what they called the *t'i-yung* dichotomy, which was an early example of looking down noses at Western materialism and praising native spiritual values. In this formula *t'i* stood for "substance," "essence," or "fundamental values," while the *yung* meant only "means" or "utility." *T'i* was of course always superior, more precious than *yung*. Advocates of the formula argued that China should adhere to Confucianism or *t'i*, but that Western technology could be adopted because it was the lower order of *yung*. Thus, as one Confucian worthy put it: "To control the barbarians through their own superior technology is to drive away the crocodile and to get rid of the whales," that is, British guns and ships.[33]

Out of this dichotomy came the basic tension in the Chinese modernization revolution between the relative importance of values and techniques. The Chinese have for over one hundred years been torn between believing that power was derived from the intensity of people's commitments to established values—first Confucianism, then the San-Min-Chu-I, and finally Marxism—Leninism—Mao Zedong Thought—and believing that power would come from the pragmatic use of science and technology. The notion that power flowed from ideology and that the most virtuous believers should become leaders was in a sense a continuation of the traditional Chinese view that power resulted from exemplary moral and ethical behavior. The fact that pragmatism has consistently been downgraded in favor of ideology is testimony to the difficulties the Chinese have had in abandoning their traditional views of power and accepting the idea that power should be seen in utilitarian terms.

The Japanese had an easier time in coming to the idea of pragmatic power. Under the formula of "restoring" the emperor, the Meiji leaders swiftly moved to select the "best" in Western practices as they set out to achieve greater national power. The transformation was made possible in large measure because Japanese traditional politics already accepted the idea of competition over power and believed that winners would replace losers in struggles, thereby creating new systems of domestic power alignment—something unknown in Confucian China where there was only the single model of an imperial bureaucratic system.

The story of colonialism in South and Southeast Asia is much too complicated to be summarized in a few words. Yet, in spite of all the differences between British, Dutch, French, and American practices, and between direct colonial rule and indirect rule through the use of traditional authorities, Western rule generally upheld the traditional Asian views that power is coequal with status and rulers have rights by ascription. Consequently the ideals of paternalistic authority and general dependency were reinforced. Sentiments that belonged to the old order were readily adjusted to fit the new phase of foreign domination.

The key difference, however, was that, except for American rule in the Philippines, Western colonialism carried the idea of a power or status hierarchy to an extreme degree through the institutions of legally based administrative bureaucracies.

The colonial bureaucracies built by the Europeans in a sense tidied up the traditional Indian and Southeast Asian proclivities to see power as the hierarchical ranking of people. The fact that in time the various civil services provided career opportunities for Asians coincided with the Asian instinct to think of power arrangements as mirroring social status. The match of old and new ideas about power was made even better because the end objective of colonial rule was essentially to preserve law and order, and thus the purpose of government remained that of upholding the social and cosmic orders.

The exception to this was American rule in the Philippines, where emphasis was placed on electoral politics rather than bureaucratic and administrative capabilities. The introduction of party politics, based on personalities rather than principles, did, however, reinforce traditional

Philippine attitudes of power as patron-client relationships, and hence did not produce so great a change in Filipino thinking as might have been expected. Power remained a matter of establishing contacts and seeking the security of dependency.

Denial of Utility, Efficiency, and Representation

This overview of the evolution of concepts of power in Asian cultures suggests that, except in Japan, the historic understanding of the nature of power had little to do with the concepts of utility, efficiency, and representation which have been central to understanding power in the Western experience. Power as ritual or status was an end value, not to be debased for utilitarian purposes. Since the goals of action were stylized acts performed in support of the collective well-being and not to promote specific policies, there was little sense that more efficient application of power would be desirable or even possible. Those with power tended to conceive of themselves as embodying the collectivity, defending a consensus, rather than representing particular interests. People tried to avoid adopting partisan positions on public "issues," but instead they generally preferred the techniques of intrigue and personalized tactical maneuvering, which were more compatible with conflict in stable hierarchical arrangements.

The aim of modernization in much of Asia has been to preserve a preferred structure of political relations while at the same time learning how to transform the concept of power into one that is more capable of achieving calculated purposes, as well as learning how to tolerate the adversary relationships of power which become inescapable as the division of labor produces greater social and political differentiation. The process of changing the concept of power from being a function of status to being a useful thing for achieving goals is profoundly difficult; it is filled with tensions because the psychological foundations of people's views about power are deeply embedded in their personalities.

The Western impact on Asia and the need to compete in an ever smaller and more technologically oriented world has forced Asian politics to use power increasingly as a means for achieving practical, collective goals. Yet cultural predispositions linger on, producing erratic ways with power. The same grip of culture makes it hard for Westerners, and particularly Americans, to think of power as anything other than something utilitarian. This has reached such a point in the United States that politics revolves around "problems," and the art of the politician is to unearth a constant flow of new problems for society. Americans have caused Asians to discover that they have more problems than they ever knew they had. Indeed, some Asians have found Americans a bit tiresome because of their habit of speaking about "problems" when they are supposed to be engaged in the pleasures of "talking politics."

3 East Asia: Varieties of Confucian Authority

T HE EAST ASIAN countries of China, Japan, and Korea—and also Vietnam in Southeast Asia—all absorbed and refined Confucian values and concepts of authority. But because of their individual cultural traditions, they also had their separate versions of Confucianism, which increasingly diverged as each country followed a different path to political modernization.

Viewed from the perspective of comparative history, the societies making up the Confucian cultural region of Asia seem at an early stage to have evolved concepts of power consistent with the requirements of modern state-building. The Confucian tradition is, after all, more this-worldly than are the guiding concepts of the Hindu, Buddhist, Moslem, or animistic cultures of South and Southeast Asia. In fact, China, a great civilization whose material accomplishments once surpassed those of the West, seems to epitomize the "hard culture" that Gunnar Myrdal, despairing of the prospects of India with its "soft culture" and otherworldly obsessions, declared to be essential for economic development.[1]

That the Confucian tradition does indeed present no barriers to modernization is suggested by the striking successes of Japan, followed by South Korea, Taiwan, Hong Kong, and Singapore, model examples of "newly industrialized nations," or NICs. That Confucianism was a compelling force that could in time drive its adherents beyond the achievements of the West has been voiced by many Western writers, from Marco Polo through Voltaire to Herman Kahn and Ezra Vogel, all of whom have been tantalized by the idea that East Asians are exceptional people, of unrealized potential. In addition, the conspicuous economic successes of the overseas Chinese living in Southeast Asia have inspired barely disguised racial explanations of the superiority of the Chinese over all other Asians.[2]

Yet China's manifest problems with every aspect of modernization over the past hundred years—from economic growth and technological innovation to modern government—would suggest that being Chinese or having a Confucian heritage is not enough to explain the successes in modernization of the rest of East Asia. In terms of the nature of power, moreover, there are significant differences between China, Japan, Korea, and Vietnam, even though they share a common Confucian tradition.

East Asian Approaches to the Concept of Power

In China, the Confucian legacy upheld the ideal that authority could be, indeed should be, an end in itself. Power was used simply to set an example of moral rectitude so that the conduct of all individuals would be exemplary. In this way virtue would be upheld and the consequence would be a peaceful, harmonious society rather than a society mobilized for grand purposes or for mundane problem-solving. Politics should be solely a matter of ethics, not the use of power to maximize values. The explicit prototype of government was the family, and therefore, not surprisingly, Chinese public life became analogous to family life.[3] The ultimate values of government were thus stability, continuity, and harmonious relations among all members. Yet in practice Chinese politics, like all politics based on family and clan, became a question of taking care of one's in-group and opposing all out-group factions, and hence politics was characterized by feuds rather than by programs.

Confucianism in China legitimized bureaucratic and imperial rule by a mandarin elite. All power and authority were presumed to fall into a proper hierarchy, in which superiors and subordinates were clearly defined. Any claims to power or authority which fell outside the single structure of government and society were seen as illegitimate—at best a part of a heterodox tradition, which was skillfully contained and hence tolerated as being too costly to stamp out, and at worst a manifestation of rebellion, deserving of the harshest treatment.

There was, however, a profound contradiction in Chinese Confucianism in that although the state could claim a monopoly of legitimate authority, at the same time individuals were expected to give total loyalty to the family and clan. The Confucian utopia was a society of perfectly managed families, each governed by ancestor worship and filial piety, over which a state authority composed of morally exemplary rulers could lightly rule. In practice, Chinese history was one of tensions between family loyalties and official obligations, between concern for one's immediate family responsibilities and sacrifices for the larger community that extended to the boundaries of Chinese civilization.

Hence in the Chinese scheme of things all legitimate power was limited to officialdom, and no significant forms of power were supposed to be at the command of any other element of the population, regardless of social station. Family or clan power was entirely an internal, indeed literally a domestic, matter. Family power became illegitimate as soon as it was transformed into social power, capable of contending with other forms of power, especially state power. Whereas in other societies merchants and gentry landlords wielded legitimate economic power, in China they were treated as though they did not, or should not, exist. Merely to suggest that landlords, for example, had local power was to imply corruption. The mandarinate made sure that officialdom had a total monopoly of power, and that no individual pushed his own special interests. That would have been a sign of selfishness, which according to Chinese Confucianism was a serious moral deficiency.

In the case of Japan, the Confucian legacy helped to legitimize a paternalistic form of elitism which produced a remarkable balance between order and competitiveness. Although, when Confucianism was first introduced, the Japanese did strive to erect a single monolithic structure of bureaucratic power, they soon reverted to their more natural feudal system, with autonomous lords commanding their separate fiefdoms. Confucianism in Japan thus became the moral basis for a system of decentralized and highly competitive power. Confucian principles dictated the struggle of the lords, or daimyos, with their samurai knights, to dominate one another, with one finally being recognized as the supreme lord, or shogun. Confucianism was thus turned into a warrior's ethic.

In the process the Japanese came to a relatively easy resolution of the dilemma of family loyalty versus state authority. The very pattern of feudalism which made it impossible for the Japanese to copy the Chinese bureaucratic system produced, paradoxically, a beneficial solution to the contradiction which had so long vexed the Chinese. In Japan family loyalty did not end with the boundaries of the family or clan but included loyalty to whatever superior authority the family acknowledged. Whereas in China the hierarchy was made up of officials, in Japan it was one of families, which were disciplined to fight for, as well as against, specific groupings.

In China, order could only mean static harmony and the repression of aggression; in Japan, order emerged out of intense military competition. In Japan, power was early associated with effectiveness, efficiency, and utility, values which the Chinese either did not overtly associate with power, or which, when it was essential, as in military situations, they submerged as far as possible by idealizing the concept of effortlessness. In short, the blending of feudalism and Confucianism produced a more purposeful, goal-directed concept of power in Japan than in the bureaucratic "virtuocracy" of either imperial or Maoist China.[4] In the beginning there was a sharp distinction between Confucian decorum and order and the instinct for excelling in feudal competitions; but in time the blend of values was so complete that the Confucian ideals maximized competitive efficiency rather than suppressing it—as is still the case in China.

In Korea, Confucianism contributed to a concept of power which accentuated the purposefulness of the Japanese approach and the elitist sense of virtue of the Chinese, a combination which has produced a bold, risk-taking style of action. Historically, Korean politics was too consumed with factional strife to permit the growth of the Chinese illusion that all of politics could be focused on achieving a stable state of harmony. Yet the Koreans took their exposure to Confucianism seriously and hence came to believe that virtue should and would be rewarded; therefore the elite could afford to take risks. At the same time, however, uncertainty as to who were the legitimate elite created a state of dynamic insecurity and produced people who were self-starters, having the risk-taking attitudes that Weber associated with the Protestant innovators of capitalism. In short, Confucianism made the Koreans aware of standards of excellence foreign to their culture, to which they could aspire, but in so doing it created aspirations for acceptance and anxiety about unworthiness which have made them audacious in carrying out enterprises that test and prove their worth. The result is a distinctive combination of discipline and lack of inhibition which make Korean political culture something quite different from a simple blend of Chinese and Japanese traits.

Indeed, more than any of the other Confucian political cultures, the Korean culture has been characterized by extremes. The Koreans have a strong attachment to disciplined and formal manners, to deference, and to a stiff and aloof style of authority; yet Korean culture also tolerates brashness and cockiness toward authority, boldness of action by leaders, and self-assertiveness by practically everyone. The gentleness of the Confucian scholar-superior can at any moment give way to brusque and often cruel assertions of authority.[5]

Korean history has provided little time for a reflective consolidation of cultural values. During the tumultuous period of the kingdoms the ruling class, the *yangban,* combined—with disastrous consequences—

the intellectual snobbery of the Chinese mandarin with the legitimized aggression of a Japanese-style feudal aristocracy. Then came the degradations of Japanese colonial rule, which for both collaborator and nationalist made viciousness seem legal and any form of conciliation seem a debasement of the individual. This was followed by the trauma of the postwar national division, the horrors of the Korean War, and finally the upsetting effects of the spectacular economic achievements under anachronistic military rule.

In the case of Vietnam, a Confucian concept of power contributed to a sense of national superiority, which was, however, flawed by having a foreign core. On the basis of their Confucian heritage and their Mahayana Buddhism, which also came from China, as well as their exposure to French culture and Catholicism, the Vietnamese conceived of themselves as superior to all other people in Southeast Asia. Theirs was a strange sense of superiority, however, because it was entirely derived from being conquered by the culturally arrogant Chinese, whose tradition, for all its pretensions of superiority, had no attraction anywhere else in Southeast Asia. Although Chinese mandarins liked to pride themselves on being able to awe "tribute" missions from Burma, Thailand, and even parts of Indonesia, the Chinese, except where their arms were victorious, had little cultural impact on neighboring regions, which were engaged in absorbing the essence of other civilizations. Southeast Asians derived their concept of the state from India, not from the equally available Chinese example; their religions came from India, and they generally rejected the versions of Buddhism which prevailed in China and Japan; their systems of law, both that of Manu and that of Adat, were taken from India and from the Arab traders. Only in Vietnam did people value the study of the Confucian classics and strengthen their sense of lineage by adopting the Confucian ways of ancestor worship. Yet, possibly because Vietnamese nationalism has such deep foreign foundations, it has had to be more assertive and more militantly fanatical, although it is also streaked with a melancholy fatalism.[6]

Thus the evolution of Confucianism in East Asia produced four distinct political cultures, each with a unique approach to the concept of power. In China, the hierarchies of virtue and the idealization of the family made authority an end in itself; in Japan, paternalistic authority was steeled by the purposefulness of intense competition; in Korea, any claim to authority legitimized audacious risk-taking; and in Vietnam, authority became associated with excelling at foreign ways while asserting nationalistic pride. These four political cultures with their different concepts of power and authority have, of course, evolved quite different patterns of modernization and political development.

Confucianism and Modernization

Of all the traditional societies of Asia, China would seem to have had the best chance of becoming an effective modern state. Blessed with a great historical tradition, a remarkably homogeneous population, a consensus about the values and the importance of government, and a strong appreciation of this-worldly concerns, it would have seemed natural for China to become the leader in the process of modern nation-building. Yet, paradoxically, the very strengths of traditional China seem in practice to have become liabilities, turning the so-called Chinese revolution into one of the longest unconsummated revolutions in history.

Western theorists in the nineteenth century were puzzled as to why China, which had once been more economically and technologically advanced than Europe, had become stagnant. Earlier thinkers, particularly the French, had been inclined to idealize Chinese wisdom and culture, presumably for having qualities they were advocating for their own culture. By the mid-nineteenth century, however, explanations for China's backwardness were being sought. Max Weber's sophisticated explanation for the failure of capitalistic development opened up a debate that still divides partisans. Briefly, Weber argued that the norms of Confucianism did not produce the same kind of psychic anxiety, and hence the same desire for achievement, as the Protestant ethic in the West. Sinologists, especially Thomas Metzger, have insisted that Weber failed to appreciate the extent to which Confucian precepts did constitute a source of tension between the ideal and the real, and therefore the Chinese situation was not so different from that in the West. By contrast, some evidence in support of Weber's view has been provided by psychological tests which suggest that Chinese feel less threatened by cognitive dissonance and hence are capable of living with the kinds of ambiguities and contradictions which presumably drove the Calvinist Protestants to economic achievements.[7]

The Marxist answer to the question why China's early successes in technological innovation did not produce sustained scientific growth, but rather were followed by decay and stagnation, has been given by Joseph Needham, who faults the class interest of the landlord-gentry in wishing to preserve the status quo. In a more complex analysis Mark Elvin hypothesizes that the rapid expansion of China's population in the thirteenth century favored labor-intensive rather than capital-intensive development, and that from then on there was little incentive for technological advancement because labor was so cheap.[8]

These economic and social issues are more than tangentially relevant to our interest in China's problems with political modernization. Fortunately we do not need to resolve them, because there are other questions which, if answered, can provide a first-approximation explanation of China's difficulties. By focusing on the political realm, and especially on Chinese attitudes toward power, we can look at China's economic and technological development from a different angle.

Politically, Confucianism undoubtedly provided the Chinese with a more secular basis for legitimizing government than existed anywhere else in Asia, or possibly in any traditional society. Confucianism upheld the ideal that rulers should be exemplary people who possessed greater skills and talents than those they ruled. Out of this belief in rule by the elite grew an imperial bureaucratic system that was one of the great achievements in human history. Thanks to its basic structure and idealized forms, the Chinese imperial system lasted for nearly two millennia, collapsing only in 1911. The Confucian scholar was trained precisely for government service, not for priestly roles, as were scholars in other traditional societies. Thus in China the highest forms of knowledge were directed toward the tasks of government and administration.

Nevertheless, in spite of these apparent advantages, the Chinese could not overcome the Confucian approach toward power which placed ritual and status above purposeful activity. In Chinese attitudes toward authority there were more than just formal ideological limits to the effective use of power, for the basic sociological and psychological patterns of Chinese culture also emphasized stability and order over action and achievement. One of the most extraordinary features of Confucianism was the way in which it elevated government and family to be the two key institutions of society, with each reinforcing the other. Crudely put, Confucianism decreed that the tasks of government would be lightened into insignificance if every family performed its tasks according to idealized standards; and government, in return, was expected to conduct itself in a way that would strengthen family authority. Thus Confucianism explicitly directed that children should be taught to have proper respect for all forms of authority.

But it is necessary to go beyond the formal doctrines of Confucianism, which were the same for all the East Asian cultures, to see how those doctrines were interpreted in each of the four cultures.

Family Patterns in the Four Cultures

Throughout the Confucian culture area of Asia, the family was considered the proper model of government. Relations between ruler and subject were seen as analogous to those between parent and child. Relations between states, such as suzerainty arrangements, could resemble those between elder brothers and younger brothers. Relationships lacking any special ties could take the form of those between clans, thus legitimizing suspicion and distrust. Because family was the model for government, it is important to understand the family patterns of the four Confucian cultures—both their common characteristics and their differences.

The first, and probably the most important, common theme was that individuals achieved their identities solely through family membership, which carried with it not only the obligation of deferring to the collectivity in critical decision-making but of acknowledging that the mortal life of the individual was less important than the immortality of the ancestral family line.

For the Chinese, Japanese, Koreans, and Vietnamese, Confucian ancestor worship generated an overpowering sense of lineage, as well as a palpable sense of biological descent. Having been made acutely aware of in-group and out-group identities, they logically concluded that "foreigners" simply could not become part of their own collectivity. By contrast, some of the Southeast Asian cultures did not even have a tradition of surnames. Indeed, overseas Chinese have sometimes justified their claim of superiority over the Malays, Indonesians, and Burmese by pointing out that because those peoples do not have family names, they must have no sense of lineage.

In all the Confucian cultures modern nationalism has tended to have a biological foundation which has reinforced the sense of the exclusiveness of citizenship. These attitudes prevail in spite of extensive exposure to the rest of the world. For example, the Japanese insistence on racial homogeneity surfaced recently when the Japanese government refused to accept many refugees from Vietnam; both the Koreans and the Vietnamese reject children of mixed blood; and the Chinese, even while formally acknowledging that the overseas Chinese may owe some allegiance to other governments, still regard them as having residual ties with the home country.

The model of the family and the imperatives of filial piety and ancestor worship have also given a sacred dimension to patriotism in the four countries. Having learned from childhood the importance of behaving correctly so as not to bring shame upon one's ancestors, those born into the Confucian tradition readily accept the notion that the living should be prepared to make the ultimate sacrifice for the ideals of the collectivity. All the mysterious questions about individual existence and mortality, which in other cultures are usually answered by religion, are resolved in Confucianism by reinforcing the individual's commitment to worshiping the ancestral spirits, whose spiritual status all will achieve in time. These spirits can be a source of assurance for the heirs of the Confucian tradition, for although they are stern and demanding, they are also just in meting out rewards and punishments.

By contrast, the Southeast Asians must cope with haunting and frightful images of the spirits of their dead. Indeed, instead of trying to maintain contact with their deceased ancestors, the Burmese, Thais, Laos, and Javanese generally perform acts which they hope will chase off the spirits of the dead. The absence of surnames in these cultures is in part a reflection of the desire to maintain distance from the frightening spirits of one's ancestors. Among Hindus, too, the otherwise strong sense of family is modified by the concept that each individual has his own dharma, his own fate, and his own prospects for reincarnation.

The second common theme of the four Confucian cultures, which had slight cross-cultural variations, was the stress on unity and stability. Just as the Confucian concept of the ideal government was an extension of the ideal family, so the prime tasks of government were the same as those of the family: to provide security, continuity, cohesion, and solidarity. In other words, government was modeled on that human institution which is directed toward self-maintenance rather than toward the attainment of external goals. Families are not normally mobilized for any collective purpose beyond that of looking after the well-being of its members. Other, larger human associations have responsibility for changing the environment and mobilizing resources to carry out specific social goals.

Thus, in a fundamental sense, Confucianism left vague any ultimate purpose of government beyond the maintenance of cohesion and stability. The upright ruler could, like a proper father, rule by example. But exactly how such exemplary role-model behavior might work to govern the conduct of others was left to the mysterious powers of "shaming"—which were considerable in Chinese culture because shaming was a principal method of disciplining children and of teaching them the horrors of "losing face." The Chinese even assumed that the powers of shaming could readily intimidate foreigners, who were expected to acknowledge the righteousness of China's positions and to appreciate China's success in upholding the cosmic order. The Chinese emperors took such an attitude toward the British delegations seeking routine diplomatic relations, and contemporary China has adopted the same posture, pointing the finger of moral condemnation at other governments while claiming perfect rectitude for itself.

In a strange way Chinese morality and government blended, means and ends became indistinguishable, and ethical conduct was not only the guide for government, but government was there to improve the ethical conduct of all. The purpose of government was to provide an environment conducive to harmonious, benevolent, and tranquil social relations; ideally, it had no interests or practical responsibilities beyond those associated with behaving as the exemplary and benevolent defender of harmony.[9]

The fundamental concept that government is analogous to the family produced the prime imperative of Chinese statecraft, the preservation of the unity of China. Chinese leaders of all ideological persuasions have agreed that the supreme goal should be to keep China as one entity, to unite all the historic territories, and to treat all ethnic Chinese as having natural ties to the homeland.[10]

Consequently Chinese rulers have always seen the reach of Chinese government as corresponding to the limits of Chinese civilization. More significantly, the emergence of modern Chinese nationalism, although it was stimulated by the Western impact, did not result in many national identities like those which rose out of the historic unity of imperial Rome and Christendom. Instead it produced the opposite reaction, a desire to perpetuate the unity of medieval China. The struggle of modern Chinese nationalism has been a Herculean effort to squeeze a civilization into the framework of a nation-state.

The historical and political consequences of this effort have profoundly shaped China's modernization. First, tremendous energies have had to be expended merely to maintain unity, with the result that little energy has remained for other objectives. Second, the fear of disunity—nearly a phobia—has prevented the emergence of competitive units within the cultural domains, which, in striving to outdo one another, might have achieved higher and more innovative goals. Had the different regions or provinces of the territory of Chinese civilization become separate entities, like the nation-states of Europe, some might have been as successful in modernizing as the competing units of Chinese culture—Taiwan, Hong Kong, and Singapore—have been. Nevertheless, it is true that by stifling the effects of such competition the Chinese were spared the terrible costs of the civil wars that Europe experienced during the rise of its separate nation-states.

Our purpose, however, is not to argue the relative cost-benefits of cultural unity and national competition, but rather to note that China's modernization path has been decisively influenced by its supreme commitment to unity. The compulsion of this ideal cannot be overstated. Westerners who do not appreciate the impulse behind it have consistently underestimated the "cost" that China is even now prepared to incur in order to facilitate the "recovery" of Taiwan and Hong Kong.[11]

Although the other three Confucian cultures shared China's emphasis on unity, they stressed it to different degrees and held different views about what should be united.

In Japan the theme of unity was more readily adapted to the smaller and essentially competitive groupings, such as clans, regions, companies, and other social institutions. At the national level it surfaced with considerable vigor during the years of Japanese imperial expansion and the military domination of politics. It is impossible to understand the reluctance of a parliamentary majority in democratic Japan to crush a minority unless one can see it as an extension of the attitude of the Japanese father toward the rest of the family, an attitude that stresses consensus and treats minority views cautiously.[12]

In Korea, because of the historic isolation of the peninsula and the homogeneity of the people, unity did not become a problem until the country was divided after World War II. As in Japan the theme of unity and harmony was expressed by subnational groupings. Koreans could afford to fight against one another, as they did during the period of the kingdoms, because they had little perception of an external threat. Yet even in terms of smaller groupings the theme of Confucian family unity was more an ideal than a practical norm. The members of the *yangban* or mandarin class were supposed to be a harmoniously united brotherhood of scholar-officials, but in fact they were an arrogant aristocracy, torn by rivalries and conflicts. In a sense they were the opposites of the Chinese mandarins in that competition usually won out over harmony and unity. In the Korean family there was no mistaking the superior role of the patriarch, and each head of household was expected to maintain order within the family and make decisions without the kinds of inhibitions that existed in Japan.[13]

The Vietnamese had a tradition of unity very similar to that of the Chinese. Beyond preserving the identity of the Vietnamese race, government was expected to provide a model of harmonious relationships. Domestic competition was regarded as unruly, as a sign that the leaders were unable to manage the affairs of the people. This view, which stressed the dignity of authority, contributed to the conclusion that the disciplined collective leadership of Hanoi was more properly legitimate than the would-be leaders of South Vietnam, who were chaotically contending over power and policy.

The need to allocate responsibilities among separate governmental authorities became a problem in all of the Confucian cultures because of their strong imperative for unity and consensus, based on the model of the father in the family. As a result of cultural differences in the degree and style of paternal authority, each culture has responded differently to the need for ever increasing specialization and differentiation of authority as modernization has progressed. The Chinese most of all, and then the Vietnamese, have had problems deciding on the proper division of authority. The Japanese have had the least difficulty, and the Koreans have fallen somewhere in between.

Of all the functions of a political system, the function of authority allocation has been the most troublesome one for China during the modernization period. The ideal that civil authority should operate like paternalistic power has caused the Chinese to feel that authority should have no precise limits and that its responsibilities are general and cannot be rigorously defined. Indeed, the ideal of omnipotent authority still persists, making divisions of responsibility awkward and the delegation of duties ambiguous. Leaders tend to see themselves as all-powerful, and the Chinese people continue to crave leaders who can solve all their problems. The tasks, however, are too numerous and demand too much specialized knowledge; consequently supreme leaders tend to reign, not rule, and to interfere in decision-making erratically. The "pragmatic" Deng Xiaoping has been as eager as the "ideological" Mao Zedong to interject his will into decisions at one moment and then to withdraw and allow events to take their own course, thus pretending to be all-powerful while at the same time avoiding total responsibility.[14]

In the Chinese family the model father, in return for striving for the well-being and unity of the family, can expect total deference and no explicit criticism. The entire family accepts the view that any "loss of face," or humiliation, of the father is an affront to everyone, and hence it is proper for him as the symbol of the family to be hypersensitive to criticism. In the political realm this attitude is translated into the general understanding that leaders are likely to be thin-skinned, sensitive to even hints of criticism, and ready to regard any questioning of their own wisdom as subversive of the common good. In the interactions of modern Chinese politics, whether under the Kuomintang or the Communist system, there have been bitter behind-the-back attacks but few open adversary relationships, except after the adversary has been destroyed. If attacks do surface, the break becomes deep and the only recourse is revenge.

At the other extreme stands the Japanese family with its interpretation of Confucian relations, based on the premise that because the family is surrounded by enemies, the duty of all its members is to uphold the family honor, even in the greatest adversity. Whereas the Chinese Confucian metaphor of state-family foresees either total respectability or utter shame—relieved only by the hope of revenge—the Japanese metaphor allows for the tragedy of defeat and hence the need for recouping honor and self-esteem no matter how bad the circumstances.

Thus the Chinese are only able to respond to defeat emotionally, seeking strength from the pangs of humiliation, while the Japanese accept the possibility of defeat and seek to learn from their failures. The Japanese "father model" is not so heroic as the Chinese hero figure, but he is expected to be the leader against overwhelming opposition. Whereas the Chinese emperors, generalissimos, presidents, and chairmen all have to pretend to be bigger than life, just as Chinese fathers must be absolute authority figures, the Japanese emperors, daimyos, and prime ministers can adopt a more reticent posture, allowing others to make the first moves, indeed soliciting views rather than determining them, as Japanese fathers are supposed to do.

The Korean and Vietnamese ideals fall between these two extremes, with the Korean coming closer to the Japanese model and the Vietnamese closer to the Chinese. Korean rulers, like Korean fathers, are expected to be embattled, needing to prove themselves in adversary contacts; but they are also expected to be masterful at all times, for like the Chinese leader-father, the Korean is supposed to be an aloof, lonely authority figure, able to cope single-handedly with all of his problems and demanding total adherence to his wishes. Yet, again like the Japanese leader-father, he is expected to be sympathetic, nurturing, and sensitive to the wishes of his followers-family, though at the same time vicious and aggressive in fighting external foes. The Vietnamese leader-father is in most respects a mirror of the Chinese model. Always concerned for the honor of the collectivity, he must be alert to slights and insults. He differs from his Chinese counterpart only in revealing his greater sense of insecurity by exaggerating, often gleefully, the significance of his accomplishments. The self-pride of a Vietnamese authority figure can easily turn into the illusion that he is universally admired.

In spite of the important similarities between the family patterns and therefore the governmental patterns of the four Confucian cultures, there were also significant differences between them.

The first and most important difference has to do with the somewhat paradoxical roles of sons and heirs. Here again the Chinese system and the Japanese system lay at the two extremes, with the Korean and Vietnamese systems in between but somewhat closer to the Chinese model. The Japanese family, or *ie,* operated under a rigid system of primogeniture which favored the eldest son; in China the inheritance was more equally divided among all the sons. The Japanese, however, allowed younger sons to break away and establish a new family line, while in China the younger sons remained subordinate to the eldest. In theory, the Koreans also had primogeniture, like the Japanese, but in practice the obligations of the eldest to take care of the younger brothers produced a more equalitarian division of shares, comparable to the Chinese family, or *chia-ting,* system. In Vietnam both theory and practice were closer to the Chinese system.

In China, birth order determined the roles and obligations of family members.[15] The eldest son was expected to assume heavy responsibilities for all of his brothers, and he also had a special obligation to protect the ancestral tablets and direct family rituals, including maintaining the parents' graves. Yet in China the laws of inheritance held that all sons should receive essentially equal shares of the estate, even to the point of dividing up the land into equal shares—by quality as well as by size. The Chinese practice of working different plots that were often far apart stemmed from the need to leave each son some of the good fields and some of the poorer fields. The ties between older and younger brothers were immutable. Throughout his lifetime the eldest brother was responsible for his younger brothers, and they in return were expected to obey him. The eldest son took over the family residence on the father's death, but he was also expected to provide shelter for his younger brothers and their families if space was available.

In Korea, theoretically, there was a form of primogeniture under which the eldest son had responsibilities for the estate, but he was expected, if resources were adequate, to look after the welfare of the younger brothers and to share the inheritance with them. In Korean families the younger brothers were free to move away from home and seek their own fortunes, often leaving the eldest son to manage the small family estate while they prospered in a new setting. Consistent with these looser fraternal bonds was the vaguer structure of the Korean clan as compared with the Chinese clan—especially the clan in South China, where the technology of rice farming created a greater necessity for cooperation among family members during planting and harvesting times than was the case among the wheat and millet farmers in North China.[16]

In Japan the more elaborately developed feudal system produced explicit primogeniture rules, quite similar to those of Europe. Family holdings were preserved. Yet, although the Japanese had the same formal rules of elder brother–younger brother relations as the Chinese, younger sons in Japan could compensate for their subordinate status by striking out on their own and then, if successful, becoming a *gosenzo,* or the founder of a new family line. Thus, although the Japanese practiced ancestor worship and conceived of everyone as belonging to a distinct line, they also provided an outlet for the ambitions of the younger sons.

Indeed, they positively encouraged younger sons to strive for success outside the family—something which was quite foreign to Chinese culture and which certainly played a part in making innovation more acceptable in Japan than in China. For example, Japanese parents or other relatives, or teachers, might refer to a younger child as having the potential to become a *gosenzo*. Younger sons might even be encouraged to aspire for material success and to become a *gosenzo*.[17]

The Japanese thus combined the anonymity of ancestor worship, in which everyone is a mere link in an unbroken chain going back to the earliest family records, with the egotistical possibility of becoming an immortal, a "founder" of an *ie*. It is true that ancestor tablets usually stayed with the eldest son, but if a *gosenzo* emerged he might get the mother's tablets, thus destroying the integrity of the original family's ancestor tablets. The Japanese system provided scope for the unexpected: a younger brother who had good fortune could suddenly supersede his elder brother and become a superior figure in his own right. Thus the apparently more rigid Japanese feudal system was actually more flexible than the Chinese system of equal inheritance.

The confusion and social disruptions of the late Tokugawa and early Meiji periods provided great opportunities for *gosenzos*. Thus in Japan social disorder could be seen as offering opportunities, while in China there was a universal dread of chaos or *luan*, and the instinctive Chinese reaction to turbulence was to reinforce family and clan ties. Since the test of becoming a *gosenzo* was material success and enough prosperity to be a worthy founder of a new *ie*, there were strong motivations in Japan to engage in economic pursuits, motivations that did not exist in China. In a sense the drive to become a *gosenzo* was analogous to the drive that Calvinism is said to have provided in the rise of capitalism in the West. According to Max Weber, the psychological force motivating European entrepreneurship was the need of Calvinists to prove themselves by prospering economically in order to allay their anxieties over whether or not they were among the "elect" according to their doctrine of pre-destination. In Japan, younger sons could also use the test of material success to confirm their need to believe that they were somehow special.

These differences between the roles of sons in Chinese and Japanese families led to significant differences in the two cultures' reactions to modernization. Public authority in China, modeled on the ideal family, concentrated on preserving unity by seeking harmony among people who had compatible but distinctive roles. Well-being was not unimportant, for it was desirable for the "family" to prosper as a unit, but more important was the obligation to reduce conflicts and preserve order. In sharp contrast, the Japanese ideal of the family, which included competitiveness and even conflict, as well as the exploitation of circumstances for self-advancement, led to the idea that government also had to be concerned with competitive skills, effectiveness, and aggressive strategies.

Yet the Japanese remained faithful to the doctrines of Confucianism even while institutionalizing their deviations from them. Not surprisingly, some Japanese Confucianists complained that young Japanese who were seeking to become *gosenzos* were developing utilitarian attitudes instead of being concerned only with virtue and abstract learning. Some bewailed the emergence of a "world of skills." When Yokoyama Yasutaka committed hara-kiri before the main gate of the government's office building in 1870, he lamented, "People do not respect uprightness but merely skill."[18] There was, however, no stopping the Japanese legitimation of materialistic advancement. Indeed, the distinctive Japanese drive to establish a new and more vital *ie* lay behind the building of such great industrial and financial companies as Mitsubishi, one of many examples of *shikon shosai*, or "a samurai in spirit, but a merchant in talent."

The differing roles of sons in China and Japan encouraged a passive approach to the outside world in China and an aggressive and activist approach in Japan. Chinese children were taught that they should do nothing that would bring shame to the family; in order to bring it honor, they were to excel in noneconomic pursuits by becoming scholar-officials. A Japanese, by contrast, could bring honor to his family by achieving material success. The reason for becoming wealthy, however, was not to live luxuriously but rather to show that one's family was substantial. In China the successful younger brother always had to be deferential to the older brother and, as in the case of the overseas Chinese, share his good fortune with his older brother, who was his generation's link to the ancestral line. In Japan the successful younger brother, upon becoming head of the new family, assumed prime responsibility for his progeny; and thus the family line, in the Japanese way of speaking, could be "fan-shaped," in contrast to the single line in China.

The second major difference in Confucian family patterns concerned the treatment of family as against non-family members. The Chinese and Japanese were again positioned at opposite poles. The Chinese were taught to recognize a vivid distinction between family members, who could be relied upon, and non-family people, who were not to be trusted except in qualified ways. The Japanese, with their more feudal tradition, acknowledged the tensions among family members and, even more important, sometimes had as retainers non-family people whom they trusted completely. In Chinese enterprises the limits of trust and of decision-making responsibilities were often set by the size of the family. In Japanese family businesses, as in the case of Mitsui, non-family members could be accepted as participants in the central decision-making process. It was thus routine for the Japanese to bring people with technical skills into their enterprises and to treat them as members of a larger "family." In China, trust was usually limited, beyond the family, to lowly subordinates, essentially "servants," who were supposedly marginal to decision-making.

These different boundaries of trust in the two cultures resulted in different views of the substantive nature of a trusting relationship. In China the idea that complete trust was limited to family connections meant that qualified trust could best be based on associations which were somehow analogous to the family relationship. Trust could thus arise from some form of shared association of an essentially ascriptive nature: hence the strong Chinese expectation that people of the same place or even the same province, and people from the same school, or better still, the same class, would be mutually supportive. Relationships were assumed to depend upon objective factors. Politically, this has meant not only that individuals with shared associations could seek special consideration from one another, but also that others could predict, on the basis of general knowledge, who had a special relationship with whom.

In Japanese culture such objective bases for connections were recognized too, but it was also possible for personal ties to extend outward to a much wider range of people. Personal encounters which might generate feelings of indebtedness, or *on*, could become the basis for enduring and close relationships. The possibility of this more idiosyncratic bonding of people has made the Japanese ties of *kankei* more personal and less publicly discernible than the comparable Chinese relations of *guanxi*. Whereas it is usually necessary to understand the precise and often subtle relationships between Japanese public officials in order to determine who has *kankei* with whom, information about the objective bonds between Chinese officials generally provides a good basis for judging who has *guanxi* with whom. Indeed, in Chinese politics even the suspicion that two leaders have *guanxi* because of some common association can be enough to force the two into a personalized relationship.

In view of the distinct boundaries set between family and outsiders in Chinese culture, it is paradoxical that family alliances have historically played a far smaller role in Chinese politics than they have in either Japan or Korea. Although the calculations behind arranged marriages at all levels of Chinese society were commonly directed toward improving family fortunes, they were rarely used to create and expand political power. In both Japan and Korea, by contrast, marriage was recognized as providing an opportunity for consolidating and advancing political power. During some periods of Korean history the specific direction of dynastic politics was determined by the patterning of marriages.[19]

The explanation for this paradox is not hard to find. Since the Han dynasty the Chinese have not had an acknowledged aristocracy, as have the Japanese and Koreans, and hence they have had no well-defined hierarchy of families. Thus the Chinese imperial household has never been supported by powerful nobles, as has been the case in Japan and Korea. Indeed, in order to prevent the emergence of powerful consort families through marriage with the emperor, the Chinese imperial practice was to insist that the Son of Heaven have grotesquely large numbers of wives and concubines. During the Ming and Ch'ing dynasties, the emperor had between seven thousand and twelve thousand wives and concubines, enough to prevent any particular family from claiming consort advantages. The only area in which the Chinese commonly used marriage arrangements for power purposes was in making alliances with Central Asian tribal leaders by giving them Chinese princesses as wives.[20]

In both Japan and Korea, by contrast, alliance through marriage was a routine method of building power and of altering the distribution of power among the elite. Aside from the fact that these two societies possessed hereditary aristocracies and hence had a natural social basis for such a form of politics, the practice reflected the more acute sensitivity in Japan and Korea to the desirability of maximizing competitive power. In China, power was presumed to be a more constant and established phenomenon, not something which needed to be constantly enhanced, as in Japan and Korea. In China, competition was indirect and implicit, for those with power could legitimately increase their share only by being more virtuous, more respected, more worthy. Power was not to be sought in order to defeat others. But precisely because Chinese political culture denied legitimacy to overt power-maximizing, both social and political relations were rife with devious stratagems and ploys, and power was based on hypocrisy. Consequently, there was a greater gap between Confucian ideals and actual practices in China than in any other East Asian culture.

Models of Family Authority in Government

In order to give a feeling for the different patterns of socialization in the four Confucian cultures, we shall use a form of ideal-type analysis to delineate the model of each family. Although family life varied greatly from one culture to another, we shall not attempt to average these differences, but shall try to achieve a distillation of the essential qualities, a blend of idealized norms and actual practices, that describes not just the typical patterns but those which were psychologically critical in giving shape to the separate cultures.[21]

The foundation of the distinctive form of paternalistic authority common to all Confucian countries was the paramount value of filial piety. Confucian doctrines emphasized that rulers should take the ideal father as their model, and subjects should similarly think of themselves as dutiful children. But although the four Confucian cultures started from this common basis, they arrived at significantly different ideals of authority because of the differences in their family practices. In particular, the role of the father figure varied sharply from culture to culture.

In China the father was expected to be omnipotent and solely responsible for the family fortunes. He was to be stern, frightening, and relatively uncompromising; he demanded obedience, and he could neither ask for sympathy nor share his burdens. Although the mother could be more sympathetic and reasonable and thus soften the harshness of the father's rule, she was obliged to reinforce his authority and to instill precisely the same values and modes of conduct. Thus she was not seen as an alternative source of authority, but instead the two were as yin and yang in complementing each other.

There was thus little scope for Chinese children to play off one parent against another, and it did not occur to them that there might be alternative forms of authority which might peacefully contend with each other. Authorities could only differ in their degree of severity and in their capacity for sympathetic benevolence. Children also were not exposed to the idea that different authorities should have different responsibilities. Instead, the Chinese child, especially one growing up in an extended family household, learned early that although authority was monolithic, it was still possible to get around it by finding mitigating personal ties, such as a special relationship with a particularly warm aunt or uncle or grandparent. The seeds of *guanxi* were thus planted early.

The only other escape from authority lay in the possibility that the father might be swayed by moods or indulge in favoritism, thereby acting inconsistently enough to permit exceptions to his rules. Authority, precisely because it was omnipotent, could have whims; and there was always the off chance that authority could be "bribed" to be more tolerant.

Though parents placed great stock in the socialization process in determining the child's development, they did not assume any personal responsibility for the ultimate outcome. Indeed, while ascribing no real role to heredity in determining personality, but leaving everything to upbringing, they at the same time believed that it would be a matter of luck how one's children turned out. Children were taught to be filial, but how their personalities evolved and whether they would later help or damage the family interests was a matter governed by fate. Chinese parents were spared any feelings of guilt.

In Japan, the father was also the supreme authority; he could, however, call openly upon others to share his responsibilities. Although he was feared, he could ask for sympathy and reveal his own sorrows and anxieties—especially when drunk. The mother was more formally deferential toward her husband and toward her sons; and yet, inferior as she was, she had her separate domain of competence and could therefore advocate different values and tolerate different forms of conduct. Thereby, paradoxically, the submissive Japanese mother was able, as the more assertive Chinese mother was not, to suggest to her children that authority might be divided. Japanese sons, more readily than Chinese sons, played off the parents against each other. More important, the distinctive role of the mother, when combined with a distant and often absent father, created a strongly maternalistic image of authority. Japanese sons were generally comfortable with such a form of authority, especially since they usually learned early that if they showed themselves to be purposeful and aggressive their mothers would be in awe of them.

Japanese parents assumed direct responsibility for the outcome of the nurturance of their offspring, and they frequently quarreled over who was to blame if the child did not live up to their expectations. Ironically, the obligation of the wife to submit to the criticisms of her husband set the stage for Japanese mothers to make their children feel guilty for any misbehavior. Moreover, children were under continuous and heavy pressures because society left no room for luck or chance, as it did in China. Thus, Japanese family relations were permeated by stronger and more openly expressed emotions than Chinese family life, in which the rule of suppressing emotions was usually only broken by manifestations of anger.

Probably the most profound difference between the socialization processes in China and Japan was that whereas in China the relations *within* the family were seen as the most important, Japanese training was more explicitly directed toward performance *outside* the family. The Chinese boy was taught to concentrate his loyalties on his family, to avoid as much as possible any dealings with outsiders, and to show passive deference to legitimate political authority. His real world was within the family. By contrast, the Japanese child learned at a very early age that his family was preparing him to contend with others, to compete against outsiders. The contemporary example of the Japanese child studying for his entrance examinations is only the most recent version of a long history of challenges that have faced Japanese sons. The Chinese child could, of course, bring honor and pride to his parents by his outside accomplishments, but the pressures for such attainment were secondary to those involved in being the dutiful son. Westerners who taught school in both countries before World War II noticed this difference: in the Chinese schoolroom students could be obstreperous and acted as though the only legitimate authority in their lives resided in their families; while Japanese students were highly competitive, quick to recognize relative ability among peers, and easy to supervise.

In Korea, as in China, the father was expected to be authoritarian: his wish was his command. He was not expected to need the degree of sympathy or understanding that the Japanese father sought. Yet, paradoxically, the Korean mother played a more autonomous decision-making role than either the Chinese or the Japanese mother, and, consequently, Korean children learned early the art of playing off the two authorities against each other. In Korea the parents' responsibility to protect the children's interests was explicitly recognized, so that socialization was more than just training in dutifulness or in sacrificing for the family. The home provided a sanctuary from which the young could go out to do battle and assume high risks, knowing that they could always retreat to their homes without shame.

Paternalistic authority in Korean culture was thus a contradictory blend of aloofness and struggle, of sternness and support. The Korean model of authority was a peculiar combination of the Chinese ideal of dignity, secure in its monopoly of authority, and the Japanese reality of competitive authority.

In Vietnam, the Confucian father figure was revered, but he was not expected to be truly effective. He was aloof, distant, and apparently not interested in mundane family problems; yet his striving for withdrawal was often compromised by the messy demands of reality. The mother was the more practical, rational decision-maker, while the father could be introspective and legitimately melancholy. The children were expected to be supportive of their parents from a very early age, and their personal successes did not reduce their family obligations.

These different models of family authority in the four cultures, which of course were not uniform but applied to specific situations in varying degrees, were translated, through the socialization process, into even sharper differences in what was expected of public authority. Indeed, the similarities between the exercise of family authority and the behavior of the political authorities in each culture were striking.

It is particularly noteworthy that in China political authority was seen as being properly aloof, distant, and unable to bend or even to ask for understanding and sympathy. These qualities were only slightly less extreme in the Korean and Vietnamese political cultures. In Japan, however, although superior authority commanded complete deference, decisionmaking could be more openly collegial, the views of lesser people could be elicited, and the ultimate authority could acknowledge a need for help and sympathy.

Thus, of the four cultures, China went furthest in upholding the ideal of an omnipotent authority who could look after the interests of everybody, and who would be under suspicion if things went wrong. In Vietnam it was accepted that ultimate authority might be withdrawn, but it was assumed that other authorities, comparable to the mother, would remain active in coping with the practical problems of social life. In Korea, with its more activist father's role, political leadership was expected to be effective, and hence was to be tolerated if all was going well; but it was highly vulnerable to criticism when difficulties arose. In Japan, the political authority could legitimately call upon its followers for ever greater sacrifices, even if the difficulties were clearly of the authority's own making; and because the leadership did not presume to have control over the total scene, it could rely heavily upon subordinates.

The supreme political authority in China was thus expected to guarantee peace and harmony among all its subjects. The well-being of everyone depended upon the performance of the top political ruler, who ideally was the soul of benevolence, without active enemies. By contrast, Japanese leaders had to be ready to cope with competitors, if not with enemies. Hence the leaders had to trust their followers and depend upon them to make the necessary exertions against very real foes.

In China the combination of filial piety and an aloof, omnipotent authority helped to create a political process in which there was almost complete dependence upon authority. Nevertheless, the demands of filial piety, which stifled the expression of natural resentment toward parents, could lead to explosions of repressed anger toward public authority if it seemed to be faltering.

It has been claimed repeatedly in China that if the country is to achieve modernization it needs stronger, more vigorous, and more virtuous authority. The Chinese have believed that their problems stem from the failings of their leader—whether the emperor, the warlords, the Kuomintang, or the Gang of Four. The psychodynamics of the same combination of filial piety and omnipotent authority explains why the rhetoric of modern Chinese politics has focused on the single theme of "revolution," even in the face of demands for stronger, more omniscient authority. Modern Chinese politics has consisted of a series of angry outbursts at the failings of the national leadership, followed by a search for leaders without weaknesses.[22] Thus Chinese intellectuals, in contrast to Western and even Indian intellectuals, have focused almost all of their attention on their national leaders and have devoted little energy to bringing about changes in the rest of society. So much has been expected of the highest elites that there has been little point in looking elsewhere.

The picture in Japan has been almost the direct opposite. Although the Japanese, from the Meiji period through the occupation, have gone through astonishing revolutionary changes, the most profound in modern Asia, their political rhetoric has remained banal and has focused largely on the themes of cooperation and group dedication. Whereas the Chinese have talked ceaselessly about "carrying through the revolution," the Japanese have spoken only of "restoration." At the same time, Japanese at all levels of society have been bringing about changes without waiting for guidance from the national leadership. Yet paradoxically, Japanese intellectuals, whenever they have been given the opportunity, have criticized the government and been pessimistic about the future. By contrast, Chinese intellectuals are instinctive nationalists, always ready to say that however bad the past may have been, the current authorities are about to produce magical results.

The Japanese style of public authority was more subtle and complex than the Chinese, largely because in Japan the father combined his requirement of family loyalty with his own quest for personal honor, whereas in China (and also in Korea) the father expected his family's feelings of dependency to be tempered with fear. Hence Japanese authority extolled achievement beyond the bounds of the family. Greatness for the Japanese required recognition by outsiders; for the Chinese it was enough to be inward-looking and respected by one's own audience. Thus in modern times the Japanese have alertly identified the world's pacesetters, and sought to impress them, while the Chinese have been more content to bask in self-praise.

Moreover, although authority in Japan could be just as domineering as it was in China, it was likely to be more paternalistic, or, perhaps more correctly, maternalistic: that is to say, Japanese authority could be very nurturing and supportive of subordinates, allowing them more scope for initiative and showing more concern for their feelings than was the case in China. Japanese children learned early that their mother's style of tentatively asserting authority could bring out the best in them, and hence they rarely underestimated the payoffs of a low-keyed style of authority that could tap the empathy of subordinates.

Chinese leaders, on the contrary, rarely asked their followers to be understanding. While in theory Chinese leadership was supposed to concern itself with the well-being of all, in practice leaders maintained their dignity and kept their distance from the common herd. The leadership style of Mao Zedong and of Deng Xiaoping has been as aloof as that of Chiang Kai-shek; and Ho Chi Minh was as withdrawn as Syngman Rhee or Park Chung Hee. One of many mistakes Americans made during their involvement in Vietnam was to demand that South Vietnamese leaders mix with their own people, just as popular American politicians do with theirs. To the Vietnamese such conduct lacked the dignity that was imperative for true authority. The Americans missed the point that the mystique of power associated with the Hanoi leaders resulted from their operating mostly behind the scenes, rarely making personal appearances but instead letting poster pictures hint their human qualities.

One particular ambivalence in Chinese political culture, which set it apart from both the Japanese and Korean cultures, had to do with the concept of willpower. In all the Confucian cultures, parents believed that their children should want to do the right thing, that they should develop a sense of purpose, and be strengthened by self-discipline and willpower. Chinese children were, however, faced with a subtle contradiction. They were taught the need for dedication and purposefulness, but at the same time they knew that their parents were anxious lest they waste their energies and physically damage themselves. Therefore activities which might bring on either exhaustion or undue agitation were to be avoided. Thus in China willpower called for spiritual and intellectual purposefulness, not physical force. Recent generations of young Chinese have tried to make the point that they represent a "new China" by dramatizing physical courage precisely because it is a quality so contrary to traditional Chinese values.

The Japanese concept of willpower called not only for moral purposefulness but for the samurai spirit of vitality and physical courage. On the Japanese political scene, therefore, disorder and social confusion were seen as providing opportunities for those spirited individuals who were prepared to take risks and exploit openings in order to accomplish great things. In China, however, bravery and boldness ranked low on the scale of virtues; courage meant demonstrating rectitude; and it was more important to show persistence than to produce outbursts of energetic activity.

Both cultures thus encouraged the work ethic, and even intense and compulsive behavior. But power meant something different in each country. The Chinese associated power not only with the positive qualities of Confucian ethics—the ideal of the patient, virtuous official—but also with the Taoist virtues of non-effort and hence with leisure and sedate physical movement. The Japanese image of power combined the Confucian ethic with the samurai's martial code of physical boldness and recklessness. The contrasts between the two cultures can be clearly seen in their different approaches to military strategy. The Japanese classic *Tosenkyo* (On the art of war) denounces the Chinese standard work on strategy written by Sun Tzu, who advocated avoiding engagement when the enemy had stronger forces. The Japanese argued that regardless of the enemy's strength, he could be defeated if the warriors' spirit was willing and determined. "Where *Sun Tzu* exhorts one to become a fox when necessary, *Tosenkyo* exhorts one to remain a lion under all circumstances."[23]

The Japanese thus turned Confucian rules of moral discipline and ethical imperatives into guidelines for aggressive action, both for the samurai warrior in making war and the *chonin* merchant in making money. The Chinese, however, maintained a sharp dichotomy between moral or spiritual attainment and material success. Confucian virtues were not explicitly linked to prosperity, which was usually seen as the consequence of either good fortune or corrupt behavior.

Whereas Japanese Confucianism valued action, the Chinese Confucianists, taking a cue from Taoism, unashamedly preferred leisure. In China the imperative of filial piety included the commandment that the son owed it to his parents never to damage himself, that is, that he should avoid physical strain and exhaustion—a caveat which in old age led to unembarrassed self-indulgence.[24] Chinese sons often agonized as they watched their once frugal fathers compulsively dissipating the family fortune in their old age.[25] The frequency with which elderly Chinese became self-indulgent suggests that behind the need for Chinese fathers to be stern and aloof there was a craving for dependency and for being nurtured.[26]

In summary, the Chinese and Japanese both professed Confucianism, but their different socialization processes resulted in quite different lifestyles. The Chinese, who accented the moral, disciplining aspect of Confucianism, and denied that ethics bore any relation to material prosperity, easily accepted the idea that if someone was fortunate enough to become prosperous he might freely indulge in conspicuous consumption. On the contrary, the Japanese, who linked Confucian values to achieving material success, looked askance at ostentation.[27] The Chinese view was, "Since what really counts is ethical standards for their own sake, there is no harm in indulging in the pleasures of wealth since good fortune is a matter of luck and unrelated to spiritual commitments." By contrast, the Japanese view was much closer to Weber's understanding of the Protestant ethic: "Since material success calls for the spiritual disciplining associated with the Confucian ethic, one must, even if successful, maintain that discipline and avoid undue ostentation."

From the Family to Friends and Foes

The Confucian valuing of family relationships no doubt contributed to the strong sense of division between in-group and out-group which characterized all four of the East Asian cultures. In China, Japan, Korea, and Vietnam the basis of social relations was the feeling that trust should automatically be extended to family members and to those in analogous groups, while all others should be viewed with suspicion. Clannishness was understood and accepted as normal behavior.

Translated into domestic politics, this spirit produced the ubiquitous phenomenon of factionalism. Because factional identity was essentially analogous to family identity, it was usually not associated with ideological or policy differences. And just as no one needed to explain or justify family differences, so officials did not need to rationalize their factional associations. It was natural to champion one's own group and oppose all others.

Raised to the national level, the Confucian spirit of family unity produced a vivid sense of the differences between the internal "we" and the foreign "they." The histories of all four cultures reveal extended periods of isolation, of fearing all foreign contacts as potentially contaminating and of feeling safer in dealing only with their own kind. The Chinese like to picture their whole modern history as a time of resisting foreign influences and struggling to preserve their own unique values. The story of Japanese isolation during the Tokugawa period and of what happened after Admiral Perry's arrival is well known. Korea, of course, was known as the "hermit kingdom" because it sought to keep out all foreign intruders down to the end of the nineteenth century. And Vietnam, in seeking to differentiate itself from both China and its Southeast Asian neighbors, developed an intense form of nationalism and xenophobia.

Although Japan, with its more competitive domestic culture, was the first to adopt foreign technologies, the Japanese have continued to treat national matters as they do family affairs, with a homogenous Japanese people competing against the outside world. For example, Japanese consumers prefer to buy Japanese products; the Japanese government has refused to accept Vietnamese refugees in any numbers; the Japanese tend to mistreat nonethnic Japanese, such as Japan-born Koreans; and the government shields the Japanese market from foreigners while collaborating with Japanese business to penetrate foreign markets.

The vivid sense of the boundaries between "we" and "they" has also been translated in the Confucian cultures into sharply different ethical norms for dealing with perceived "friends" and "foes." Not only do "friends" become those who share a sense of "we-ness" while enemies are "theys," but the distinction also justifies doing to outsiders things which, if done to friends, would be completely unethical. Thus "theys" are lesser people who can be treated as potential, if not actual, foes. They are simply "barbarians," "foreign devils," *geijin*.

Governmental Structures in the Four Cultures

Confucianism, based upon the ideal of paternalistic authority, held that the ideal government would be rule by superior men who were guided by the wisdom of the classics and organized as a hierarchy of bureaucratic authority. Ruling entailed the persuasive influence of moral example and the expectation that lesser people, like children, would be shamed into emulating the ways of their superiors. Thus the purpose of governmental power was more to uphold respect for status than to implement innovative concepts or policies. The ideal ruler did not impose his preferences on others, but rather inspired everyone to seek his or her own moral perfection; yet all was done within the terms of a hierarchy in which superiors lorded it over their subordinates. The test of Confucian political power was the number of acts of obedience that superiors could extract from subordinates. The more subordinates a superior commanded, the greater was the impression of his power; the higher the status of a superior, the more subordinates he would have to obey his commands.

Only in China was the Confucian ideal of bureaucratic power actually realized: the Chinese imperial system, for all of its compromises with the ideal, was a reasonably well structured hierarchy of mandarin officials who had proved their command of classical knowledge through competitive examinations. The Japanese tried only briefly, during the Taika Reform period (646–858), to replicate the Confucian bureaucratic model. Thereafter they reverted to their native feudal structure of loyalties which allowed for competition among locally based power groupings. Centralization could take the form only of a ranking of feudal lords, who had to yield to the one among them who was militarily their superior, the Shogun. In Japan, as in the West, there was constant tension between the ideal (the Confucian principle that government was a matter of morals and ethics) and the real (the need for military skill and strategy); and the ideal of a hierarchy of Confucian scholars gave way to the more utilitarian principles of superior-subordinate relations dedicated to intense competition.

China's success in realizing the ideal and Japan's success in combining Confucianism with its more natural structures of power contrasted sharply with the problems that plagued Vietnam and Korea as they tried to achieve the Confucian ideal of government.

For a thousand years, ending in 939 A.D., Vietnam was ruled directly by the Chinese. Thus the principles of both Han and Tang government were well understood as Tonkinese power spread south from the Red River Delta first to Annam or Central Vietnam and finally to Cochin China and and the Mekong Delta. The Nguyen dynasty, based in Hue, sought in numerous ways to replicate the Chinese system. Mandarin officials were recruited on the basis of examinations in Confucian doctrines; the government was divided into exactly the same six "boards" as the Chinese—civil appointments, rites, war, finance, public works, and punishment or justice—and at the local level there were district magistrates and provincial governors.[28]

The result, however, was not the stable, almost static, governmental structure of the Chinese. Faced with the threat of China on the north and the imperative to conquer the central highlands and the south, which had once been part of the Khmer Empire, the Vietnamese military officers had greater influence on empirical decisions than their Chinese counterparts. Moreover, the expansion into new lands and the opportunity to seize territory led to a more vigorously entrepreneurial approach to government. This resulted in internal feuds among the mandarins and ceaseless struggles to take over the throne. Samuel Popkin notes that "in the four hundred years prior to the French takeover, there were fifty emperors and pretenders who exercised (or attempted to exercise) power in the northern half of Vietnam—an average of one every eight years!" Indeed, in spite of their pretensions to the gentlemanly conduct associated with Confucian authority, the Vietnamese court and country were not far removed from primitive power. In the nineteenth century alone, more than 450 local uprisings occurred, cholera may have killed 20 percent of the population, and bandits and marauders roamed the countryside.[29]

The Vietnamese concept of power was in theory one of authority based on ethical appeals, but in practice it assumed that people would seize all they could get and hold on with fanatical tenacity. Those who succeeded could expect threats of physical harm, but it was worth the risk because a loser's life was hard and dangerous. At the court Confucianism was practiced conscientiously as emperors sought to discipline their ambitious mandarin officials. In the countryside the traditional Vietnamese inclination toward ancestor worship made certain aspects of Confucianism, especially those related to the authority of the father, easy to accept. But there was perpetual conflict between the drive for orthodoxy and the heterodox religious movements. In the case of Buddhism the court eventually managed to gain control by the ingenious but un-Chinese tactic of arranging that the emperor should appoint the monks, thereby making them his agents.[30] Various forms of animism survived and provided the basis for more localized power groupings. In theory, and usually in practice, the "authority of the emperor stopped at the village hedges," and the emperor rarely trusted the local authorities because they could be troublemakers. At the local level, as well as at the court level, there was constant contention as villagers and their headmen sought individual advantages, especially with respect to land holdings and irrigation rights.[31] In short, at all levels of Vietnamese society people accepted the principle that power should be based on rules of morality and propriety—those set down in the Confucian classics for the mandarins and those of filial piety for the common people—but in practice people connived for advantage, often preferring force to finesse.

In Korea under the Yi dynasty (1392–1910), the tension between morality and force was even more extreme than it was in Vietnam. The Koreans did not institute a pure form of estate-based feudalism as in Japan (or Europe), for they did not have an orderly system of fealty relations. They had, however, a hereditary aristocracy, called *yangbans*, who made up about 10 percent of the population. The *yangbans*, who were superior to all other classes, were landowners, but they were not obligated to look after their subordinates although they exacted deference from all who were their inferiors.[32] Nor did they engage in martial competition with one another in order to expand or protect their estates.

The introduction of Confucianism only made the *yangbans* more arrogantly contemptuous of everyone beneath them. They took to the idea of leisure and avoided all forms of exertion as though these were the accepted prerogatives of the aristocracy, unlike the Japanese aristocracy, who rejoiced in personal combat. As a nonmilitaristic aristocracy, the *yangbans* initially claimed status and power on the basis of birth and aristocratic pretensions, and then, after the introduction of Confucianism, a thin overlay of scholarship. *Yangban* superiority called for the avoidance of anything resembling peasant activity. No matter how poor a *yangban* might be, he still could demand that villagers work his fields before they looked after their own. Only *yangbans* were supposed to ride on horses or donkeys: a nobleman was "by custom forced to perch himself on an extraordinarily high saddle—presumably a compensation for the smallness of the animal—where he would be safeguarded by a retainer walking on each side, as well as by a retainer leading the horse," while a commoner could only ride in the presence of a *yangban* when going to his own wedding or his grave. The methods of ensuring that the *yangbans* were indeed different from others seemed to focus on questions of locomotion. In what must be one of the more extreme and unlikely ways of asserting status, the *yangbans* in effect reinvented the chariot, but one with only one wheel. They insisted on being taken about on a type of unicycle that looked like a chair set on top of a single wheel from which protruded two poles, one pushed by a man behind the contraption and the other pulled by a man in front. On each side hovered clusters of servants "to avert a possible catastrophe," and the whole scene was enough of a spectacle to announce that greatness was passing by.[33] The Chinese sedan chair and the Japanese palanquin may have suggested a greater aura of dignity, but the *yangban*'s vehicle was in a class by itself.

When the *yangban* aristocrats took on the ideals of the Confucian mandarins—and their competitive examination system—the result was a catastrophe for Korea. The elite that resulted was too large to fit into either the land available for estates, which they all still expected to have, or the bureaucratic posts available for assignment, which now they also expected to get. The Japanese avoided that problem, when they briefly tried out the Chinese system of recruitment through examinations, by a policy of limiting competition to members of the samurai class only. In Korea, the compounding of aristocracy and meritocracy brought an elite population explosion which could only be contained by ruthlessness; and the Koreans came to see power, even in its Confucian-ethical guise, as entailing a series of struggles unrelated to either serious policy choices or ideological disagreements.

The story of factionalism in the Yi dynasty makes the medieval Europe of Barbara Tuchman's *Distant Mirror* seem almost genteel. The dynasty began with a series of "massacres of scholars" in 1498, 1506, 1519, and 1545, when certain factions of *yangbans* connived with the king to exterminate other *yangbans* who were cluttering up the higher reaches of the bureaucracy by passing the Chinese-type examinations and then expecting not only to hold official posts but to have the estate lands which had always been the right of *yangbans*.

The politics of factionalism steadily increased as more aspirants to *yangban* status, having passed the Confucian examinations, clashed with the ever expanding numbers of progeny of *yangban* fathers.[34] By 1575 the court was split between Easterners and Westerners, designations with little geographical meaning. In 1575 the Easterners won out, but immediately split into Southern and Northern factions. Then in 1591 the newly victorious Northerners split into a lesser and a greater faction, each of which, as its fortunes rose, subdivided further. The lesser separated into the *tak,* or "muddy," and the *chong,* or "clean," factions, while the greater splintered eventually into six factions—the *kol,* or "far right," the *chung,* or "center," the *chong,* or "clean," the *pi,* or "far left," the *yuk,* or "left," and the *tak,* or "muddy." In 1623 the Westerners returned to take over court politics, only to disintegrate instantly into an array of factions which, in order to distinguish between the like-minded *yangban* clusters, took on such meaningless labels as the "merit," the "clean," the "elder," the "younger," the "positive," the "negative," the "older doctrine," the "newer doctrine," and even such popular proper names as Pyok, Si, Wan, and Nak.[35]

These factional conflicts, carried out with uninhibited ferocity, had a certain elegance since they were rarely justified by either policy or ideological argumentation. They were like sporting events in that their purpose was only to produce winners and losers. Sometimes feeble issues were raised, such as whether the mourning for the queen should last for two years or three years, or whether the crown prince should spend his morning or his afternoon in study; but, in general, *yangbans* felt it was beneath their dignity to articulate the reasons for their loyalties and hatreds.[36] Members of different factions never spoke to one another and they never passed on documents or memorials drafted by a member of another faction. Their practices made it impossible for the hierarchical bureaucracy to function as an instrument of coherent rule. That the Korean government endured in spite of this is proof that a bureaucracy, as long as it engages in enough infighting, need not do anything to stay alive.

The vigor and ruthlessness with which the factions struggled reflected not only the benefits of winning but also the costs of losing. If the winners were to take over both the losers' official posts in the bureaucracy and their properties as *yangban* estate owners, it was usually necessary to kill the losers. In this zero-sum game of Korean politics, played out as though conforming to the ground rules of Confucian ethics, the winners felt none of the compulsions that victorious political leaders normally have to smear the reputation of the losers in order to justify their own vindictiveness. Rather, it seemed that everyone understood the stakes involved and that neither winners nor losers felt any need for explanation.

Chinese Confucianism was important in shaping Korean politics because its ideas and ideals centered the politics of the *yangbans* on the court and bureaucracy. A traditional aristocracy like the Japanese daimyos and the European feudal lords would have associated power with their landed estates and offered only symbolic allegiance to the king.

Instead, as Gregory Henderson has demonstrated, Korea developed a "politics of the vortex," in which everything focused on the capital. Once the *yangban* class accepted the idea that their special privileges depended not just on their inheritance but also on royal approval in the form of bureaucratic appointments, it was no longer possible for them to opt out of the struggle at the capital. If any one of them had tried to do that, he would have been attacked by all the others, who were playing by the rules of the imported Confucian bureaucracy.

The Politics of Dependency

The differences between the four Confucian countries, important as they were, were not so great as to obscure the fundamental similarities in their concepts of the politics of dependency.

First, power was supposed to flow inexorably from the morally superior; however, superiority did not arise from exceptionality but rather from conformity to the established ethical norms. The higher the elite, the more the presumption of ethical excellence; and hence the greater the tendency to see the machinations of day-to-day politics as evidences of ethical failings, that is, as a politics of corruption. Leaders should be perfect, but all too often they were bad—not that their politics was foolish or that they were misguided, but rather that in their private lives they were less than exemplary.

It must be emphasized that in the Confucian tradition power was never associated with a Puritan sense of morality. The Confucian relationship of ethics to politics has no counterpart in Western thinking, which assumes a dichotomy between private morality and public obligation and responsibility. Whereas, according to the Confucian norms, the private conduct of the ruler determined his power and legitimacy, his private conduct did not encompass what Westerners call private morality, that is, sexual conduct, truthfulness, and temperance. Instead, rulers had innumerable concubines, were never held to their word, and could enjoy unlimited food and drink. Yet at the same time, the Confucian tradition ignored the idea, best expressed by Max Weber and Reinhold Niebuhr, that there is a difference between personal morality, based on the imperatives of private salvation, and public morality, which calls for an ethic of responsibility for the fate of the collective. In the Confucian scheme the private morality of the ruler did indeed determine the collective fate, but his private morality had a public face; that is, he was to be a role model, adhering to the rules of public propriety, displaying benevolence, and having compassion.[37] In short, the test of ethics for the powerful was the same as that for the father: his treatment of the sub-ordinate, the weak—his children.

Second, power was seen as emerging out of the relationships between superiors and inferiors. The social and political order was perceived as arranged hierarchies, and power was by definition the dynamics in the relationships of specific superiors and subordinates. Only in Japan was there a sense that power might arise from competition between groups of near equals. As a consequence, the operations of power tended to follow patterns common to highly personalized relationships. Superior power was expected to act in ways which would inspire awe, deference, and even fear, while the weaker sought to manipulate, trick, cajole, humor, and generally play on the sensibilities of superiors. The play of power, even at the very center of the political system, could be completely absorbed in the limited interaction of superior and subordinates—of emperor and ministers, for example—without having any effects beyond their personal interactions. Because the interactions between superior and subordinates were largely limited to ensuring that each side continued to abide by its respective rules of conduct, they did not extend to sub-stantive policy issues affecting the society at large.

Given this framework for thinking about power, the process of building political power in the bureaucratic politics of China, Korea, and Vietnam tended to be incidental to the career progressions of officials. Some of-ficials tended over time to accumulate ever larger circles of subordinates who took them as mentors, protectors, and patrons. These officials would gain the reputation of being powerful, and hence would be treated with increasing deference, with the result that their status would rise and their claims to dignity would be widely recognized. Other officials who were loners could command little authority, even if they had the advantages of seniority and age.[38]

The third distinctive characteristic of the East Asian approach to power, which in this case included Japan, was the practice of treating formal government as the sole legitimate basis for power. Those outside of the ranks of officialdom and the ruling class were not acknowledged as having any proper claims to power. To the extent that pressures from society infringed upon the sphere of government, these pressures were seen as manifestations of corruption.

It is true that in certain regions of China the gentry did constitute a formidable class and that magistrates acknowledged their importance and recognized them as a collective force. As one magistrate said, "Please one *shih* and the whole group of *shih* will be pleased; humiliate one *shih*, and the whole group of *shih* will be resentful."[39] Yet even the gentry could not make demands that would shape imperial policies; they could only act in a defensive manner, trying in each particular locality to protect their interests by asking for special considerations in applying regulations. The merchant class was in fact politically impotent, having no regular channels of access to the world of officialdom.[40] In Japan, feudal distinctions allowed for more explicit recognition of the legitimacy of merchants to control the economic sphere, but when it came to politics and government the *chonin* had no rights of power.[41]

Thus in all the Confucian cultures there was a strong sense that wealth should not be translated into political power. This did not mean, however, that the well-to-do were politically helpless, for they could usually find ways to protect their interests. But the norms that excluded economic power as a legitimate source of influence ensured that the wealthy did not become patrons of the less fortunate, who might have difficulties with government authorities. Consequently, the clustering of informal power which was basic to the making of power in Southeast Asia did not emerge in the East Asian cultures.

The Confucian principle that political power resided only in formal government also meant that religion did not generally provide an alternative center of power. In China the Buddhist monasteries were a political force only for limited periods; and in Vietnam, where Buddhism had a strong appeal, the mandarinate neutralized its potential political influence by insisting that the government should appoint the monks and abbots. As a consequence of treating formal government as the only proper arena of political power, the Confucian cultures never experienced the clash between church and state that took place in Europe, nor did they extensively exploit religious mysticism in order to generate greater authority for their secular power holders, as was the case in South and Southeast Asia.

The fourth major characteristic of Confucian patterns of power was the strong notion that those in power should use their own exemplary conduct as a means for influencing the behavior of others. The idea that model behavior by rulers should elicit comparable behavior among their followers was, of course, a function of the paternalistic version of authority that saw everyone as indoctrinated with the ideals of filial piety.

The ruler was expected to be both a model and a guardian—a belief which had two consequences. First, rulers found it desirable, indeed necessary, to glorify themselves as exemplary figures. Hence leaders seemed larger than life, but at the same time they were depicted as carrying out, in model ways, routines known to everyone. Second, people who were not capable of responding properly to the influences of their model rulers were seen as being less than human and deserving of hard punishment, and torture was thus legitimized.

The Confucian model of paternalistic authority stressed the banding together of ruler and subject, with each clearly needing the other. As father figures the leaders needed to picture themselves as looking after their children. Confucian paternalism, however, had a general stance that precluded the explicit quid-pro-quo concerns which typified the Southeast Asian pattern of paternalism.

4

Southeast Asia:
From God-Kings to the Power
of Personal Connections

T O GO FROM East Asia to South and Southeast Asia can be a jarring experience. In East Asian countries the populations are homogeneous, and their similarities in physical appearance are accentuated by the traditions of uniformity in dress. Merely by observing the people moving along the streets of China, Korea, and Japan one can see that these cultures still value the Confucian norms of conformity. The teeming cities of South and Southeast Asia, by contrast, are filled with colorful crowds, dressed in unusual varieties of clothing. And going from one part to another of any South or Southeast Asian country one comes in contact with a series of different cultures. From the South Asian subcontinent eastward, people of different ways of life have long lived side by side, preserving their separate traditions and thereby defying the anthropologists of acculturation who hold that inefficient ways yield to more efficient ways when cultures meet.

Tropical Asia is characterized above all by diversity.[1] Certainly it lacks a unifying cultural force comparable to Confucianism in East Asia. Yet, despite the significance of this factor of diversity, two elements have decisively shaped the South and Southeast Asian attitudes toward power, and hence their experience of modernization. The first, which applies to all the countries except Thailand, is the shared experience of colonialism and the reaction to it, which resulted in various versions of nationalism. The second is the pervasive force of religion—Hinduism, Buddhism, Islam, or Catholicism—which in some respects has become stronger with modernization and certainly continues to exert a decisive influence on the people's imagery of power.

The colonial experience of all these countries has left physical marks as well as cultural reactions that are quite different from the East Asian response to the West. Consequently the peoples of tropical Asia have more complicated and more ambivalent sentiments about Western cultures. Although as a reflection of their colonial heritage a higher proportion of these Asians speak a Western language—now mainly English—they also seem at times to have greater psychological barriers against foreign ideas. Colonial rule also meant that—except in Thailand—traditional authorities were in varying degrees cast aside, and therefore the forms of government that were adopted after independence represented newfound aspirations and not traditional customs and practices. The colonial period stifled whatever inherent political creativity may have existed in the various countries, introducing instead an administrative rule designed by foreigners.

Independence, of course, brought a relegitimization of traditional values, especially as the search for nationhood intensified and moved beyond the initial effort to show the former colonial rulers that their subjects had mastered the Western art of government. Thus the assertion of religious identity became a way of accepting forms of Western political institutions while maintaining national distinctions. The combination of the colonial ruler's former monopoly of ultimate power and the ambivalences about the West inherent in the new nationalism no doubt helped to strengthen religion as the basis of group identity in these cultures. Whereas in East Asia religion is usually muted and often seen as a thing of the past, in South and Southeast Asia religion has been omnipresent. In South Asia the partition of British India followed, of course, the lines of religion, producing ultimately Islamic Pakistan and Bangladesh and an India which professes secular ideals but is still profoundly Hindu. In Southeast Asia the elites and masses are bound by ties of common religious identities. Not only does every village in Thailand have its *wat* (temple), but even in bustling Bangkok people stop at shrines on the busiest sidewalks to say a prayer. In Malaysia and Indonesia the appeals of Islam, far from receding in importance as cosmopolitan urbanization has progressed, have taken on new force for college students. In Burma and the Philippines, Buddhism and Catholicism are respectively the daily concern of almost everyone.

As we focus now on the evolution of concepts of power in Southeast Asia, our starting point will be the heritage of a bifurcated image of authority: one part informed by the models of authority and power introduced by Western colonial rule, and the other rooted in the traditional cultures that have been kept alive by the vitality of religious beliefs in the region. The notions about the nature of power associated with most of the nationalist movements were, paradoxically, quite Westernized because their inspiration was the anticolonialism of the more Westernized elites.[2] Yet the day-to-day politics of the post-independence period has seen a revival of the more traditional concepts of power.

Thus, in a sense, religion has competed with the secular nationalism of anticolonialism. For example, in the Islamic countries of Indonesia and Malaysia the more Westernized and secular national leaders, while still respecting religion, have recently been concerned about the dangers of fundamentalist revivalism and therefore have sought subtly to restrain the influences of religious spokesmen. The continued challenge of religion to nationalism has been possible because the ending of colonial rule came relatively easily and did not require a sustained and broad political mobilization of all the people. Consequently, the political elites who took command in each newly independent country were not so representative of all the people in their respective countries as they would like to have been.

Although it was commonly said in the 1950s and 1960s that nationalism was the dominant force in Southeast Asian politics, it was a limited, elite-based nationalism, articulated by the few who had a vision of modernizing their countries. Since in each instance the individual leaders represented some particular ethnic community, their attempts to identify themselves as spokesmen for the collective nationalism were seen as a threat to the identity of other ethnic or cultural communities. For example, in Burma the more U Nu advocated his version of Burmese nationalism, the more he was seen as threatening the identities of such non-Burmans as the Karens, Shans, Chins, Kachins, Mons, Arakanese, and other hill peoples, to say nothing of the Chinese, Hindu, and Islamic minorities.[3] Similarly in Indonesia, though it might have seemed to the world that Sukarno was orating for Indonesian nationalism, to the peoples in the outer islands he was speaking only for a Javanese elite. Indeed, in order to avoid the problems inherent in making the language of any one group the national tongue, the Indonesians went to the extreme of adopting as the official language Bhasa Indonesia, which was not the native language of any major group in the country.[4] Even in the Philippines national integration is not a given fact, and the strains of allocating scarce resources have made the Moslems in the south as well as others, feel that Manila has been cheating them.

Thus neither the collective bonds of secular nationalism nor those of traditional religions, strong as they both were, proved adequate to solidify the new national power in the postcolonial countries. The problem was one of creating a new understanding of political power which could provide legitimacy for the governments and some degree of consensus as to how power should be established and be used to carry out policies. The problem was profoundly complex in Southeast Asia because of the profusion of historic memories of what power should be. Power could be part of the cosmic order, could rest in god-kings who ruled essentially as theater, or could be synonymous with status—thus leading to the general conclusion that power should never be applied to mundane matters. All of these ideas combined to make it far from clear to Southeast Asians just what their governments should be doing.

In the colonial era these historic images of power had been incorporated with surprising ease into patterns of rule which were premised upon the legitimacy of rulers and subjects as parts of the natural order though with completely separate ways of life. Western colonial rule had generally meant little direct governmental involvement in people's daily lives, especially in Indonesia and the unfederated Malay states, where indirect rule was practiced, allowing traditional sultans and local potentates to preserve their prerogatives.[5] This is not to say that during the colonial era there were not extensive changes in the economy and society as urbanization accelerated, plantations were established, educational systems were introduced, and Chinese traders penetrated villages and hinterlands.[6] The point is rather that colonial authority, with its stress on law and order and on constitutional development, reinforced images of power as status, not of power as utility.

Colonial rulers, in spite of their unpopularity, seemed in many respects to be adhering to traditional concepts of power. Colonial officials could manifest the fearful wrath associated with the personalized power of the precolonial rulers and at the same time could act as though they were bound by strict regulations that were not unlike the sumptuary laws of ancient Southeast Asian kings.[7] Colonial rule also reinforced the idea that power should be hierarchically arranged and that order called for the avoidance of any form of competition among contenders. Finally, colonial rule upheld the ancient principle that power should not be diffused throughout society but held as a monopoly of the ruling class, a distinct elite, born to rule.

With independence, however, these similarities did not resolve the more fundamental questions as to what should be the basis of legitimacy of the new governments and what should be the objectives in their management of power as they sought to build new nations. From the beginning there were two contradictory approaches to solving these problems of handling power. The first was to humanize the idea of power by identifying it with the personalities of the father figures of independence.

Thus power became associated with the charismatic appeal of Aung San and U Nu in Burma, Sukarno in Indonesia, and later Ramón Magsaysay in the Philippines. The second approach was to build power out of the impersonal institutionalization of hierarchies, mainly the bureaucracies left behind by the colonial rulers, but also the armies and in some cases the political parties. The power of bureaucracies became essentially the negative power of immobilism, of maintaining hierarchies by inaction.

The concepts of power associated with both approaches—the charismatic leader and the bureaucracy—were not foreign to their respective cultural traditions. On the contrary, they were almost ideally matched. U Nu was the devout Buddhist the Burmese admired; Sukarno had the flair for the dramatic that inspired Indonesians; and Magsaysay was the hail-fellow leader whom the Americans had taught the Filipinos to see as ideal for democracy. And in South Asia, Nehru was the aloof, reflective, and somewhat arrogant Brahman, precisely the kind of man whom Indians associated with greatness. The behavior of the bureaucrats in each of the countries also conformed to the respective standards of government conduct in the different cultures.

It was common in the 1970s to speak of the charismatic leaders as the "first generation," who helped to solidify the sentiments of national identity, and of their successors, the technocratic leaders, as the "second generation."[8] It is true that the charismatic leaders were not followed by equally skilled rhetoricians, and certainly Sukarno, for all the damage he did, did lead the Indonesians to a strong sense of nationhood. Yet it would be wrong to see the events as entirely the result of different generations of leaders. In fact, at independence the Southeast Asian countries were left with trained bureaucracies; the people were accustomed to a well-ordered officialdom and understood that government involved more than just a spectacle of posturing leaders.

A conflict between politicians and bureaucrats dominated the first years of national independence.[9] Only the latest in a series of conflicts over the concepts of power and government, this one was rooted in the colonial period, when some Southeast Asians had committed themselves to careers in the various colonial services while others had joined the anticolonial nationalist movements. Those who trained for the colonial civil services were not necessarily sycophants of their European masters. Most, in fact, pictured themselves as learning the skills essential for eventual independence and as being at the forefront of the drive for self-government. They were thus in the happy situation of seeing their own advancement as identical with their people's movement toward independence. The nationalists, who from the beginning competed with the administrator-technocrats, benefited greatly from World War II and the Japanese occupation.[10] These men later became the politicians and charismatic leaders of the new national states.

The problem, therefore, throughout non-Confucian Asia was not that independence brought entirely new or foreign models of authority figures. The leaders and their governments did adapt to essentially traditional expectations as to the nature of power and authority. But these traditional images of power, which gave the governments remarkable legitimacy and stability, were not adequate for modernization or appropriate for implementing new policy objectives. This is the central paradox of Southeast Asian modernization. Although the governments of Southeast Asia, with the exception of the Philippines, have generally faced less intense debates about the purpose of government than have the heirs of the Confucian traditions,[11] these countries have not used this apparent advantage to establish a core governmental authority with effective executive power such as the Confucian countries have had.

The Contrasting Responses of Burma and Thailand to the West

At the level of conventional historical analysis Burma and Thailand would seem to have been much the same: both had absolute monarchies; both peoples were deeply committed to the same type of Theravada Buddhism; the economic base of both societies consisted of similar agricultural technologies; and although in the last wars between them the Burmese were the victors, their respective military capabilities were much the same.[12] Yet the two countries have had quite dissimilar political histories, for the Burmese succumbed to colonial rule while Thailand remained free. This difference was not limited to the two countries' nineteenth century responses to the West, for Burma has had continuing problems with political modernization while Thailand has had considerable success.

Thailand, the one country in South and Southeast Asia which escaped colonial domination, might seem to offer a "scientific" control case for testing hypotheses about the effects of colonialism. To the limited degree to which Thai developments differ from those of its neighbors, we can assess aspects of the colonial impact. Particularly striking are the essentially ambivalent Thai attitudes toward Western culture which, though less intense, seem close to the Chinese-Japanese pattern of viewing the West as both a danger and a source of useful technology.[13] But the skillful strategy of the Thais in exploiting Western colonial rivalries—especially that between the British as they advanced into Burma and the French as they moved from Vietnam into Cambodia and Laos—brought into Thailand large numbers of foreign advisors, thus providing the Thais with some of the intimate "teacher-student" interactions with Westerners that were common to colonial settings. Therefore, although the Thais remained independent, they did not have the same "arm's length" relationship to the West that the East Asian countries had.

From the time of their first sustained exposure to the West, the Thai rulers understood that the Western countries were competing nations which could be balanced against each other. Historically the Chinese were the supreme masters of the art of "playing off one barbarian against another," a skill they developed in manipulating relations among the nomads of Inner Asia. But this strategy was not a success in coping with the West because the Western governments were able to turn the tables on the Chinese by insisting upon most-favored-nation treaties. Instead of being able to give favors to some and withhold them from others in a strategy of playing one power off against the other, the Chinese Imperial Court discovered that a concession made to one required equal treatment for all the others. The Thais escaped this problem by initiating closer relations with representatives of all the Western countries, who then jealously went about neutralizing each other. Thus in time the Thais had foreign advisors in nearly every ministry of their government, but they were from different countries and hence never united as a coherent foreign influence.

The Burmese and the Thais responded very differently to the encroachment of the West because their concepts of power were very different. Their experiences did not reveal any significant differences in their rulers' rational understanding of the advantages of Westernized techniques of government, but they did reveal differences in the rulers' ability to adjust the concepts of power of their respective cultures to the new realities.

In the mid-nineteenth century both countries had exceptional kings, absolute monarchs who were regarded by their subjects as omnipotent. In Burma, King Mindon, judged by J. S. Furnivall as "probably the best sovereign of his line," introduced numerous reforms, including the use of regulated coinage, a new tax system, and the ending of some royal monopolies, all of which showed how much he had learned from foreign practices.[14] In Thailand King Mongkut engaged in very similar reforms, and his successor, King Chulalongkorn, carried the reforms even further.

Before King Mindon's time the first Westerners to visit the Burmese court had been confronted with the same issue of protocol that vexed visitors to the Chinese court, that is, the kowtow problem. In Burma it was the "shoe question": all visitors, including foreign ambassadors, were expected to take off their shoes and approach the royal presence on hands and knees. The Burmese conceived of their king as the most powerful ruler in the world. "Their armies were invincible; there was no land they could not conquer. Their king, lord of the white elephants, was also lord of the universe. Their neighbors were their vassals: Chinese armies had been humbled in the field and China was now sending tribute; Manipur and Assam lay open and India, just beyond, was at their mercy; Siam had been successfully invaded."[15]

The Burmese fantasy about the omnipotent nature of their god-king's powers became a dogma which could not be challenged by anyone in the court or among the local nobility. As John F. Cady has noted, the magical properties associated with kingship in Burma were particularly intense because they involved not only Hindu concepts about the magic powers of court regalia and beliefs about the cosmological importance of the hallowed precincts of the capital, but also the Buddhist belief in the king as the ultimate patron of the *Sangha*, or the sacred order of monks.[16] Every ceremony at the court had to evoke awe for the mystical power of otherworldly forces and the unpredictable potency of magic. In this atmosphere of fear of the unknown and unknowable, court politics came down to infinitely refined calculations and excruciatingly contrived schemings. Safety called for precise conformity to all rituals, with everyone striving to outdo everyone else in praising the omnipotence of the god-king. Thus, after the British defeated the Burmese forces in the first Anglo-Burmese war in 1824 and forced the king to pay a substantial indemnity, the official chroniclers felt compelled to describe what had happened in as stark an act of psychological denial as can be found in any account of international relations: "In the years 1186 and 1187 (Burmese era), white strangers from the West fastened a quarrel upon the Lord of the Golden Palace. They landed at Rangoon, took the palace and Prome, and were permitted to advance as far as Yandabo; for the King, from the motives of piety and regard for life, made no preparations whatever to oppose them. The strangers had spent vast sums of money on their enterprises, so by the time they reached Yandabo their resources were exhausted, and they were in great distress. They then petitioned the King, who in his clemency and generosity sent them large sums of money to pay their expenses back, and ordered them out of the country."[17]

As D. G. E. Hall has pointed out, the Burmese paid a high psychological price for their blinding pride: "King Bagyidaw became subject to recurring fits of melancholia, which ultimately led to insanity. The cruel loss of face that it had suffered made the Court not less but more arrogant. There was the same elementary ignorance of the outside world, the same refusal to learn. Above all, Burmese pride continued to revolt against the humiliation of having to carry on diplomatic relations with a mere viceroy [in India]."[18] Within the Burmese court the ultimate proof that the king had divine powers was the fact that his actions and words were never constrained by common sense. To submit to the dictates of reason would have been to lower oneself to a subservient position and to deny the magic of kingly powers. Loyalty called for an unquestioning faith in magic, and hence powerful forces of irrationality flowed through the traditional Burmese political system. The higher the status of an official, the more readily he would put forward absurd ideas in his effort to prove that he was above the limiting constraints of everyday logic.

In the hierarchical structuring of power, superiors lorded it over subservient subordinates. In every relationship the decisive question was, "Who is the superior, who the inferior?" Every official was prepared to act with shameless servility before his superior and with aggressive contempt and haughty disdain toward his subordinates. No one was secure anywhere in the hierarchy, and even at the top the tensions were great. The royal council, called the *Hluttaw*, or "the place of release," promised a degree of security, which in fact did not exist, for the four senior ministers, or *wungyis* ("great burden-bearers"), and their four junior ministers, or *wundauks* ("supports of the great burden-bearers").[19] As G. E. Harvey has observed, the *Hluttaw* never achieved "the independence and security of even a tsardom cabinet [for its members were] liable without a moment's notice to be flung into jail . . . merely because the king was displeased for some trivial reason."[20]

Thus the Burmese glorification of power, their profound concern for status, and their fear of being seen in a subordinate role all combined to make them deny the realities of the European challenge and to seek safety in isolation.

By contrast, the Thai kings were quick to evaluate the relative power of the Europeans and to conclude that much could be gained from the Westerners merely by being flexible and civil. As King Mongkut pointed out in criticizing Vietnamese behavior: "The Annamites have been deaf, dumb, and stubborn as were the Siamese in previous reigns. Their stubbornness caused them to turn small incidents into serious ones, with the result that their country became a French Colony in the end."[21]

The Thai kings, like the Burmese kings, were thought to be demigods, though without the detailed rationalization of Hindu cosmology; and they could also be autocrats. Yet they were seen as protectors of their subjects, teachers and guides of their officials, and students of the scriptures of their Buddhist monks. The record of violence and cruelty of the Burmese kings was not matched by the Thai kings. For example, none of them sought, as did Thisi-thu-Dhamana, to increase his powers through an elixir made from six thousand human hearts. Whereas the last Burmese king on coming to the throne in 1878 sought to eliminate all possible contenders by executing his eighty half-brothers and half-sisters—since royal blood could not be shed, he had his relatives tied up in sacks and trampled by white elephants—the Thai kings used their marriages, and those of their relatives, to expand and enhance their dynastic power.[22]

Status was important in the Thai aristocracy, but the rules governing relations among officials were more precise, gradations more stable, and subordination less of a threat than among the Burmese. Unlike the ubiquitous Burmese fear of losing power, the Thais institutionalized a sedate form of losing status: with each generation the heirs of the king and of the highest nobles lost a grade in the aristocracy until with the fifth generation the offspring became commoners.[23]

Thus the key difference between the two countries was that in Burma the idea of power revolved around profound tensions between superiors and inferiors, with subordinate roles carrying deep anxieties, while in Thailand inequities were not only acceptable but a dependent relationship could offer considerable security. It was quite possible, in fact, to show deference even while confidently manipulating those who presumed themselves to be superior.

The initial skill and good fortune of the Thai kings in preserving their independence and in pursuing modernization policies on their own initiative ensured that Thailand not only avoided the trauma of foreign rule but created a substantial structure of power under the monarchy which in time took the form of a plausible modernizing bureaucracy. The structuring of power under the monarchy proceeded with remarkable smoothness as the Thais developed clearer status differences and gradually separated their civil from their military bureaucracies.

Indeed, unlike the Burmese with their ambivalent feelings about power relationships, the Thais found status rankings to be extremely congenial, with inferiors readily accepting their stations and not appearing to envy those above them. This characteristic of the Thais has long been noted. For example, Lucien Hanks and Herbert P. Phillips reported, "Group cohesion [among Thais] depends on status inequality. It is difficult for an equal to give anything of value to an equal or to command his 'respect.' Indeed he stands as a potential competitor for favors. Group solidarity requires . . . framing unambiguously the relative rank of each [member]."[24]

No doubt the fact that Thai society was not disrupted by colonial rule as Burmese society was, has made it easier for the Thais to accept status gradations and to find their relative rankings with a minimum of confusion. Yet there are certain basic psychocultural differences which also help to explain the continuing pattern of Burmese and Thai differences.

Burma: Distrust of Dependency

Burma's basic political problems since independence have been psychological and cultural. As anthropologist Manning Nash observed in the early 1960s, "Burma does not suffer from many of the handicaps besetting other Asian and African lands. It is not plagued with overpopulation . . . Its future is not caught in those dismal 'vicious circles' that seem to make economic and social development a virtual impossibility. If Burma does not succeed in developing a modern economic, political, and social structure, it will be a failure of human effort, a matter of social and cultural variables, a case of organizational and ideological inadequacy."[25]

The Burmese have not been able to avoid a faction-ridden politics except through an immobilist autocratic military regime. Either they have engaged in self-destructive squabbles with everyone seeking more power, or they have retreated into their private domains, leaving the leader supreme but ineffectual. Superiors cannot trust their subordinates, even to the extent of sharing with them their policy designs; and subordinates distrust their superiors because they do not expect to be properly rewarded for their loyalties or their efforts.

In 1948 U Nu became Burma's first prime minister at independence, following the bizarre murder of the "father of the country," Aung San— an act which exemplified the Burmese habit of carrying personal power rivalries to the point of total ineffectualness. On the eve of independence, assassins burst into a meeting of most of the cabinet-designates and machine-gunned Burma's new leaders. On making their getaway they stopped for one beer, and then a few more, until their celebration was interrupted by the pursuing police, to whom they confessed that they had been hired by the disappointed politician U Saw, who coveted Aung San's role.[26] This was not the last time a Burmese politician calculated, "If someone is going to enjoy high status, why can't it be me?"

Soon after being called upon to step into the breach, U Nu began to display his mastery of Burmese political culture even as he unsuccessfully coped with the forces of Burmese disunity. On the surface the most obvious obstacle to national unity was the special demands of the various ethnic minorities. The Karens immediately mounted an armed struggle for an independent state, and since a disproportionate number of the British-trained officers were Karens the uprising created a major crisis for the new Burmese army. Other independence movements and armed conflicts were started by the Shans and by the Burmese Communist party, which in the fractious state of Burmese politics soon became two parties, the White Flag and the Red Flag. As serious as these challenges were to Burmese nationalism, they were far from fatal to U Nu's leadership, mainly because of Burmese political tolerance for inordinately large gaps between official rhetoric and publicly recognized facts. More than half the country was outside the control of Rangoon, except when infrequent army patrols were sent, hurriedly, through the troubled territory; but the government would simply ignore that fact, declaring that all was well and the country was successfully following its own "road to socialism."[27]

U Nu's insurmountable problem, and that of his successor, General Ne Win, was not the innumerable insurgencies but rather the inability to build unity among the most ardent supporters of Burmese nationalism. It was in the nature of Burmese political culture that the more brilliantly U Nu conducted himself, the more he created enemies among his associates. The more he learned about appealing to the rural masses, the more the political elite felt he had to go. U Nu learned early that successful development programs and projects, which might elate American development economists, brought no rewards in Burmese politics. But as he concentrated more and more of his attention on the patronage questions which were the very essence of Burmese politics, he discovered that the Burmese politician's calculus meant that for every friend bought, a multitude became enemies. Burmese politicians seemed unable to reason that "if the other fellow got something today, maybe if I am loyal I will get something tomorrow." Instead they adopted the logic that "if he got something today, I should have had it yesterday." In short, the more U Nu succeeded in building loyalties among some elements in his party, the more estranged others became. The result was rampant distrust in a political culture in which everyone was too "wise" to accept as truth any statement by any politician.[28]

U Nu's initial approach in seeking unity followed one of the cardinal principles of Burmese political culture, which holds that statements of ideology should be used to soothe the aggressive passions of others and to convince them that one is blissfully innocent of malice toward anyone. Thus, in one of his early speeches, U Nu declared that he was a "Marxist" and that the government would carry out a fifteen-point program, which in its details would have been more radical than that initiated by either Lenin or Mao Zedong in their first steps toward socialism. But then he reassured all non-Communists that the goals would have to be achieved by "education" and not by government fiat; that "the propagation of the writings of Marxist authors, such as Marx himself, Engels, Lenin, Stalin, Mao Tse-tung, Tito, and Dimitrov," would not be the work of the government or of his party, the AFPFL, and that "anti-Marxists" would be free to propagate their views.[29]

When the appeals of Marxism began to fade, U Nu generated ideological statements based on Buddhism, which had the same quality of being, happily, unexceptionable, but also, sadly, unworkable. The purpose, however, of U Nu's rhetoric remained typically Burmese: it sought to reassure the people that the speaker was motivated only by kindness. But since Burmese politicians fancied that they were too sophisticated to believe in such a benign idea of power, they were certain that behind the gentle words lay deviousness.

Examined more closely, U Nu's problem, like that of his successor, was that the Burmese political process contains profound ambivalences about the purpose of power. On the one hand, the culture exalts qualities associated with the possession of power: gradations of status are never blurred; the meritorious are honored with enthusiasm; dignity in demeanor is rewarded with appropriate awe; and all manifestations of aloofness and haughtiness by superiors are not only tolerated, they are respected. On the other hand, the mere suggestion that someone desires power is a scandal, as is any intimation that one of high status should display any familiarity with the details of policy matters. Hence there should not be, and usually cannot be, any manifest connection between having power and making decisions. The Burmese feel that decision-making should be left to such low-status figures as astrologers, junior officials, and foreign advisors. One who gets to the top should be spared all the inconveniences and strains associated with making choices that might trigger unpleasant emotions in others.[30]

To understand the profound ambivalences that the Burmese have about power, it is necessary to appreciate three fundamental cultural concepts which take on great significance because they are central features of the Burmese socialization process.

The first is the concept of *pon.* Any Burmese from villager to high official can aspire to be recognized as a man of *pon,* a person of quality, deserving respect. According to Nash, "The idea of *pon* is mystical; it is close to the idea of grace, charity, election, destiny. The presence of great amounts of *pon* (all males have some) is a fact of social inference. It depends upon the meshing of community opinions, on the one side, and the mundane success and power of a man, on the other."[31]

A man of *pon* exudes authority and has a commanding presence, but he must also manifest both a respectable degree of religiosity and more than a suggestion of sex appeal. At the same time, he must carry off all of these assertive traits with fitting modesty. The point, however, is that anyone can hope to be recognized as a man of *pon,* and whether he does or does not succeed stems largely from his *kan*—"the summary of all of his past deeds and misdeeds."[32] *Pon* is thus an attribute of one's personal identity, but it is incumbent upon others to acknowledge the degree to which an individual has it.

Thus the first source of Burmese ambivalence about power is the gap between the judgment of the individual and that of others concerning how much *pon* he possesses. Although in theory *pon* is acquired in the same impersonal and unbiased manner as are Buddhist merits and demerits, in practice almost every Burmese learns early that with a little guile one can sometimes enhance one's *pon*. But then comes the consciousness that some people may be maliciously withholding recognition of one's claims to *pon*. What should be one's own precious possession is thus dependent upon others. The seeds of mistrust are planted early.

A second, related concept is that of *awza*—in a sense, *pon* in a social or group context. In any group there is always one individual and only one who has the *awza*. Just as everyone aspires to *pon*, so those who feel they are blessed as men of *pon* will strive to have the *awza* in any group in which they may find themselves. Burmese, from the moment they join a group, are generally skilled in spotting who has *awza*, and having done so they set out to calculate their own chances of replacing that person. The process of determining who has the *awza* is entirely implicit: one could never ask openly who has it, or claim it for himself. Consequently the competition is subtle and must be tacitly carried out.

Awza, more than *pon*, contains contradictory qualities. He who has the *awza* must be both assertive and modest, active and passive, authoritative and decisive—and yet kindly and attentive. The blending of all these traits is made even more complex by the need to be equally knowledgeable about this-worldly concerns and otherworldly matters.

Thus the very nature of *awza* compounds the Burmese ambivalences about power. Since the phenomenon is entirely subjective, each individual is free to picture for himself the ideal blend of traits, and misunderstandings can arise as to who in fact has the *awza* in any specific group. The more subtle contenders can become frustrated when the more obtuse fail to appreciate their superior qualities, while those who are action-prone can become irritated by those who are more inclined toward refinement.

Ultimately the concept of *awza* is what makes a Burmese believe that if only he were recognized by everyone else as having the *awza*, everything would be perfect.[33] Justice would be done. Moreover, the group should feel eternally in his debt for giving it his blessing of *awza*. Yet, in the normal flow of social life, a Burmese rarely achieves such a blissful state of affairs and consequently life does seem unfair. Thus, to the extent that *awza* defines the Burmese concept of power, it is clear that to have power should be ecstasy, and not to have it is a gross injustice. Since its possession depends upon one's judgment about the subjective and unarticulated attitudes of others toward oneself, concern about *awza* intensifies the Burmese feeling that others are not to be trusted.

The combination of the gratification of being a man of *pon,* the thrill of having the *awza,* and the horror of being seen as having neither of them would produce unruly behavior and unseemly struggles on all levels of Burmese social life if it were not for the third concept, that of *ahnadeh,* which the Burmese insist is unique to their culture. *Ahnadeh* is a physical sensation which wells up from the stomach and paralyzes the individual so that he cannot press his self-interest but must defer to the wishes of others. *Ahnadeh* is described by most Burmese as being, at least initially, a warm physical sensation, but as it wears away it can leave one angry and embittered.

The Burmese frequently rationalize their failures in the business world by citing their susceptibility to *ahnadeh,* which they say the Chinese and Indians never experience, but which leaves the Burmese unduly tender-hearted and generous at the wrong moments. An example of *ahnadeh* at work, once reported in the Rangoon press, concerned a man who saved up his *kyats* to buy a bicycle. Just as he was at last going to town to make the purchase, his neighbor asked to borrow a few *kyats,* triggering his *ahnadeh* and forcing him to lend the money, which left him without enough for the bike. Frustrated, he returned home to brood; but when his *ahnadeh* receded, he jumped up and in a fit of anger killed his neighbor. Among other examples is the well-recognized fact that a subordinate will not respond to unjust criticisms by a superior while experiencing *ahnadeh,* and that a boy who is tongue-tied in expressing his affection for a girl is said to be with *ahnadeh,* while a girl who is yielding to the wishes of a boy is also influenced by it.[34]

Although Burmese claim that only they know the sensations of *ahnadeh,* they are convinced that not all Burmese necessarily experience it. Indeed, perversely, it is the man of *pon* who is supposed to be the most sensitive to it. Here is another source for the profound Burmese feelings of ambivalence toward power. The very individuals who are supposedly most susceptible to the inhibitions of *ahnadeh* are also most likely to have the *awza.* Hence it is easy to have resentment toward one who acts as if he had the *awza,* for it is natural to think, "If only I had not been checked by my *ahnadeh,* he would not have the *awza,* which must mean that he doesn't have *ahnadeh* and hence is unworthy of having the *awza.*"

Such resentment can either fuel an urge for revenge, expressed in the frequent outbreaks of apparently unprovoked violence against leaders, or it can be assuaged by the rationalization that one has *ahnadeh* and is therefore truly a superior person, as shown by the frequency with which the Burmese withdraw into their private domains.

These competing sentiments seem to cause the Burmese to have visions of either being exalted in power, and thus completely above the competition, or so correct in their humble stance as to be shielded from the wrath of others. Yet at the same time they know that these polar positions are also the most vulnerable: the one who stands out above all others, no matter how timid and benign his actions, will be the target of the ambitious and vicious; and he who completely humbles himself invites the attacks of those who cannot resist the pleasure of having an easy victim.[35]

Obviously these sensitivities generate fantasies which make it difficult for hierarchical institutions to operate effectively. Thus, in spite of their exaggerated interest in, and glorification of, power as a personal attribute, the Burmese have not been able to establish significant state power. Their nationalist, umbrella party, the AFPFL (standing for the long-forgotten English name of Anti-Fascist People's Freedom League) degenerated first into two competing factions, quaintly named the "Clean" and the "Stable," and then into untold subfactions. The army, as the institution of last resort for national unity, has also had its factions of colonels.

Burmese elite politics became a process in which leaders had to reassure themselves daily that they possessed high status and therefore should command deference from everyone. Consequently, every slight was translated into a calculated affront by a scheming enemy. Thus the Burmese have learned to avoid anyone they imagined to be their enemy and to concentrate their attentions on those who seemed spontaneously to enjoy honoring them. The result was an array of political potentates surrounded by their deferential entourages. Those with truly high status, according to their official ranks, found it nearly impossible to have civil dealings with those whose status was almost as high as theirs and who therefore might be taken as their peers. Consequently, high officials have only been able to work comfortably with low-status people, and this has reinforced the common belief that leaders inevitably surround themselves with incompetents.[36]

When in 1962 General Ne Win pushed aside U Nu, arrested most of the civilian politicians, and instituted military rule, nothing much changed because the political culture endured. That physical force, and not just public shaming, had been used to destroy the enemy had minimal effect. Even after General Ne Win had locked up the politicians at the Mingladon air base, he still felt a need to shame his enemies by saying that as prisoners they constituted an indecent drain on state resources because they asked for expensive foods and cigars—to which one politician's wife responded, with startling boldness, that she would be more than happy to pay such expenses if only the state would let her husband go home. In time, of course, the politicization of the Burmese army took place and factions began to appear among the officers as they found that they got on more comfortably with some leaders than with others.

There is no need to document General Ne Win's failure to transform the Burmese economy into a post exchange in which everyone could buy things at less than market value. Few Burmese made the effort to find out why the scheme would not work; it was enough for most that the new leader was dispensing a benign ideology and that he did not want to make enemies. Although the structure of the army set limits to disunity, the expectation that the army would provide a more coherent leadership only made the symptoms of disharmony seem worse.

Thus, neither U Nu nor Ne Win was able to project himself as a charismatic unifier of Burma. Instead, the basic features of Burmese political culture generated divisions within the elite which made effective public policies impossible. The monotony of the two leaders' respective ideologies signaled to everyone that they did not intend to initiate novel departures, and therefore the political stratum could concentrate on dividing itself into a variety of subgroupings. Thus after each jarring transition, whether to national independence or to military rule, the return to equilibrium always produced a situation in which a select number of relatively autonomous leaders sought the happiness of non-decision-making while their dutiful supporters sought the security of dependency.

The enduring Burmese ambivalences about power must have deep roots in the Burmese personality. Anthropologists report that the Burmese socialization process carries to great extremes the pattern of a threatening father and a doting mother. Rather than being distant and aloof, like the Chinese father, the Burmese father is more often remembered as being harsh, chastising, and at times even cruel. Above all, he can release his hostile emotions within the security of the family he presides over, something he is careful not to do publicly. To this extent he is like the Japanese father, who can express emotion at home and ask for sympathy. The Burmese mother, however, unlike the supportive and somewhat worshipful Japanese mother, is reported to be at one moment the most loving and enthusiastic mother of any Asian culture, but at the next moment, as the mood changes, she can abandon the child. It has been hypothesized that very early Burmese children experience intense affection and are made to feel that they are indeed the center of the universe, but then they find that the source of all their enjoyable emotional warmth can be withdrawn without explanation. Hence nothing is enduring. Later they learn the same lesson in cognitive terms when they discover in the doctrines of Buddhism that nothing lasts, that all things are in a state of flux. The result is a profound sense of distrust.

Hence the Burmese are troubled with a deep sense of insecurity, which, when translated into social relationships, becomes the ambivalence of both wanting and fearing power and of both wanting and fearing dependency. In contrast to the Confucian cultures, which teach children that if they adhere to clearly prescribed rules they will be rewarded or at least will avoid punishment, Burmese learning experiences do not provide clear-cut guidelines for behavior. Children learn only that they should please their parents and not cause them trouble, but the Burmese notion of the obedient child, the *lein-ma-deh* child, is defined more in terms of emotions than according to propriety.[37] Whereas in Confucian cultures it is expected that correctness of behavior and adherence to set rules can and should guarantee positive responses, in Burmese culture that goal can only be achieved by manipulations of the emotions. Hence laughter, playfulness, coyness, stern posturing, and feigned anger are the ready tools of Burmese social interactions, and there are fewer of the calculated stratagems and clever ploys than in the Confucian cultures.

Thailand: Gentle Dependency in a Military Dictatorship

The Siamese monarchy was not untouched by Hindu lore. Like the Burmese god-kings the Siamese kings were thought to be divine; in both countries the white elephant was a symbol of power and good fortune, and Indian astrology and numerology were adopted.[38] The Thais, however, were also influenced to a minor degree by contacts with the Chinese. Indeed, exposure to Chinese pretensions of greatness may have contributed to King Mongkut's wisdom in dealing with the arrival of the Europeans. The Thai court had much earlier accepted the Chinese proposal that the Son of Heaven be declared an "elder brother" to the Thai kings.[39] The Thais found that a suzerain relationship with the Chinese court was in no way threatening, but that, on the contrary, they could exploit the Chinese sense of self-importance, thereby getting more from the pompous Chinese mandarins than they gave in "tribute."

In short, the Thai kings, without giving up any of their claims to mystical and supernatural power, were able to see the benefits of a dependent relationship. Consequently when the Europeans arrived, the Thai court instinctively sought ways to exploit the Westerners' exaggerated sense of their own importance. First King Mongkut and then his son Chulalongkorn brought in foreign advisors from England, Denmark, America, France, and Prussia.[40] Whereas the Burmese, like the Chinese, resisted the demand for diplomatic relations with Western countries, the Thais welcomed foreign embassies and even accepted the idea of extraterritoriality so that the Westerners could be regulated by their own laws. The lifting of the nineteenth century "unequal treaties" was the work of Francis B. Sayre, son-in-law of President Wilson, who served from 1920 to 1927 as Siam's Foreign Office advisor, and who believed he ought to do well by his "client."[41]

The successors to Chulalongkorn, benefiting from the balance of foreign forces he had established both within the governmental ministries and vis-à-vis the surrounding colonial powers, were content to reign without provoking anyone with either reforms or revivals. The kings Rama V and Rama VI did not find it demeaning to ape the European aristocracy and to import into Bangkok gaudy Western uniforms and rugby football.

Thai autocracy then began to drift into decadence. The mixture of incoherent reforms and arbitrary insistence upon past practices finally became more than the army officer corps—who had been mainly trained in England—could endure. The result was the 1932 coup, the first of the Third World coups, as they would later be called. Yet, what the officers wanted from their bloodless act was only a constitutional monarchy. Their goal was to stabilize the Throne and to introduce progressive policies that would bring Thailand into line with its neighbors, all of which were by then under colonial administration.

Perhaps Western historians, in what came to be denounced as their "Euro-centric" view of events, have tended to be unfair to Thailand, stressing its leaders' propensities to shift with the winds of international politics—accommodating to the Japanese in World War II and then, after Japan's surrender, welcoming relations with the United States. Yet, whatever the moral judgments, the fact remains that whereas Burma had trouble with the advent of the West, and still has trouble with modern world culture, Thailand coped easily with the initial arrival of the West and has continued to accommodate to the modern world.

The explanation lies in part in the differing attitudes in the two cultures toward superiors and inferiors, in short, their notions of power. The difference, bluntly put, is that the Burmese see all relations as essentially hierarchical and feel threatened thereby, while the Thais, who also see relations in terms of superiors and inferiors, rejoice in that fact. Whereas the Burmese feel profoundly threatened by being in a dependent role, the Thais appreciate the payoffs of dependency. Indeed, the only problem for the Thais has been uncertainty about whether it is better to be the dignified superior or the self-seeking inferior.

In contrast to the Burmese craving to be a man of *pon* and to have the *awza*, the Thais find gradations acceptable because of their positive view of the subordinate's role.[42] Thais may also, of course, be ambitious for leadership, but they give more recognition to the rewards of follow-ership than do the Burmese. This is possible because the Thais instinc-tively understand that there are psychic exchanges between leader and follower which bring substantial benefits to both. Indeed, in many cases the benefits for the subordinate are so great that it becomes difficult to determine whether the patron or the client is in the more advantageous position. Thai culture makes explicit the idea that people are vulnerable, indeed helpless, if they do not have a benevolent superior. It is the security provided by such a superior which gives an individual the necessary "will" to accomplish things. In return for this gift of "will," however, the "little person" must express "awe" of the superior, which in turn ensures a continuous flow of benevolence.

The linkage that provides for the exchanging of "will" and "awe," which has been analyzed by Herbert Rubin, starts with the superior having to manifest what the Thais call *metta*, a form of kindness and compassion that is heavily colored by pity.[43] Nobody who is a leader can escape from being a true father—that is, from exuding sympathy and wise understanding. Hence the greater the power of an individual, the more kindly should be his actions. The spirit of *metta* ensures that the superior will evidence gentleness—a trait, surprisingly, that is more im-portant in superiors than in subordinates.

Even more important, *metta* certifies that a superior is endowed with *karuna*, which is a passion to be helpful and to lead others in constructive ways. The critical test as to whether a leader has *karuna* is his ability to guide subordinates without damaging their self-esteem. When the leader has *karuna*, the follower is not threatened by accepting a state of de-pendency. The quintessential quality of leadership is thus the ability to protect the fragile feelings of the weak. Power is the protective nurturance of the lowly, that is, the ability to inspire the less powerful. The inter-actions between the superior and the inferior must not harm the latter.

When a *phuunoj* or "small person" is exposed to a superior with *karuna*, he will be instantly filled with *kamlungjie*—that absolutely es-sential sense of will, of the vitality and energy necessary for all manner of activities. *Kamlungjie* is essential in order to overcome the natural lack of self-confidence which is innate in all honorable people. Those who are naturally self-confident and therefore are not in need of *kamlungjie* are regarded as dangerously anti-social, even as candidates for the crim-inal class. Normal people, by contrast, are driven to find *kamlungjie* so that they can face the vicissitudes of life.

On experiencing *kamlungjie* the energized subordinate reciprocates by being possessed with *krengjie*, a sensation which in this context can best be described as "awe" for his benevolent superior. Just as the Burmese insist that only they know *ahnadeh,* so the Thais claim that only they have a natural feeling for "making *krengjie.*"[44] The subtle skills expected of a superior are matched by those of the subordinate who can make *krengjie.* Basically *krengjie* is a subjective state, as is the Burmese sensation of *ahnadeh,* but it differs from the Burmese concept in that it calls for a positive manifestation. The subordinate needs to communicate, with the greatest subtlety, that he is making *krengjie.* To be gauche about it, to make a show of deference, would not be sincere, and hence not *krengjie.*

Every member of Thai society is expected to be able to make *krengjie* to those with whom they interact. Indeed, in Thailand anyone can *krengjie* another in the sense of displaying considerateness. In the superior-subordinate relationship the leader's passion of *karuna* can take the form of *krengjie* if it involves showing extra consideration toward the subordinate; but the key to the relationship is the absolute need of the subordinate "to *krengjie*" the superior. The follower's *krengjie* is a fine balancing of his own humbleness and self-effacement with his respect and deference toward the superior who is the source of the blessing.

The act of *krengjie* is absolutely essential to the idealized superior-subordinate relationship because it protects the benevolent leader from what might otherwise become the insatiable demands of his followers for ever more favors of *kamlungjie.* The Thais seem to need this wall of distance so as to prevent inferiors from becoming intolerable nuisances who pester their patrons for benefits.

American culture does not have a comparable appreciation of the need of leaders for some such protection, a balance between kindly support and impersonal distance. In American culture the use of distance and aloofness is seen mainly as tactics ("He is too busy, or too important, to answer my phone call"), or as annoyance on the part of the powerful ("How can I get past his secretary?"), and not as a matter which needs to be ritualized in order to civilize power relationships. Some Americans in positions of authority like to assert that they are always "accessible," but in Thai culture subordinates have an instinctive understanding that such a leader needs to be protected from his follies so that he will not waste his time or his charms on meaningless matters. Power should not be indiscriminate. It is the distance provided by *krengjie* which makes it possible for the Thai leader to appear to be evenhanded with his subordinates, allowing no one of them greater intimacy than another. A proper leader should never have to give way to strong emotions: he is expected always to manifest *ubekka* (unimpassioned impartiality), which he can only sustain by appearing to be immune to self-interest.

The Thai approach to personal relationships produces remarkably stable power structures. Even when Thai politics was characterized by periodic coups d'etat, the transfers of leadership occurred with a minimum of fuss because each of the participants appreciated the importance of adhering to his respective status role.[45] The guiding principle was that leaders who failed to inspire *kamlungjie* would in time lose not only their followers but also their legitimacy in the eyes of the elite.

Power in the Thai political culture is thus seen as the magnet which draws out of people a desire to act. It is not supposed to be harsh or repressive. Subordinates need inspiration, not discipline.[46] Thus, in all power relationships there is considerable sensitivity to the subtleties of dignity and self-esteem. Traditional Thai concepts of power are not consistent with the ideas associated with executive authority in Western command relationships. The Thais emphasize the need for the superior to be a nurturing figure, not a forceful, threatening one. Power is certainly not seen in utilitarian terms.

Thus in both Burma and Thailand a magical and sacred concept of power evolved into a view of power based on status relationships: one of tension between superiors and inferiors in Burma, but one of mutual support in Thailand. Neither culture accepted the idea that power should be used systematically and efficiently for collective practical purposes. Yet, the Thai concept of a bonding relationship, with relative merit as the essence of power, did facilitate a pyramiding of power which greatly accelerated the establishment of a modernizing state structure.[47]

Indonesia: A Bureaucratic Polity Based on Patron-Client Ties

In its early history Indonesia had several imperial power structures, headed by god-kings not unlike those of Burma and Thailand. By the time the Dutch arrived, however, power had been fragmented throughout the archipelago. Instead of a single reigning court, various rulers and sultans dominated Java, Sumatra, and the outer islands. Colonial government consisted of a pattern of indirect rule in which local authorities made treaties with representatives of the Dutch East India Company to provide governing assistance. The spread of Dutch rule was thus a gradual and uneven process. In Java alone, the Dutch, who made their first penetration in 1619, took 211 years to complete the process. They did not govern Bali until 1914, some 295 years after they had begun to rule in Indonesia. It was in 1798 that the Dutch government replaced the company as the agent of colonial rule.[48]

Although the Dutch centralized much of their administration, their practice of indirect rule and their policy of "like ruling over like" meant that the immediate forms of power experienced by most Indonesians were still elements of local authority. Furthermore, Dutch policy tended in the main to preserve traditional forms rather than replacing them with Westernized institutions.

Consequently Indonesia came to independence in 1949 without the memory of an indigenous and traditional structure of national power.[49] The concept of national power and national administration was almost entirely a foreign import. In terms of people's immediate understanding of power in their personal relationships, however, the Indonesians probably had more vivid traditional and mystical concepts of power than any of the other Southeast Asian peoples. Although the building of a sense of nationhood called for the use of European concepts of power, the actual play of power in human relationships remained very traditional. Thus political parties, national bureaucracies, and the military services were all modeled on Western forms, but their practices followed the traditional rules of power relationships.

Indonesian political development took the form of first experimenting with constitutional democracy, then settling on the charismatic leadership of Sukarno, and finally—after a bloody coup attempt—arriving at a bureaucratic polity that was shored up by the military hierarchy but that operated primarily according to traditional patron-client roles. The linkage between elite politics and the rural masses was also based on networks of patron-client ties. As Karl Jackson has demonstrated, political integration in Indonesia "depends on a system of traditional authority relations animating village social life and connecting each village with the world of regional and national politics existing beyond the village gate. Virtually all Sundanese villagers are organized into networks of dyadic, personal, diffuse, affect-laden, and enduring superior-subordinate relationships."[50]

In the first years of independence the Indonesian political class sought to emulate European democratic politics by dividing themselves among several ideologically differentiated political parties; and then, in the forum of a parliament, they made every effort to form and to tear down cabinet combinations. Within a matter of twelve years the Indonesians had no less than seventeen governments. The process was self-generating and self-contained in that the Indonesian politicians avoided, no doubt to the great envy of their European counterparts, the European practice of holding regularized elections to determine who should play the game of power. Indeed, by the time the Indonesians did hold a general election in 1955 the parliamentary process was so discredited that the stage was set for a new version of democracy—Guided Democracy, established under the hand of the charismatic Sukarno.

It is not surprising that a newly independent country should have had difficulties operating a highly complex parliamentary system. It is surprising, however, as well as significant, that party identification remained fixed in the case of individuals, but that party ideology was easily negotiable when it came to forming a coalition in order to make up a government.[51] The NU (Nahdatul Ulama, or Moslem Teachers party) made several alliances with the secular PNI, or Nationalist party, while rejecting ties with Masjumi, the more moderate, broadly based Moslem party. Thus Ali Sastroamidjojo of the PNI formed a cabinet in 1954 with a strong secular tilting but with the necessary support of both NU and Masjumi. Wilopo of the PNI formed another cabinet while being allied to Masjumi and the PSI, or Socialists. Sjarifuddin of the Socialists formed a government by allying with Masjumi. The shifting combinations of parties did not, however, blur the party labels of the individual politicians. Sjahrir remained always a Socialist even after the party had practically disappeared; Sjarifuddin was to be remembered as a Socialist even though he was killed while leading a band of two thousand Communists during the Madiun rebellion; Sukarno was labeled a PNI even while ruling independently; and Hatta was always an independent in spite of working closely with several parties.

All of this points to the importance of individuals and their personal networks of followers as opposed to formal party organizations. Although Wilopo and Sastroamidjojo were both identified as PNI, they had their own groups of followers, and judging by the lack of intimacy in their relationship, they might as well have belonged to different parties. Even more telling was the fact that the two Moslem parties, NU and Masjumi, were to remain deeply antagonistic to each other in spite of many shared values.

After Sukarno ended parliamentary democracy and inaugurated Guided Democracy, it seemed that Indonesian politics was moving into line with Indonesian cultural practices. Sukarno increasingly denounced Western norms and scorned the idea that "50 percent plus one should rule." In particular he attacked the idea of having a political opposition that "opposes the government out of its own interests." In praising instead the ideal of "governing by consensus" Sukarno spoke frequently of the Javanese ideas of *gotong-rojong* and *musjawarah,* community mutual assistance and discussion leading to consensus.[52]

Although Sukarno's style captured many elements of Javanese culture, it also violated some of the basic taboos. Consistent with Javanese concepts was Sukarno's uninhibited acceptance of power as an inherent personal right. Leaders are different from common people, according to the Javanese concept of power; therefore the top ruler can flaunt his superior status and no one should question his right to use his status to advantage. Sukarno also captured the essence of the Indonesian style of communicating by slogans and symbols. By acting as though the code words and acronyms he invented had a potency of their own, he appealed to the Indonesian inclination to seek magic formulas. Sukarno caught the spirit of the *wayang*, or shadow plays, when he talked against the "Old Established Order" and when he posed as the brave ruler surrounded by evil forces. In doing so he drove home the ideal that the *satria*, or Javanese warrior, must always be loyal to his king even when, or more correctly, especially when, the king has done wrong.[53]

At the same time, Sukarno violated numerous Javanese norms as President Suharto never has done. Sukarno was much too blatant and crude to be the ideal Javanese leader. He exposed his emotions in ways that appalled the traditional Javanese. Too often his behavior suggested that he was seeking revenge for the slight he had felt when the Dutch father of his first love refused him permission to marry his daughter while they were still in high school.[54] Sukarno repeatedly set impossible goals for Indonesia and then found that he had been confounded by conspiracies. His behavior would have been more consistent with Javanese norms if he had set modest objectives and then been lavish in extolling his good fortune in achieving them.

Although Sukarno appeared to be tapping the emotional roots of Javanese culture with his theatrical politics, he was only touching some of the inherently contradictory Javanese views about power. His sense of drama did help to unite the country, but his excessive display of emotion violated the Javanese notion that true power is a subtle matter, and that the real leader should be one who can maintain a balance between his inner emotions and his formalistic and almost ritual-like moves.

Indeed, according to Clifford Geertz, the Javanese tend to think of every person as being preoccupied with coping with both an inner world and an outer world, in both of which their goal is to be unexceptionable. With respect to the "inside" dimension of their personal lives, or *batin* (to use the Javanese word), and the "outside" aspects of life, or the *lair,* the ideal is to maximize refinement, conformity, and modesty, and to reduce vulgarity, self-glorification, and conspicuousness.

More specifically, the goal with respect to the inner self is to master all feelings and ensure that one's passions are kept under control. At no point should an individual be overwhelmed or even seriously influenced by his inner feelings. Needless to say, Javanese cannot always achieve this ideal. At times the burden becomes unbearable, and they explode: it is, of course, the Malays and Javanese who have given us the word *amok,* as in "running amok." Yet the Javanese ideal is to deny unruly feelings as much as possible and to subdue one's emotions so that they will be like "a low background hum"—never shrill, never jarring.

With respect to the outer world, or *lair*, the goal is to achieve a sense of smoothness and refinement so that one is never abrasive and, most important, always carries out one's social role in the prescribed manner. When one does have to act, the hope is that nothing one does is in any way influenced by private feelings. When one does have feelings, they should not show; and when one reveals oneself, there should be no stimulus of affect. Perfection in manners requires the complete inhibiting of the self.

Thus the Javanese have, according to Geertz, a "bifurcated conception of the self, half ungestured feeling and half unfelt gesture." They do not want their inner world to intrude upon their outward activities, nor do they want their social relations to disturb their inner sensitivities. With respect to both the inner and the outer worlds, the goal is that of a proper ordering of certain positive values, all of which are related to the Javanese concept of *alus*, which means "pure," "refined," "polished," "exquisite," "ethereal," "subtle," "civilized," "smooth." At the same time, everything must be done to avoid suggesting the concept of *kasar*, which means "impolite," "rough," "uncivilized," "coarse," "insensitive," and "vulgar."[55]

All of this points to the overriding Indonesian need for the psychological suppression of individuality and for the comforts of dependency and conformity. Among the Balinese, for example—again according to Geertz—the ultimate horror is stage fright, for in that state one is separated from one's role and the true identity is starkly revealed. The goal in life should be to fit one's assigned role so perfectly that it is possible to mask individual identity and be known only for one's success in carrying out social obligations. In Bali people believe that it is the role which endures, not the memory of an actor who has personally interpreted the role. It is Hamlet who belongs to history, not the variety of actors who come and go, craving to be remembered for their infantile desire for attention.[56]

General Suharto, the Javanese mystic who succeeded Sukarno, has come so much closer to embodying the essence of Javanese culture that he has made Sukarno appear to be almost a foreigner. For example, Suharto has mastered the art of masking his feelings while at the same time calibrating them to such a fine point that he can choose his responses to stimuli with great delicacy. After impassively receiving a foreign ambassador who, unfortunately for his country, conveys his message too aggressively, Suharto can instruct his chief of staff that, because he does not wish to have his emotions so aggravated, he will not see that man again for a year. Again, Suharto can ignore criticism that verges on being explicit, and that hence is in bad taste by Javanese standards, until long afterward, when the inevitable opportunity for revenge arrives. At the same time, however, a questioning of one of his decisions which is so elegantly phrased as to seem a compliment can bring an instant response, and more likely than not an adjustment in the desired direction.[57]

The ordering of the politics of a nation-state according to such elaborate and courtly rules of conduct can create great problems for effective administration. The use of cryptic modes of communication among people of highly tuned sensitivities makes it almost impossible to place blame unambiguously and accurately. Moreover, the pervasive belief that mystical and otherworldly forces can always come into play in human affairs expands the domain of the plausible to the point where the implausible hardly exists. To those who are in subordinate roles or are outside the system it may seem obvious that things are not right, but it is extremely difficult for them to concentrate criticism on a specific superior. By contrast, those at the top can make anyone a scapegoat. The result is an environment in which actions are not related to clear purposes, and the leadership can make startling moves for apparently whimsical motives without raising many eyebrows. In Indonesia it was concluded long ago that the best way to operate the government was to have only vague theories about the relationship of cause and effect in human affairs.

These and other features of Javanese culture generate expectations among Indonesian officials that dangers abound and that they must move with infinite care until they reach the security of a close personal relationship. In terms of the cultural norms, safety can be found only through disassociating oneself not only from the people with whom one has no ties but also from what is actually taking place. These prescriptions have been turned to structural ameliorations; that is, the Indonesians have sought to gain security by agreeing that power should be hierarchically arranged so that each person can find his niche in a system of pyramided clusters of patrons and their individual clients.

This is what has led Karl Jackson to speak of Indonesia as having a bureaucratic polity.[58] In other connotations that term might suggest impersonal norms, administration directed toward public policy accomplishments, and orderly efficiency. But in Indonesia a bureaucratic polity only means that all the dormant power in society is concentrated in government hands: those who control events have official positions, and government employment provides the highest security in return for the least effort.

At the heart of this bureaucratic polity is the idea of reciprocity between patron and clients. Senior officials have their networks of dependent junior officials. Power moves as the patterns of personal relations among the senior officials change; and the exaggerated responses of their respective subordinates often create the illusion that great changes are certain to follow new elite appointments, even though such an expectation has little historical validity.

It should be apparent by now that the Indonesian pattern of superior-subordinate relationships is closer to the positive Thai model than to the distrustful Burmese example. But whereas the Thai principle of exchange involves a highly subjective quid pro quo, that is, *kamlungjie* for *krengjie,* Indonesian relationships, for all their fascination with subjective matters, can include very materialistic transactions. Yet the Indonesians are explicit in describing their ties as paternalistic, and hence as belonging to a non-materialistic level of relations. The tie between leader and follower, between patron and client, is known as *bapakism,* a relationship involving a *bapak,* or father, and his *anak buah,* or children. The *bapak* has to assume extensive responsibilities for his *anak buah,* and they in turn owe him the incalculable debt of *hutang budi,* a form of indebtedness which they can strive ceaselessly to repay but which continues to endure, sometimes even into the next generation. In this respect the Indonesians develop feelings of obligation in their social relationships which are similar to the Japanese sentiments of *on* and *giri.* But quite unlike the tacit Japanese style, the Indonesian bonding of superior and inferior quickly becomes an explicit relationship.

The game of Indonesian politics is only secondarily one of *bapaks* seeking to gather more clients. It usually revolves around *anak buahs* who are seeking out *bapaks.* Therefore much of the initiative in Indonesian politics may, surprisingly, come from subordinates who are striving to gain the recognition of higher officials. The analogy with the natural family is complete to the extent that once someone has declared that he owes *hutang budi* to a particular *bapak* figure, the patron cannot easily dismiss him. Thus Indonesian political leaders, like real fathers, will talk about being cursed with incompetent "children" whom they cannot, of course, get rid of. Nevertheless, President Suharto, clearly a master of the patron-client game, has frequently violated this rule and banished from his inner court *anak buahs* who had grown too powerful by becoming major *bapaks* in their own right.

Certain key distinctions (as well as similarities) between Sukarno's and Suharto's ruling styles can be understood only in the context of the subtle dynamics of these Indonesian forms of patron-client relationships. Indonesians, nurtured in the tradition of Javanese etiquette, are not so taken in by the abjectly servile posturing of subordinates as to believe that masters can be carefree and have no restraints. The Indonesian rules of conduct acknowledge the likelihood that the few who are capable of being true patrons must assume great risks in dealing with the dangerous uncertainties of the outside world. By contrast, the subordinates, the servants, in return for flattering the ego of the master and thereby giving him the necessary strength to carry on, are able to gain complete security—something the master is denied because he must always be proving himself against adversaries in antagonistic encounters.

The patron needs his clients, not as a general needs soldiers to be risked in battle, but as pilots need enlisted men to maintain the planes in which the officers risk their lives while the enlisted men remain safely behind. The pattern of power in these patron-client ties can be, and usually is, so complex that it is not at all certain whether it is the few patrons or the many clients who are manipulating the relationships. The Javanese would insist that only the patron has power, according to their definition of power; yet they will also acknowledge that clients can usually get their way if they are smart. Such successes, however, are not seen as manifestations of power, for power is a matter of status and not a means of achieving purposeful ends.[59]

Patrons must always follow the wishes of the supposedly dependent clients, for the patron is no less dependent on the relationship. Clifford Geertz points out that Indonesians are unable to say no, and that anyone who is on to a good thing has to share his good fortune, even to the point of self-destruction. He cites the example of an enterprising man who starts a cigarette factory in a village and ends up having to put everyone in the community on the payroll, thus bringing inevitable bankruptcy on himself. The same sequence is repeated over and over in Indonesian political life as leaders are worn down by their inability to insulate themselves from the pressures of growing numbers of clients. In this connection, Indonesians grumble that the Chinese among them are less disadvantaged in business because they only have to give jobs to their relatives.

Sukarno's method in handling patron-client power was to act as the bold "father" of the whole country who was fearlessly confronting the "outside," dangerous world. He sought to give psychic rewards to all of his "children." They could feel that they could "stand tall," that they were bigger and stronger than before, while it was he who had assumed the risks. But in the end he was the loser, for the world saw him as a buffoon, a conceited dictator, while his own people with smiles remembered him as something of a show-off, having forgotten the brief emotional charge he had given them.

Suharto's conduct has been equally tied to the patron-client ideal, but he has adhered more closely to the Javanese ethos that values modesty and reticence. Rather than dealing at a symbolic level, Suharto has specific clients, and rather than pretending that as master he can do anything and everything, he has acknowledged that in most practical matters it is the servants who should be burdened with decisions. Thus, in contrast to Sukarno with his flamboyant all-knowing manner, Suharto has exploited the traditional patron-client model to legitimize divisions of authority based on technical specialization. This is no mean achievement because, as we saw in the case of the Confucian cultural tradition, one of the most difficult problems of political modernization is that of moving from traditional to modern expectations—from the view that the highest authority should be all-powerful and intolerant of specialized authority to the view that technical skills call for divisions of authority which may transcend the highest authority.

Thus in a strange way Suharto, who is more traditionalist than Sukarno was, has been more successful in bringing to Indonesian public life the seemingly modern notion that the top political authority should not intervene in technical matters that call for special knowledge and skills. Thus Suharto has given scope to Western-trained technocrats who, as his clients, carefully treat him as their deserving patron. Similarly he has given direction to such state enterprises as Pertamina, the oil empire, and to a growing generation of "client businessmen" who got their start through government concessions. Following a more traditional pattern he has also helped, and then protected, the members of his family who have pursued entrepreneurial ambitions.

As patrons both Sukarno and Suharto have performed the critical role of appearing to be rulers capable of making history. Each, however, in coming to terms with his prevailing clients, has had to accept their views as to how far change can go, since it is the obligation of clients to preserve continuity. More important, both leaders have had to appear to be generous with the resources available to the state. Sukarno in his day played to the hilt the role of the bountiful, but also profligate, Javanese ruler as he dissipated state resources on symbolic monuments. When he had nearly killed the goose that was laying the golden egg, he was replaced by Suharto, who found that with the revival of the economy he could distribute substantial rewards to his clients. All the key elements in the polity were able to obtain their expected shares even during the period of austerity when inflation was being brought under control. The Indonesian belief that all who are well off should be ready to share their good fortune has made it hard to draw a sharp line between "socialistic redistribution" and corruption. This spirit of sharing has made it easy for the Indonesians to array their principal patrons in hierarchical order and thereby create the structures of relatively stable bureaucracies. Relative ranking is not the problem that it has been in Burma.

Still, the existence of a stable structure of national power has not meant that policies are readily or efficiently implemented. On the contrary, the very essence of the Indonesian concept of power is that it is too precious to be contaminated by purposeful activities. Power is something to be had, not to be used. Power is status; it is a matter of being above others and of being treated in a deferential manner. It is not a utilitarian matter. People want power in order to have it, to rejoice in its possession. In contrast to the Western practice of seeking to constrain those with power by holding to the ethic of limiting power to those with worthy purposes and thereby making power holders responsible for the causes they support, the Indonesian way of checking the evil effects of power has been to uphold the idea that power should not be used at all. The powerful should be content to welcome the psychic deference they receive, and they should, in material terms, show unlimited generosity toward their clients.[60]

This need to provide for clients, rather than any ambition for policy results, is what usually drives Indonesian leaders to establish private empires. Ideally, a private bureaucratic empire is completely self-contained, does not threaten anyone, and expands only at a rate consistent with the increasing number of one's clients—and with a readiness to have subordinates who are publicly acknowledged and who are thereby patrons in their own right.

An impressive feature of such sedately growing "empires" is that the leaders rarely seek to intervene in the domains of others. Few attempts are made to draw away subordinates who have allegiances to other leaders. Those who are acknowledged to be leading patrons have a tacit understanding that they would only bring trouble upon themselves if they encouraged the practice of demoralizing another's subordinates in order to recruit them. Any subordinate who might suggest a willingness to shift his allegiance would be suspect, since his mere hinting of disloyalty would be enough to label him a dangerous opportunist whom nobody would want.

These practices have brought to Indonesia a fairly stable power structure with little capacity for coherent and integrated national policies but with many islands of impressive bureaucratic performance. Pertamina, for example, has resembled a small state within a state, prospering from its control of oil revenues, using an inordinate share of those revenues to expand its own activities, and yet incurring little envy from others because they accept the legitimacy of such domains.

Philippines: The Limits of a Bargaining Polity

Philippine politics has also been built around patron-client ties, but the logic of power calculations has been quite different from that in the other three countries. The Philippines came to independence with considerably more experience in popular politics than either Burma or Indonesia; their economy had been more severely damaged by the war, but the former colonial ruler was more ready to give material assistance.

American colonial policy was strikingly different from that of the British, Dutch, or French. Almost from the beginning of American rule the Filipinos were taught that politics meant elections, not careers in the civil service. With this rule came the free-for-all spirit of grandiose promises, back-room deals, and patronage. With independence the Philippines did not inherit bureaucratic structures comparable to those in Burma, Indonesia, or even Thailand. Instead, government during the Commonwealth period was the city-hall politics of mayors and congressmen dealing with constituents, and of presidents distributing favors to deserving provinces.[61]

The Nacionalista party, formed in 1907, is the oldest political party in Southeast Asia. Orderly progression toward independence was disrupted by World War II and by the troublesome issue of collaboration with the Japanese occupation forces. The Tydings-McDuffie Act of 1934 had promised independence on July 4, 1946; but when the Japanese attacked the Philippines in 1941, President Manuel L. Quezon and Vice-President Sergio Osmeña were evacuated to Washington, where Quezon died during the war. In the Philippines his protégé, Manuel Roxas, escaped from Bataan, joined the resistance forces on Mindanao, was later recaptured, and subsequently worked for the Japanese puppet government that was headed by José Laurel, a former senator. As a result of General Douglas MacArthur's intervention, Roxas was cleared of collaboration charges, although no hearings were held, and the reconvened Congress elected him president after the Americans had displayed their lack of confidence in Osmeña. In the subsequent wrangling, largely over the issue of collaboration with the Japanese, Roxas took his following out of the Nacionalista party to form the Liberal party. From that date to 1972, when President Ferdinand Marcos imposed martial law, Philippine politics revolved around the competition between these two parties and their extensive use of pork-barrel tactics.

From the beginning of independence the issue of collaboration seriously tainted the legitimacy of the Manila government. Furthermore, the blatant use of government for personal aggrandizement by the wheeling and dealing politicians added to the population's mood of cynicism. In this environment the Hukbalahap movement spread across the main island of Luzon. By 1950 signs of disintegration were widespread, the government in Manila seemed threatened, and the army was demoralized. At that point Ramón Magsaysay was made the secretary of defense, and by 1953 his charismatic leadership had brought him to the presidency. In the process he resigned from the Liberal party to accept the nomination of the Nacionalistas.[62]

Magsaysay's brief presidency, which ended in an airplane crash in March 1957, lasted long enough to prove that charisma in the Philippine culture was very different from charisma in Burma or Indonesia. As a vigorous, generous-spirited leader, Magsaysay devoted all his energies to the practical, bread-and-butter problems of the Filipinos. In contrast to U Nu's ideological appeals and symbolic projects or Sukarno's international posturing and monument-building, Magsaysay talked of the practical problems of barrio people. Instead of setting up bureaucracies or institutions for implementing public policy, Magsaysay seemed to suggest that he personally could help everyone with his or her special problems. When he was secretary of defense, his spacious office at Camp Murphy was always filled with visitors, who were never kept waiting at the door as he welcomed all and circulated among them like a host at a cocktail party. And so it was on special days in Malacañang Palace after he became president.

In his style of dealing directly with individual problems, Magsaysay was following the standard rules for Filipino politicians, who conceived of government in pork-barrel terms and believed that their paramount role was to take care of their constituents. What made Magsaysay different was that he dramatized his willingness to help the poor and not only the sugar industry and other special interests. Because people felt that his promises of help were not just words, they idolized him.

Thus, ironically, both cynicism and idealism in Philippine politics have been associated with the same ward-heeler style of politics. Everyone assumes that those in power will be helpful to somebody: cynicism mounts when it is assumed that only the few are benefiting; and idealism takes over when it is believed that the brokering is fair and generous to the many.

The brokerage role of the Filipino politician is based on the key element of that political system, namely, a continuous process of bargaining which creates a distinctive form of patron-client tie.[63] In contrast to Indonesian politics, where party labels become permanently attached to individuals even though the party itself may have disappeared, Filipino politicians readily change party identification in order to move with the winner. Local political leaders feel that they have to be accepted by the top leaders in Manila if they are to continue to get what their local constituents expect.[64] Instead of the unquestioning loyalty demanded of subordinates in the Burmese cliques, it is assumed in the Philippines that everyone is looking out for himself, ready to advance his own well-being in any way he can. Those leaders who are cut out of the game because of the whims of electoral politics must look to other sources for the support they need in order to keep their followers from drifting off to seek their fortunes elsewhere.

Filipino politicians must tread a very narrow path: they are expected to boast of their skills in using government to help their constituents, while at the same time upholding the concept of *delicadeza,* that is, not being crass or vulgar in their use of power. Jean Grossholtz has observed, "The difference between what is acceptable and what is contemptible seems small to the observer but makes a great difference to the Filipino politician."[65] Mrs. Imelda Marcos, for example, has been considered grossly vulgar by the elite because she has too blatantly used pork-barrel methods to seek grass-roots support. The standard Filipino answer to the politician's self-identity question, "What are we in power for?" usually demonstrates that the difference between "service" and "corruption" is only a matter of who happens to be benefiting. This is shown by President Quirino's claim that his fellow party member Senator Avelino once publicly pleaded, "Why did you have to order an investigation, Honorable Mr. President? If you cannot permit abuses you must at least tolerate them. What are we in power for? We are not hypocrites. Why should we pretend to be saints when in reality we are not? We are not angels. And besides, when we die we all go to hell. Anyway, it is preferable to go to hell where there are no investigations, no Secretary of Justice, no Secretary of the Interior to go after us."[66]

To a large extent the style of politics in the Philippines can be directly traced to American influence. The combination of the rhetoric of democratic idealism and the materialistic calculations of the ward heeler bear the stamp, "Made in USA." Through the American-introduced educational system the Filipinos learned the language of democracy. They also learned the pork-barrel methods of American congressmen, with the added nuance of not only delivering public largess to their own districts but also giving private rewards to their favored supporters.

After independence Philippine politics became a caricature of American politics. It also illustrated the important psychological fact that idealism and cynicism are two variations of essentially the same psychic defense mechanism in that both make the user appear superior to reality. Filipinos, like some segments of American youth, are at one moment idealists and at the next moment cynics, and they are usually unsure which of these is their real identity. Nevertheless, Philippine concepts about power include some strong traditional attitudes which have, no doubt, helped to determine which aspects of American political culture will be accentuated, even exaggerated, and which ignored.

The Filipino concept of *utang-na-loob* is a modified version of the Indonesian *bapakism*. According to this system of obligations anyone who receives help from another should feel personally obligated and should try to reciprocate, but the personal bonding is not so intense or so enduring as the Indonesian ties. By contrast, the Filipinos give much more explicit recognition to the collectivity formed by *utang-na-loob* relationships. They speak of *tayu-tayo,* or "our group," with all of its traditions of collective loyalty.[67]

These concepts go back to the pre-Spanish era when Filipinos were living in scattered settlements which they called *baranguys* after the boats that had brought them from Malaya and Sumatra. Each settlement was controlled by a *datu* or headman and a council of elders. Because the settlements were strongly individualistic, the *datus* were in constant warfare with one another, and no larger units of power were created until after the Spanish conquest. Moreover, Spanish colonial rule reinforced the concept of *tayu-tayo,* for the Filipinos became hacienda peons under the domination of *cacuques,* or chiefs. Those living on the same estate were assumed to be bound not only to their master but also to one another as an extended family.[68]

The Filipino concept of power, *mga malakas,* has a more active connotation than the Indonesian view of power as pure status. To have *mga malakas* is to have privileges and to be exempt from regulations and restraints. Whereas in Indonesia power suggests skillful adherence to precise dictates of custom and convention, in the Philippines it implies a capacity to ignore convention and not to have to follow rules, which are there only to keep the common herd in check. Filipinos assume that privileges and favors do not come as automatic blessings, but that they must be sought in a competition called *palakasan,* a term which describes quite well the game of Philippine politics.

The Philippine elite is thus not a stable hierarchy of patrons, each with his own set of clients, but rather a dynamic society of people, all of whom are competing to gain more privileges, to appear to be more above the law than others, and to be more deserving of honor and respect. People who have known each other from childhood are constantly joining together, then feuding—looking up to some at one time and then looking down on them, as the game goes on. Leaders have none of the Confucian obligations to be models for others. On the contrary, the proof of leadership is that one does not have to be the prisoner of laws. To bend the regulations in order to help clients is the norm. At the same time, in their dealings with one another the members of the elite are expected to adhere to strict codes of honor. The defeated politician is never to be insulted— not only because of the code, but because of the probability that he will in time recoup his fortunes and seek revenge.

The much freer spirit of patron-client relations in the Philippines reflects the fact that the individual Filipino is given a less secure position in his family and community than the Thai or the Indonesian. Elsewhere in Asia siblings generally have well-defined status positions according to their order of birth and their sex, and even in the extended family the boundaries are usually clear. In the Philippines, as Carl Landé has noted, every sibling in a sense has a different "family" because kinship is extended by a system of godparents or *compadrazgo*.[69] Thus brothers and sisters each have their separate *compadres* to look to as their benefactors. Furthermore, in Philippine family culture equal importance is attached to the families of both parents, and the family is seen as extending to at least third and fourth cousins. Each child in a way learns that he or she must take the initiative to establish a special set of relations with a distinctive combination of relatives in order to create his or her own unique "family." Every child thus starts life in search of those who will treat him or her as a favorite child, and by the time children are ready to venture beyond the world of the family, they are well primed to seek out patrons.

Philippine social life consists of an endless process of establishing contacts and advancing one's interests. This process of social life easily blends into political life, so that a politics of personal connections becomes the normal way of advancing one's well-being.[70] New relationships are always possible, and old ones are never totally cast aside. There is surprisingly little resentment if an old friend moves on to new friendships, for if the new ties pay off for him it will always be possible to remind him of his old friendships.

The Philippine system produces a far more complex pattern of relationships than the more discrete circles of Thai and Indonesian patron-clients with their bonds of single loyalties. In a sense Philippine politics is a system of intersecting patron-client networks. Not only do loyalties change with shifts in political fortunes, but individuals may try to maintain ties with competing camps.

Since the American style of colonial administration did not create the kind of institutionalized bureaucracy that colonialism brought to Indonesia or South Asia, the Philippines has had no structural basis for the creation of a bureaucratic polity around which the patron-client networks might organize themselves. President Ferdinand Marcos's decision to institute martial law in 1972 was in part a reaction to an almost complete breakdown in government authority which had opened the way for widespread lawlessness. Indeed, the Philippine patrimonial style of government has failed to produce commanding authority in the political system. People feel obligated to respect only those with whom they have paternalistic ties; others, regardless of their formal office or reputation, can be ignored. Deference is given only when there is something to be gained in exchange. Politicians are contemptuous of each other if they have no personal ties; citizens are generally scornful of those with high status and have little respect for professional competence.[71]

In seeking to rise above the frustrations caused by the insatiable demands of their clients, Philippine leaders go to great lengths to achieve heroic dimensions and to live out their fantasy that reality can match their idealistic rhetoric. Because World War II, the trauma of Bataan and Corregidor, and the drama of MacArthur's return meant so much to Filipinos, the image of the hero bulks large in their political imagination. By becoming war heroes Filipinos shed the psychology of being colonial subjects. Moreover, by posturing as war heroes many sought to become illustrious public figures. The benefit which President Marcos received from his wartime activities nearly thirty years after the war suggests the extent to which Philippine political culture has been frozen in time. The culture of the American GI still colors Filipino behavior, just as the jeep, in its rainbow guise as "jeepnees," is still the main mode of transportation in Manila.

Because the patrimonial pattern of politics has produced diffuse authority instead of an effective bureaucratic polity, as in Indonesia, the Philippines has been slow to use technocrats even though more Filipinos than Indonesians have been trained as economists and social scientists. Under martial law President Marcos did enlist technocrats in his government, but they have not had the impact that Indonesian technocrats have had.

In a perverse sort of way Marcos's dictatorship represents a faulted attempt to create in the Philippines a bureaucratic polity along the lines of those in Indonesia, Thailand, and South Korea. But neither the traditions of the colonial era nor those of the native culture have provided Filipinos with the attitudes about power necessary for establishing such a polity. Marcos has, moreover, succeeded in destroying the democratic institutions, and in more ways than by repression and the denial of human rights. Martial law ended any hope of elections and with it the reason for being of the political parties as competing patronage machines. Immediately after independence, praise was heaped on Philippine democracy because the opposition party was able to win every national election. It seemed that the Philippines would soon join Japan and India as Asia's model democracies. What was occurring, however, was not competition over the popularity of policy alternatives. The dynamics of Philippine elections was based on expanding and contracting patronage networks built upon unstable patron-client relations. Before each election the opposition was able to make grandiose promises of patronage to more and more potential clients—especially to those who were disappointed that they had not obtained more for supporting the winner in the previous election. Then, when the opposition did win on the basis of inflated promises, there were again huge numbers of disappointed people who were ready to shift their allegiance to the defeated government party in the next election.

Martial law, which brought this process to an end, revealed in short order that the Philippine parties lacked both the ideological and organizational basis to survive. Without the possibility of patronage promises the leaders had nothing with which to hold together their parties. But martial law also exposed the obstacles to creating a coherent structure of governing power in the Philippine political culture.

Family Patterns and Dependency Syndromes

The four Southeast Asian cultures illustrate, with variations, the type of political power that is built upon the dyadic relations of patrons and clients, in which subordinates and superiors manipulate each other in their quest for security and deference. A description of the family patterns in these cultures will show that the basic socialization processes have helped to maintain and even reinforce traditional attitudes about dependency as the essential element in power relationships.

The Philippine family system, which forces children to seek out personalized security relationships, is the most open and dynamic of all the Southeast Asian patterns. In terms of mere size the Philippine family resembles the extended family idealized in Chinese culture, though it lacks those precise and formally recognized relationships between each child and all of his uncles, aunts, cousins, nephews, and nieces. Especially in the upper class Philippine family each child must not only find his or her special ties but must compete for attention—a fact which seems to have left most Filipinos remarkably tolerant of anyone who is showing off.

In the other three Southeast Asian cultures the key family relationships tend to be within the nuclear family, and thus they usually extend only to grandparents. Although children are taught that they should put their trust in their family members, the traditions of family honor tend to be weak, as is consistent with the practice of having no family surnames. In Indonesia the Dutch helped to preserve the traditions of aristocracy by faithfully distinguishing between the *prijaiji* class, or traditional aristocracy, and the non-*prijaiji*, or commoners, but after only a few years of independence the Indonesians had largely forgotten that there was such a distinction.[72] In Burma, all formal recognition of the former noble families ended during the period of British rule. Thus today in both Indonesia and Burma there is no formal ranking of families. Yet in practice there does seem to be evidence that although all people are classed as commoners, those from the older aristocratic families have continued to be disproportionately successful, especially in governmental and academic jobs.

Paradoxically, in Thailand, in spite of the enduring monarchy, the aristocracy has also almost disappeared. Because the recent Thai kings have practiced monogamy, the ranks of the nobility have not been replenished fast enough to offset the rule that fifth-generation heirs must become commoners. In practice the rankings of families is largely determined by the relative status of their principal figures, and therefore achievement criteria bulk as large as family background.

In these last three cultures the socialization process begins on a positive note. All of them are child-centered: people find great happiness in babies, lavishing warmth and nurturing support on them. Within each country, of course, there are great differences in terms of subcultures, classes, and urban-rural conditions, but in all of them childhood is unquestionably the happiest period of life. Nevertheless, there are variations on this common theme. In both Thailand and Indonesia children are treated in an understanding but not overly emotional fashion, whereas in Burma there seem to be greater vacillations between effusions of love and attention, on the one hand, and disinterestedness which amounts to abandonment, on the other.

Thai culture inculcates an orderly sense of life's stages, without any sharp breaks. From the outset the purpose of socialization seems to be to instill in the child the two prime values of Thai culture, serenity and happiness: the first in the form of *choei*, that is, a cool, relaxed, unemotional approach to anything that might be stressful; and the second in the form of *sanuk,* or the ability to have a good time. All processes of learning are gradual, from toilet training to mastering the precepts of Buddhism. Even before the child has learned to speak, he or she is taught the gestures of respect and deference to those older and superior. The child is encouraged to imitate the mother in performing respectful gestures, to everyone's glee. Thus early in life the Thai discovers the need to defer to elders and the pleasures of so behaving. Older children are treated respectfully by their parents, in the sense that they are rarely scolded in the presence of younger siblings.[73]

In Indonesia there is the same appreciation of the helplessness of infants and small children. The Indonesian "baby is handled in a relaxed, completely supportive, gentle, unemotional way." The universal belief seems to be that children need to be protected. Hildred Geertz reports, for example, that all children in the town of "Modjokuto" were put to sleep every evening by what is called *dikuloni*, in which "his mother lies down with him on his mat and puts her arms about him, cuddling him till he is asleep . . . sometimes it is not the mother; sometimes it is an older sister or grandmother or his father, but always there is someone." Until the child is five or six it is assumed that he cannot really learn and hence needs no punishing. He is said to be *durung djawa*, "not yet Javanese," and hence *durung ngerti*—he "does not yet understand."[74]

The anthropological reports on Burmese child care suggest significant differences: instead of having the relatively unemotional but supportive style of the Thai and Indonesian mother, the Burmese mother can be enthusiastically loving and playful, but then, at a whim, she may lose all interest in the child. Among the adults the child often becomes a plaything that can be suddenly set aside. The Burmese infant is thus at one moment "told" that he is special, an object of worship; and then at the next moment he "learns" that the one who had just obeyed his commands is not to be trusted.[75]

In all three cultures an early phase of learning about the nature of power and the operation of cause and effect in human affairs consists of being told about the spirits that, though invisible, are everywhere. Although the formal religions of these cultures are Buddhism and Islam, the people live in a world surrounded by animistic spirits and otherworldly forces. Again, however, there are subtle differences which to some degree explain the differences in the three approaches to power.

On first examination it would seem that the Burmese belief in *nats* is almost identical to the Thai concept of *phi,* or "spirits." Yet when we look more closely, it becomes clear that the Thai *phi* are more benign and less capable of doing mischief than the Burmese *nats*.[76] The Thais, not unlike the Japanese Shintoists, believe that *phi* exist everywhere— on every hill, in every tree, in all the forms of nature. By contrast, the Burmese believe that there are twenty-eight principal *nats*, and that, while some are good and others bad, it is imperative to propitiate all of them. Thus the Thais come to identify with otherworldly forces in the context of their familiar surroundings, while the Burmese must cope with more abstract concepts.

Moreover, the Thais teach their young that there is a great difference between *phi pop,* or ghoulist spirits, and *chao thi,* or guardian spirits of the home. Thais learn early that there are good and bad spirits, and that good is clearly related to the home and family ties. The Burmese tend instead to stress the probability that one is more closely encircled by malevolent forces than by helpful ones. The Burmese child, once he reaches the age of reason, is constantly told that the spirits, both visible and invisible, that govern events are likely to be his enemies, while the Thai child, who grows up with an equal respect for otherworldly forces, believes that magical powers may work to his advantage.[77] The Thai child, in fact, is taught that adherence to the exact rules of etiquette will protect him from the awful forces of evil spirits. In Burma some attempts have been made to elevate etiquette to the level of protection from terrible vulgar forces, but the Burmese rules of conduct have never equaled those of the Thais or of the Indonesians. Indeed, the Thai stress on learning correct modes of behavior for every type of situation is clearly linked to the idea that one can actually achieve security and tranquillity. The object of etiquette is to ensure smooth relationships so that everyone can realize the Thai ideal of aloofness, which is *chai yen,* or a "cool heart," or *choei,* relaxed indifference. The Burmese might like to have the same degree of security; but the social norms in Burmese culture are less precise, and hence they provide less psychic security.

As for Indonesian children, they are introduced to the idea that power is not limited to the people they know even before being exposed to the grim dictates of Islam. In a strange way Indonesian adults seem to want to pass on their pre-Islamic beliefs to their offspring before sending them to the discipline of the Islamic schools. Consequently Javanese children are taught not only that the world is filled with all the forces let loose in the Ramayana, but also, "There is but one God, and Mohammed is His prophet." Power becomes, from earliest childhood, synonymous with both the mysteries of contending forces and the awe of a monotheistic belief. Early in life the Indonesian is introduced to the idea that miracles can occur without a clear cause. Power is thus both awesome, dangerous, and malevolent, and also merciful, compassionate, and kind.[78]

In spite of these differences all three cultures share the idea that miraculous things can happen by acts of magic that are otherworldly in nature. Thais, Indonesians, and Burmese all believe that there is something to the idea of the auspicious moment, and they fear the inauspicious. The Burmese had to set the time of their independence at an awkward but auspicious moment in the morning, according to the dictates of astrologers; Sukarno, the friend of "materialistic" revolutionaries, felt it right that the first Indonesian Five-Year Plan, drafted by a poet, should have eight chapters, seventeen sections, and 1,945 paragraphs, because the date of Indonesia's independence was August 17, 1945; and the Thai court is not ashamed to admit that the movements of the king are governed by astrological calculations.

In a world governed by invisible forces, each of the three cultures tries in its own way to reassure its young. The Thais probably go to the greatest lengths. They teach their children that each individual has three components: a material body, or *kaj*, that exists because of karma, the sum of previous merits and demerits; a "free" or "body" soul, or *khwan*, which is in the body but also floats about and can become a haunting ghost on death; and the "ego" soul, or *winjam*, which experiences reincarnation after death.[79] At every stage in life the Thai will have ceremonies designed to help strengthen his *khwan*. A timid person is said to have a "tender and delicate *khwan*," and when someone panics it is said that his "*khwan* is lost." In addition to the lofty search for merits to improve the destiny of one's *winjam*, one can seek the more immediately practical objective of "making *khwan*" and thereby strengthening one's capacity to cope.

The point of these observations about cultural differences in the earliest responses to a dependent situation and to the fantasy life that young Southeast Asian children are inducted into as soon as they are capable of cognitive reasoning is to illuminate how in all three Southeast Asian cultures—omitting only the Philippines—children are given profound feelings about their dependency upon, and vulnerability to, omnipotent but also whimsical external forces. Through their earliest nurturing experiences they get a strong taste of the ecstasy of being at one with a universe which they can command by a mere cry. But then they must learn that their world is filled with powerful and dangerous forces. For Burmese children the transition is the sharpest, and it apparently leaves them as adults with a greater distrust of authority than is the case with either Thais or Indonesians. The Thais, who have the smoothest process of maturing, value dependency and are not so threatened by being in a subordinate position as are the Burmese. The Indonesians go through some of the same shocks that the Burmese experience when they are sent to religious schools, but Indonesians are also presented with rules of conduct which they can rely upon for safety even when they are in a subordinate position.

These cultural differences seem to be vitally important in explaining the different patterns of village life. In Thai villages there can be, as Charles Murray reports, a very high level of cooperation, with everyone collaborating to maintain the village *wat*, or temple. Either there is "tithing," with each individual contributing according to his ability and the better-off assuming greater responsibilities, or everyone is concerned only with "investing" to better his own lot and thus the whole village tends to fall apart.[80] In the Thai culture, it seems, the norms of etiquette and the gentle superior-subordinate relations hold if there is a general sense of cooperation; but once that collective sense of belonging is shattered, the Thais can suddenly become self-oriented and antisocial. One result is the high rates of crime associated with parts of urban Thailand.

Burmese villagers seem to lack the Thai potential for cooperation. The larger temples are located in the cities, and the religious enterprises are supported by the wealthy, who make their contributions to gain merit. In the villages themselves, those with the *awza* have usually established links with the national political process—at one time through the AFPFL political party and later through the government bureaucracy. By claiming ties with higher authorities, such local leaders are able to exploit their position in the community. They are often not especially popular, but the people have to turn to them when they have problems. Thus local power is seen as being similar to higher government—as one of the four evils of life, along with thieves, floods, and fires—and any sense of village participation is overshadowed by threatening pressures from above.[81]

In Indonesia, as Karl Jackson has found, the villages are coherent units under the leadership of their headmen.[82] The process which holds them together is that of *bapakism,* which can at times produce factional strife rather than cooperation. In contrast to the Thai stress on friendship and the art of friendliness, and to the factional tensions of Burmese culture, the Javanese seem to achieve day-to-day tranquillity by avoiding strong intimacies and seeking to be evenhanded. When Robert Jay studied Javanese villages, he made the surprising discovery that the villagers had no concept of special friendships.[83] People just interacted and did pleasurable things with whoever happened to be around. But if the tranquillity of community life was broken, the Javanese could hold deep grudges and seek violent revenge, as they did in 1965 when they slaughtered thousands of Communists after the failure of the PKI coup attempt. Thus, on a continuum between community cooperation and more individualistic competition, Indonesian villages generally fall between the cooperative Thais and the fragmented Burmese villages.

5

The South Asian Subcontinent: Hindu and Muslim Power and the Rewards of Narcissism

T HE COMPLEX CULTURE of the Indian subcontinent, or South Asia, presents a tradition comparable to Confucianism, one that has had a greater effect on the history of Asia than any of the influences emanating from other parts of Asia. Not only did India introduce Buddhism to Tibet, Central Asia, China, Japan, and Southeast Asia, but its Hindu and Mogul cultures introduced the concepts of god-kings and sultanates which shaped the traditional systems of Southeast Asia. Although Sinic culture has had an impressive impact on Korea, Japan, and Vietnam, it has come in a poor second to the Indian culture in attracting other peoples.

This appeal of Indian ideas and cultural practices is hard for us to understand because of our difficulties in explaining Indian thought in any systematic manner. Indian culture and philosophy, which abound in contradictions, ignore the canons of logic and the rules of cause and effect, and label and categorize things without going on to seek analytical explanations.[1] This jumble of ideas in Hindu religion, the references to convoluted otherworldly events and the propensity to assert, at random, moral superiority would seem to make Hindu culture much too parochial to influence anyone who is not born into it.

The problem of understanding the evolution of ideas about power in the subcontinent lies not only in the complexity of traditional Hindu beliefs, but also in the complications added by the waves of foreign conquerors who brought in their own distinctive ideas about power and authority. Indeed, the introduction of these ideas was second only to the successful diffusion of Hindu cultures into neighboring Asia in making India distinctive. But traditional concepts proved to be remarkably durable in spite of India's acceptance of the ideas of foreign rulers. The Hindus' fondness for ambiguity and their capacity to compartmentalize government from society have made it possible for the Indians to pile ideas about power upon each other layer by layer without any noticeable blending or compromise. They have maintained a purity of traditional concepts, even while they have been acquiring a greater knowledge of Western or British ideas than any other Asian people. In India, traditional and Western ideas and institutions coexist without challenging or threatening each other.

Thus, in terms of political modernization and development, not only does India represent a great Asian tradition, but in modern times it has become the archetype of the democratically developing ex-colonial country. Indeed, as soon as India recovered from the shock of the communal slaughter that followed partition, it became the unquestioned leader of and model for the newly emerging nations. In the 1950s most theorizing about the "newly developing countries" was actually a barely disguised description of India. India's problems, preferences, and proclaimed policies were applied to the other newly independent countries. This was particularly true during the early cold war years when India was seen as the democratic alternative to Communist China—as its competitor, in spite of Nehru's protestations of India's special friendship with China.

Probably not enough attention was given at that time to the fact that India was the champion of neutralism (later nonalignment) vis-à-vis the two superpowers, for Indian politics had long involved playing off two powers against each other: the British Raj against the traditional rulers, the maharajahs against the nizams. One power may have been stronger than the other, but the duality of authority did encourage ploys and tactics which surfaced as national policies in Nehru's foreign relations. Undoubtedly, the experience of using different approaches in seeking to manipulate domestic power contributed to India's glibness in its relations with Washington, Moscow, and Peking.

India's misjudgment in approaching different types of foreign power first came home, and with a devastating effect, when in 1962 China successfully invaded India and destroyed its claim to Third World leadership. Nehru's foreign policy was shattered, ironically, by the country he had championed in the belief that he could thus prove India's leadership. The second blow to India's foreign policy came about when its long-professed goal of striving to reduce tensions between Washington and Moscow, on the one hand, and Moscow and Peking, on the other, was outpaced by the establishment of détente by the powers themselves and the opening of U.S.–China relations. India's international significance was diminished; and furthermore, the Indian style of dealing with dual power centers left New Delhi dependent upon the USSR even to the extent of initially withholding criticism of the Soviet invasion of Afghanistan and of being the only non-Communist country to recognize the Vietnamese puppet regime in Kampuchea.

India's decline in international politics seemed dramatic because in the early years of independence its stature had been inflated by its many well-wishers. American economists, anxious to justify larger foreign-aid appropriations, frequently overstated India's potential for rapid economic growth.[2] Many observers of India were impressed by the fact that the country seemed to be blessed with three exceptional advantages for building effective national power: a national leader who combined charisma and sober policy interests, a national political party that apparently could aggregate local interests while steadfastly championing national programs, and an administrative service staffed by talented civil servants.[3] The combination seemed to provide the necessary elements for dynamic development.

In the domestic management of power, much as in foreign policy, the Indian government has not been notably successful in implementing its ambitious development policies. Nevertheless, the Indian concepts of power have contributed to the country's remarkably stable democratic order. Indeed, stability is precisely what India has had, not only during Nehru's lifetime but also during the rule of his daughter, Indira Gandhi. Although the interlude of Lal Bahadur Shastri's government, Madame Gandhi's Emergency Rule, and the brief period of the Janata party administration brought uncertainty and drama, India has had far greater stability than most developing countries. Stability, however, has not been translated into effectiveness in carrying out programs. This contradiction between India's success in maintaining political order under a democratic system and its failures in policy implementation is a consequence of the Indian views about power, which accentuate dependency.

Roots of an Amoral Polity

The origins of Indian concepts of power can be traced to the ideas underlying the god-kings and the state as theater, ideas which have been central to the Burmese, Thai, and even Balinese theories of power. All of the key concepts of legitimacy in the major Southeast Asian systems came from India. Behind Buddhism, and later Islam, lay the Hindu idea that one's fate, one's karma, was determined by behavior in a previous existence; and, according to Hinduism, the individual was born into a station in life in which he or she had to follow precise rules of conduct and deference to superiors and of avoidance of contamination by subordinates.

Yet, the same ideas that in Southeast Asia linked secular power and divine authority produced in India a separation between the sacred and the secular that is unique in history and that surpasses the secularization of government under Confucian doctrine. The ultimate irony is that this justification for freeing secular power calculations from religious imperatives was made possible by the perversity of the Indian caste system, whose absence in Southeast Asia produced a unique blend of sacred and secular authority.

Simply stated, the caste system in India decreed that certain people could be rulers but that they need not at the same time be supreme religious figures. Of the four varnas, the Brahmans as the religious leaders— the "twice born"—were of course the elite, but this gave them neither political power nor material benefits. They were free to pursue their religious obligations without bearing social burdens. The Kshatriyas, or princes and warriors, were distinctly second in importance even though, according to their varna, they governed society. The Hindu concept of kingship did, in caste-ridden India, make a distinction between the equally sacred rights of priests and kings—a separation which had to be blurred in cultures that rejected caste but accepted Hindu theories of kingship.[4]

In simple terms again, the respective rules of conduct, obligations, and customs for all the people have been determined by their dharma, that is, by fate as determined by their conduct in previous incarnations. The rules of conduct vary according to the station of the individual and especially his varna and his *jati,* that is, his caste category and his subcaste grouping. The ideal of behavior was not to aspire to some universally admired standard, but to adhere to one's own particular lot. Thus, according to the code of Manu the lawgiver, called the *Manusmriti,* "It is better (to discharge) one's own (appointed) way incompletely than to perform completely that of another; for he who lives according to the law of another (caste) is instantly excluded from his own."[5]

Paradoxically, out of this need for differentiation the Indians gained a sense of specialization which, in Asia, was akin only to that of the Japanese, with their sense of feudal hierarchy. In Hindu culture those with recognized power did not have to pretend that they were the same as everyone else. Nor did they have to be, like the Chinese, moral models for their subjects. By acknowledging that different rules governed different ranks, the Indians escaped from the ubiquitous hypocrisy of Confucian China.

This was possible because the caste system had the perverse liberating effect of separating status and power to a degree unknown in other Asian or Western societies.[6] People who belonged to a high caste or subcaste could have less power than those of lower status. Indeed, the Brahmans, or priests, who had the highest status, were seen as having explicitly less power than the Kshatriyas, or kings and warriors.

This gap between power and status was possible because Hindu culture was more explicit than any other in declaring that gradations among people should be based upon the boundary lines between purity and defilement, between cleanliness and abomination.[7] In most cases the dividing line between *jati* (subcaste) categories was that of family and food. One could only marry a member of the same *jati*. One's food had to be prepared by a certain type of person, and, more particularly, there were rules as to who could give and who could receive food—that is, who could nurture whom. Superiors had the right to be served first, but they were expected to pass on leftovers to subordinates—wives, children, servants, and other dependents.

This distinction between status and power in Hindu culture opened the floodgates for rulers to be pragmatic, indeed, Machiavellian, and even ruthless. Free of the constraints of having to appear as saints and holy men, roles reserved for the Brahmans, Hindu rulers could concentrate on managing power. Since it was their dharma to be rulers, Hindu kings were expected to be masters in using force to uphold the social order. It was above all their duty to punish people in order to make sure that they performed their caste-determined roles in a proper manner. As the code of Manu states, "The whole world is kept in order by punishment, for a guiltless man is hard to find; through the fear of punishment the whole world is called to enjoy its blessings."[8]

The code of Manu made it clear that kings should harshly punish transgressors, not because it was in their nature to be harsh, according to their dharma, but rather because maintenance of the social order required a temporal force to uphold the divine laws of the universe. As Manu decreed, "If the King did not, without tiring, inflict punishment on those worthy of being punished, the stronger would roast the weaker, like fish on a spit, the crow would eat the sacrificial cake and the dog would lick the viands, and ownership would not stay with anyone, the lower would [usurp the place of] the higher ones."[9]

The ruler's obligation to coerce through punishment was the basis of the rules of *danda*, which were necessary to uphold the social order and to help people achieve their dharma, their duty, which if properly carried out would bring moksa, or salvation.[10]

The power of kings was thus not constrained by the rituals of the divine order—as in the Confucian and the Southeast Asian worlds—but power was critical in helping all other classes of people to find their divinely ordained salvation. Kings were not bound by the dictates of priests, but their actions helped maintain the cosmic order. The requirements of state routinely compelled kings to commit such immoral actions as killing their enemies, actions which were forbidden to others. At the lowest levels of the social order there were also people, such as butchers and leather workers, who had to violate the imperatives not to kill which bound others.

Thus, just as Confucianism stood out in world history for advancing a secular concept of legitimacy and authority, so Hindu thought was precocious in recognizing that statesmen should not be constrained by the same rules of morality and ethics that bind ordinary citizens. The logic embodied in Max Weber's "Politics as a Vocation" and Reinhold Niebuhr's *Moral Man and Immoral Society* is the same as the traditional Hindu view of power and its responsibilities, namely, that those with power may have to engage in unsavory activities and even violate the social taboos so that others can follow their dharma and gain salvation.

According to traditional Hindu thought, the state has six basic functions: to protect the people from internal and external dangers; to maintain the common law as embodied in the customs and usages of the land; to uphold the social order; to levy taxes; to promulgate laws and resolve conflicts; and to promote the people's happiness by performing the proper rituals and sacrifices.[11] The concept of *danda,* however, stressed punishment and the ruler's power to coerce.[12] Indeed, there was a great enthusiasm for the idea that rulers needed to punish and actually hurt people for their own good. According to Manu, "Punishment alone governs all created beings, punishment alone protects them, punishment watches over them where they sleep; the wise declare punishment to be identical with the law."[13]

This legitimization of violence and coercion which lies at the core of the Hindu concept of power seems to stand in sharp contrast to the spirit of nonviolence which runs through Hindu religious thought. Yet this contrast is the key to the Indian idea of power, which insists that there should be a division between religion and politics. Louis Dumont's dictum that Hindu society was based upon the separation of status and power stresses this divorcement of religious principles from statecraft.

Most Western observers of India, who have been awed by the pervasiveness of religion in Indian life, have mistakenly concluded that in Indian politics morality must also play a major role. It is true that since Gandhi's time Indian leaders have routinely articulated moralistic themes. Nevertheless, as Ashis Nandy has pointed out, Gandhi's espousal of satyagraha or nonviolence contradicted the traditional Hindu concept of statecraft as entirely amoral and centrally concerned with the uses of coercion.[14]

Two features of Indian political culture directly relate to this extreme separation of status and power, of religion and politics.

First, while religion was the supreme force that held society together and dictated people's obligations and duties, politics had an ambivalent place in their minds. On the one hand, power was the ultimate force in upholding the social order, so that rulers had to perform society's dirty work by using coercion. Dharma, the set of rules imposed by one's karma, is eternal and immutable; and therefore what happens in politics is ephemeral, a mere diversion for rulers. Serious souls should concentrate on their own inner lives and not let themselves be distracted by the play of politics.[15] On the other hand, because of the ruler's obligations of *danda,* and precisely because power is the last resort for upholding the social order, there can be no limits to the power of the state. Because rulers had to be concerned about whether their subjects were following their dharma, they were permitted to pry into the private lives of their people. As a result the Indians did not develop the notion of individual rights until British rule was imposed.

Thus, while the Hindus could think of power and politics as matters of only secondary importance, they could at the same time accept the right of power to penetrate every aspect of their lives and to dispense punishment, from which there could be no appeal. As stated in *Narada,* "Whatever a king does is right, that is a settled rule because the world is entrusted to him on account of his majesty and his benignity towards living creatures. As a husband, though feeble, must constantly be worshipped by his wives, in the same way a ruler, though worthless, must constantly be worshipped by his subjects."[16]

Second, the separation of power and status opened the way for sophisticated, and completely amoral, thinking about the art of statecraft. Indian philosophy was far ahead of all Asian, if not all Western, schools of thought in elaborating pragmatic strategies for ruling and for the practical uses of power. Of course, among the "hundred contending schools" in Chou dynasty China there were some Legalists and Taoists who went beyond the moralism of the Confucians and Mencius, but even at their hardheaded and relativistic best they were no match in cleverness for the Indian advisors of kings. In Indian philosophy there was a well-defined category of knowledge called the *dandaniti,* within which the state became an effective instrumentality for making the ideal of dharma a possible goal for people in their respective castes. In practice it was an increasingly refined body of thought about statecraft. Bhaskar Anand

Saletore has identified some nineteen great thinkers in this tradition, starting with Manu, the omniscient sage and lawgiver, who lived about 1900–1800 B.C., and ending with Asia's great Machiavellian, Kautilya, the prime minister to Chandragupta Maurya, founder of the Mauryan empire, and the putative author of the *Arthasastra,* the quintessential volume of *dandaniti,* who lived about 400–320 B.C.[17]

Kautilya premised his advice on the Hindu notion that the state was created by divine and not human action, and that the ruler's duty in applying his *danda* was dictated by the ideal of helping people to achieve their dharma. Except for these concessions to the sacred, Kautilya limited himself to the nature of reason, and in his *Arthasastra* he sought to collate all previous wisdom on the subject. He recognized the need for occasional deception and trickery. He did not, however, believe only in force or in the ruthless application of laws. He praised explicitly the value of voluntary support: "The acquisition of the help of corporations [that is, local communities] is better than the acquisition of an army, a friend or profits."[18]

Kautilya set as the objective of state power the creation of a strong, centralized government, supported by an extensive bureaucratic machine but sensitive to local usages and customs. Such a structure of power was presumed necessary to protect against both external and domestic enemies and to guard against the eight providential visitations of fire, flood, pestilence and disease, famine, rats, tigers, serpents, and demons.

Hindu thought not only justified harsh and oppressive acts (people could benefit from being punished, even for acts they had not committed, because they certainly had done other wrong deeds), but it also gave considerable attention to the idea that while governments may be troublesome, not to have them would be the ultimate disaster. The absence of government would mean not only the horrors of anarchy and the emergence of primitive power, but also the abomination of living in a society without castes or divinely ordained distinctions. The pure and the impure might mix, and all the evils of contamination would appear as boundaries and taboos were violated.

As the *Ramayana of Vahmiki* explains, "A kingdom without a sovereign is like a river without water, a forest without vegetation, or a cow without a cowherd . . . No man loves his own kind in a rulerless state, but each slays and devours the other daily, like fish. Atheists and materialists, exceeding the limits of their caste, assume domination over others, there being no king to exercise control over them . . . The king, discerning good and evil, protects his kingdom, for bereft of him, the country is enveloped in darkness."[19]

Thus rulers and kings were absolute necessities. That they were also thought of as divine figures was of secondary importance. By contrast, the god-kings of Southeast Asia, although they thought of themselves as adhering to Hindu concepts of kingship, were wholly sacred figures. But according to the *Narada,* the Indian king was the eighth of the sacred objects, preceded by a Brahman, a cow, fire, gold, clarified butter, the sun, and the waters.[20] When the divinity of kings is ranked with water and clarified butter, it is easy to agree with Professor Basham that "divinity was cheap in ancient India."[21]

Political Power and the Inner World of the Self

Although power was seen as second to status in Hindu culture, this did not mean that rulers were necessarily trivial or humble people. On the contrary, the Hindu doctrine of illusion, or maya, which held that physical things are of little importance because the real world, that of the spirit and of the dharma, is invisible, in a perverse way legitimized ostentation and luxury for those who could afford them—as rulers usually could.

This would have led to a completely cynical political elite except for the fact that the rulers themselves were Hindus and thus believed that their own spiritual development was important. Indeed, the Hindu concept of power always had a highly subjective dimension which required those with power to appear as being also concerned with moral improvement, not only through punishing others but by employing moralistic language themselves. Ashis Nandy argues, "Contrary to popular belief, concern with power was never low in traditional India; if anything themes of power were ubiquitous . . . The uniqueness of the Indian concept of power lay in its strong 'private' connotations. The most respected form of power was power over self . . . There is always some pressure on the rulers to indulge in the language of conspicuous asceticism and self-sacrifice and to render even the most trivial politics as part of a grand moral design—as if power over one's own self, over the self-seeking instinctual self—legitimizes one's political powers."[22]

Thus, paradoxically, the traditional amoral approach to statecraft has, especially in modern times, encouraged the aspiring Indian leader to legitimize his search for power by suggesting that his inner life has made him peculiarly sensitive to morality questions. This tendency became more conspicuous under British rule. The Indian response to colonial domination was probably the most ambivalent of any in Asia. Because power and status were traditionally separated, the initial incursion of the British into the political realm was not seen as threatening, especially since they were simply replacing the foreign Mogul rulers as yet another foreign conqueror. In time, however, as more and more Indians became Westernized, there was a steady erosion of self-esteem, accompanied by a tendency to "identify with the aggressor" and to demean Hindu culture.[23] Particularly during the Victorian era the Indians seemed to think of themselves as morally backward, an attitude which was magnified by a sense of British racial supremacy. In time, however, came the predictable backlash, as the Indians began to assail those who fawned over British ways and to revitalize traditional Hindu culture. The traditionalists' interpretations of Hindu values were, of course, heavily colored by Western values; their objective often was to assert that Indian culture had once had themes comparable to those admired in British culture, but that were superior to the foreign imports.

According to Nandy, the highly Westernized Mahatma Gandhi believed he was reviving a purer form of Hindu culture when he introduced the idea that nonviolence was central to traditional Hindu statecraft—which of course it was not. Gandhism also brought to the center of the political culture "traits that had come to be associated with femininity, primitivism, passivity, and cowardice."[24] He thus challenged both those who had accepted British values and those who had engaged in the first round of Hindu revivalism and had sought to prove that Hindu culture traditionally had as many virtues as British culture.

The combination of British rule and a successfully led Gandhian independence movement brought many changes to Indian views of power, two of which are particularly noteworthy.

The first was that British rule and Gandhian independence reinforced each other and produced the Indian style of moralistic political rhetoric. The British never accepted the idea that rulers should be amoral—on the contrary, they suggested that that tenet of Hindu culture was a major source of Indian backwardness. And, of course, Gandhi saw moral power as the supreme form of power. The twentieth century brought stirring forces for change; but instead of completely altering Hindu political culture they encouraged politicians to use the language of morality without in fact making moral imperatives the basis for policy. What emerged was a form of amoral politics carried out in an atmosphere of verbal moralizations. Certain features of Indian socialization made this possible, and the change opened the way for Indian politicians to give expression to their powerful feelings of narcissism.

This moralizing posture seems to have had less to do with seeking to impose universal moral constraints on all citizens than with wanting to impress others with one's own superiority. Foreigners have often been baffled by the moralizing of Indian politicians. In most cultures there is an element of aggression in moralizing which is usually seen as provocation—"Don't you preach to me!" or "What gives you the right to criticize my behavior?"—and therefore foreigners infer an element of hostile intent behind Indian moralizing. In fact, much of the moralizing by Indian power holders is a form of narcissism, of self-congratulation for being so apparently virtuous. It is true that politicians in all societies are prone to admire themselves.[25] Yet the Indian case seems to be especially extreme because of their socialization experiences. In fact, the combination of British rule and Gandhian response turned Indian political culture inside out by making it appear to be moralistic, when in fact it still contained many of the amoral, but subjectively gratifying, qualities of traditional Hindu political culture.

The second major change brought about by the British and by Gandhism was that the status of politics in Indian culture was elevated so that it became the sovereign activity. As a result people turned to politics for help with all sorts of problems. Raising the status of politics has gone against Hindu tradition, but it has been accepted because it has introduced into Indian political culture the idea that power can be turned to utilitarian goals.

Unfortunately, like so many adaptations of Western cultural features in former colonial lands, the Indian enthusiasm for the idea of using power for significant policy purposes turned out to be an acceptance of form more than substance. The immediate postcolonial leadership in India went further than the leadership of any other newly emergent country in believing that state power could be used for achieving practical goals—especially since many of the Indian leaders had been exposed to the British socialist thinking of the 1930s, which envisaged a benign form of state planning and technocratic rule. But even before the end of Nehru's rule it was obvious that state power in Indian culture was not performing as its advocates had expected. Instead, Indian politicians showed a marked propensity to indulge in enthusiastic planning, utopian speculation, and wishful thinking while usually failing to carry out the implementation: virtuous talk, big plans, but little delivery.

This failure to perform up to expectations has been extensively studied. It is a failure which not only has seriously affected the lives of hundreds of millions of Indians but has hurt the cause of Third World development by debasing the most supportive theories of aid to developing countries.

At one time India seemed to have the administrative capabilities to carry out even the most grandiose development plans. For, superimposed on the traditional Hindu belief—that expressed in Kautilya's *Arthasastra*—in the need for an elaborate bureaucratic machinery of state, the British built an administrative service which was the wonder of the colonial world, if not the entire world. Yet, there were elements in Hindu political culture which undermined the effectiveness of even this amazing hierarchy of dedicated men.

The problem was that, as well trained as the service was, it could not escape the Hindu belief that matters of the spirit were more important than objective factors. In dealing with power, the Indian bureaucrats became bogged down by their Hindu propensity to defer automatically to rules of rank and status. Just as each person, according to his station and caste, was expected to adhere strictly to all the laws of his dharma, so the bureaucrat also had to prove his worth by faithfully obeying the administrative regulations. The rituals of administration became the presumed source of governmental power, and effective government meant carrying out each action in the correct way.

To make administrative matters worse, superiors felt no need to praise subordinates who were merely following their dharma, and nobody needed to be honored for doing what he must. Instead of giving praise, superiors were expected, in the spirit of Indian rulers and of their *danda,* to scold, punish, and heap ever more work on their subordinates. Subordinates were not expected to make judgments about priorities. Proof that one took one's "duties" seriously could in fact be best demonstrated by concentrating on trivia and giving greatest attention to matters of form without regard to substance.[26]

Hindu concepts of power were well suited to the development of elaborate administrative structures, with all manner of hierarchical gradations, elaborate regulations, and formal procedures, which, nonetheless, remained frustratingly ineffectual in implementing policies. Indeed, the Hindu personality seems to be most at ease with activities associated with visionary planning and grandiose designs.

Much as the Indian politician satisfies a narcissistic urge by moralizing, so he seems to feel that he can display virtue and win accolades by the wonders of his planning proposals. And just as he does not expect others to be bound by his moral pronouncements, so he does not really expect his plans to materialize—for, after all, the physical world is only maya, illusion; the real world is of the spirit—the realm of utopian speculation, which so easily becomes wishful thinking.[27]

The problem of consummation is overriding in Indian politics, and to understand fully all of its dimensions we must appreciate some key aspects of Indian personality. One consequence of this Indian tendency to separate thought and action and to place greater value on the inner and invisible world than on the outer world is that Indian leaders, for all of their narcissism, do have an extraordinary capacity to criticize national developments. Indeed, Indians are often harder on themselves than foreigners are. Self-criticism is a part of self-analysis, which, given their narcissism, can become an all-absorbing activity for Indians.

Unquestionably, Indians surpass all other Asians, except possibly the Japanese, who have their own fascination with self-analysis, in engaging in honest self-criticism.[28] The Chinese may ask visitors for criticisms of what they have been shown, but if any foreigner is so naive as to oblige, the Chinese become defensive and treat the response as a hostile act. Southeast Asians prefer to practice denial, ignoring opportunities to elicit praise by pretending that they have nothing worthy of criticism. Indians, on the contrary, do not find it humiliating to engage in self-analysis, and indeed some individuals, especially academics, have made a practice of seeking personal applause by harshly criticizing Indian developments before foreign audiences.

The fabric of Indian politics, however, is more than a series of grand designs that never quite materialize but become instead the target of self-criticism. That is the pattern at the highest level, but there is another level of Indian politics—that of the daily give-and-take of quid-pro-quo arrangements. At this level, power becomes the capacity to be nurturing and supportive, to give favors and to receive praise and homage.

Here, as in Southeast Asia, the logic of dependency gratification produces a complex web of patron-client ties which become the essence of political power. As Myron Weiner has demonstrated, the Indian party system is not built around ideological or policy-oriented parties, but rather it grows out of a system of patronage politics. The "internal conflicts of the party are not related to ideological disputes or, for that matter, to disputes over major questions of public policy. Caste and kinship ties and, above all, factional affiliations related to the need for status and prestige or to the desire for material rewards have been the crucial factors in intra-party conflict."[29]

The Indian patterns of patron-client ties are significantly different from those found in Southeast Asia. In India there is not the same intensity of commitment as in the Indonesian concept of *hutang budi,* nor is there the subtle exchange of "will" and "awe" as in Thailand. Indian superiors enjoy authority, while subordinates because of their narcissism are content to be obsequious. Inferiors, however, require material benefits. Yet there is still the psychic distance in which relations can be broken without shock. Among Indians, friendships exist with few ups and downs—people can be separated for long periods, and when they again meet it is as if they had never been apart. It is the same in Indian politics when factions split, for in time they may rejoin if that seems to be mutually advantageous. The logic of patronage permits such combining and recombining as long as the ties are based on clearly defined rewards. But if any hint of malice enters the picture, or there is a suggestion of treachery, the parties become permanent foes and recombining is nearly impossible.

Thus the approach to power in India becomes bifurcated, with the political sphere divided between the politics of grandiose design and the politics of patronage. This bifurcation has produced two levels of public life. Beyond the unfulfilled pronouncements of grandiose plans lie ceremony and formalities. In no other country of Asia do purely ceremonial offices and functions achieve the dimensions that they have in India. The Indians have transformed, and even expanded, the grandeur that the British Raj and the Mogul emperors employed to inflate the awesomeness of their ruling power. But the Indians now apply that grandeur to purely ceremonial affairs. For example, the magnificent building which once housed the ruling British viceroys has become the residence of India's president. Though the office of president is purely ceremonial, the four hundred acres of grounds now house over ten thousand members of the president's staff and all their hangers-on. This may not seem superfluous when compared with the extravagances of the Chinese emperors, but the Chinese emperor was presumed to be the ultimate ruler, the source of all power, and not just the symbol of collective greatness, as is the case with the Indian president.

If it were not for the cohesion of the patronage networks, Indian politics would appear to vacillate between peaks of unaccountably optimistic yet doomed expectations and low points of confused anarchy. In fact, however, in this society of nurturing superiors and their dependent inferiors it is possible for people to find satisfying rewards in spite of the failed grand designs.

This is not a bad formula for preserving a rough-and-tumble form of democracy. Elections open the doors for leaders and followers to make or renew pledges of mutual support; and once the returns are in, another set of doors is opened to allow late joiners to make up for their mistake of working for the losers. After the 1980 victory of Mrs. Gandhi's Indian Congress party the Indian press ignored the consequences of the Soviet invasion of Afghanistan, which had coincided with the elections. It focused instead on the Indian politics of state governments, which were "toppled" as state legislators crossed the aisles to form new state governments that would support the party of the new government in New Delhi. These politicians understood that power means access to the distribution of central government resources. For them the governmental process took one elementary form: the central government collected whatever surpluses it could from society, and then, following the flow of patronage chains, the resources were redistributed. This is a system well understood by the governments of many American cities, but none has ever operated on so grand a scale as those in contemporary India.

It is paradoxical that the Indians have been able to achieve political stability but have not been able to attain policy effectiveness. Policy is always secondary to patronage, although the Indian tolerance for ambiguity makes the gap between the politicians' rhetoric and their practices seem less hypocritical.

It would be wrong to suggest that the Indian bureaucratic structure, its party organization, and its charismatic leaders are totally incapable of coordinating their actions to carry out large projects. A total mobilization of effort can take place for a time, as, for example, when Mrs. Gandhi's government decided that India would make itself a showplace for the 1983 Asian Games—a policy objective which, because it was attended by much ceremonial grandeur, had appeal on the higher plane of Indian concepts of power. The enterprise called for the construction of six gigantic stadiums—including the world's largest domed stadium— a games village of 853 flats and twelve five-star hotels, all at a cost of three billion six hundred million rupees, according to officials, or up to ten billion rupees by unofficial estimates.[30] The successful completion of this huge construction effort was proof not only of the organizing skills of the Indian civil service but also of the effectiveness of the patronage system, as large numbers of contractors and suppliers, who allegedly had made payoffs, benefited handsomely from their contracts.

Thus, while there is constant grumbling about government policies, the system of rewards in distributing the bounties of government is usually adequate to keep complaints within bounds—indeed, much of the carping which enlivens Indian public life comes from those who are left out of the patron-client system. For example, the demands for changes in state boundaries and for the creation of new states have been inspired by minority communal leaders who feel they could command more patronage resources if they had their own states.

It becomes apparent that an exceptionally stable system has been built upon a remarkable set of bargains: (1) the rank-and-file politicians can expect to receive generous material rewards in exchange for disregarding their leaders' failures in implementing policies; (2) common citizens can accept the inadequacies of governmental performance in return for being left alone by government and for being entertained periodically at theatricals and ceremonies; and (3) the intellectuals are given research grants and freedom to carry on their work in return for withholding criticism of the government. The stability of the power structure rests upon the ways in which Indian attitudes about power correspond to the same fundamental features of Indian personality. For although it might seem that there is a contradiction between the leaders' self-absorption and inward-looking narcissism and the followers' outward-looking search for material benefits, in fact the two complement each other because they are manifestations of similar dependency needs.

Psychological Bases of Grandeur and Dependency

The tendency toward narcissism and other traits in the Indian character has its origin in the socialization process. Although the typical Indian family has many elements in common with other Asian families, particularly in regard to extended family ties and arranged marriages, there are also some striking differences which may be significant for an understanding of the unique features of the Indian political culture.

Whereas family and caste are at the core of Indian society, the family is not a close-knit unit, partly because of the abyss that separates men from women, husbands from wives, and hence fathers from mothers.

Those who are well informed about child rearing in India seem to agree that the Indian baby is fully indulged and nurtured, that he is constantly handled, and his every whimper brings a response. Although the Indian mother may not have the playful moments with her baby son or daughter that a Burmese mother has, she does give the baby loving support and nurturance. The father is a distant figure, having nothing to do with the infant, and he plays a stern and aloof role as the child grows older.[31]

Unquestionably the nurturing mother is the dominant authority figure in the Indian family. Whereas in the other major Asian cultures the father is acknowledged as the supreme authority, the Indian mother tends to "become the ultimate symbol of authority as well as the ultimate target of defiance." Morris Carstairs, Philip Spratt, and Sudhir Kakas all concur with Nandy in stressing in varying degrees the essentially feminine quality of authority in Indian culture, which they also trace back to the way in which the Indian mother seeks to manage the growth of her children. According to Nandy, "the mother-son relationship is the basic nexus and the ultimate paradigm of human social relations in India."[32] This close tie between mother and child, and especially mother and son, has several profound consequences for the Indian view of power.

First, the nurturing responsiveness of the mother must be the source of the ubiquitous phenomenon of narcissism in Indian culture. The Indian infant experiences the complete bliss of feeling that he is one with his surroundings and that his environment is automatically responsive to his every wish. He need only cry to give expression to his wishes, and they soon become realities. He is led to feel that all of this is possible because he is so exceptional, so special, and so deserving of being the center of the universe. Consequently, when the shock of separation occurs following the arrival of a new baby, he does not seek autonomy and individualization but strives to recapture the wonders of that first idyllic and blissful state of being one with the universe.[33]

The shock of being abandoned by the mother in favor of younger siblings is made more complicated because the child is then taught to deny his own identity in favor of that of the family and the *jati*, a collectivity to which he must yield his individuality without gaining much attention in return. Understandably, the first and most basic reaction is one of withdrawal, of believing that to be alone must be the supreme ideal. But this need for withdrawal is overwhelmed by the more fundamental desire to be recognized again as being exceptional, worthy of everyone's attention—hence the Indian's propensity for aloofness, for not being truly gregarious while at the same time wanting to be the center of attention, or for feeling that nobody fully appreciates his qualities.

A key feature of this tendency toward secondary narcissism is that the individual is less troubled by the feelings of guilt that arise from having one's conscience fixed by a demanding authority figure. (Hindus do feel guilt, but less intensely, for violating the impersonal laws of dharma, learned at a much later age.) Thus morality is not so strongly identified with suppressed hostility toward a disciplining father and with the complications of the Oedipus complex as it is for people who are forced to have more strongly developed superegos. For the narcissistic personality the preferred way of demonstrating inherent goodness is to express moral values and to be free of aggression. The moralist with a strong superego behaves in exactly the opposite way, seeking, with aggressive vengeance, to be the collective conscience. Thus Indian moralizing is more an act of self-expression and self-absorption than a serious attempt to impose standards on the community. Indeed, Indians can be completely impervious to community problems and feel no urge to correct "injustices" because they are completely engrossed in their own moral development.

That the Indian child has a very distant relationship with the father and must learn to yield completely to family and caste authority may also be the root of Indian passivity toward authority.[34] As young children Indians learn that it is best not to fight for their "rights" or to protest mistreatment because the road is smoother if they simply submit to parental and caste authority. Thus, early in life, they develop the ability to feel no shame in bowing to authority, but in doing so they reserve the knowledge of their own inner goodness and thereby prepare themselves to set out in search of their own self-fulfillment. They yearn to escape from all external constraints and to become unified with the great, harmonious forces of the universe—that is, to reexperience the exhilaration of infancy when they were one with the environment and could totally command the loving mother. This is the origin of the search for a guru, a kindly guide in seeking perfection in the inner self, according to the rules of dharma, which are more pure than one's everyday *jati* rules.

Second, the shock of losing command of one's mother and of having to settle for the impersonal collective identity of the family and the *jati* creates a sense of confusion about the true meaning of right and wrong, success and failure, praise and shame. In contrast to the Chinese child, who also must learn to cope with an extended family but who is given precise standards of behavior which, if followed, will bring praise and protection, the Indian child must operate under a complex body of taboos, rituals, rules, and contradictory ideas which can inhibit action and encourage withdrawal into introspection. Starting with their religious training, Indian children are presented with a universe of gods who are simultaneously creators and destroyers, men and women, both honest and treacherous. Then come all the rules about the dangers of defilement and pollution. Clearly, the physical world is filled with hazards; it can only be hoped that the spiritual world is supreme, for that is the only one that can be mastered by the self alone.

Finally, and most shattering, the Indian child is confronted with the horrible contradiction that in spite of all the wonders associated with the nurturing, loving mother, women are impure, a likely cause of contamination, a lower form of life that can bring destruction by dragging one down to their level. This contradiction gives rise to a profound ambivalence about women which is second only to the overriding influence of narcissism in shaping Indian political culture. The mother is the ideal of authority; yet women turn out to be sources of destruction. As children learn about the need to abominate impurity and to seek absolute cleanliness, they are hit by the discovery that their own mother is unclean. Whatever ambivalences they may have had about receiving less than deserved attention from the mother are heightened by this revelation.[35]

Thus, because the Indians have turned the mother into such a basic symbol of authority, they grow up with profound ambivalences about authority in general. On the one hand, they expect authority to be nurturing, sympathetic, and supportive. It should also be all-embracing and concerned with harmony and therefore with group cohesion. On the other hand, authority can be associated with all that is negative in the Hindu cultural view of the nature of women, and so it can be self-centered, vain, and worse, fickle—a source of pollution and, at times, of harm because of its indifference. The Indian ambivalence is well described in

Nandy's analysis of the contradiction between looking down on women and admiring womanliness.[36] Long before Gandhi extolled nonviolence and what Indians consider to be feminine virtues, the Hindus had already infused the word *mata*, "mother," with a "strong affective charge. It is invariably linked with the sacred cow, *gau-mata;* and it is as a symbol of motherhood, succoring, gentle, and the antithesis of violence that the cow is liable to be worshipped with a show of feeling which leaves non-Hindus embarrassed and bewildered." At the same time women are an abomination, a destructive, contaminating source "for carnal temptation, for seduction from the ideal values represented by [one's] father and [one's] *guru.*"[37] Out of this clearly established contradiction in Indian culture Nandy arrives at an explanation for the Indian practice of sati, or the widow's self-destruction. Sati had as its unconscious psychological rationale the idea that "the husband's death was due to the wife's poor ritual performance and was her self-created fate . . . the wife brought about the death of the man under her protection, by her weak ritual potency and by deliberately not using or failing to maintain her latent womanly ability to manipulate natural events and fate."[38]

It is impossible to exaggerate the confusion experienced by Indians as a result of holding to a feminine ideal of power while also seeing women as corrupters and destroyers. There is profound ambivalence about sex and masculinity. Hindu culture is filled with contradictions between erotic art and the ideals of celibacy. The folklore holds that men are weakened by the loss of semen, yet a man needs the nurturing of a dutiful wife. Understandably, Indian males seem to be obsessed with anxieties, which have the cumulative effect of inclining them to separate their fantasy about women from their actual sexual activities. While men exercise their imaginations with robust sexual fantasies, much as politicians busy themselves with idealized planning, they show great timidity in actual relationships. Consummation is indeed the great cultural problem.[39]

In addition to the testimony of psychologists that Indians are prone to ambivalence about sex, another indication of repression is that only the Indians among all the peoples of Asia have continued the tradition of arranged marriages, even among their modernized, educated classes. Among today's Indian college graduates the convention is still the arranged marriage, something which Chinese and Japanese graduates rejected more than sixty years ago. The persistence of the arranged marriage suggests a tendency to accept authority and to reject autonomy in favor of dependency. As Edward Shils has noted, this extraordinary divide between, on one hand, an extensive, and even intimate, exposure to the liberating ideas of Western, secular culture, and, on the other hand, the obligation in one's private life to be married to perhaps a completely traditional and religious woman has made the Indian hypersensitive to the idea of being rootless, of being pulled in two directions.[40]

These elements of private life are important in Indian public life because they contribute to the Indian acknowledgment of a deep division between the subjective, inner world of the spirit and the mind and the real world of substantive things. Not only is the divide greater than in other cultures, but through the socialization process Indians also learn that the subjective world is the more important. Thus they have no difficulty in accepting the religious doctrine of maya, the belief that the seemingly diverse physical world is mere illusion.

It might seem that this Hindu life of the mind should have produced a politics in which ideology was at the core of power. Yet this is not the case. Ideology does not play a major role in Indian politics because all Indians are legitimately preoccupied with their own inner worlds, and they do not feel that what they find there, either in terms of conscience or insight, should necessarily be binding on others. Thus the articulation of ideology becomes more a private than a public matter. One is not compelled to agree or disagree with the abstract views of another.

What is more important in Indian politics is to discover whether one can or cannot have a rewarding, and generally submissive, relationship with another, regardless of his or her idiosyncratic doctrinal pronouncements. Power is determined by dependent relationships, not by inspiring ideologies. It did not seem anomalous to Indians that in some districts the landlords joined the Communist party because the peasantry had already preempted places in the Congress party and the other ostensibly bourgeois parties.

Yet it is unlikely that these commitments will last. There are no binding ties in the Indian politics of patronage, for Indian personal relationships do not generally include the emotional bondage that *guanxi* ties have in Chinese culture, or the obligations of *giri* and *on* in Japanese culture, or even the patron-client relationships of Southeast Asia. In most of Asia reality is centered on physical phenomena or, at the most, abstract social relations; but in India the actual is ephemeral and illusory, and therefore reality can only be found in the self and in withdrawal from human ties. In China self-cultivation has always meant improving one's sensitivities in human relationships. The Confucian values of *jen* and *li* demanded a humanitarian approach to personal relationships. But the Hindu ideal of self-cultivation has been in the direction of spiritual attainment and withdrawal from human relationships. The Chinese universe is centered on mankind and secular concerns, while at the center of the Hindu universe is the Absolute. The Chinese sages sought wisdom in balancing good with evil, thus achieving harmony and reliability in human affairs. The Hindu saint, on the contrary, "renounces the normal human emotions of love and attachment and abjures sex. To remain detached is his ideal; any sign of attachment in himself is evidence of his weakness. Whereas the Chinese sage is recognizable as a human being, a Hindu saint is not."[41]

Both the Chinese and Hindu cultures encourage a separation of emotion from action, and they place stress on repressing the passions. In the Chinese case, however, starting with the childhood socialization process, the need to mask one's emotions is related to becoming more effective, particularly in dealing with others. By controlling one's feelings, the Chinese expects to become more competent and successful in this-worldly affairs. The Indian ideal of controlling emotions has the opposite objective of making action irrelevant and unimportant.

The *Bhagavadgita* is the authoritative Hindu statement of the ideal of dispassionate withdrawal from worldly concerns, as expressed in such verses as: "He whose mind is untroubled in the midst of sorrows and is free from desire amid pleasures, he from whom passion, fear, and rage have passed away, he is called a sage of settled intelligence" (verse 56); and "He who is without affection on any side, who does not rejoice or loathe as he obtains good or evil, his intelligence is firmly set in wisdom" (verse 57). The *Bhagavadgita* goes further, however, and says that one should not be concerned about the consequences of one's actions. Verse 47 decrees: "To action alone hast thou a right and never at all to its fruits; let not the fruits of action be thy motive; neither let there be in thee any attachment to inaction." One surrenders to the rules of one's dharma and thus need not be concerned about the outcome of one's actions. The attraction of this verse for Hindus "lies in the fact that if there is no personal motive behind an action, the doer cannot be held responsible for his own actions. The very surrender of the right to the fruits of one's actions confers on the doer freedom from all responsibility. And is not the relief great, even if the price be greater? . . . So, freedom from guilt, responsibility, and anxiety are the gains for the loss of the right to receive."[42]

Nevertheless, in the political realm the traditional concept of *danda* did require that rulers act so as to maintain the social world, and hence they could not escape all responsibilities because of their own dharma. In the increasingly secularized politics of India, tensions have been rising over the question of power and responsibility. In a sense, the traditional view about the rulers' responsibilities through their obligations to *danda* have been supplanted by legally defined rules and regulations. The transition from sacred obligations to secular laws has not, however, been complete or truly satisfying, and the idea that one might be able to escape from responsibility for one's actions is alluring to Indian power holders. It is not surprising, therefore, that among the moralizing critics of Indian politics the theme of corruption is just as popular as the failure to consummate policies.

The Muslim Dimension

The concept of power in the subcontinent cannot be treated as though it were only a Hindu cultural phenomenon. This would certainly be inaccurate in view of the history of Islamic Mogul rule, the importance of Pakistan and Bangladesh, and the existence of 61 million Muslims in the Republic of India. Indeed, the approximately 190 million Muslims in South Asia make up the "largest regional aggregate of Muslims anywhere in the world."[43] Furthermore, given the intensity of the animosities between some Hindus and some Muslims, it would be absurd to subsume Islamic ideas of power under a discussion of Hindu concepts.

Yet heuristically it is helpful to begin with the more amorphous and contradictory concepts of Hindu culture and then to contrast them with the more sharply defined character of Islam. This is a legitimate procedure because historically Muslim rule in India did achieve a remarkable balance with Hindu culture, and both cultures were equally affected by British concepts of power. The emergence of Bangladesh also suggests that the Bengali sense of identity turned out to be stronger than the more general appeal of Islam. In short, in spite of sharp differences there are common threads in the two cultures, especially with respect to the concept of power.

During the Mogul period, Percival Spear has written, although "there was no assimilation of Muslims to Hindu, there was a gradual development of mutual toleration (with interludes of persecution) and of a workable *modus vivendi*. Hindus were freely employed and came to dominate the revenue and financial services. Hindu philosophy exercised its spell on Muslim scholars . . . The air and water did not combine, but they interspersed on the fringes and developed curious eddies within themselves."[44] The Moguls added grandeur and cultural excellence to India's concept of elitehood; the Red Fort, the Taj Mahal, Jama Masjid, Fatepur Sikri, and the palaces of Agra gave a new visual dimension—a dimension which the British enhanced in building New Delhi.[45]

In contrast to the diffuse and contradictory nature of Hinduism, Islam has well-defined characteristics: a Creed, a Book, and a Brotherhood. The Creed is the Prophet's words, "There is no god but Allah and Muhammad is his Prophet." The Book is the Koran with its precise rules for all aspects of life; and the Brotherhood is the principle that all people have in their being the essence of God and all who share the faith stand equal before God. It would seem that from these fundamentals no two religions could be further apart than Islam and Hinduism.

Yet, there were certain doctrinal views which brought them together, especially with respect to the acceptance of authority and one's place in society. Although not the same as dharma, the Islamic concept of *din* has the similar quality of holding that all things and people have a fixed nature, determined by divine force. The concept of *din* goes beyond human destiny, and encompasses all of nature; therefore it can be said that it is the *din* of water to flow down hill, of gases to rise, of magnets to attract iron.[46] The *din* of Islam thus becomes both a law of nature and a set of rules for correct behavior. But in contrast to the pluralistic Hindu concept of *dharma,* which asserts that everyone has his or her own nature and appropriate rules of conduct, the Islamic concept of *din* applies to all people, as a single absolute set of rules. Whereas among Hindus diversity is tolerated and everyone has his or her caste-specific dharma, with Muslims total conformity is expected, and deviants are seen as an abomination to nature and to God—hence the Muslim sense of the unity of the universe and the Hindu acceptance of diversity.

Another overlapping but significantly different theme is that of the concept of the state and the obligations of rulership. Islamic doctrine, like Hindu, attaches great importance to the role of political authority in upholding the "divine order" of society. The key difference, however, lies in the division between sacred and secular authority. In Hindu culture the concept of the king as having a necessary function which must be carried out according to amoral statecraft opens the way for the building of a secular authority that is not the prisoner of priests and religious leaders. In Islam, of course, there can be no such neat division because everything is governed by an all-pervasive religion. Here is the origin of the ideal of the "Islamic state," and of a government that in every act seeks to implement the words of the Prophet as recorded in the Koran. This tension in Islamic theory works itself out by glorifying government and causing leaders to act as though they have all the authority of God behind their actions. The *khilafah* as the Islamic state becomes the "representative" of Allah, "the Sovereign," "to whom alone belongs all the Power." Laws of the state are expected to be manifestations of "higher laws." The concepts of authority are thus absolutist and totalistic. The powerful can act with confidence that to some degree they embody the Divine Will.

Yet, the all-pervasive character of *din* also means that every human being is also a "representative" of God, and that all Muslims are bound together in a common brotherhood, the *umma*, which unites the faithful and decrees that all people must be individually respected. Decision-making should also reflect the spirit of the brotherhood. The Islamic concept of *shura*, or "consultation," holds that there should be community discussions about interpreting the Koranic law. Out of these and other theological concepts about the individual and the community have developed the doctrine that the Islamic state should be a populist community, a "perfect democracy."

Thus at the heart of the Islamic concept of power lies a contradiction between authoritarian rule and populist democracy. This tension was heightened in the subcontinent as Muslims under the British identified with both a martial tradition and the idea of a rule of law. The stress became even greater in the last days of the British Raj because the Muslims' belief in their superiority was threatened by the prospect of becoming a minority in a secular democracy dominated by Hindus. The drive for partition was fueled not only by fear but also by the ideal that a true Islamic brotherhood in the subcontinent could produce the dual, but contradictory, phenomenon of a strong (authoritarian) state and a populist democracy. The history of Pakistan and of Bangladesh has shown the inadequacy of the idea that Islamic faith alone is enough to overcome the absurdity of a country made up of two wings two thousand miles apart.

Just as with the Hindus, the socialization practices of the Muslims reinforce certain features of the formal political theories and thus give a psychological dimension to the Islamic views of authority and power. Although the Muslim practices take a different form, the pattern of socialization produces a type of narcissism not too different from the Hindu, but the ambivalence toward authority is based on conflicting sentiments toward a demanding "brotherhood" rather than a stern father.

Briefly stated, Muslim socialization begins in an environment dominated by the mother, in which there is almost no contact with the father. This is the case because, regardless of wealth or the number of wives, the ideal of the harem has persisted. Living accommodations are reserved for the women and children, and the man stays away from the house (or, if large enough, from the women's quarters) from the end of early morning prayers until the last prayers in the evening. The child experiences extremely close physical associations with the mother, with weaning not taking place until well into the second year. Suddenly, at the age of five or so, the child is taken from the mother to spend his entire day in the "brotherhood" of an Islamic religious school. He then must learn to make his way in a situation that mixes stern discipline, protestations of friendship, and the intimidations of older children. The longing to recapture the security of his early years becomes the basis of a form of secondary narcissism—the self is good and deserves to be honored rather than separated from the force that it had once been able to command. At the same time the child develops profound ambivalences about the concept of brotherhood—the ideal seems an acceptable alternative to the ties with the mother, but in practice one is not always treated as a true brother. Thus the Islamic ideal of authority becomes that of the brother, not the father figure, but it is an ideal that is not always fully trusted. Because the "brotherhood" can be the source of pain, aggression can be directed against the ideal, but that is wrong behavior and therefore the aggression must be suppressed. Leaders and followers are supposed to share a common destiny and to be united both religiously and psychodynamically in the ties of brotherhood; but one can never be sure whether the others are living up to the ideal—especially because one has experienced hostility toward that ideal oneself.

Thus, for all their differences, the Hindu and Muslim political cultures in the subcontinent share the concept that leaders see themselves as peculiarly virtuous and are distrustful of others because they suspect that those others do not appreciate their superior worth. Leaders, in short, need the reassurance of admiring followers. The followers are in their way equally dependent as they seek the security of either an understanding guru or an idealized brotherhood.

6

The Riddle of Japan: The Combining of Competition and Consensus

JAPAN'S HISTORICAL EVOLUTION from centralized feudalism through an authoritarian state to a democratically ruled industrial society seems at many turns to have paralleled Europe's development. Yet a closer inspection reveals that Japan's modernization differs markedly from European examples. Whereas in Europe the end of feudalism led to an intense sense of class conflict between the reactionary-conservatives remembering an aristocratic tradition and the Marxist defenders of an underclass in search of revenge, the postfeudal Japanese have opted for an American consensus style of politics which Louis Hartz attributed to America's freedom from a feudal past.

The story of Japan's transition, during the Meiji Restoration, from Tokugawa feudalism to a modern bureaucratic state has been told many times.[1] The central themes, however, remain the same: the astonishing speed of the change from a shogunate system to a modern bureaucratic state; the lack of any charismatic leadership; the ease with which opposition elements were brought into line; and, finally, the Japanese people's sudden change from being almost completely isolated to becoming frantic searchers abroad for "better" ways of doing nearly everything in the political and economic realms, while at the same time preserving most of their own social customs.

These themes lead to a monumental question. How was it possible for the Japanese to abandon an exceedingly rigid, feudal, clan structure and adopt a merit-oriented bureaucratic polity without great bitterness? In other words, how could they move from a society in which power was the monopoly of specific classes and ascriptive groups to one in which power was associated with consensus—a consensus that presumed to encompass the entire nation?

Viewed in terms of evolving concepts of power, the symbolic restoration of the role of emperor as supreme authority concealed a much more significant development in the ranks of the samurai class. At the beginning of the Tokugawa era the daimyo lords needed their samurai warriors to defend their fiefdoms and to expand their power through military alliances. Samurai of all ranks thus formed the ruling class; and as the only ones allowed to carry swords, they were in a sense above the law. Yet at the same time, as members of the dominant class, they could not demean themselves with activities associated with the lower classes. The success of the shogunate in bringing peace to what had been a war-torn Japan made the samurai class not only increasingly irrelevant but also a drain on the resources of the daimyos.[2]

Peace had the effect of "civilizing" the samurai. At the beginning of the Tokugawa period they were illiterate, physically active warriors, but as their role grew superfluous, except as members of an aristocracy, they became increasingly well educated, and even learned in Confucian doctrines.[3] Thus, while a minority of the lower samurai dropped to being *ronin*, that is, wandering samurai who owed fealty to no lord because their daimyos were bankrupt, the majority took on new skills. Some of these further strained the resources of their daimyos, as, for example, by participating fearlessly in Edo's "floating world" of entertainment; but others identified themselves with the problems of their fiefdoms and applied their growing skills to the problems of administration of the clan lands.

In a sense the samurai were prisoners of their aristocratic, ruling-class status. They could not easily take on leadership roles in other fields, although some did sell their samurai status as the system became more corrupt. Precluded from assuming even local forms of power, such as becoming village headmen, the lower samurai had to worry increasingly about how to make the national system work better.[4] Thus, well before the Meiji Restoration, some of them were running the major *hans*, or daimyo estates.[5]

Because the lower samurai, as a warrior ruling class, were concerned about status deprivations, they grew increasingly interested in becoming civilian rulers. Their improved education had made them into pragmatic Confucianists who took seriously the idea that rule should be by merit. Thus the Restoration was carried out by lower samurai who were committed to the ideals of recruitment according to achievement standards, but who also had some feelings of loyalty to their class and their daimyo lords. Consequently, with the final collapse of the old system after Perry's visit in 1854, the older elite were not ruthlessly pushed aside but were "pensioned off" with bonds and symbolic peerages. Because of the Confucian emphasis on symbolism over reality, it was easy for the daimyos to avoid losing face. Although they gave up power, they preserved a kind of status and also acquired capital, which many used to initiate significant economic enterprises.

This acceptance of the right of subordinates to push ahead without seeming to threaten the formal superior is the essence of the Japanese family system. The mode of commitment to the *ie* is such that, without directly challenging the father's authority, sons can assert themselves and younger brothers can even start new "branch" lineages by becoming *gosenzos*. Then the father can bask in the glories of his sons' achievements without having to make it appear that they are following his dictates. Such a relationship is generally impossible in the Chinese family system, in which the father must at all times seem in command and the sons must appear docile and find achievement only behind a mask of passivity. For the Chinese the rules of Confucian filial piety make loyalty the supreme value, even to the point of hobbling merit and effectiveness.

Hence, in a form very different from the ending of the old regime in Europe, the Japanese executed a smooth transition to the bureaucratic state. At the same time, the Japanese lower samurai interpreted Confucianism in ways significantly different from those of the Chinese, so that the ideology became a stimulus for state-building and not the obstacle it was in China. This was done largely by a shift in the emphasis placed on the Confucian values of merit, virtue, and loyalty.

Merit versus Loyalty in Building Power

The version of Confucianism held by the lower samurai during the late Tokugawa and the early stages of the Restoration was, in a contradictory fashion, both more liberating and more of a practical guide than was Chinese Confucianism. During the Tokugawa period Japanese Confucianists were aware that their version of feudalism (*hoken*) was closer to the arrangements that Confucius himself had written about than was the Chinese bureaucratic system. In liberating themselves from Chinese orthodoxy, the Japanese went further and concluded that to understand the "Way of the Sages" it was appropriate to think of the Sages not as specific, historical personages, but as types of political wisdom.[6] Hence, although they felt comfortable with a more sophisticated version of Confucian thought than was possible in modern China, the lower samurai found it easy with the coming of the Restoration to push quickly for a centralized bureaucratic structure in which the concept of recruitment by merit meant achievement standards which were not mere manifestations of virtue. In Japan, modernization meant a meritocracy; in China, the appeals of a virtuocracy lingered.

The 5 to 6 percent of the population who were samurai soon filled the ranks of the newly centralized bureaucracies and became a new kind of local authority. All this not only gave them new scope as a ruling class, but it also required that they abolish the class restraints of the feudal order.[7] The striving for competence that was rooted in their martial tradition of feudal competition, together with their Confucian appreciation of merit, made it possible for the lower samurai to adapt with alacrity to the idea of hierarchical power arranged as civilian and military bureaucracies based on achievement standards.

Like younger sons seeking to establish their own lineages, the lower samurai who carried out the Restoration were bold risk-takers who did not feel the need to cling to the protection of their former ascriptive status as the born elite. Merit meant to them achievement in terms of competence in doing things, not in pretending to superior wisdom or virtue. Even during the Tokugawa period the Confucian samurai had come to the conclusion that a loyal servant should be his own judge as to what was in the best interests of his lord and should act accordingly, and therefore he should not necessarily follow literally his lord's orders.[8] Former feudal rankings gave way quickly to recruitment and promotion according to skill and competence.[9] Power meant effectiveness and decisiveness in bureaucratic actions. This was possible because, as Harry Harootunian has noted, "toward the latter part of the Tokugawa era, a crucial distinction was made between loyalty and competence in bureaucratic performance. Once this distinction was articulated . . . then it was necessary to establish which of these two standards was more essential to the political ends of society. While loyalty was still a highly valued virtue in the definition of the ideal official, it was no longer sufficient to serve as a criterion of recruitment or as a basis of promotion. Loyalty was still loyalty but ability needed proof."[10]

The concept of merit that the lower samurai held as their ideal was derived from Confucianism, but it was almost the opposite of Chinese orthodoxy because it was based above all on universalistic standards. The Japanese Confucianists took seriously the idea that merit called for scholarship and that scholarship should be based on knowledge, and that knowledge should be universal, not limited to any doctrine or orthodoxy. Thus in the words of the Charter Oath of 1868, which restored the Meiji Emperor: "Evil customs of the past shall be broken off and everything

based upon the just laws of Nature. Knowledge shall be sought throughout the world so as to strengthen the foundations of imperial rule."[11]

Yet, in a strange way, the idea that it was legitimate to seek for elements
of power abroad released in Japan the forces of nationalism. Prior to the
Restoration loyalties were parochial: there was little sense among the
general public of any need to unite against foreign threats until Perry's
arrival; and even then the response was that it was the duty of the
shogunate to cope with the "black ships," while the other daimyos and
the samurai, to say nothing of the general public, could exploit the Ba-
kufu's dilemma. The Restoration was touted as calling for the reestab-
lishment of a true *jinsei,* a "benevolent government rooted in normative
principles of political organization, obtainable in all times and places."
Generalized and practical knowledge, that is, *jitsugaku,* was to become
the basis for judging the standards of merit, *jinzai,* for recruitment of
leaders who would give Japan a *jinsei.*[12]

The Japanese concept of power was at the time more external to the
specific resources of the actors than it had been under the feudal arrangements. Their search for knowledge was premised on the idea that
there were certain natural laws in the universe, not unlike the Tao or the
Way, but now called Science, which, if adhered to, could provide truly
exceptional power. Thus the Japanese appreciated surprisingly early the
value of impersonal forces, which were, however, absolutely lawful and
hence not capable of whimsical actions, as were the invisible forces with
which Southeast Asians had to contend. But, as Albert Craig has observed
in studying the writings of a leading Meiji intellectual, this insight into
the importance of natural laws governing both the physical and social
worlds did not produce a deterministic or fatalistic view of history, but
on the contrary was coupled with the idea that each individual is independent, capable of autonomous achievements, and that society exists
for the good of all.[13]

A vivid sense of nationhood, a completely new passion, was thus built
up in a context of ever greater awareness of universalistic norms, laws,
standards, which were definitely associated with what was foreign to
Japan. In a peculiar way, therefore, the Japanese made the essentially
parochial force of nationalism into something which could parade in the
uniform of cosmopolitanism.

All this was possible because the Japanese were able to compartmentalize and thus differentiate what others have tended to see as contradictory and as calling for relative preferences. Not only were they able
to infuse the parochialism of nationalism with the attractions of cosmopolitanism, but they were equally able to separate completely the issues
of merit and loyalty so that the value of the one did not compromise the

obtaining of the other, as has constantly happened in the modernization of China. Loyalty could be taken as a self-evident value, like the obligation to identify with one's *ie;* but once that was acknowledged, loyalty still had to be manifested through recognizable achievements. Although, as in all Confucian cultures, loyalty called for conformity to the group norms, exceptionalism was easier for the Japanese because the model of the supreme leader, the father, did not always have to pretend to omnipotence. Without a sense of being threatened, he could ask for and welcome the ideas and efforts of his sons (or subordinates).

Even more important, the Japanese image of authority was strongly colored by the effective role of the mother. Japanese paternalism is really a form of maternalism, for although the father is the nominal head of the family, in practice the mother is the authority model—and increasingly so as Japanese men become absorbed with their work and play, and hence are not a daily factor in the early formative years of the children. Thus, although we often speak of the Japanese "paternalistic" form of authority, the style in fact is that of the nurturing mother.

Conformity remained a part of face-saving, and one did not needlessly defy it, for it provided other bases for the quid pro quo which made individual exceptionalism possible. In China, by contrast, loyalty could not be satisfied in any other way than by dutiful conformity because the "father" who set the norms supposedly had all of the appropriate answers to all questions. For the Chinese, merit meant not primarily technical skills, but virtue and correctness in thoughts and manners.

A Bifurcated Approach to Power

This Japanese way of living comfortably with contradictions, which Ruth Benedict encapsulated in her title *The Chrysanthemum and the Sword,* has involved more than just compartmentalizing the dichotomies of the parochial and the cosmopolitan and of merit and loyalty. Above all, in their political modernization the Japanese have preserved stability by separating two quite different concepts of power and seeing no contradictions between them. At one level the Restoration initiated a vivid sense of a national polity in the concept of *jinsei.* National power quickly became the bonding together of a whole people in an enlarged *ie,* based on ethical principles of striving constantly for greatness and perfection. At this manifest and formal level, power was seen as flowing from ideological beliefs and grand normative principles—first in the doctrines of Japanese imperialism and the force of the Bushido Code, and then, after Japan's defeat and the American occupation, in the ideals of democracy.

At the other level the Japanese continued to understand that power resided in the bonds of very personal relationships built upon the emotional attachments associated with the traditional concepts of indebtedness and mutual obligations—of *on* and *giri*. At this more intimate or latent level of personal connections there have not been any comparable changes, but the enduring strength of the system of quid-pro-quo bonding is impressive.

During both the imperial and the current democratic periods, the bifurcation in Japanese politics has distressed the intellectuals. Depending upon their politics, they have had mixed sentiments about the manifest level and almost unanimous contempt for the latent level. Even Japanese political scientists, for reasons that no doubt are related to their Confucian heritage, have had a peculiar bias that favors reverence for the ideological plane, with its stress on symbolism and spiritual values, and a contempt for loyalty in personal relationships, which they scorn as a shameful holdover from "feudalism." The intensity of the reaction against Ruth Benedict's study of the Japanese was in no small part provoked by Japanese intellectuals, who were strangely embarrassed because she publicized attitudes and practices that they associated with "feudal" Japan and therefore regarded as past and properly forgotten. Fortunately, however, Japanese, like Americans, have a fascination with analyzing their own national character—indeed, they have a name for such work, *nihonjinron*, or "theories of Japaneseness," and gradually Japanese intellectuals have also begun to speculate about the character of the more personal level of power relationships, usually with a high degree of self-criticism, but more recently with a touch of pride.

During the prewar era the imperialistic stress on the need for every Japanese to sacrifice himself for the greater glory of the Emperor and the Japanese nation obscured the continuing importance of face-to-face relations and peer pressure in individual behavior. And during the war the phenomenon of kamikaze pilots on suicide missions made it appear that the Bushido ideology was all-powerful. This, as well as the fact that there was no study of Japanese army morale comparable to the Shils and Janowitz analysis of the importance of personal pride and small-group identification in upholding cohesion in the defeated German army, led the Americans to believe that the Japanese were motivated mainly by the public factors of politics and ideology. Later, during the occupation, the speed with which Japanese responded to the American demand for democratic institutions and practices seemed to be further testimony that as a nation the Japanese were extremely sensitive to the wishes of the highest forms of authority.

Yet over the postwar years it has become increasingly apparent that the Japanese respond not just, or even primarily, to the ultimate forms of public authority but also to their more immediate power relationships. The continuing successes of the Liberal-Democratic party (LDP) and the falterings of the more ideologically oriented opposition parties show this to be the case. Indeed, as Gerald Curtis has discovered by examining Japanese election campaigning, the successful Japanese politician must rely very heavily upon the power of personal relationships in Japanese communities.[14]

In today's electoral politics two concepts seem to dominate the calculus of power. The first is the "hard vote" or *koteihyo*, votes by those who are in some way personally bound to the candidate because of considerations of *on* and *giri*. They may have either a direct tie to the candidate—as a personal friend, a former classmate, or even a relative—or they may be more indirectly associated through a chain of personal ties.[15] The key quality of this "hard vote" is that it is automatic, little affected by issues, and can be counted on at all times. It is governed by the strong Japanese feeling for the "norms of reciprocity." The second concept is that of the "gathered vote" or *matomari*, in which the members of a local community have a feeling that they should vote together, and therefore their leader can "gather" their votes and deliver them to the politician with whom he has personal ties. This is possible because of the strong feelings of "village solidarity and the idea that voting is regarded as an obligation to the community."[16] The sum of the "hard votes" and the "gathered votes" gives the successful modern politician his support base, or *jiban,* the most important of the "three *ban* or *sanban* which Japanese believe are essential in politics—the other two being financial resources, *kaban,* and a public reputation, *kanban*."[17]

The same bifurcated concept of power is found on the administrative side of the Japanese system of government. Although it may appear that the Japanese state is highly centralized, with the top ministerial leadership deciding everything, in fact the local authorities have considerable autonomy, not only in dealing with the center, but, as Richard Samuels has reported, in their horizontal relations with one another.[18] Also, within the bureaucracy lower divisions and lesser bureaus do have considerable freedom to initiate actions and to assume responsibilities. Although the central authorities set the tone and provide general guidance, action is possible at the ground level without complete surveillance. Hence local authorities are indeed true authorities.

To summarize, in the Japanese bifurcated view of power there are two opposing forms of power: first, at the latent level, power that is the sum of the intensity and the reach of direct, personal relationships, built on all the forces behind the powerful human sentiments of obligation, reciprocity, and of not letting one's side down; second, at the manifest public level, the motivations inspired by highly abstract and grandiose values, such as the idealism of aggressive nationalism or that of a pacific form of democracy. In modern times the Japanese system has been able to operate both with and without great emphasis upon the second dimension of power, but it has always needed the first.

An appreciation of the dual levels of power helps to explain many of the key features of Japanese political culture as documented through survey research by Bradley M. Richardson, for example: high voter turnout and strong partisan identification coupled with minimal understanding of the political world; and a low degree of satisfaction with politics but a high sense of personal efficacy in influencing politics.[19] The data show that the Japanese are quite at home with the personalized level of power, but that they feel unsure of, though not really alienated from, the larger political system.

The Inarticulateness of Power

The primacy of the direct, personalized, and hence locally based forms of power has had far-reaching consequences for the language of politics in Japan. At certain periods, however, and more important, among certain elements of society, the shame of such "feudal" types of relationships has produced an exaggerated enthusiasm for escaping into revelries of expansive idealism. This occurred, for example, with the heady experience of transforming the rules of samurai conduct into a national ethos of sacrifice when emperor worship, Shinto beliefs, and martial values were written into the Bushido Code which every Japanese was supposed to be able to follow. The same emotions about collective power seem to be a motive force behind the quasi-Marxist ideology of those Socialists who would seemingly want to lose all touch with the realities of Japan's society and economy.

In the mood of the occupation-imposed democracy the Japanese have carried the idealization of the formal system to such an extent that they have sought to divorce it from any reality of power. Thus, for example, cries have been repeatedly raised in the Diet about the "tyranny of the majority" whenever the opposition is particularly troubled about losing a vote. This same articulated antipathy to power, a product of the idealization of the formal system, has led to elaborate hypocrisies about military matters, which range from pretending that there is no army or navy to near-sacred formulas about levels of defense appropriations.

Such a divorcement from the realities of power would have led long ago to disaster for the Japanese political system if the political culture had not had the other level of power—that which remains directly and intimately associated with human relationships. Japanese politics functions smoothly as a system of personal ties and obligations that are supported on all sides by concrete commitments. The entire structure of the Liberal-Democratic party is built upon personal factions which are decisive in determining who shall lead the party and hence become the prime minister. The existence of factions that are based almost entirely upon quid-pro-quo sentiments, and not on the idealistic norms of the manifest or formal level of politics, explains why the former prime minister, Tanaka, who has been convicted of taking bribes but is still on appeal, can continue as a dominant force in the LDP, running for re-election and increasing the number of his factional supporters. Tanaka has simply done too many things for his constituency and for his Diet followers for them to abandon him now.

Yet, at the same time, the supremacy of the reciprocity system of power-building has led to an inverse-ratio rule in Japanese political articulation: those with the real power can remain silent while the weak dominate the course of public discussions. It is considered proper in Japan for those with no real power but with a penchant for verbosity to be allowed to dominate political discourse—much as Japanese children are allowed to monopolize breakfast table talk.

Consequently election campaigning reaches a lower intellectual level in Japan than in any other major democratic country. During the inordinately frequent national elections the candidates have their pictures posted on state-established billboards, their sound trucks roam the streets screeching their names and begging people to be good enough to vote for them, and at formal meetings the candidates' speeches are carefully crafted to avoid saying anything relevant to policy. An incumbent's aim in meeting his constituents is to reassure them that he has not forgotten his obligation to them, and that they should not forget theirs to him. Since it would be unseemly for him to be too specific, he needs to use evasive language, but language which will not suggest that he has become dangerously interested in national problems that are far removed from his constituents' interests. The challenger also must avoid expressing excessive interest in distant matters, and for the same reason. The study *Election Campaigning Japanese Style,* by Gerald Curtis, was an eye-opener for many non-Japanese because it documented the low-keyed and non-issue-oriented approach of the successful Japanese politician at the very time that the Japanese media were filled with the lofty views of the inevitable losers.

Elections must be called frequently, not to force the ruling party to explain and justify its governing responsibilities, but rather to let it demonstrate that it is solidly based on the more important level of personalized relationships and hence its performance at the national level is of secondary importance. The standard political posture of the successful Japanese politician is to avoid explaining what has been done in government, or what is intended, and to concentrate on the more becoming practice of merely apologizing for not having been able to do more for his constituency. Instead of adopting the American politician's dictum, "Never apologize, never explain," Japanese leaders follow the rule, "Merely apologize, so as not to have to explain."

The Japanese press has steadfastly filled the void created by Japan's inarticulate leaders. Yet, in a perverse way, the financial and technological success of the main Japanese newspapers has made them at times nearly irrelevant to the workings of real power in Japan. Because the most successful papers have become national institutions, they underreport the local news and so ignore an important level of power in Japanese politics. They are prisoners of the national level; and even worse, since the real power figures prefer silence, they often give voluminous space to the opinions of the insignificant. Japan has been spared the tensions that the United States has undergone between government and the media partly because Japanese politicians skillfully establish close personal relations with particular journalists who are assigned to cover them. Indeed, most of the important politicians have a special room in their own homes reserved for the press, where every morning and often late at night they hold relaxed, off-the-record sessions with the intimate group of reporters that covers them. As a result of this arrangement the press does get substantial inside information, but its criticisms consequently are less ad hominem than in the United States and consist more of general and ideologically oriented attacks. The behavior of the Japanese press has enabled Japanese politicians to carry on in their quiet ways with power. By creating the impression that a great deal is happening when nothing much is, and by touting a vocabulary of issues that are peripheral to matters of real power, the press ensures that Japanese power holders can comfortably occupy their preferred place behind the scenes, pretending to be out of sight.[20]

Compulsions of Group Identity

In spite of the criticisms of Ruth Benedict by practitioners of *nihonjinron,* her interpretation of the sources of the intense Japanese commitment to personal ties still stands up well. She perceived that the Japanese socialization process created strong memories of the warmth and security of the family, and that training in social conduct gave particular significance to feelings of indebtedness and obligation, partly because through such reciprocal relationships it was possible to recapture the security of the family.

The social anthropologist Chie Nakane has further refined the picture of the individual's place in society by stressing that the Japanese must learn early to balance their vertical ties with superiors (parents, teachers, supervisors, and employers) against their horizontal ties with peers, who for their part define the boundaries of the group, organization, or company that will become the basis for the individual's identity.[21] The security of the individual thus involves having the combination of a nurturing authority figure and a collectivity to which loyalty is owed in return for the self-esteem it provides. According to Nakane, Japanese tend to find the warmth and security of their original family membership in their adult group identification. These groups include their circles (*kai*), cliques (*batsu*), factions (*ha*), and professional worlds (*dan*). And, of course, as the literature on Japanese management practices constantly stresses, there is also the identification with one's company and even one's department.[22]

Because the Japanese have such a vivid feeling for the boundaries of their group identification, they tend to treat in-group and out-group people in completely different ways. They can be exquisitely refined in handling the slightest differences in status with exactly the correct etiquette, but then can be extremely rude to those to whom they have no obligations—a fact which Benedict used to explain the brutal behavior of Japanese troops in China, and which is now used to explain the subway behavior of the Japanese and their conduct as tourists.

Masao Maruyama, the foremost analyst of Japanese ultranationalism, has suggested that for the Japanese, group identification is so complete as to make them lose all sense of individualization and to be unaware that superiors and subordinates may have different interests—subordinates become completely identified with their superiors, and superiors feel at one with their subordinates. The result, according to Maruyama, is an authoritarian political culture. The members of each group are so absorbed with their own group identities that they generally give little thought to the real interests of the nation, and therefore they can easily be manipulated by a small number of leaders using the basest appeals of nationalism. He pictures Japan as having a *takotsubo shakai* or "octopus-pot-like structure," meaning that the society is a stack of octopus-pots, or a hierarchy of groups that are largely absorbed in their own worlds and have only limited communication with one another.[23]

This picture of the intensity of group identification is somewhat overdrawn, for it fails to take into account the blend of loyalty and competition which makes Japanese political culture distinctive among the Confucian societies. Other Japanese observers, with their eyes on contemporary, successful Japan rather than on fascist Japan, have recognized that the spirit of cooperation and group identity, which is modeled on the ideal of the *ie,* is balanced by an alertness to the needs for contention and faction-building, which is modeled on the *mura* or village.[24] The dual qualities of *ie,* warm group belonging, and *mura,* factional competition, are thus used to explain the capacity of Japanese to work together in an organization while also being aggressively competitive in a larger context—but not so competitive as to destroy the ultimate unity of the "village," or, in general terms, the nation.

Although the spirit of the *ie* is probably the key source of Japanese group identification, the intensity of the commitments suggests that other factors must be at work. Lewis Austin has noted that in the Japanese religious traditions there are no sharp distinctions between this world and another world. Consequently, all the powerful sentiments of awe, respect, and obedience, which in the West have been diffusely and differentially focused on sacred as well as secular institutions, are concentrated almost entirely upon here-and-now relationships.[25] There is thus tremendous psychic attachment to concrete role relationships. Indeed, George DeVos has documented the fact that the Japanese concentrate extraordinarily intense emotions on the performance of each specific role.[26]

The most telling evidence for this view comes from the work of Takeo Doi, who analyzed the Japanese craving for a dependency that involves the indulgence of others, a sentiment he epitomized by the word *amae.*[27] According to Doi, this craving goes far beyond merely seeking to recapture the security of childhood in the *ie,* in that the dependent expects the superior to express indulgence, sympathy, and a distinctively Japanese quality of "sweetness." The superior must be not merely supportive, but also comforting and kindly, a blend of the mother and father forms of paternalism. Takie Sugiyama Lebra has carried the analysis of *amae* beyond Doi's by noting the qualities expected of the one who accepts another's *amae,* a role she calls *amayakasu.*[28] To play this role successfully requires a large capacity for patience, sympathy, and, above all, duty.

The craving for *amae* means that superiors, by suggesting that their subordinates have let them down, can exploit the high susceptibility to guilt feelings of the dependency-oriented Japanese. The Japanese mother seems constantly to use the technique of professing "hurt feelings" as a means of disciplining her children. Japanese leaders also use the pressures of guilt to extract better performance from their subordinates.

The Warm, Unassertive Leader

Because primary power in Japan tends to be built up from local bases through patron-client ties which are heavily influenced by strong dependency sentiments, leadership style has to be strongly paternalistic and emotionally sensitive to the feelings of subordinates. The first, and usually the all-consuming, obligation of leadership is to maintain group morale, and above all not to impose an independent will or even to determine policy directions.

Indeed, the great paradox about power in Japan is that although the culture was profoundly shaped by a warrior-samurai tradition, and although the country has carried out imperial conquests and now, because of the ties between government and business, is considered to be a dynamic economic force, the Japanese have never embraced the idea of leadership as decisive executive power. To the Western mind it was inconceivable that Japan could have initiated the Pacific war without a decisive, ultimate leader, and hence it became necessary in the West to make Tojo into a kind of dictator comparable to Hitler and Mussolini, when in fact Tojo played a much more subtle and indirect role. Still today, Americans tend to assume that there must be czars behind Japanese industrial policies, and that MITI (the Ministry of International Trade and Industry) must dictate policy.

The truth is that the Japanese have never had an ideal of leadership comparable to the American concept of chief executive. As Austin points out, "Even the word 'leader' has had to be imported into Japan and naturalized imperfectly as *rida*—or even more implausibly as *wan man rida*."[29] In the hierarchically ordered society superiors could expect deference, but in return they were not expected to push their views but rather to work for consensus.

Indeed, the essence of Japanese decision-making has been the operation of consensus-building. Historically, the introduction of modern state bureaucracies produced a complex system of decision-making which was quite different from the Western model of executive command and control. In the system of *ringi,* decision-making began when a lowly subordinate in a department drafted a policy proposal, which would then be passed up the chain of command, with superiors acknowledging and possibly editing, but not exactly approving it; yet by the time it reached the top it would have come close to being the consensus. The document would then be transmitted to another department, where it would be immediately sent down to a lowly official who would start the process of reacting by drafting a reply which in turn would be passed up that hierarchy. If after the process of consensus checking the proposal arrived at the top accompanied by heavy criticism, the head official would have to tell his opposite number at the initiating department that there seemed to be "a few problems." At this signal that official would declare promptly that the proposal was only the work of a lowly person and that nobody should pay any attention to it. Thus nobody in either hierarchy would have "lost face" except the initial draftsman, and such was the inescapable risk of being a neophyte. By contrast, however, if the proposal met with a positive response, everyone would celebrate because the two hierarchies would be integrated in a total consensus. Anything which might fall between the two poles of rejection and consensus would have to be subtly classed, at the last moment, as one or the other, and consequently there would be no need for bureaucratic infighting. All results would be either consensus or rejection, and since rejection would be based on the follies of a lowly subordinate, it would be no cause for embarrassment.[30]

The contemporary Japanese bureaucracy has adopted more Western ideas of businesslike behavior, but there is still a great deal of leaning over backwards to achieve consensus and avoid firm decision-making. For example, before it is possible to initiate a new policy or drastically change an old one, it is usually necessary to go through what is called *nemawashi,* or "root trimming," which means that everyone involved must be attended to, much as every root of a tree must be trimmed and all must be brought together in a ball before the tree can be successfully transplanted. In short, prior to new actions everyone must be contacted and made to feel a part of the new consensus.

It is not only in small-group organizational contexts that Japanese superiors are supposed to be sympathetic, nurturing figures. The same qualities are expected of prime ministers and cabinet officials. In the postwar period Shigeru Yoshida asserted dominant leadership for a brief two-year period, but the result was internecine fighting, repeated elections, and finally his removal as head of his party for "being an anti-party bureaucrat of the old school, arrogant, antidemocratic, and a practitioner of 'secret diplomacy' at home and abroad."[31] Subsequently, both Nobusuke Kishi and Yasuhiro Nakasone ran into severe criticism for being unduly assertive by acting in ways that would seem in American politics to be almost mouselike.

Aside from the universal Japanese dislike of being conspicuous, there are two major reasons why those who get ahead in the Diet and become plausible candidates for cabinet office are, by the standards of most political cultures, humdrum personalities. These are, first, the requirements associated with the politics of factionalism in the LDP and, second, the very large number of cabinet and Diet members who have begun their careers as civil servants.

First, the politics of factionalism within the parties and the Diet requires that leadership at the highest level of Japanese politics be governed by the same rules of reciprocity that shape small-group behavior in face-to-face settings throughout Japanese society. Leaders always have to be sensitive to the needs of their factional members, providing them with necessary support and making sure that their egos are protected. The more powerful the factional leader, the more time and energy he must give to responding to the wishes of his band of followers; for if he were to appear to be seeking glory for himself, he might find his power base quickly eroding. By the time any Japanese politician reaches the top he has almost certainly become a master of tending to the *amae* needs of all kinds of personalities.[32]

Skills in sustaining harmony and avoiding conspicuousness are required not only for managing interfactional relationships but also for the complicated art of negotiation among factions in the LDP. Most cabinets consist of coalitions of representatives of the major factions; and since not all factions may be included, the Japanese will use the term "mainstream" in referring to those factions in the governing cabinet and the term "anti-mainstream" for those left out of the government. Thus at the heart of Japanese government there is a politics of alliances which would be difficult to operate if the leaders were prima donnas.

The need to maintain balance among the factions also means that no one can expect to be prime minister for long, and therefore leaders begin grooming successors even before they themselves reach the top. Only Yoshida has had two terms (1946–1947 and 1949–1954), but he was active in grooming both Hayato Ikeda (1960–1964) and Eisaku Sato (1964–1972). Ikeda in turn brought Masayoshi Ohira (1978–1980) into politics. Sato's faction was eventually taken over by his chief lieutenant, Kakuei Tanaka (1972–1974). Moreover, Sato's brother, Nobusuke Kishi (1957–1960) helped build up Takeo Fukuda (1976–1978).[33]

Second, it has been demonstrated by Bradley M. Richardson that a large proportion of politicians have had long and distinguished careers as bureaucratic administrators. Richardson has calculated that from 1976 to 1979 about 70 percent of the Diet members were former bureaucrats or local politicians; that in the 1960s at least 50 percent of the main cabinet positions were held by former bureaucrats; and that in some administrations (Suzuki, Fukuda, Miki, and Tanaka) from 61 percent to 71 percent of the cabinet were former bureaucrats.[34]

Civil servants who know that they will not become bureau chiefs or department heads make a practice of retiring at fifty-five and starting a new career, often in politics, and this suggests that the Japanese political elite includes an inordinate number of people who have a deep technical knowledge of the workings of government. The result is a politics of "insiders" of a kind unknown either in the rest of Asia or in Western democratic societies. (Those who do not turn to politics tend to have a second career in the particular industries they have dealt with as officials—practicing *amakudai* or "descent from Heaven"—and thereby ensuring that government-industry relations in all fields will be intimate and smooth.) Most of the successful politicians who have been civil servants are graduates of the Japanese elite universities, which also helps to explain why they are not only superior intellects but also masters of the social graces. The brighter the Japanese, the greater the skill in masking cleverness.

To the extent that these ex-bureaucrats set the standards for elite political behavior, they reinforce the Japanese leadership style as low-keyed, nonabrasive, and highly sensitive to the opinions of peers. Whereas in other political cultures there tend to be significant differences between the operating modes of administrators and of popular politicians, in Japan it is the style of the bureaucrat which sets the whole political tone.[35]

Diffusion of Responsibility

Because the Japanese paternalistic style of authority has in recent years been praised as a valuable approach to industrial management, attention has been diverted from what historically has been considered to be its major weakness: its tendency to diffuse responsibility so much that accountability for the use of power is often impossible. Consensus in the making of decisions can strengthen unity, raise morale, and ensure agreement on purposes; but it can also result in a tolerance toward drifting, uncertainty in a crisis, and a general avoidance of responsibility. Japanese leaders may be quick to make ritualized apologies for personal failings, and hence win approval, but they are not usually put on the spot for their use of power. This attitude toward responsibility can culminate in the "resignation" of a superior official because something had gone wrong over which he had no control—as when the head of Japan Air Lines resigned after a crash caused by a pilot's error. In such cases, although the official brings honor to himself and the issue is symbolically resolved, nothing has been done to acknowledge the real responsibility.

Power holders are usually evaluated less for their accomplishments than for their ability to preserve harmony. Consequently, in the Japanese attitude toward power the sentiments of the weak tend to take precedence over the responsibilities of the strong. The result is a form of leveling of power, so that the members of the opposition may paralyze the majority simply by crying "tyranny of the majority" and suggesting that the rules of the game have been violated because they are about to lose. Again, the craving for dependency and *amae* is so great that Japanese find it not unreasonable to expect their opponents to respond to their desires, a phenomenon that may explain the unusual strength of the opposition in the Diet. It may also explain why the Japanese, on the basis of their views of the appropriate powers of a "junior partner," felt that their alliance with the United States should give Tokyo a major say in Washington's foreign policy.

The very skills which leaders develop in reading the emotions of their followers can complicate the workings of power. Japanese tend to be keenly aware of the differences between a person's open statements (*tatemae*) and his inner thoughts and intentions (*honne*). Therefore the good leader will frequently discount the formal acknowledgment which would have certified a consensus and will probe instead into latent discontent.

These factors are not necessarily causes for serious trouble, so long as events are working out well—as they have so often in recent years in Japanese industry. But they can cause problems when more decisive and accountable decision-making is needed.

Probably the most striking aspect of modern Japanese history is that great events seem to have taken place without the action of clearly responsible power. The Japanese invasion of Manchuria was the work of junior officers who exuded such a spirit of dedicated nationalism and emperor worship that their superiors, including the civil authorities, felt they had to go along and in a sense uphold the consensus.[36] The story of Pearl Harbor and of the eventual surrender aboard the USS *Missouri* shows more drift than decisive leadership.[37] Indeed, once it is possible to separate the "forest" from all the "trees" in Gordon W. Prange's detailed account of Japanese and American actions in relationship to the Pearl Harbor attacks, the most significant conclusion has to do with the vagueness of Japanese accountability in decision-making and the consequent American difficulty in pinning responsibility.[38] In the Japanese navy the lower-ranking officers pushed their own strategic concepts and dictated the pace of decisions, while their superiors, who allowed them scope, held only a veto power which, everyone understood, would be too awkward to use.

In democratic Japan diffusion of responsibility has become even more common because of the Japanese tendency to believe that democratic decision-making should be not only consensual but also gentle and considerate. For example, the authorities were completely impotent in the face of radical student takeovers of university campuses in the 1960s. At Tokyo University administrators stood helplessly aside while students took over key university buildings and occupied them for more than a year, destroying property and preventing normal academic activities. Similarly, at Narita airport the Japanese government is having to spend millions of yen a month in elaborate defense against terrorist attacks by "radicals" supposedly defending the "rights" of farmers who, they say, were wronged when "consultative procedures" were not followed in the decision to extend runways.[39] In most democracies the authorities could not have been so easily paralyzed because they would have quickly moved to resolve the matter by court action.

In Japan, however, power is not so used. Drift is preferable to decisive action if action might create disharmony. Just as the Japanese Diet leaders are not exhilarated in the same way that a Lyndon Johnson or a Tip O'Neill would be at the prospect of pushing through a measure and winning by "50 percent plus one" of the vote, so the Japanese administrative authorities will avoid firmness with malcontents even when the public is being greatly inconvenienced. Their sensitivity to *amae* means that in Japan probably more than anywhere else "squeaky wheels get the grease."

In Japan policy actions must move at a sedate pace if disruptive choices are to be avoided and precedents are to be followed. As John Campbell has reported, the Japanese Finance Ministry always has the goal of avoiding favoritism and striving to achieve "balance" (*baransu*) among all concerned.[40] The Finance Ministry officials, who are the cream of the civil service elite, like to believe that they are not just stifling criticism among contending claimants for resources, but that they are maximizing the abstract ideal of *baransu*. Thus supreme power in Japan denies itself the customary pleasures of aggressively putting down some and elevating others, according to its whim, in favor of dutifully striving for an essentially neutral ideal of *baransu*.

The Driving Power of Dependency

Left to its own devices, the Japanese style of leadership would be a formula for political failure. Its successes come from the responsiveness of Japanese followers to the most offhanded blessings of superiors. They do not need discipline; the most subtle cues given by those above are enough.

Paternalistic authority works in Japan because the desire for dependency on the part of subordinates is so great that it often drives them to superhuman efforts. The fear of letting down the side, of breaking with the consensus, of not meeting the expected standards provides the main psychological drive for generating what must be the most impressive political and social power in Asia. The need for acceptance, which began under the set rules of a rigid but contentious feudal system, and which was redefined first for a militaristic imperialism and then for a capitalistic democracy, has compelled individual Japanese to strive for levels of achievement which have made their respective group identities successful, and these in turn have been the building blocks of national power.

In the "learn from Japan" movement that stimulated American thinking about industrial relations in the early 1980s, attention was concentrated almost entirely upon management practices, thereby overlooking the critical fact that Japanese workers had attitudes toward authority that were quite different from those of American workers. Japanese factories were presented as being filled with dedicated and efficient workers, thanks to the skills of their benevolent superiors.[41] But revelations about the actual conditions of work on a Toyota assembly line have shown that rigid, authoritarian controls can be applied to Japanese workers because their dependency ethos allows them to accept uncomplainingly speed-up pressures and overtime demands that would be completely unacceptable to Western workers.[42] The workers' loyalties and their trust in the "fairness" of their superiors make them tolerant of ceaseless demands for greater efficiency and commitment to the factory.

That power in Japan is built upward from the motivations of subordinates and local networks of relationships explains in no small measure why historically the Japanese have gone through dramatic changes in the forms of their political systems without experiencing similar changes in social dynamics. The same patterns of mutual dependency between superiors and subordinates were at work when the Japanese made their distinctive adaptations of Confucianism, of imperialism, and finally of American-imposed democracy. With each adaptation leaders and followers alike have deferred collectively to what they have taken to be a better, larger system, even while preserving the essence of their own basic approach to power.

This appreciation of power as associated with dependency explains why the Japanese, of all the non-Western peoples, have had fewer traumas over the clash between traditional values and modern ways. At the personal level, which involves not only their private lives but also their bonds of reciprocity, the Japanese have been able to adhere pretty much to traditional patterns, while in the public domain, where form takes precedence over substance, they have been able to be fashionable, going along with what is most useful. Change has thus not been a fundamental challenge to their basic understanding of power. Only those intellectuals and politicians who have lost their social anchoring and have become captivated by ideological passions are troubled by the contradictions between Japan's formal beliefs and its private practices.[43] As long as their dependency needs are met, most Japanese feel secure enough to indulge in whatever modernization has to offer—particularly if they can do so under the blanket of conformity.

For the future, it is a major question whether the motivations inspired by dependency can continue to be a driving force in Japanese society and politics. If what has driven the Japanese to their competitive successes is, as some have suggested, a sense of inferiority to the West, then their achievements may diminish their motivations. Thus in time the Japanese may be infected by the "English disease."

But if they are driven exclusively by the needs of dependency, the realization of various forms of achievement may have little effect on their maturation; their psychological needs are only marginally related to the payoffs of "success," and the achievement of recognition may only fuel the craving for dependency. This is quite a different situation from that in Western cultures, where the prime value is the achievement of autonomy and independence. In such cultures the motivation for achievement, as suggested by Max Weber for economics and Harold Lasswell for politics, can be a strong need to prove oneself in response to feelings of insecurity; and therefore, as Joseph Schumpeter and Daniel Bell have argued, success in entrepreneurial systems can eventually erode motivation and produce a crisis of stagnation.[44] The psychology of dependency in Japan may produce other problems, but this is not likely to be one of them. Those who are "successful" will become the nurturing paternalistic authorities always ready to respond to the dependency needs of their circles of clients.

Indeed, the alacrity with which the Japanese have adopted paternalistic, in fact patronizing, attitudes as a result of their successes is already apparent in Japanese foreign policy. Although they have also been quick to tie their foreign aid to the sale of Japanese products, they have taken a very positive attitude toward providing help to developing countries. Aid to the weak and the poor is the most popular aspect of Japan's foreign relations. At the same time, other countries, especially Korea and some of the Southeast Asian nations, have been irritated by what they perceive as smugness and a sense of superiority in the paternalistic ways of Tokyo.

Diffuse Power and Unfocused Leadership

Japan's politics of dependency has produced a system of technocratic managers but no great political leaders. Its failure to produce such leaders to be known outside Japan as the country has become a world power reinforces the idea of Japan as "an economic giant, and a political pygmy," recalling General de Gaulle's disparaging remark that "Japan is a nation of transistor salesmen." Greatness achieved without the benefit of great men suggests to some a form of Oriental deviousness. Outsiders cannot find any one individual who is worth studying in order to get a better understanding of the country he represents. In an era which has produced Roosevelt and Churchill, Hitler and Stalin, the Japanese have had to make do with leaders of the status of the post–Civil War American presidents. The closest thing the Japanese have had to a charismatic leader is their emperor; and the fact that he is, and has always been, devoid of real political power only reinforces the conclusion that power in Japan is generally not in the hands of identifiable actors.

The Japanese have developed an array of techniques for dealing with the problems of power which call for leadership in other societies. Whenever the government is confronted with tough decisions or awkward issues, the prime minister calls for new elections so that everyone can see again where the roots of power lie. When the problems are less extreme, the government simply allows bureaucratic procedures to take over and dispose of the questions. Issues which might generate confrontations are passed on to mediators or middlemen who seek to achieve compromises. Above all, the Japanese are prone to fall back upon the tactics of delay, hoping that time will work to create consensus—which it often does because of the preference for dependency over assertiveness. The fear of being conspicuous, of being the object of criticism, or of being merely out of line is enough to dampen passions.

One technique common to most democratic societies, that of turning to law and the courts for resolving difficult issues of political power, is almost unknown to the Japanese, whose aversion to litigation goes well beyond that of any other civil society. The combination of dislike for the precision of legal contracts and the desire to avoid confrontation means that too often there is imperfect communication and that parties completely misunderstand each other because no one wants to be direct or explicit. In negotiations between politicians, as between businessmen, there is a great deal of irrelevant talk, and then at the last minute a few quick exchanges take place about the business at hand. The parties then separate and each one is left to puzzle out its version of what was decided.

Even when the Japanese have had apparently strong leadership, the realities of power have usually not matched the image. The Tokugawa Shogun was supposed to be the supreme authority who ensured the peace; yet the stability of the two and a half centuries of the Shogunate flowed more from the readiness of the daimyos to adopt their respective dependent stations than from the power of Edo. Similarly, during the American occupation General MacArthur was in effect worshiped, but the actual policies were carried out largely by Japanese who were always alert to the wishes of the Americans.

The Japanese concept of power, which minimizes the accountability of leadership and stresses the dedication of followers, has made Japan appear to its neighbors as a mindless giant, not to be trusted. The imperial thrusts of Japan in the interwar years had an inexorable quality: no one seemed to be calling the tune, and therefore there was no one with whom to negotiate. The same is true today as Japan, in spite of its economic impact on other countries in the region, does not see fit to provide any responsible authority capable of dealing with foreign complaints. The Foreign Office will say it is a matter for MITI, and MITI will say it belongs in the private sector.

In the meantime, foreigners feel that the Japanese are excessively clannish and very self-centered and nationalistic in their team spirit. Japanese officials profess to be powerless to force open Japan's markets to foreign competition. They say that the Japanese public resists foreign products, sometimes because private associations have their own "high" standards of quality control, sometimes because of bureaucratic regulations which have the power of "law." Although the Japanese are capable of expressing a collective sense of shame at being disliked by foreign countries, this does not have much effect on Japanese behavior. Authority is too diffuse, and those in high formal positions have to be materialistically minded in order to protect the interests of the members of the Japanese national "family."

Thus the Japanese formula for "success" in modernization has included some disturbing elements, especially for other peoples. The Japanese way of organizing power so as to maximize both loyalty and competitive competence, and of keeping personalized, locality-based, and face-to-face relationships strong, has worked to produce highly efficient and technically skilled bureaucratic institutions. Government has been more by administration than by an open political process. Decision proceeds with an inexorable, impersonal drive, but also in a spirit of maternalistic benevolence. The language of politics is muffled, the voices most heard are those of the weak, and the themes are often irrelevant. What is most important may be expressed in such cryptic ways as to be meaningless to all except the insiders. From time to time leaders make what they consider to be bold initiatives, but to foreigners these moves seem very timid.

The Japanese have thus transformed their centralized feudalism into a modern bureaucratic state with a minimum of tension over authority and the character of power. The result is a stable, highly integrated political system which operates in a slow, sedate manner. Yet it is a government staffed with men of abundant talent and considerable energy, so that technocrats can quickly make necessary adaptations to prevent problems from reaching a crisis stage. In this way the Japanese have learned how to master dependency and to use paternalism to inspire collective efforts which are hard to achieve in more individualistic, ego-centered cultures.

7 | China: The Illusion of Omnipotence

Unlike the Japanese encounter with modernization, which turned a heritage of Confucianism to productive economic and political purposes, China's encounter with modernization has been one of history's great balancing acts, whose outcome is still far from certain. Westerners from Voltaire to Napoleon, from Henry Adams to Richard Nixon, have believed that when the "Dragon awakened" the "world would shake." From the reformers of the Ch'ing dynasty to Sun Yat-sen's revolution, from Chiang Kai-shek's proclaiming of a new republic in Nanking to Mao Zedong's victories of 1949 and on to Deng Xiaoping's call for "seeking truth from facts" in order to achieve the Four Modernizations, friends of China have lived in the expectation that it was about to command a respected place in the modern world. More important, hundreds of millions of Chinese have believed that China's historic sense of greatness would soon be shared by a world that was awed by the accomplishments of the "new China." Yet, although China's achievements have not been trivial, they have consistently fallen short of the expectations of both Chinese and foreigners.

Few peoples have gone through such violent travails as the Chinese, whose society has been torn by ceaseless wars and revolutions; and yet, amazingly, the culture is devoid of any sense of tragedy. Politically the Chinese are undaunted optimists. No matter what nightmare they have just survived, they are always ready to proclaim that they are on the threshold of a new day that is certain to bring miracles of national accomplishment. Their capacity for complaining about past mistreatment—which can be considerable—suddenly disappears when they think of the country's future. All the broken promises of their past leaders are forgotten as they accept unquestioningly the new leader's vision of a bright tomorrow. No other political culture relies so much on the psychological pleasure of suspending disbelief. Chinese who welcome enthusiastically Deng Xiaoping's promises of pragmatism will make bold to criticize the faults of their former idol, Mao Zedong, but it would not occur to them that timely and penetrating criticism of present policies might be constructive and not a sign of disloyalty.

In spite of the giant ups and downs in Chinese expectations, the country has on the whole made progress, and it will certainly continue to do so. But the political attitudes of the Chinese are not geared to the benefits of mere compound interest; their political rhetoric is tied to a faith in the almost magical powers they expect to find in authority. Therefore, we must ask why Chinese cultural attitudes have both raised and shattered the hopes of those who want China to become a modern society— to project constructive power abroad and alleviate the problems of its massive population at home. The problems of ruling a billion people are so overwhelming that maybe we should ask nothing more, and yet there is no avoiding a deeper question: why has the mentor culture of Confucianism repeatedly tied itself into knots in its responses to modernization? Certainly one factor to be considered is the Chinese people's exaggerated idea about what centralized power should accomplish.

There Can Be Only One Authority and It Is China

In contrast to the Japanese approach to power, which evolved out of feudal pluralism and was based on primary relationships, the Chinese started with the ideal that all power should emanate from above, from the center, from a single supreme ruler. In contrast to the near anonymity of the low-postured Japanese leaders, the Chinese have consistently made their top leaders into larger-than-life figures. Sun Yat-sen, Chiang Kai-shek, Mao Zedong, and Deng Xiaoping are names that dominate the history of modern China, while only the aficionados of Japanese history can recount the names of those involved in carrying out the Meiji Restoration or can list the prime ministers who made the Japanese economy the third greatest in the world.

Around the supreme Chinese leader, power clusterings have always existed, but in a state of semi-illegitimacy. Local authorities have been either the delegates of the supreme authority, the obedient agents of centralized power, or the unprepossessing protectors of parochial concerns. In traditional China the power of the local magistrates came entirely from their role as representatives of the imperial court, and today local cadres are equally the disciplined servants of the central authorities. Magistrates and cadres might be aware of local concerns, but their authority was and is based entirely upon their identification with the central authority. Similarly, in the bureaucratic hierarchies of the past and present, lesser officials are expected to act only according to directives from above.[1]

The Chinese conviction that all power should reside in the central authority—a fact that is acknowledged by the entire population—has been one of the most powerful factors in shaping Chinese history. It has preserved a unitary political system in China, and it has made the Chinese uneasy whenever their cultural world has been sundered by contending political authorities. In large measure the central authorities could claim omnipotence because most Chinese were already under the discipline of more immediate, and essentially private, systems of authority: they were ruled by their cohesive families, their revered clan associations, or other private groupings which kept them in line and reduced the burdens of official government. As a society which was predominantly rural, China was largely governed by village institutions. Unquestionably these local systems of authority and power were decisive in shaping Chinese society, but it was equally true that they were content to protect their particular interests through informal and often devious means without trying to reshape national authority in order to make it supportive of those interests.

The inherent weakness of local, geographically based authorities has made China unique among political systems in that historically its political economy has not reflected significantly the profound geographical differences in the country. The economy of south China has been based on rice culture and a related technology, while the villages of north China have been organized around wheat and millet farming; the culture of east China has been the product of massive cities with their distinct economic interests, while west China has been closer to a nomad culture. Yet for all of these striking differences, which reflect a geographically diversified land, at no time in history has Chinese politics revolved around them. Political issues have usually emanated from the center; but if pressing concerns are raised in one part of the country, they are either quickly suppressed or are taken over by the central authorities and made into national concerns, relevant for the whole country.[2]

During Mao Zedong's rule the ideal of national autarky was carried out to the point of trying to make every province self-sufficient. The stated goal was the absurd idea that eventually every province would have its own automobile industry, and the ideal was that there should be no inequalities among the provinces. As extreme as these pronouncements were, they represented, in a sense, only the codifying of what had long been the tacit understanding of Chinese politics: that the central authorities should benevolently care for all parts of the country with equal concern, and that no part should push for special favor. Local interests should never openly challenge the authority of the capital.[3] The secret of the Chinese ability to preserve the notion of a centralized authority lies in a combination of cultural factors.

First, and perhaps most important, has been their exaggerated ideal of the great man as leader—the emperor, generalissimo, chairman—who is an amplification of the Confucian model of the father as the ultimate authority in the family. Just as the father's word was absolute in the family, so the ruler could tolerate no challenging authorities. Should any lesser figure wish to assert authority, he would have to protect himself by proclaiming even more loudly the greatness of the supreme authority. Those who were most vociferous in extolling Mao Zedong's greatness were usually advancing their own power surreptitiously. Lieutenants at the center and leading cadres in the provinces could promote themselves by posing, not as starring players, but as cheerleaders for the one great man. This, of course, is the technique used by young Chinese sons and their mothers if they are inclined to take initiatives. They defer to the family elders and acknowledge that the father is omnipotent, and only after they have demonstrated their subservience can they safely push their own interests.[4]

Second, the centralization of power has been made easier by the strong Chinese sense of racial identity, which in modern times has meant national unity. In spite of their awesome linguistic and other cultural differences the Chinese have long had an overriding sense of their common racial roots. Awareness of the importance of one's own ancestry seems to have made the Chinese feel that they have a bond with all people of Chinese blood. The historic Chinese sense of cultural greatness was readily translated in modern times into strong feelings of nationalism. When Chiang Kai-shek rallied the nation to fight against the invading Japanese in July 1937, his appeal was to racial pride: "Weak militarily as we are, we cannot neglect to uphold the integrity of our race and ensure our national existence . . . If we allow another inch of our soil to be lost, then we are guilty of an unpardonable offense against our race."[5]

This vivid sense of racial identity, which inspires the illusion among Chinese that it is better to trust other Chinese than "foreigners," is reinforced by a third factor that helps to uphold the ideal of centralized power: a near-pathological fear of factionalism and social confusion or disorder.[6] The Chinese are generally convinced that disaster will follow if brothers fight, if villages have feuds, or if there are factions in their elite politics. Everything should be harmonious, at least on the surface. Needless to say, in China families do fight, villages do feud, and factions abound, but the Chinese, unlike the Japanese, have never been able to channel these inevitable tendencies into constructive payoffs of competition and pluralism. The reason is that they have not been as tolerant of locally based power as the Japanese have been. The Chinese persist in believing that power should not be bifurcated, as it has been in Japan, and they doggedly refuse to recognize the realities of this major segment of their social and political life.

They have had some success in this attitude because they attach such great importance to ideology and symbolism—a fourth reason why the Chinese have been able to uphold the myth that legitimate power comes only from above. They have a long and well-established tradition that government and politics should be thought of only in terms of moralistic ideology. For two millennia the ideology was Confucianism, and then when the imperial system collapsed there was a desperate search for a new ideology in which to cloak their politics. For a while it was the San-min-chu-i, which in its mummified form is still official dogma in Taiwan—proof that in Chinese political culture ritualistic symbolism can easily prevail over reality. Then for most Chinese came Marxism–Leninism–Mao Zedong Thought.[7]

The reasons why the Chinese cannot talk straightforwardly about power in their politics, but must turn politics into an ideological question, are complex; but they do go to the heart of Chinese political psychology. Briefly the problem is that in the socialization process the unrelenting emphasis upon filial piety prevents the Chinese in early life from expressing aggression against the natural targets of authority; instead they must learn to separate their feelings from their actions, suppressing the former and controlling the latter by strict rules of etiquette. In compelling people to repress all aggression the culture puts a moralistic cloak around discussions of power. Thus politics must be discussed only in ideological terms, even though in practice aggression does surface, resulting in hostility, backbiting, self-pity, and presumed mistreatment.[8]

In Japan, Confucian ideology with its stress on sacrifice of self for the interests of the collectivity elevated the vision of the samurai from their particular ties to feudal lords to the higher plane of national loyalties. In the case of China, the Confucian stress on "altruism" forced people to make the jump from loyalty to family to loyalty to the emperor, without legitimizing any intervening interests. Consequently, even after the collapse of the imperial system the assertion of self-interest was considered scandalous by Chinese political thinkers.[9] Aside from the family, the only other legitimate interest was that of the state.

Since in early life ideology is so closely related to basic feelings toward the supreme authority, it is understandable that in China orthodoxy has always meant justification of a single national authority. As relief from this pressure for extreme filial obligation the Chinese have understandably produced heterodoxies that have performed the cathartic function of releasing tensions, thereby making it easier for people to conform ritualistically to the formal imperatives of the official orthodoxies. At times, as in the purges under Mao, the Chinese defenders of orthodoxy have demanded total commitment, but in general the practice has been to tolerate hypocrisy and require only that there be no open or blatant challenge to the established ideology.

The Crisis of Competing Authorities

To stress that all legitimate power in China comes from above, from the center, the *chung-yang,* is not to say that in practice there were and are no local forms of power. Of course there were. Power existed in the gentry families, in clan organizations, in village councils and county offices, and above these always stood the middle level of provincial governments, some of which ruled over populations larger than those of some European countries. Not only were all of these forms of power so subservient to the center that whatever autonomy they sought was seen as illegitimate, but their style of handling power was identical to that at the center. In the past, local authorities, acting for the imperial authority, have behaved like miniaturized imperial courts. Today's local cadres are also expected to model their behavior on the standards of the Center, even as they carry out the Center's policies.

Chinese emperors were constantly troubled by their awareness that at the local level officials and even pretenders to officialdom were acting for personal gain when they claimed to be acting in the name of the central authority. Emperor Hung Wu, the founder of the Ming dynasty, found it necessary, for example, to issue an imperial edict on the need to dismiss excessive local staffs, which read in part: "Among those with no redeeming features, the worst are the riffraff found in the prefecture of Su and Sung. It is indeed a great misfortune that these ne'er-do-wells can cause such great disturbance among the cities' inhabitants . . . These idle riffraff . . . just hang around, concerned only with establishing connections with the local officials . . . They work for the local government, calling themselves the 'little warden,' the 'straight staff,' the 'record staff,' the 'minor official,' and the 'tiger assistant'—six types in all, each with a different name . . . At this time, if I were to thoroughly eradicate this riffraff, in addition to those already imprisoned, I would have to deal with no less than 2,000 people in each of the prefectures . . . They utilize the prestige of the government to oppress the masses below . . . What a difficult situation this is! If I punish these persons, I am regarded as a tyrant. If I am lenient toward them, the law becomes ineffective, order deteriorates, and people deem me an incapable ruler . . . To be a ruler is indeed difficult."[10]

This same problem, and much the same sentiments, might easily have been expressed by Mao Zedong in his frustration with the conduct of local cadres. The Deng Xiaoping regime's decision in 1983 to carry out a "rectification" program over several years was inspired by a conviction that local authorities were not acting in tune with the policies of the Center.

We push this point with full awareness that recent scholarship, which has greatly expanded our knowledge of local government, has shown that there was much vitality outside the domain of the central authorities. John H. Fincher in particular has done impressive work in seeking to illuminate the reformist and democratic aspirations in local government immediately before and after the fall of the Ch'ing.[11] For all of Fincher's sympathetic account of efforts at widespread local elections, the fact remains that the democratic movement failed in China; it failed because the culture favored a centralized form of power. Indeed, in the end his analysis supports our interpretation that Chinese culture was uncongenial to a variety of forms of legitimate power. We can agree with Fincher that "societal" forms extended to the highest levels—the Manchu rulers were in fact an imperial clan of between seven and eight hundred people, and the subsequent politics of cabinet membership involved patronage circles—and that the central "government" reached down to the lowest levels when it came, for example, to tax collection. Yet the difference which we are trying to stress remains: whatever was "societal" was traditionally regarded as illegitimate by the Chinese mind.

In any case, the era of the warlords, which did give China a period of pluralistic, competitive politics involving provincial power bases, was such a humiliation to the Chinese that it drove them once again to centralized politics. Thereafter the problem of accepting diverse and lo-calized authorities became more serious. Increasingly Chinese saw their "national salvation" as the single goal of "strengthening the nation," which meant, given their cultural predispositions, total consensus in terms of a single national authority. The Kuomintang leaders felt the need to keep in line all provincial authorities and dissident voices, and the Chinese Communists have been even more stringent in demanding conformity to the wishes of the Center. For example, Premier Zhao Ziyang in his 1984 visit to the United States explained the "Anti-Spiritual Pollution" movement on the grounds that the realization of the Four Modernizations required that all Chinese "concentrate their energies" and "not allow other considerations to keep them from the national tasks." It is simply inconceivable to Chinese leaders that diversity and a pluralistic power structure might produce more creativity and faster modernization. In Chinese culture single-mindedness is an unquestioned virtue.

As a consequence of these attitudes the most fundamental problem of power the Chinese have had in achieving modernization is that of recognizing the need for division of authority. The situation is acute with respect to two types of power-sharing: first, the continuing problem of centralization versus decentralization; and second, the more subtle need for political leaders to respect the authority of experts who have specialized technical knowledge.

The Fear of Local Kingdoms

As they have moved toward modernization the Chinese have had increasing trouble with decentralization. The old fear of weakening cultural and ideological orthodoxy has been compounded by fears that "national salvation" and the search for national "wealth and power" would be compromised by any substantial decentralization of authority. To the Chinese any surfacing of autonomous power groupings, whether based on geography or on economic or technical achievement, has been taken as a sign of dangerous centrifugal forces. China's experiences during the decade of civil strife in the warlord era reinforced their distrust of pluralism.

This uneasiness about decentralization contributed to an interesting and distinctive Chinese interpretation of the concept of "revolution." In most cultures the idea of revolution is associated with the shattering of authority so as to liberate people and provide greater freedom. In China the slogan of "complete the revolution" has always been directed toward creating a stronger, more enveloping authority. The Chinese ideal of revolution is not, "Let's get rid of father so we can all do our thing," but rather, "We need a stronger, better father."[12] The calls to action of the Taipings, the Boxers, and of Dr. Sun Yat-sen were all made on the note of revolution. Chiang Kai-shek, whatever his shifting ideological orientations, believed that his North Star was that of "carrying out the revolution." Although outsiders view Mao and Deng as ideological opposites, both have seen themselves as committed "revolutionaries." The concept of "revolution" for all Chinese has been one of creating a truly dominant authority. Whether they are political reactionaries or radicals, Chinese have wanted "revolution," by which they mean an ever stronger authority, but one that is more morally committed to a partisan view of what is best for China.

Chinese nationalism is not one of singing the praises of a richly diverse culture but one of insisting that all should "march to the baton" of a single political authority. That the Chinese stress their homogeneity, their valued unity, without embarrassment may seem to others appalling conformity. There have been no spokesmen for political or cultural diversities among the Chinese peoples. The forty-odd million minority peoples are depicted always as being on the brink of falling into step with the Han majority.

The culmination of the Chinese distrust of pluralistic decentralization is the fear that, either inside or outside the Chinese bureaucratic structure of centralized power, "independent kingdoms" will be formed. Moreover, this fear has been heightened precisely because such kingdoms do inevitably take shape. In part this is because the country is so vast and the population so large that no single authority can penetrate all dimensions of the polity. The formation of such kingdoms is also a response to the Chinese need for greater security than can be provided by the impersonal system of rule; people need to establish more particularistic ties, based on bonds of mutual trust or *guanxi*, which are better able to offer security. There is thus in the Chinese political system a profound contradiction between the doctrine of legitimacy, which requires consensus and no special relationships, and the informal patterns of behavior, in which people do seek out factional ties. The need for such ties becomes greater as the higher officials advance, for as they approach the heights of power they are likely to feel increasingly vulnerable and to need the protection of patrons.[13]

Such "kingdoms" or factions breach the Chinese norm of conformity to the authority of the supreme power. They are therefore compelled to operate in devious ways, behavior which only reinforces the idea that the lower ranks of power are deceitful and a danger to the public good. Indeed, any attempt to organize special interests or to mobilize subordinates to express views contrary to those of the Center is taken in Chinese political culture to be an example of the sin of "self-centeredness," or *geren zhuyi*. This is the case whether the faction or "kingdom" protects only its own members or tries to represent a larger constituency. Indeed, if a "kingdom" tries to articulate popular concerns, it may be seen as tampering with the affections of the public, whose loyalty should lie with the central authorities. As a result, any form of power not associated with the Center appears to be scheming, devious, and subversive, reinforcing the tendency of legitimate power to stress its identification with morality and orthodox ideology.

By the mid 1980s there were signs that the policy initiatives of the regime in the area of political economy were forcing what had been largely informal, *guanxi*-based factions to begin very gradually to articulate local economic interests. Apparently what happened was a paradoxical development in terms of the logic of Chinese political culture. During the Mao era the party was extraordinarily successful in penetrating the whole of society, and therefore the local cadres were able to carry the messages of the Center to all localities. These messages were usually consistent with traditional Chinese politics in that they called for conformity to the behavioral standards of the central authorities and for obedience to the wishes of the ultimate ruler. Under the Deng administration, however, there was a shift away from essentially normative policies, which would call for universal conformity, to policies related to efficiency and utility. In order to carry out the wishes of the Center, cadres found it increasingly necessary to take into account the marginal advantages of their local resources. As a result different localities have begun to favor different policy mixes.[14]

If this trend were to continue, and if the Chinese leaders were to acknowledge openly the possibility of different localities having different interests, it would be a true revolution in Chinese political culture, probably more profound than Mao's ideological revolution, which continued to hold in place the Chinese tradition of honoring consensus and conformity. So far the leadership has not been prepared to publicize the idea that policies which favor some parts of the country may work against the interests of other parts. The most they are prepared to say is that some places may move ahead more rapidly than others and that they need not be held back in their modernization efforts so as to preserve equality. This is, however, a first step toward a more pluralistic and competitive situation.

Denial of Specialization: Ambivalence toward Intellectuals

The traditional Chinese belief that legitimate power should appear to be omnipotent and omnicompetent has made it difficult for technically skilled Chinese to find scope for their skills in government. Historically, of course, the Chinese political system was distinctive because its elite, the mandarinate, claimed status based on superior knowledge, as tested in the highly competitive examination system. Yet, paradoxically, with modernization one of China's most difficult problems has been the question of how much power and what form of power should be permitted to intellectuals. Precisely because the Confucian scholars were so closely identified with the traditional system, it has been awkward for modern intellectuals to find a comfortable role in Chinese politics.

Indeed, from the beginning of the republican period to the present the Chinese political elite have had the lowest proportion of educated people of any political class in Asia. This first became clear when the warlords were calling the tune in organizing the cabinets in the "phantom republic" period.[15] And in the Communist period the members of the Politburo and the State Council have consistently had less education than the prime ministers and cabinet members of Japan, the Southeast Asian states, or India. Moreover, in such countries as Korea, Indonesia, and Thailand, which have military rulers—and even in the Philippines under Marcos— it is more usual for technocrats to be employed in government than it is in China.

The issue is not only that the supreme authority must appear capable of handling all problems without the assistance of subordinates. It is also that China's intellectuals have been unsure as to what role they themselves should claim. Now that they think of themselves as modernized, they seem to be uncertain as to how they should relate to the Chinese political orthodoxies. In the declining years of Manchu rule, Westernized intellectuals could assert the idea that they should learn "Western technologies to preserve Chinese values"—that is, the *t'i-yung* dichotomy. Yet the more the Chinese intellectuals sought to "reform" the Chinese political system, the more difficulty they had with Chinese predispositions about power. As Benjamin Schwartz has demonstrated, the effort of Yen Fu to translate Western liberal thought invariably resulted in distortions which exalted the state and national power in ways quite different from those described by the original Western authors.[16] Western concepts in translation have taken strange forms. John K. Fairbank has observed, "To say that liberalism rests on individualism under the supremacy of law is more sensible and gratifying than to say, as one does in Chinese, that the doctrines of spontaneous license (*ziyu-zhuyi*) rest on the doctrine of self-centeredness (*geren zhuyi*) under the supremacy of administrative regulation (*falü*)."[17]

This is not the place to recount the history of the Chinese intellectuals as they confronted the hostility and violence of warlords, Nationalists, and the Communist authorities. Jonathan Spence has told the story of

huge public, of being correct for the nation—which is a magnification of the traditional Chinese fear of shaming the family and striving only to bring honor to it.

This personalizing of nationalism has contributed to a sense of the theatrical in which the self is cast in a heroic mold; and it makes the Chinese vulnerable to national slights, which are turned into personal insults because the individual is so completely identified with the collectivity. Chinese who lack the boldness to imagine themselves in heroic roles tend to accept their timidity, but, to escape disgrace, they must be just as alert to national slights as to personal insults.[24] Thus no hint of offense to China's national honor is too slight for some official to take note of it and insist that redress is called for in order to preserve "face" for the one billion Chinese.

The psychological dimensions of patriotism in China are significantly different from those in either Japan or India, to say nothing of those in the easygoing Southeast Asian countries. Nationalism in Japan resembles patriotism in China in that the self serves the larger collectivity, but the Japanese are less interested in heroics than in being victorious in practical competition, and the Japanese sense of the heroic is less like grand theater and more like a quiet commitment to a larger cause.[25] The Indian sense of nationalism, which is partially impelled by feelings of past mistreatment, differs even more from the Chinese in that it glorifies parochialisms by elevating them into universalistic values. Indians display their deep feelings of nationalism by simply making the Indian experience the common theme for all the Third World countries. Hence they can forget everything else and dwell only on India as the center of the larger issues of world politics.[26]

Chinese nationalism, as explained by Joseph Levenson, was sustained in modern times by the belief that Chinese culture had unique values that were the essence of Chinese superiority, while the West had only technology—again the Chinese *t'i-yung* dichotomy. This distinction was plausible as long as Confucianism was the formal ideology of China. But later when Mao Zedong took the "foreign" ideology of Marxism-Leninism, added his own "Mao Zedong Thought," and claimed that the result was the "essence" of Chinese civilization, to be defended against foreign contamination, he performed a feat of legerdemain that was one of his most astonishing achievements. Mao's heirs have continued to proclaim that in their ideology they have values that must be defended against "foreign" influence, as they did in the "spiritual pollution" campaign of 1982–83.

Given the upheavals of Chinese society in modern times, and the repeated rounds of attacks on Confucianism and on the "remnants of feudalism," it is hard for Chinese to identify any formal values which they can call the "essence" of their civilization. Yet somehow the Chinese persist in believing that they are culturally distinctive. Of course they are, largely because of features of their social life, their language, daily habits, and simply their ways of doing things; but most of what adds up to "Chineseness" lacks the quality of grandeur to which the Chinese feel they have a claim. Often embarrassed about specific details of their everyday culture, the Chinese usually end up basing their feelings of nationalism on either explicit or implicit concepts of racial identity. The importance of family line, of course, makes it easy to give a biological dimension to their concept of Chinese nationalism.

To question Chinese nationalism then becomes the same thing as challenging one's family. It is simply impossible for Chinese intellectuals to stand back and try to get an objective or critical view of their government. Because the paternalistic style of authority employed by the leaders makes it seem improper to criticize them, the government finds it easy to co-opt intellectuals.

Thus Deng Xiaoping's reforms seem to be having two results. On the one hand, they are forcing local interests to challenge the traditional supremacy of the conformity rules of the Center. On the other hand, the continuing tradition of suspicion toward the foreign-trained Chinese intellectuals, who might help in exploiting the marginal advantages of localities, not only limits their effectiveness but compels them to try to be totally patriotic—that is to say, to be champions of the central authorities.

This major contradiction is enough to raise questions about how smooth China's continuing modernization is likely to be. But in addition, other traditional and still persisting Chinese attitudes about power are creating further problems. The most troublesome are the complications caused by attitudes of dependency toward paternalistic authority, which have grossly distorted the Chinese economy by requiring massive, uneconomical subsidies.

The Comforts of Dependency

It would take us well beyond the boundaries of this study to examine in detail the Chinese centrally planned economy and the regime's efforts to decentralize and create initiatives through various forms of "responsibility" systems. But we do need to take note of the distortions created in the Chinese economy by the extensive system of subsidies and the "irrational" price structure, because the source of this problem, and, more important, the obstacles to its solution, are closely related to our central theme—the importance of cultural perceptions of authority and power in determining patterns of modernization.

The Communists under Mao were not content to base their claim of legitimacy upon their ideological message. They sought further to justify their power by responding to the profound cravings of dependency on the part of the Chinese masses. Their goal was to promise a secure existence, based upon job security, the "iron rice bowl," and most of the necessities of life at below-cost prices. In the initial years of Mao's rule, standards were set which at the time were only slightly out of line with economic reality. The state, as a paternalistic authority, procured grain from the peasants at one price and sold it to urban dwellers at a slightly lower price. In time, however, in order to raise agricultural production and provide resources for investment in irrigation, fertilizers, and machinery, and to give the peasants a greater incentive to produce, the procurement price for grain had to go up even though the expectations of the urban population, and their frozen wages, did not allow for a significant rise in procurement prices for grain.

Similarly, the price of medical care had to stay constant in order to maintain the image of a paternalistic state, although the costs of health care went up. Housing had to be provided at rents that in theory covered maintenance but in practice did not, and therefore the state found that it was not collecting enough to replenish the housing stock. Yet it could not raise rents because the psychology of dependency was so firmly fixed that any increase in housing costs would have been taken as a breach of promise by the paternalistic authority. In addition, subsidies for nearly free goods and services came to cover everything from textiles and bus fares to meat, cabbages, and even scallions. By 1984 the cost of subsidies totaled more than 40 percent of all state expenditures.[27] The strain on the state was enormous, seriously limiting its capacity to make desired investments for modernization.

Thus the belief that the rulers should be paternalistic and that the public has the right to be dependent made the Chinese government a prisoner of its own pretensions of bountifulness. Now the Chinese people are enjoying some comforts, and any hint of a rise in the prices of subsidized goods or services could create pandemonium.

Those trained in economics would say that the situation calls for only one thing: bold leadership, to cut back on subsidies, to raise the wage scale so that people could individually pay for what they bought, and to readjust prices drastically to make them reflect market preferences more accurately. This is clearly impossible, however, because the majority of the urban population have indicated that they prefer a system in which they can confidently depend on a solicitous paternalistic authority over the autonomy that would result if they earned higher wages but did not have the security of the subsidies. Higher wages would be appreciated, but higher prices would be intolerable.

What then is the solution? In the short run, it is for the leadership to display the traditional complement to paternalistic authority, namely, the evasiveness of aloofness, an escape into dignity, and even a distancing from the humdrum matters of the day that is often indistinguishable from irresponsibility.

Diffusion of Accountability

The concerned but distant "father" that underlies the Chinese style of paternalistic authority is free to keep his own counsel and to have his private plans, which everyone assumes will be for the good of the family. He does not have to share his worries with others, nor is he expected to bare his breast and admit to past mistakes.

What this kind of authority figure can do is to retreat, to seek solitude, and to leave current problems to others. The expectation is that they will in time call him back and ask him to take full charge again. The idea that ultimate authority can thus be slightly withdrawn from the immediate scene, but still be omnipotent, makes it seem not at all odd that Deng Xiaoping, China's strong man, does not officially hold any of the supreme posts in either the party or the government. This makes it easier for him to diffuse accountability, which is the ideal Chinese leadership practice.

Although in Chinese politics it is quite acceptable for the ultimate power figure to vacillate between ruling and reigning, those who carry on while the top leader withdraws are not expected to take initiatives, but only to continue the routines. Since power is not meant to be shared, there can be little delegation of authority. The ultimate authority can return to the action and denounce what has transpired in his absence, much as a master returns to criticize what his servants have been up to while he was away. There is thus no real sense of accountability; no one asks, for example, why the leader appointed unworthy stand-ins.[28]

The absence of strict accountability for the leader's actions in Chinese political culture does not mean tolerance for irresponsibility. Rather the relationship of leaders to the public is modeled on the relationships within the Chinese family, in which the father is assumed to be working for the well-being of the family as a whole even while keeping his plans very much to himself. The Chinese father is expected to be aloof and distant, invulnerable to all but the most subtle hints of criticism. To challenge the father's decisions would be equal not just to questioning his judgment, but worse, to suggesting that he has been disloyal to his family and hence to his ancestors. The Chinese child does not have the American child's option of intimidating his father by suggesting that he has been "unfair" by not treating all his children "equally." Children thus learn early that it is not wise to question their parents' conduct; they must instead concentrate on deporting themselves according to the rules of ethics they have been taught in the hope that their exemplary conduct will shield them from the wrath of parental authority. In China it is the parents who use shame to control their children, and not the other way around; and therefore in the adult world those who use shaming to influence the behavior of others usually fancy themselves to be powerful figures.

Very early in their learning experiences Chinese children discover that authority can be influenced more by playing on emotions than by logical reasoning. The threatening father can be humored, or more likely, can be moved by pity or by teasing into taking a relaxed view of the rules. Similarly, in the adult world one tends to use flattery in dealing with authority and to beseech the powerful to be lenient. Chinese children discover that their parents will shamelessly favor one child over the others, and the one that is the favorite can change from day to day according to the moods and emotional state of the father. In short, authority can be whimsical, easily won over by bribes and personal inducements—that is to say, authority is human and not bound by legal rationalism.

The possibility that parents will express their feelings in their relations with their children opens the door not just to disciplining anger and preferential treatment, but more important, to the expression of the warmest and most positive feelings allowed by a culture which otherwise seeks to suppress most manifestations of the emotions. Whereas in Chinese culture most relationships, including even those between husbands and wives, must be carried out with a minimum of demonstrable affect, it is acceptable for parents, and particularly for fathers, to exude pleasure toward their children. Childhood is supposedly the happiest period of life not only because it is free of care and responsibility but also because it is the time when one can be the center of attention and the object of effusive affection. The obvious pleasure that parents get from indulging their children seems to leave the children with a permanent sense of worthiness that can later manifest itself in what others may perceive as Chinese arrogance. The "Middle Kingdom complex" is in part nurtured and sustained by the Chinese child's warm experience of having once been the center of his universe.

Thus the profound sense of security derived from these earliest childhood experiences compels many adult Chinese to seek to recapture a comparable sense of dependency upon paternalistic authority figures whom they perceive to be easily moved by emotional appeals. Gaining the indulgence of authority by being an appealing object of pity is seen as being much the safest course of action in dealing with people who otherwise must be aloof rulers. Above all, Chinese are usually certain that security cannot be found in trying to hold authority accountable. One can display one's own virtues by citing ideological texts and doctrines, but it is never prudent to try to hold the authorities accountable even to the rules that they themselves have issued.

Politics as Surprise, Intrigue, and the Work of Unidentified Forces

The Chinese view that legitimacy should be the monopoly of the supreme authority, together with the feeling that such an authority should only be loosely accountable, highlights the Chinese belief that there is a gray area beyond the domain of politics as defined by the current orthodoxy. Both the common people and the politically sophisticated share the view that much goes on in public life which is not consistent with established doctrines and ideologies.[29] This view is reinforced by the extraordinary value the political elite consistently place on secrecy. The presumption that deception yields high payoffs makes the Chinese suspect that political enemies are hiding behind "sinister plans" and, as the People's Daily has frequently charged, "acting in a wholeheartedly sneaky way."[30]

Chinese politics has consistently operated under the assumption that power is not in fact a monopoly of the formal institutions of government. Yet both in the past and under Communism there have been no codifications of the rules concerning how such informal types of power operate. Since everyone must defer verbally to the formal ideologies of the moment, no one is free to articulate standards for the informal workings of power. The only public discussion of this aspect of power is the rhetoric of condemnation.

The Chinese dilemma of power is not the clash between the ideal and the pragmatic, as in the Soviet Union, or between morality and reality, as in the United States; it presents a much more complex set of contradictions. It stems from the initial belief that rule should be by (virtuous) men and not by (impersonal) law—a cultural belief which makes it difficult for the Chinese to institutionalize authority since they are reluctant to invest power in impersonal arrangements. The dilemma arises because the stated regulations of conduct for officials take the form of private moral precepts geared to formal and public rules, without any recognized guidelines for the informal operation of power. This gray area is large in Chinese politics precisely because the Chinese demand rule by men, not by law.

The only way the Chinese can publicize the actual workings of their politics is by using moral condemnation, which inevitably involves personal corruption. The Chinese press presents national politics in two ways: either government is functioning well, with the leadership providing wise guidance and keeping all of its institutions in order; or evil men are engaged in devious and corrupt practices, and as scoundrels they deserve ruthless punishment. The normal picture of politics found in other countries, in which ordinary politicians are trying to implement unexceptional ideas, is completely missing in the Chinese public version of politics.

All this heightens the element of surprise in Chinese politics. The unexpected constantly occurs because it is improper to examine beforehand what is taking place in the ill-defined area of informal power relationships. The associations, alliances, and conflicts which are the essence of routine political analysis and discussion in other countries are taboo in China. They can only be spoken of as sinister and corrupt activities after the defeated parties have been exposed.[31]

Surprise is also important because the secrecy that shrouds informal political relationships makes it exceedingly difficult even for the participants to read the map of the distribution of power in the polity. People simply do not know how much power different actors command. Therefore figures presumed to be centers of power may turn out to be straw men, while others can suddenly surface, supported by more associates than anyone knew they had.

This uncertainty about power makes the unexpected more likely, which in turn causes the Chinese to emphasize more than Westerners do the importance of "luck" and good or bad "fortune" in calculating the nature of power. Similarly, politicians in few other countries attach as much importance to the factor of timing in the determination of political outcomes. Chinese politicians are profoundly sensitive to the fact that the power at their disposal is in constant flux. If the timing is right and the moment propitious, their actual power can be miraculously magnified many times—hence the implausible ambitiousness of Lin Biao's coup attempt, the expectations of the Gang of Four, or even the dreams of glory of the hapless Hua Guofeng. But if the timing is wrong, power will of its own accord dissolve into nothing.[32]

Anticipation of the unexpected has taught the Chinese that the force of history is beyond the reach of any of the principal actors. They accept the idea that the locus of power is external not only to themselves but to everyone else as well.[33] Indeed, all aspects of Chinese political culture, its mores and countermores, converge to reinforce the idea that considerable, indeed decisive, power lies beyond the command of any actor—a form of free-floating determinism which one can hope to benefit from, but which nobody can control. The traditional Chinese concept of legitimacy as the Mandate of Heaven located ultimate power in a mystical realm. The instinct of power holders to avoid accountability suggests that they do not believe that they have as much power as they pretend to have. The concept of rule by example requires that there be intermediary forces which will ensure that respect is translated into deference. Subordinates seek the mystique that will bring them power beyond their station, and finally, those who are weak have faith that their virtues will be rewarded.

The belief that power can exist beyond the control of anyone was once formalized in the Taoist doctrine of the Way, and in the principle of non-effort or wu-wei. In modern times the Communists have recreated it in their almost magical beliefs in the "dialectic" and in the Marxist linear laws of "history." In recent years China's foreign policy has been more constantly and delicately adjusted than most foreign policies to judgments of the changing flow of international power relationships. Whether it was at the time of "East Wind prevailing over West Wind," or of "one superpower rising and the other in decline," the Chinese objective always has been, in the words of the *People's Daily*, "to Ride on the Wind to Break through the Waves."

The quest for modernization reflects the Chinese belief in the power of external forces. Non-Marxist intellectuals once argued that just as in the West the Golden Age of Greece and the Roman Empire were followed by the Dark Ages which ended in the Renaissance and the beginnings of the modern age, so would China have its "renaissance." "Modernization" was thus inevitable.[34]

Personal Dedication and Loyalty

Psychologically, the Chinese faith in benign forces beyond the immediate command of any actor manifests the positive sense of dependency, nurtured by the feeling of belonging to a group that is basic to Chinese socialization. As members of collectivities to which the individual must submit, the Chinese are taught that the power of the group is substantially greater than that of the sum of its members. They assume that the dedicated and loyal commitment of each individual to the collectivity, manifested by correct personal conduct and deference to the symbols of authority, can help to bring good fortune and unexpected success to the collectivity, whether it be the family, the class, the party, or the country.

These attitudes produce a unique Chinese blend of single-mindedness and wishful thinking. In China people work tirelessly while always suspecting that their fate is in the hands of others. One can therefore hope, or more correctly gamble, on luck. Hence the ambivalence about effort and willpower in Chinese political culture. Sometimes Chinese leaders are keenly sensitive to the dangers of dissipating their energies and seem anxious to find strategies that will bring success with a minimum of effort or risk—another example of the value of deception and surprise. At other times they call for a maximum expenditure of effort by demanding that the masses display willpower and determination.

Their belief in dedication and single-mindedness makes the Chinese contemptuous of those who are less fervent. Any behavior that might divert them from single-mindedness is considered both improper and a sign of disloyalty. Therefore those who do not join in the collective spirit of dedication become legitimate objects of scorn, as well as victims of rebuke by the group.

Mao initiated cycles of mass mobilization campaigns to teach the people that willpower and enthusiasm would bring about miracles. Under Mao's successor the great campaigns have ceased, but the call for dedication continues. The leadership seems to have forgotten the historic Chinese work ethic that has always existed in spite of the Taoist belief in non-effort. It was only the officials who, contrary to their Confucian teaching, venerated leisure. Mao himself seemed to believe that purposefulness was not enough, that there had to be enthusiasm as well as a manifestation of loyalty, if the collectivity was to achieve extra benefits beyond the sum of individual contributions.[35]

It is probable that the root of Mao's problem was the Chinese cultural trait of separating emotions from action, which required children to suppress their natural feelings of aggression, especially toward a domineering father, and learn to act according to prescribed norms. Because of this squelching of emotional spontaneity, Mao could never be sure of the true sentiments of his people. Hence he instigated more and more campaigns to prove that they were loyal to his authority.

Other leaders besides Mao have had the same problem, although their attempted solutions have not usually been so extreme. The issue of loyalty has been a central problem of Chinese politics. Leaders tend to believe that total loyalty ensures success, while failure usually raises suspicions of treachery. The psychological core of the attitude is the Chinese masking of emotions.

Ideology: Obstacle to Rational Use of Power

The political effect of a socialization process that separates feelings from action has been to impose upon the otherwise pragmatic and materialistic Chinese a belief that politics should be highly moralistic if not socialistic. This contradiction has led most observers to characterize the Chinese as vacillating between "ideology" and "pragmatism" when factions inclined to one tendency or the other have gained ascendancy. To understand this phenomenon it is important to appreciate that the contradiction is not solely between groups but also relates to the character of individuals. Those identified as "pragmatists" in the post-Mao era profess an interest in ideology; their opponents, who are usually classed as "leftists," have proved to be skilled in the "pragmatic" art of bureaucratic maneuvering. A cloak of morality is needed because the idea of applied power is associated with feelings of aggression, which have been deeply repressed in the Chinese socialization process.[36]

The Chinese predilection for ideological discourse is quite different from the Russian or Bolshevik tradition of intense concern with doctrinal matters. Although there are extensive areas of congruence between Mao Zedong Thought and conventional Marxism-Leninism, there is a key difference between the ways in which they relate power to ideology, a difference that goes far to explain the diverging development of Chinese and Russian Communism. In the Soviet tradition, doctrinal issues are assumed to be matters of supreme importance because, first, beliefs are held to be decisive in governing action, and second, doctrinal issues are supposed to be foolproof tests for separating the faithful from the traitorous heretics. Hence battles over ideological statements are the normal way of determining policies and of distinguishing friend from foe. The Chinese certainly are not insensitive to Lenin's cardinal question of strategy, that of determining the "who-whom" issue of friend and enemy, as witness Mao's skillful adoption of the traditional Bolshevik style of debate in his polemics with Khrushchev. Yet, the more common Chinese use of ideology is to employ high sounding sentiments as a way of asserting the sense of moral superiority that is associated with legitimacy. Of course, the Chinese also use ideology in their disputations and in anathematizing their opponents.

The gap between words and actions, between doctrinal theories and practice, in Chinese political culture is wider than in almost any other culture. The Chinese tolerance for what others might consider to be hypocrisy is really their way of avoiding the troublesome problem of allowing later actions to become the prisoner of earlier words. Some students of Chinese Communism believed for a long time that Mao Zedong had achieved a higher degree of unity of theory and action than Lenin and the Russians had ever realized, but we know now from the revelations about the Cultural Revolution that Chinese rhetoric even in that supposedly ideologically supercharged era bore little relation to actual practice.

Thus, whereas in Soviet culture, and generally in Western culture, correctness about doctrinal questions has a value in itself, in Chinese culture there is a more relaxed view about basic matters of faith and belief. One need only reflect on the contrast between the Western and Chinese religious traditions to sense the great difference between the Chinese and Western Communist approaches to the role of ideology. In the secular realm the Chinese scholarly tradition did include careful analysis of textual questions, and at times different interpretations of a single word did divide the mandarin community. In general, however, the Chinese did not assume that policy changes flowed directly from doctrinal arguments, but rather they saw disputes over interpretations as the forum for power struggles.

For both Confucian and Communist Chinese, ideology has been important, not only as a guide for action, but also as a way of making the moral claims associated with leadership, and more important, of protecting discussion of politics from the very threatening possibility that explicit talk could lead to the chaos they associate with factional strife. Such talk is threatening because it comes close to bringing into the open the feelings of aggression which the Chinese have been taught to suppress.

In consequence the Chinese leaders profess their ideologies largely to legitimize their claims of authority. It is their way of asserting that they are superior and hence deserving of deference. Masters of morally respectable ideologies can treat disdainfully those who cannot articulate their passions with grace. Logical contradictions and, even more important, contradictions between words and actions need not compromise the legitimacy of a leader, so long as his protestations have the vital pretension of moral authority which signals that his instincts of aggression are under control. Historically, there have been few great conflicts involving the splitting of doctrinal hairs among Chinese who professed to share the same ideology, and there has certainly been nothing to compare with the turbulent history of Western Marxism and, more particularly, of Russian Bolshevism. In Chinese Communism the leaders have contended and the losers have been purged, but the conflicts have been over matters of power and status and only secondarily over doctrinal questions. The losers have, of course, been denounced for their ideological failings, but more as part of a ritual of condemnation than as a defense of the purity of doctrine. Even the Great Cultural Revolution, which seemed in the West to be an example of ideological madness, was largely a conflict over power in which the cultural restraints of aggression were broken and the passions of hatred flowed freely. Although the Red Guards proclaimed ideological purity and the need for blind faith, their understanding of ideology was more simplistic than that of any other group in the entire history of Communism.

Thus we find an interesting paradox. The Chinese have a great need for ideology, yet in practice they seem to ignore the content of ideology; they do what advances their self-interest without amending the substance of their ideology. They can profess, as Deng Xiaoping's administration has done, a dedication to "socialism" and even to international Communism, while acting in ways totally inconsistent with what Westerners consider to be true socialism. Doctrine thus becomes both a way of masking one's feelings of aggression and a means of confusing opponents about one's motives. For Chinese Communism this has meant that ritualized talk about the importance of ideology is comforting to all concerned, but in practice a great deal of tolerance has been shown to what passes as being consistent with ideology. The existence of personalized rule, rather than institutionalized procedures, makes it normal for ideology to be whatever the supreme ruler says it should be. The Russians, by contrast, must uphold the purity of ideology, the sacredness of the party, and the abomination of overt dissent, even while they accept suppressed cynicism and corruption. The Chinese leaders simply claim that what they want is ideologically good, frequently ignoring the problems of consistency and logical contradictions. They are able to do this because as national leaders they can and must claim to be both omnipotent and morally supreme.

Consequently, in Chinese politics there is a continuous problem of the purposeful use of power. In manipulating power, the leader tends to go to extremes: sometimes he is the masterful "teacher" who "effortlessly" achieves results either by shaming others or by using ploys and tricks; and sometimes he is the ruthless aggressor who dispenses harsh, or even cruel, punishment. The two extremes can be rationalized when good people are made to do the right thing merely by being shamed; when a person is not hurt by shame, then he must be truly evil and an object of severe punishment. The psychological transition must be made from the controlled use of moral pressure to outbursts of aggression which can be legitimately released.

Shaming is a very blunt instrument, especially for purposes of public policy. Nevertheless, it is difficult for the Chinese to initiate even routine administrative policies or programs without giving them a strong moral or idealistic gloss, followed by suggestions that anyone who fails to comply with the policy is morally deficient. Such is the logic of paternalistic authority. The rule must be total conformity. Yet at the same time leaders are expected to be clever—to have tricks which will cause the evil ones to do themselves in of their own accord.

This style of leadership produces a gap between moralistic and hopeful rhetoric and constant maneuvering and experimentation. Beneath their respective ideological covers Mao Zedong and Deng Xiaoping have been each other's equal in shifting policies while trying to come up with ingenious solutions, none of which they could live with for long.

Their grand ideological visions and restless attempts to be clever have made the Chinese exploit the human potential of hope more than any of the other Asian political cultures. Daily politics in China is made up of responses to people's cravings for a better life that promise miraculous changes just around the corner. The "pragmatist" Deng and the "visionary" Mao have both used these cravings to strengthen their hold on power. No modern Chinese leader has gained an audience by being an objective realist. Mao's pure-minded revolutionary society and Deng's prosperous economy have both caused the multitudes of Chinese, as well as supposedly knowledgeable foreign observers, to suspend disbelief and rationalize wishful thinking.

Chinese politics has also exploited an emotion which is the opposite of hope, namely, fear, when leaders have adopted draconian measures to compel compliance and punish deviance. The mechanics of fear in Chinese politics blends the terror of being out of step, of being singled out in contempt, with the horrors of physical torture and exile to the countryside. It is hard at any one moment to evaluate the role of fear as an aspect of power in Chinese politics because the culture invariably deals with the matter in terms of the past, rather than identifying fear as part of the present. People feel free to protest, or more correctly, they feel they must conform in protesting, how terrifying life was in a previous period—that is, how cruel the Gang of Four were, how awful the Cultural Revolution was, how vicious the Kuomintang was before Liberation, how dangerous the warlords were, how heartless the Manchus were. Yet there is a strange silence as to whether fear exists in the present. Foreigners who visited China in the early 1970s learned years later that many people who enthusiastically greeted them were living all the while in fear of the Gang of Four and their followers. In the mid-1980s Chinese intellectuals were not explaining to visitors how they felt about the campaign against "spiritual pollution," and bureaucrats were equally evasive about the "rectification" campaign against the "three types of persons": those who had risen to higher positions by following the Lin Biao and Jiang Qing cliques and who held that "it is right to rebel"; those who had serious factionalist ideas; and those who had engaged in "beating, smashing, and looting."

In short, power in the Chinese political system remains a crude, blunt instrument, generally inappropriate for a government striving to solve the complex problems of modernization. Each act of authority, each proclaimed policy, tends to be enveloped in affect, either blind hopefulness or diffuse fear, or a blend of both, and consequently the precision of rational authority is missing. Thus policy is usually thought of in imprecise ways; it either turns into heroic statements or is reduced to slogans. The translation of public rhetoric into operational or administrative language is usually imperfectly done.

This Chinese approach to power explains why the basic rhythm of Chinese politics is an alternation between the tightening of authority and the relaxing of controls. The political pendulum has not swung between left and right so much as between clamping down and letting up. It is, of course, the hope of the centralized authorities that relaxation of direct controls will produce spontaneous public behavior that will conform to their ideas of what is desirable—much as the Chinese father hopes, but without much confidence, that his children will act in the ways he desires even when he is not supervising them. Since precise guidance is impossible, the major question for authority concerns what should be the limits of benevolent tolerance before total control again becomes necessary.

This problem goes beyond the difficulties that policymakers have in efficiently directing governmental power. It also affects the way in which critics evaluate the performance of those in command of national or local power. They seem to have little ability to point out the technical failings of policies, and thus they usually have little to say about what needs to be done next. Their criticisms are generally moralistic rather than analytical. Moreover, in modern times Chinese intellectuals, writers, and journalists have rarely asked probing questions about the Chinese condition. By contrast, Indian intellectuals do not hesitate to ask why their country has failed to achieve their lofty aspirations. Russian intellectuals, and not only the dissidents, also ask themselves the "why" questions: "Why has Russia gone wrong?" "Why is there no hope?" "Why is there no real political option for Russia?" "Why do Russians fear chaos more than slavery?"[37]

Given the trauma suffered by educated Chinese in the last thirty years, it is astonishing that they seem intellectually and emotionally satisfied to blame all that went wrong on the Gang of Four and Lin Biao. Even those who have defected or are in a secure situation tend not to ask operational questions about policies and the uses of power. For example, in the late 1970s during a period of liberalization Chinese writers produced what they called "Wounded Literature," stories of the suffering caused by the Cultural Revolution, which the Chinese considered to be bold reflections but which, not only by Western standards but by those of other Asian cultures, seemed almost evasive in explaining what had gone wrong.[38] Their explanations of events in their national history tended to do nothing more sophisticated than to point out the personal faults of particular leaders. There has been no lack of intellectual ability or human sensitivity; rather, the problem is that in Chinese culture there is no tradition of the articulation of systematic uses of power for policy objectives. The Chinese tend to think of power as scheming maneuvers and ploys—activities that can hardly account for the profound movements of history.

Moreover, introspection is neither a well-developed nor a respected activity in Chinese culture. The individual is expected to focus on his relations with others, not on his inner state. The Chinese tradition of autobiography allows for only a recounting of experiences, not the elaboration of feelings. The soul-searching novel is yet to appear. Chinese intellectuals give the impression that they must constantly guard against looking inward for fear that they might find something too frightening.

Bureaucracy: Hierarchies Plus What?

The Chinese view of power as something other than a means for achieving utilitarian ends has created problems in the operation of the bureaucracy. It has always been easy for the Chinese to establish bureaucratic hierarchies because they have an instinct for recognizing fine status differences and their social order is a continuum of rankings from the lowest person to the highest official. Yet, once the hierarchy has been established, so much energy is expended in the interplay of relations between superiors and subordinates that at times there is little left over for accomplishing anything else.

The problems of policy formation and implementation in China's bureaucracies have been analyzed so extensively that there is little need to dwell on all the recognized difficulties.[39] Both Mao Zedong and Deng Xiaoping have railed against "bureaucratism," but neither leader has had the knack of reducing his grand pronouncements to an effective guide for administrative performance. Consequently Chinese bureaucrats have not tended to seek their own personal security by accomplishing goals, but by proclaiming achievements and treating the symbolism of policies as a reality.

Richard Baum has summarized five characteristics of Chinese thought which have impeded the rationalization of science. These can also be used to explain the obstacles to using power effectively in the bureaucracy. "There are, first, an ongoing intellectual tradition of *cognitive formalism* that has its historic roots in the metaphysical pseudoscience of classical Chinese philosophy; second, a methodological tradition of *narrow empiricism* that has characterized much of Chinese scientific inquiry over the past two millennia; third, a pronounced quality of dogmatic scientism in the ethos of epistemology of Chinese communism; fourth, a persistent legacy of *feudal bureaucratism* in the political culture of modern China; and fifth, a dominant behavioral style of *compulsive ritualism* deeply engrained in the process by which Chinese children are socialized to become responsive, compliant adults."[40] These features combine to make Chinese officials believe that in their hierarchical arrangements they should receive the right instructions so that in a formalistic way they can respond with the one current answer to whatever the situation demands. When the demand is for creativity, the response tends to be not an act of imagination but a display of dedication, a commitment to the symbols of loyalty, and the easing of general commands to subordinates.

Chinese leaders, in trying to get more out of their bureaucracies in order to advance modernization, have repeatedly engaged in administrative "reforms." Their concept of reform has led them to call for a reorganization in which the number of ministries is reduced and departments are shifted about. The results of such reforms have not been impressive because they have not touched the key hierarchical relationships or the cultural attitudes about power and action. Indeed, the reshuffling of organizations often has had negative consequences, for it has increased insecurity and made officials look inward to find security in their personal and particularistic ties. It has also often made coordination more difficult by reducing even further the weak flow of communication between the separate hierarchies.

In spite of Chinese bureaucratic inefficiency, the bureaucracy sometimes works well. This usually happens when two significant conditions are met: first, when the policy has been reduced to very simple and explicit guidelines; and second, when there is a clear basis for a paternalistic-dependency relationship between the bureaucrats and the respondents to the policies. For example, the elaborate system of rationing and of managing the various subsidies can be smoothly carried out because the regulations can be codified and the recipients can see a paternalistic authority acting in support of their dependency needs.

As long as these two conditions are met, policies which might seem to go against the grain of Chinese tradition can be successful. The most striking example of this is the policy of limiting families to one child. The rules are easily communicated, and the government can be seen as acting with a full array of rewards and punishments, ensuring that if the parents conduct themselves correctly they will be treated with favor, and if they do not they can expect disciplinary action.

More often, however, bureaucratic problems hamper policy implementation because only the grand goals are set forth and the operational concepts are missing. The Chinese ideals of authority and power do not call for the ability to design operational programs.

The Elusive Goal of Modernization

These Chinese approaches to power have meant that, while there has been a consensus in favor of modernization in the form of building national power and economic growth, there has not been any real public discussion about alternative ways of seeking the goal. More important, the Chinese have been unable to allow open competition of values and power; that is, they have had to try to modernize without the benefit of real politics, or genuine political processes. Their fear of competition makes them distrustful of factionalism. More energy goes into checking deviation than into exploring alternative policy approaches. The appeal to dedication and to loyalty inhibits imagination and stifles creativity.

These problems have plagued the Chinese from their first reform efforts of 1898 to Deng Xiaoping's "pragmatic" reforms after the era of Mao Zedong. The continued theme of hope and expectation has been sustained by a deep craving for a better and stronger authority which can somehow solve the nation's problems. Leadership has been all-important because the Chinese have such an exaggerated need for authority. The individual who has no dependable *guanxi* connection feels helpless, and the public is wholly dependent upon its leaders. Yet too often the leaders of modernization have been reduced to elucidating moralistic ideologies and alluding to ingenious but secret magical solutions. The history of twentieth century modernization attempts is a story of abiding faith in official cleverness. The incessant railing against bureaucratism is the Chinese way of expressing frustration arising from the exaggerated expectation of what governmental authority should be.

Beginning with the idea that the superior Chinese should easily be able to outwit the "barbarian," especially by using his own technology against him, the Chinese have continued to believe that there must be some clever formula, some simple trick, that would restore China to greatness—and even turn the tables on the threatening West. In Deng Xiaoping's China, cleverness has focused on "reverse engineering," that is, obtaining a model of a foreign technology, figuring out how it works, and by sheer hard work replicating it at what is expected to be a lower cost. Although, in one area after another, from building aircraft engines to manufacturing mining equipment, the approach has not worked, the Chinese have not been discouraged. Ever in search of more advanced technologies, they ignore the fact that their past failures occurred largely because they had not yet built up the necessary base of fundamental skills and technology. Just as with political power, the Chinese approach is to try to work down from the top, rather than to build upward from solid foundations.

Mao's exaggerated promises and exhausting campaigns, which brought little progress, have resulted in skepticism if not cynicism, especially among the younger generation. Although this disillusionment with past failures could take an unhealthy turn, it could be a blessing in disguise. It could have a positive effect if the Chinese began to feel less morally and culturally superior to others, less thin-skinned about accepting advice and criticism, and hence more open to the competition of ideas.

So far, however, all the traditional Chinese instincts for conformity and for centralized power remain. Talk of reform is easy, as it always has been, but the centralized bureaucracy remains firmly in place. Deng Xiaoping has suggested that experiments in decentralization should be tried, but the China of the mid-1980s remains a centralized state. The attempts at bringing in foreign entrepreneurs through joint ventures or direct investments are significant liberalizing steps which may open the way to greater changes. Yet there are still signs that any little problem could trigger off a tightening of centralized controls.

Premier Zhao Ziyang summarized the value of decentralization, but the greater importance of centralization, in his report to the sixth National People's Congress in June 1983, when he said: "It is wrong to exercise excessive and rigid control over specific economic activities of enterprises which hamstring their initiative. A proper measure of flexibility is entirely necessary. But major economic activities that concern overall interests should nevertheless be centralized. Any attempt to weaken such centralization means retrogression rather than progress and cannot ensure the growth of our economy along socialist lines."[41]

If the leadership could conquer its fears, check its monopolistic bureaucracy, and allow greater relaxation of centralized controls, the result might be a surge of competitive achievements with the more fortunate provinces exploiting their comparative advantages. Such provinces as Guandong, Fujian, Zhejiang, and Hopei might in fact be able to join the NICs (newly industrialized countries). Forced into competition, they might follow the path of Taiwan, Hong Kong, and Singapore in casting aside the inhibiting concepts of power inherent in Chinese culture and focusing on the down-to-earth qualities of economics.

What is equally likely, however, is that the passing of Deng Xiaoping will bring attention back to the Center, causing the Chinese to worry about the future until they once again have a supreme leader who will satisfy their need for dependency. Unfortunately for China's modernization, the favored provinces are not likely to exploit the opportunity for autonomous development which any serious contendings between post-Deng factions might offer. Chinese culture, especially after the ideological impact of Marxism–Leninism–Mao Zedong Thought, is less ready than ever to accept divisions of authority and precise accountability. The dependence upon the collectivity is as strong as ever. Indeed, nearly every area of reforms is certain to run into the obstacles of subsidies, job security, and seniority arrangements, and into anxieties about the unknown consequences of change, all of which are sustained by the cultural feelings of dependency.

Thus it seems likely that China's route to modernization will continue to be the extremely difficult one of trying to achieve goals within a political system which is highly centralized, disciplined by a moralistic ideology, and heavily dependent upon authority. The fate of a billion Chinese will rest upon the personal qualities of its next supreme leader. The real "tragedy of the Chinese revolution" is that even with all the shocks the country has gone through, its culture is still one of extreme dependence upon authority. Yet, as China becomes more open, increasing numbers of Chinese will certainly come to realize that while they were absorbed in their illusions of revolutionary heroics their neighbors were racing ahead of them in modernizing. Although the shock resulting from the stupidity of the Cultural Revolution and the Maoist excesses has not been so great as the KMT's humiliation at losing the Civil War, it has been great enough to instill a degree of humility in a culture that has always been obsessed with its own greatness. Therefore the potential for significant change exists. Increasing numbers of Chinese have the ability to think through their country's problems and arrive at undogmatic solutions.

The question that will be decisive in determining not only the future of China but the stability of Asia is whether people of such minds will win out in the post-Deng succession struggle, or whether power will slip back into the hands of conservative bureaucrats anxious to preserve traditional Chinese attitudes toward power and authority.

8

Korea, Taiwan, and Vietnam: Forms of Aggressive Confucianism

A CLOSE EXAMINATION of development in the small Confucian countries of Korea and Vietnam reveals variations on a common tradition that are just as great as those between China and Japan. A brief look at Taiwan's approach shows, too, that whereas Korea and Taiwan are frequently treated as very similar cases because they are both successful NICs that have relied upon export-led growth, they have followed significantly different development paths. And of course a comparison between Taiwan and the Mainland uncovers important, shared features of Chinese culture.

Korea's evolution falls somewhere between the Chinese and Japanese patterns of Confucianism. Although the Koreans accepted the Chinese ideal of a virtuocracy for their ruling mandarins, the Korean *yangbans* were openly competitive in their use of power, much like the Japanese samurai. While the Chinese system had a strong emperor figure and a disciplined, if not always dutiful, bureaucracy, the Koreans had a relatively weak king and a strong aristocracy which did not always take gracefully to the idea of being part of a bureaucratic hierarchy; in this sense the *yangbans* resembled the competitive daimyos of Japan.

By contrast, the Vietnamese, in spite of their deep hatred for their longtime Chinese rulers, came closer than all the other non-Chinese Confucian societies to emulating the Chinese system of power. This was particularly the case with respect to the Chinese ideal of rule by a bureaucracy staffed with mandarins well-versed in the Confucian classics. There were, however, two fundamental differences. First, power in Vietnam tended to have a geographical, regional base, and family alliances and marriages were openly used to build power constellations in ways unknown in China. Second, beneath the level of the mandarin officials, who were oriented toward the Confucian court at Hue, the great bulk of the Vietnamese population had ideas about power that were still strongly influenced by the historic Southeast Asian traditions.

Korea: A Risk-taking Culture

Ever since gaining independence from Japan, the Koreans have experienced a crisis of authority. Its roots resemble those of the Chinese authority crisis: the Koreans also believe that their difficulties can be traced to the inadequacies of the ultimate political authority, who should be able to handle all problems, as should the ideal father in the family. Everything in Korean politics has to be played out at the center of highest authority, thus leading to what Gregory Henderson has called a "politics of the vortex."[1] As Harold Hinton has said, "Korea was probably the most centralized and uniformly administrative state in traditional Asia."[2]

The Korean crisis, however, is even more complex than the Chinese, for contemporary Korean culture includes contradictory views of the basis of legitimacy. Traditional attitudes that favor a strong, domineering style of authority are still very much alive; but highly educated Koreans also believe in democratic ideals and the obligation of authority to respond to popular sentiments. The result has been a recurring problem of legitimacy. Koreans create this problem for themselves by simultaneously wanting their leaders to be supermen and insisting, perhaps more than in any other Asian culture, that everyone has a right to assert his or her views and to be treated with respect. There is dependency upon authority, but there is also the feeling that the dependent ones should be secure enough to assert themselves. As individuals, therefore, Koreans can suddenly drop their deferential style and become combative defenders of their rights. Hence the popular image of Koreans as the "Irish of the East."

Although the Korean *yangban* as a bureaucratic scholar-official was modeled after the Chinese Confucian scholar, hereditary advantages gave him a sense of security in ruthlessly demanding his rights. According to Pak Chi-won (1737–1805), a *yangban*, no matter how poor, could not engage in manual labor. Pak wrote in the *Tale of a Yangban*, "Even though a yangban be poor and rusticated in the country, he is still a law unto himself; a man who can demand his neighbor's cow so that his fields be plowed first, and who may require the people of the district to weed his fields. Should someone slight the yangban, the wretch will be seized and lye will be poured down his nose, and he will be tied down by his topknot and his beard will be torn out hair by hair, and no one will attend his grievances."[3]

Although the combination of Japanese colonial rule, the struggle for independence, and the social dislocations of war have eliminated the *yangban* as a class, the idea endures that every right and prerogative owed one should be asserted, so that not only superiors but also common people are quick to claim their privileges. At the same time, encounters that might develop into clashes of will are usually effectively checked by the strong sense of social solidarity. The fear of social isolation, strong in all the Confucian cultures, may be most intense among Koreans.[4]

It would be disingenuous not to take note of an element of cruelty in the Korean use of power. Cruelty bulked large in the struggle of the *yangbans*. It surfaced frequently during the period of Japanese occupation when Koreans were recruited by the Japanese *kempeitai* to carry out torture, particularly in China during the Japanese occupation of that country; and the brutality of the Korean War and the continuing sense of national insecurity have "legitimized" the Korean officials' use of harsh methods against perceived foes. As in traditional China, the need to suppress feelings of aggression in most social contexts seems to have produced psychic pleasure in torturing others when aggression becomes legitimized. In addition, those with power tend to have a vivid sense of a great divide between their own virtue and the wickedness of their opponents, so that it seems only proper to strike the foe as hard as possible and to make him suffer.

It might seem that Koreans operating in a world filled with such dangers would be extremely cautious in their dealings with the powerful. It is true that they tend to be formal and correct in the presence of authority. Yet one of the striking contradictions of Korean political culture is that in spite of manifest dangers, the Korean tends to be willing to take high risks. This boldness and audacity are apparent in many aspects of Korean behavior. In decision-making, Koreans will routinely plunge ahead in adventurous fashion with little apparent anxiety over the possible consequences.[5] This spirit of risk-taking became an even more notable feature of Korean elite behavior after the Korean War, evidently for two reasons.

The first reason is that the Koreans seem to have gone through what Martha Wolfenstein first described as the "disaster syndrome" as a result of the North Korean invasion and the widespread destruction and loss of life in the ensuing war.[6] According to this syndrome, people who survive a major disaster in which friends and neighbors are killed usually go through a definite sequence of psychological states: first, they become numb, dazed, and generally ineffective, as did the Korean people and their leaders immediately after the war ended; and then comes a period of experiencing guilt for having survived while others died. In order to overcome such feelings of guilt the survivors begin to convince themselves that somehow they must be special since they were not among the victims. In time this produces a sense of being invulnerable to danger and hence a greater readiness to assume risks in the future. This syndrome helps to explain why refugees who were uprooted by the partition of India turned out to be conspicuously greater risk-takers as entrepreneurs than comparable people who had not been uprooted.[7]

Having suffered as much as they did, but in the end surviving, the victorious Koreans, both government officials and civilians, soon came to see themselves as exceptional and destined for great things. The war experience also taught them a great deal about organizing themselves in disciplined ways to perform difficult tasks. Thus, while the whole society was exposed to the model of military effectiveness based on ideals of duty, sacrifice, and responsibility, the people were also encouraged to think in bold terms and to believe that, as surviving Koreans, they were somehow unique and capable of great achievements.

Second, because the Koreans were given tremendous support through American aid, they came to count on a safety net to save them from any disaster. From 1953 to 1962, American aid funded 70 percent of Korea's imports and 80 percent of all its fixed capital investments.[8] The massive amounts of aid Korea received after the war created a completely new world for Koreans, giving them the feeling of security which their cultural need for dependency made them crave. By contrast, during the pre–Korean War period of American occupation, there was little guidance or support, and consequently political developments were somewhat aimless.[9] The one noteworthy achievement of the American military government was the introduction of an effective land reform program, made easier by the redistribution of former Japanese-owned lands.

The massive amounts of U.S. aid during the 1950s and early 1960s greatly strengthened an already effective state bureaucracy, originally created by the Japanese during colonial days, and encouraged a lasting pattern of close relations between private entrepreneurs and the government. In the view of many people the intimate relations between AID, the Korean government, and Korean business produced an aura of corruption, if not the actual thing.[10] This contributed to a paradox of power: the Korean state has steadily become stronger, with nearly every element in the society looking to it for protection or support; but at the same time the legitimacy of the government has steadily come into question.

Paradoxically, Korea has what is customarily classified as a "strong state" system, but it also has a fragile basis of governmental legitimacy. Each of the main leaders has in different ways contributed to this contradictory pattern of development. President Syngman Rhee took over the state bureaucracy and then built up his Liberal party through the National Agricultural Cooperative Federation, which had been created by the U.S.-inspired land reform measures. In the urban areas, Rhee built political power through a trade union movement which was dominated by the Liberal party. Rhee's approach to government was that of using patronage to build up dependent relationships, and then demanding ever greater sacrifices to his authority. By 1952 he was caught up in feuds with leaders in the National Assembly, who recognized his increasingly autocratic tendencies. In the same year he finally forced the Assembly to extend his term as president and then, in 1954, to amend the constitution to remove the previous two-term limit on the president's tenure.[11] That he did not get the required two-thirds majority placed his subsequent presidency in doubt. The aging Rhee responded in ever more Confucian ways, stating that government should not be ruled by laws but by superior men. In the July 1960 election for the National Assembly, the opposition Democratic party gained a two-thirds majority over Rhee's Liberal party, but it soon split into contending factions, as is typical of Koreans without a strong leader. Student demonstrations forced Rhee from office, and then on May 16, 1961, a military coup brought to power Park Chung Hee.

Although Park began his rule by coup, he sought to legitimize it by resigning from the army, forming the Democratic Republican party, and winning a presidential election in October 1963. Park, in time, followed Rhee's pattern of first using irregular methods to amend the constitution to give himself another term, and then forcing through, under martial law, a new constitution, the *Yushin,* or Revitalizing Reform Constitution. Besides compromising the legitimacy of his rule, Park concentrated ever greater powers under his direct control in the Blue House. As opposition grew, he increasingly relied upon a combination of patronage, successful economic policies, and the coercive powers of the Korean Central Intelligence Agency.

As Park's rule became more centralized and authoritarian, he shifted the base of Korean dependency. The safety net of national security continued to be the United States, but he tried to reduce Washington's leverage on his policies by seeking economic help from the Japanese government and foreign banks. "Outstanding debt jumped from about

$300 million in 1965 to over $13 billion by 1979, though it is a testament to Korea's export performance that the debt service ratio remained relatively constant over the entire period."[12] The bureaucracy restricted direct foreign investments, forced an increase in exports, and channeled loans to favored industries and enterprises, with the result that in a few years Korea built up a series of large industrial-financial conglomerates under close government support, a system which was in many respects similar to the Japanese *zaibatsu* monopolies supported by MITI. This combination of government-encouraged monopolies and aggressive foreign borrowing of necessary capital has helped the Korean economy to grow even faster than Japan's did at a comparable stage, because the *zaibatsu* had to depend solely upon capital from domestic, although always understanding, banks.

Chalmers Johnson is correct in seeing many similarities between the Korean and Japanese approaches to government-business relations, in which "soft authoritarian" states guide capitalist development according to planning that is consistent with market forces.[13] Yet the differences are also significant. In many respects MITI has had to be more "low-postured" in trying to influence Japanese industrialists than the Korean authorities have been. Moreover, there are striking examples of Japanese industry disregarding MITI and still achieving success—as, for instance, in automobiles and early electronics—something that would have been impossible for Korean industrialists to do. In contrast to MITI's conservative bias, the Korean economic czars have generally been aggressive risk-takers.[14] Indeed, the strategy of the Koreans in moving from import substitution to export-led growth by heavy use of foreign loans has had a degree of audacity that was generally lacking in Japan.

The rapid success of Korea's export-led growth strategy under President Park Chung Hee heightened the importance of the technocrats within the bureaucracy, but they in turn were totally dependent upon the Blue House for all final decisions. Even huge Korean industrial combines or "groups," such as Hyundai Heavy Industries, with some $7.6 billion annual gross sales (or nearly 9 percent of Korea's total GNP), have generally remained passively dependent upon the Blue House.

After Park's bizarre assassination in 1979 and Chun Doo Hwan's coup the next year, the same emphasis was placed on one-man rule, accompanied by increasing public doubt about the legitimacy of the "indispensable" ruler. Chun Doo Hwan, like Park, resigned from the army, changed the constitution, and pledged that he would seek only one term as president. Unlike Park, however, he was given no honeymoon period, for skepticism about his promises and cynicism about his legitimacy followed him into the Blue House.

Korean Progress under a Legitimacy Crisis

Korea's basic political problem is therefore legitimacy. Most of the criticisms of the government of President Chun Doo Hwan resemble the normal griping in any developing country; but they have become magnified in Korea by being articulated in a context of widespread skepticism about the legitimacy of the president's rule. Enumerating the sources of this legitimacy problem will show why it is difficult for the government to resolve the matter.

First, after the assassination of President Park Chung Hee it was expected that his increasingly repressive rule, furthered by his self-serving authoritarian constitution, would be replaced by a liberalizing trend—many Koreans even dreamed of a utopian democracy. For a few months in late 1979 and early 1980 it seemed that such a dream might come true. But soon realistic Koreans began to realize how quickly their economy faltered when it lacked decisive government guidance. The use of economic arguments to justify Chun's move to power made the utopian believers permanently suspicious of all economic justifications for governmental actions. An extreme but numerically not insignificant element of the Korean intelligentsia even went so far as to convince itself that economic progress per se was reactionary. Yet the establishment of the Fifth Republic in June 1981 did signal a new era in Korea's economic and political development. The uncertainty following the assassination of President Park was replaced by a period of renewed economic growth and political order. Still, however, the question of the legitimacy of the new presidency continued to haunt public acceptance of the new order.

The second reason for discounting the government's legitimacy has been its exasperating practice of constantly reminding the people of the threat of invasion from the North. Most Koreans, on sober reflection, admit that North Korea is a serious security threat, but the ceaseless harping on the problem over so many decades has led educated Koreans to dismiss the government as narrow-minded and rigidly conservative, if not reactionary—hence their pursuit of the unrealistic goal of "reunification." People who are cocky, self-assured risk-takers cannot live in a permanent state of anxiety over foreign invasion.

The third and most serious source of the legitimacy problem is that every thinking Korean has been able to see through the sham of "opposition" parties, manufactured by clumsily disguised government moves. There is no shortage of Korean politicians eager to become the loyal, and even responsible, opposition to the government, but as things now stand the country is saddled with party leaders who, to put it graciously, have obligations to the government. Ungracious critics would say they are simply in the pay of the government.

The idea that an authoritarian government might help its image in the world, if not among its domestic public, by establishing synthetic parties was not original with President Chun Doo Hwan. On the contrary, it has a long, if unimpressive, history.[15] Chun's approach to "organizing" the "opposition" parties was, however, reminiscent of tactics employed in the factional strife among the *yangbans* of the Yi dynasty. In determining who should be the leaders of the opposition parties, he brought together politicians who resented having to work together and who dissipated their energies in plotting new combinations which the government simply disallowed. More specifically, he selected pliable leaders but saddled them with bright, ambitious, and relatively incorruptible subordinates, a move which ensured that no one could trust anyone else. Thus, in contrast to the imperial British, who believed that "divide and rule" was the ultimate formula for perpetuating their domination, Chun Doo Hwan hit upon the more entertaining stratagem of "combining to confound." Paradoxically, however, the government's blatant involvement in the affairs of the "opposition" parties has compelled those leaders to be aggressive in articulating antigovernment sentiments, which has further undermined the government's legitimacy. Thus, during sessions of the National Assembly when the otherwise controlled press is freed to report "debates" among the Assembly members, the "opposition" feels compelled to hyperbolize. Similarly, when Korean opposition leaders go abroad, they are quick to exploit the occasion and make speeches which contain uninhibited attacks upon the legitimacy of the Korean government.[16] Given the behavior of the government-blessed "opposition," the rhetoric of some of the main dissidents in Korea has been almost redundant. The effect, however, has been to make the illegitimacy of the government conventionally accepted.

Although many critics of the Republic of Korea might argue that the prime source of the government's legitimacy problem is its human rights record and, particularly, its treatment of dissidents, it is surprisingly hard to determine the extent to which the activities of the dissidents have hurt the government. Unquestionably, their arrests, fasts, and self-exile have damaged the ROK's international reputation and contributed to the tendency to group South Korea with the "pariah countries" of Taiwan, South Africa, and Israel. Yet, domestically, the acknowledged suffering of the leading dissidents has not as yet made them into martyrs, largely because they are publicly known to have a variety of personal failings. These "warts" would hardly be noticed in other societies, but, ironically, the Korean crisis of legitimacy, which has caused Koreans to be excessively cynical and to honor only perfection, has also made them cynical about the most dedicated critics of government. Thus people tend to allow their loyalties to gravitate to the extremes—either they are mindlessly committed to authority, or they are anxious to be more cynical than the others, finding hope only in manifestly hopeless causes.

Chun Doo Hwan's legitimacy problems, like those of Park Chung Hee, have been due only in part to his own failings. At a fundamental level these questions of legitimacy arise from the contradiction between the Korean concept of authority and the Korean craving for dependency. The legacy of being more Confucian than the Chinese has made the Koreans, first, idealize authority to such a degree that they fancy their rulers should be paragons—moralists more than strategists—and, second, assume that they could escape all their personal troubles if only their rulers would behave correctly. In short, while they may appear to be ready champions of authoritarianism, they are also prone to believe that authority should be completely nurturing and that most forms of suffering can be traced to the failings of authority. Chun Doo Hwan has thus been caught in a bind: to gain legitimacy he had to inflate his image of authority; but the grander his pretensions of omnipotence, the more he was criticized for not alleviating people's problems.

Furthermore, Chun Doo Hwan has had a peculiarly lonely role as leader, for in the Korean political system there are not many pillars of society to reinforce the legitimacy of the country's top man. In a sense, Korea has a "king" without any "nobles" to broaden the basis of authority and reinforce legitimacy. The bureaucracy itself is dependent upon the Blue House; both ministers and local leaders derive their authority from the president, on an almost personal basis, and thus they are not in a position to evoke commitments to the legitimacy of the system. The normal institutions of such an establishment do not have sufficient autonomous power to perform as champions of the legitimacy of the national political system. The press is weak and vulnerable and hence not to be trusted as a supporter of legitimacy; business leaders and industrialists are much too dependent upon government to be seen as having separate voices of national leadership; academic leaders have had to be agents of government policies too often to be an autonomous moral and intellectual force for the larger well-being of the nation. And, of course, the president's reliance upon the army only negates his claim that Korea has a civilian government rather than military rule.[17]

Since the president is aware of his problem of legitimacy, he tries to project an image of individual leadership which in turn isolates him further, and the enterprise becomes one of building a castle on sand.[18] Because the Korean image of authority calls for a larger-than-life figure, a benevolent philosopher-king who is wiser than any other man, Chun Doo Hwan feels that he must try to rise above himself to achieve a fictitious hero's guise. The need to inflate brings on a need to be reassured, to be surrounded by obedient but respected advisors. His need to project grandeur and his feelings of insecurity explain why he took along the cream of his government talent on his tragic October 1983 visit to Rangoon, where North Korean terrorists set off a bomb which killed his key officials.[19]

As Chun has gained self-confidence in his presidential role, he has become more imperious. He has behaved more formally and ceremonially in public and has shown less inclination to visit the countryside, thereby becoming more and more isolated from his subjects. His aloof manner tends to remind Koreans that his road to power was by military coup and the Kwangju repression. But the attempt to build authority has gone beyond projecting the image of President Chun. In this homogeneous society which has withstood the travails of war and occupation, the government has still felt the need to strive for conformity and enthusiasm for the national identity. The result has been the controversial Saemaul Undong, a movement initiated by President Park and designed to mobilize the countryside and generate rural development.[20] Even though it is clearly a blend of military authoritarianism and Confucian moralism, the movement, at one extreme, has hit responsive chords among government cadres, who hope they can be shielded against criticism merely by displaying dedication; and at the other extreme, it has appealed to the peasantry, who concentrate on the economic payoffs of its developmental drive. To the urban population, growing larger and more sophisticated every year, it seems a bit sophomoric. And to some Westerners, the Saemaul Undong appears to be a vulgar blending of Confucian emperor worship, Maoist fanaticism, and an embarrassing mirror image of the glorification of Kim Il-sung's campaigns in North Korea. Although it is hard to judge the enduring impact of the movement on Korean political culture, it seems likely that, in true Confucian style, Koreans are able comfortably to separate the ideological rhetoric of the movement from its practical aspect, its positive impact on rural life. Given the capacities of the Koreans, who, like the Chinese, can divorce ideological rhetoric from practical calculations, it seems surprising that the government continues to spend so much effort to promote the ideology when practical payoffs are what count in the countryside. Yet, ideology remains a necessary fig leaf for power in a Confucian culture. The lasting commitment of the government to the Saemaul Undong movement must therefore be understood as a manifestation of the need to strengthen the legitimacy of a state which in its dependence upon outside support may seem to some to be less legitimately nationalistic than North Korea.[21]

The common theme in the authority crises of Presidents Syngman Rhee and Park Chung Hee was that they insisted on clinging to power beyond their established terms of office, even to the point of illegally changing the constitution. And part of President Chun Doo Hwan's problem is that the Korean public doubts his pledge to serve for only one term. Had his predecessors stepped down at the proper time, they would have been remembered as greater figures. In both cases the longer they clung to office, the more sullied their reputations became.

This insistence by leaders upon staying in power even when it means downgrading their historical reputations is an interesting aspect of power in almost the whole of Asia. Since Asian politics is generally more genteel than, say, African politics, where to fall from power can lead to financial oblivion if not death, and since there are no great monetary reasons for persisting in office, it seems that nothing would be gained and much, including the pleasures of leisure in later life, would be sacrificed by clinging to power for so long. Not only in Korea, Taiwan, Vietnam, China—all Confucian cultures that revere age—but also in the case of President Marcos in the Philippines, Ne Win in Burma, Lee Kwan Yew in Singapore, and Suharto in Indonesia, one can see the same phenomenon: leaders refusing to step down at the moment of their greatest glory, but insisting instead on holding onto power even though it can only hurt their image in history. The only exceptions are first, Japan, where the office of prime minister is rotated so that each can in turn become an elder statesman whose reputation is secure, and second, Malaysia, where Tungku Abdul Rahman gracefully stepped down when he felt he was faltering.

The explanation for the Asian tilt toward superannuated leaders is not just the cultural tendency to revere age. More significant is the fact that the leaders themselves want to cling to power at all costs because they still have traditional notions about power and therefore believe that it means status and not heavy responsibilities. In the private calculus of most Asian leaders the gratification of being thought the supreme figure for the moment outweighs any calculations as to what history may say of them.

Beleaguered Authority—Alienated Korean Public

At the opposite pole from the government's problems of legitimacy stands the alienation of the Korean public. In spite of impressive economic achievements and dramatic improvements in the standard of living, the Korean people are more preoccupied with their frustrations than thankful for their benefits.

Two major themes are central to this alienation. One is style and rhetoric, which can be quickly explained. The other involves complex frustrations which take various forms in different areas of Korean society.

Korean conformist culture permits open expression of anger and displeasure, but the Korean concept of manliness does not include the prescription that one should hide one's disappointments. This Korean style of complaining makes it difficult to determine the validity of publicized grievances. At the same time, however, the desires of the Koreans for political change have been shattered more than once, for there are no easy alternatives to the current arrangements. Change in Korea can be only incremental. The constraints of having an implacable foe to the north, of being a divided nation in an ideologically warring world, of having to give primary importance to the security forces and to the domestic intelligence agencies, all conspire to make it unrealistic for Koreans to dream of ideal forms of government.

Students and intellectuals in particular are frustrated by these limits to change. Their denunciations only make the authorities feel more beleaguered, and hence more inclined to be heavy-handed. Because student demonstrations were involved in previous changes of government, the authorities are more inclined to repression than to co-optation. Yet, as long as the Korean economy continues to grow, the standard career line for students is likely to be similar to that in Japan: intense study in order to get into a top university, a few years of undemanding student life, and then a job in industry that again demands conformity. The few who have remained politicized have so far been easily controlled.[22]

Many foresee a rocky future for the Republic of Korea with labor as the major explosive force after the students. Since 1961 economic growth has been the basis of the regime's claim to legitimacy, and therefore throughout the 1970s everything was done to maintain labor peace. Indeed, as the economy made dramatic gains, managers competed for labor and wages rose rapidly. Then came the recession of the early 1980s, followed by governmental concern that Korea might lose its competitive advantage because labor costs might threaten the country's balance of payments. Thus, although the constitution of the Fifth Republic guaranteed labor's right to organize, the government passed laws which restricted the labor movement.[23]

The government advanced the doctrine that as a Confucian society Korea did not need the "wasteful" confrontations of Western labor-management relations. There should instead be harmony, cooperation, and a common dedication to the national welfare. In 1980 the government established labor-management councils which were expected to achieve this ideal of harmony by bringing together labor representatives and management officials in a highly paternalistic context. By 1983 the unions had lost their capacity to challenge the combined forces of management and government, and union membership was down by almost 20 percent.[24]

Modernization has thus brought increasing tensions to Korean society, which the government seeks to alleviate by appealing to traditional sentiments. Viewed by Westerners without knowledge of its cultural heritage, Korea might seem to be a "strong" state caught up in an adversary relationship with "society." The authoritarian ways of the Blue House might suggest that the Korean "state" is also highly "autonomous," in the jargon of some recent writings on political science.[25] Such conclusions would, however, be incorrect, for they would overlook the extent to which the shared cultural attitude toward the nature of power serves to blend, and hence integrate, "state" and "society" in Korea. Some elements of the society seem to be in a mutinous, if not outright rebellious, mood, anxious to assert their autonomy and achieve a sense of independence. In fact, however, group cohesion is still strong, and those who are apparently rebellious are playing out recognized roles, often in a stylized manner. The picture is one of confrontation between an isolated authority and an alienated population, but much of this is theater. Authority is supposed to be isolated and distant, and in the end the unruly public expects that authority will save it from its own self-destructive tendencies.[26] Behind all the signs of confrontation lies a deeper bonding of reciprocal dependency. Should Chun Doo Hwan fall from power, he would probably be succeeded by someone with a similar style of leadership.

The ultimate strength of the Korean system lies less in particular institutions or social groupings than in the people's tenacious sense of solidarity and national pride. Koreans are contentious, prone to divisive attacks and self-righteous assertions of their individual rights; but they are still deferential and they believe in self-sacrifice. Hence conflicts which at one moment seem to be taking the community to the brink of civil strife can suddenly be contained in favor of the higher imperative of disciplined harmony.

Students who have been actively engaged in disseminating poisonous rumors that their professors are government agents can, on being reminded of their obligations, become suddenly deferential. But it is just as likely that the reverential students will suddenly assert unorthodox views. Similarly, workers can be on the verge of a strike and then reverse themselves, even making sacrifices for the interests of the enterprise. They will explain that it is like being a member of a family, that the intensity of their criticism is legitimized by their loyalty to the collectivity. These contradictory characteristics make it hard to anticipate developments in Korea, especially since the dominant pattern is to pull back into a disciplined mode just before the reckless instinct assumes command, although at times the controls are too weak to prevent the damaging act from occurring.

The basic Confucian concept that authority should be omnipotent, which is at the root of the Korean legitimacy problem, makes it difficult for any occupant of the Blue House to build coalitions in the society and thereby to construct a broad-based establishment. The Korean view of power makes delegation impossible; indeed, the contrary forces prevail in that all decisions must flow up to the Blue House, making it the perennial target for criticism.

Taiwan: An Antipolitical Confucianism

It is conventional to think of South Korea and Taiwan (that is, the Republic of China) as similar. Both are impressive examples of newly industrialized countries which have benefited from policies of export-led growth; both are a part of a divided nation and thus feel threatened by their implacable conational enemies; both are authoritarian states with a strong leader, a dominant party, and a weak opposition. In both countries the military has a decisive voice in national affairs.

Yet the contrasts are perhaps more significant than the similarities, and they are certainly paradoxical. For example, Korea is probably the most culturally homogeneous country in Asia, while Taiwan is divided between the mainlanders, who arrived in 1949 rather like an occupying force, and the native Taiwanese. In Korea tensions exist between ruler and subjects, while in Taiwan relations have steadily eased and there is a broader-based establishment. Whereas the Korean presidents have consistently run into legitimacy problems, Taiwan's president, Chiang Ching-kuo, who came to power largely because he was the son of Generalissimo Chiang Kai-shek, has steadily built up the legitimacy of his rule. Also, there are substantial differences between the economies of the two countries. Korea, which has the base for a more diversified economy and a considerably larger domestic market, has much more government involvement in economic decisions; Taiwan, aside from its few state-run enterprises, offers much greater freedom to private-sector entrepreneurs.

The political divergence in particular calls for an explanation. How was it possible for the government of Taiwan, with its Confucian attitude toward authority, to evolve in a way that allowed increasing pluralism and modest tolerance toward the opposition? When the Kuomintang

(KMT) forces arrived in Taiwan in 1946 under the command of General Ch'en Yi, they treated the Taiwanese as a lesser breed, virtually crushing any sign of political awareness. The abominable behavior of the Mainland armies, which assumed that all Taiwanese were Japanese "collaborators," exemplified the imperialistic attitude of Confucianists toward "outsiders."[27] Two other examples of this contemptuous and vicious behavior toward subjugated peoples are that of the Japanese militarists in the heyday of the "East Asiatic Co-prosperity Sphere" and that of the Vietnamese in relation to the Laotians and the Cambodians. But even though the mainlanders began their rule in Taiwan with a Confucian elitist "we-against-them" mentality and with a continuing fear of Communist infiltration, they gradually revised their attitudes about power, especially after Chiang Ching-kuo succeeded his father.

The relationship between mainlanders and Taiwanese is an extraordinary case of an ironic interplay of power and ethnicity. It also demonstrates that economic and political power need not be interchangeable or reinforcing, especially if the culture associates authority with propriety, as does Confucianism.

On their arrival in Taiwan the KMT met problems far greater than that of showing their superiority over the Taiwanese. Chiang Kai-shek brought with him an army which had been humiliatingly defeated by a supposedly inferior Communist army. Chiang had to recover some degree of "face" with the United States, and he knew that many Americans were enthusiastic about land reform. In Taiwan it turned out to be easy politically to conduct a massive transferral of land holdings, since some of the large estates had once belonged to the defeated Japanese and other large land holdings were owned by Taiwanese. There was no effective opposition to land reform. Yet under American influence, the government of the Republic of China (ROC) opted to compensate Taiwanese land owners with government bonds, as the American occupation had done in Japan.[28]

The result was a double miracle. Taiwan soon had the most equitable rural scene in all of Asia, and the Joint Commission on Rural Reconstruction, consisting of Americans and KMT officials, saw to it that the newly independent Taiwanese farmers had all the infrastructure necessary for them to prosper. In the meantime the former Taiwanese landlords became an astoundingly vigorous entrepreneurial class, using their bonds as capital for the first stages of the Taiwan economic miracle.[29]

In the 1960s and 1970s a strange inversion of economic and political power took place. The two million mainlanders who had accompanied the defeated Chiang Kai-shek to the island were of two classes. The vast majority had been common soldiers, mostly unaccompanied by families, and hence a substantial proportion intermarried with Taiwanese women. The minority, who were officers and officials, were frozen into bureaucratic salary jobs. Given the aura of corruption which accompanied the defeated KMT to Taiwan, they had to prove that they were honest officials by living only on their salaries, and this left the private sector open for the Taiwanese to become the economic elite. The result was a pattern unimaginable in traditional Chinese political culture: the political elite came to have a lower standard of living than those who were not connected with government. This turned the world upside down in a way which had not been done even in Communist China, where cadres and high officials continued to live, as in traditional China, well above the level of those outside the government.[30]

When Chiang Chin-kuo took his father's place in 1975, he seemed to have control of all the elements associated with traditional authority in Chinese political culture. He could invoke the only recognized ideology, the San-Min-Chu-I; his bureaucracy was disciplined and without corruption; and he had massive military and police power. Yet he could have become a vulnerable and beleaguered leader because his 2 million mainlanders were outnumbered by some 16 million Taiwanese, who dominated the economy and were not particularly dependent upon government in their export activities. Moreover, the very success of the government in achieving income equality meant that the rural people were so prosperous that they were living as well as the lower bureaucrats and soldiers.

This peculiar situation, which reversed the basic socioeconomic logic of traditional Chinese political culture, forced President Chiang Ching-kuo to break with some of the basic Chinese authority practices. He had to reduce the tensions between mainlanders and Taiwanese, which meant ending the political monopoly of the mainlanders and attracting Taiwanese into politics. Moreover, he had to accomplish this on terms that would not encourage the idea of "Taiwan independence," mainly because any such movement would certainly have seemed provocative to Peking and thus would have heightened his security problems. There was not much he could do to improve the economic lot of mainlanders since the largest Taiwan industrialists preferred to hire Taiwanese.[31] He could only give mainlanders positions in the state-owned enterprises, but these operated on bureaucratic salaries, and, with only a few exceptions, at a loss to the state.

Several factors facilitated President Chiang's efforts to bring the Taiwanese into established political life. The KMT itself increasingly became a Taiwanese party, so that by the early 1980s its mix was almost the same as that of the population. Even more important, the pattern of local

elections meant that most KMT candidates were Taiwanese. Young mainlanders could only look forward to administrative chores, while their
Taiwanese peers began to monopolize public life as well as private
enterprise.

Because the KMT did not abandon its traditional Chinese authoritarian
instincts, it could only compromise with the idea of an opposition; but
paradoxically its compromises have facilitated the growth of a sophisticated opposition. The old guard of the KMT insisted that they would
recognize only the two "official" opposition parties—one of which was
the China Youth Party, whose leader was nearly ninety. Therefore the
opposition politicians had to become "independents," or *dang-wai* ("outside the party") figures. Ironically, by not allowing the *dang-wai* to be
an organized party, the KMT has given them vitality, because their prima
donnas have been spared the divisive, indeed the impossible, task of
determining their relative rankings, as would have been necessary if they
had been bound into a single hierarchy. Another result, even worse from
the KMT's point of view, is that the game has been tilted against the
moderate *dang-wai* and toward the more extremist elements.[32]

During the late 1970s and early 1980s, the Taiwanese electorate became quite clearly divided, with 70 percent favoring the KMT and 30
percent the various *dang-wai* candidates. Consequently, people both within
and outside the KMT came to believe that Taiwan was moving toward
a modified Japanese party system, with the KMT performing the role of
the LDP, even to the point of having factions, and the *dang-wai* being
the equivalent of the Japanese opposition parties. Unquestionably, the
KMT has found that it must act with the cautiousness of the LDP if it
is to maintain any semblance of consensus.

At the same time, as threadbare as the San-Min-Chu-I has become,
the KMT continues to seek moral justification through its ideology—the
Chinese are not comfortable with power unless it is cloaked in a moralistic
ideology. Hence the pure pragmatism of the LDP model is still beyond
the grasp of the Chinese in Taiwan. Ironically, a key to President Chiang
Ching-kuo's success in inducting Taiwanese into the established political
process has been the pretentious myth that the "Republic of China" is
the "legitimate" government of all China. During the first twenty-odd
years of KMT rule in Taiwan, this claim of ROC "sovereignty" was used
to justify mainlander rule over the local Taiwanese, but in the 1970s a
gradual reversal took place and the myth came to serve the opposite
purpose. The pretension that the government was a "sovereign state"
made it safe to recruit Taiwanese into the ruling class. The myth of
sovereignty ensured that the Taiwanese who participated in politics would
accept a social contract to treat mainlanders as equal nationals even

though the logic of numbers gave increasing power to Taiwanese in electoral politics. Furthermore, the myth of sovereignty has meant that the provocative idea of "Taiwan independence" could be repressed without repressing Taiwanese participation in politics.

There was a time when KMT leaders manifested intense hostility toward the first political stirrings of the Taiwanese, and especially of the *dang-wai,* characterizing them as traitors and agents of the Communists, if not outright Communists; but since hitting upon the formula of "sovereignty," they have found it possible to tolerate, though with obvious distaste, the existence of the *dang-wai.* The process thus has been a gradual and subtle one, with the KMT inching forward toward accepting the *dang-wai* and the *dang-wai* agreeing that the test for political participation should be the acceptance of the principle of ROC "sovereignty." The *dang-wai* people thus know how far they can go, and they generally understand that "independence" is taboo.

They are, however, able to preserve their integrity by refusing to follow the KMT in glorifying "reunification." The Taiwanese use code words, such as "the future of Taiwan should be determined by the people of Taiwan," to stand for the idea of "self-determination" and "independence." This calculated play with symbols is indicative of the degree to which the KMT has had to bend to the opposition, and of how far the opposition has gone in resisting KMT desires. The compromise solution which calls for everyone to agree to the basic principle of ROC "sovereignty" saves face for the mainlanders, and it ensures that the rising tide of Taiwanese power will not produce a Taiwan-oriented independence movement, but rather will lead to a Chinese-oriented Taiwan autonomy, thus maintaining the status quo. The irony is that these developments have also produced a formula that is the least provocative to the PRC, since the alternative of allowing Taiwanese power to become a drive for Taiwan independence is totally unacceptable to Peking. Hence, it is desirable for all concerned that the litmus test for Taiwanese to become political participants is that they be socialized into believing in the supreme principle of ROC "sovereignty."

To attribute reality to symbols is traditional in Chinese political culture, but the integration of the Taiwanese into the political process could not have occurred without a significant change in attitudes toward political power. Specifically, it required a downgrading of authority, indeed of all government, and a tolerance for the other aspects of social life. The KMT leadership had to accept the idea that their initially superior political position did not give them the traditional Confucian claim to authority in all areas of life. This fundamental change in Chinese political culture, which has not occurred in China itself or in Korea or Vietnam—

and never really existed in Japan—took place in Taiwan for several reasons.

First, the transition was facilitated by the unique character of the ethnic divisions between mainlanders and Taiwanese. Whereas in most ethnically divided societies the social differences are basic and politics often serves as the main avenue for bridging differences, in Taiwan it is the other way around. There is little social distance between the Taiwanese majority and the mainlanders: intermarriages are common, occurring in nearly 60 percent of the extended families. The only area of tension is politics. Hence measures taken to reduce political strains in the political realm have had dramatic payoffs in integrating the society.[33]

Second, the KMT has a serious problem of political generations. The oldest generation (seventy and over) was well educated and had some experience of the world. Those in the next generation (in their sixties), who ought to be in the line of political succession, are distinguished only for their loyalty to their elders, whom they accompanied in the retreat from the Mainland; they are conspicuously lacking in technical skills and political sophistication. So it is the members of the third generation, now in their forties and fifties, who as the educated and technocratically skilled people are needed to rule Taiwan's complex and modern society. Moreover, mainlanders and Taiwanese place a traditionally Chinese value on education. As incomes have risen, so have college enrollments, and consequently those in the youngest generation are even more pluralistic in their thinking and less unquestioning of political authority than their elders.

Indeed, Taiwan is possibly the best working example of the theory that economic progress should bring in its wake democratic inclinations and a healthy surge of pluralism, which in time will undercut the foundations of the authoritarian rule common to developing countries. By the 1980s Taiwan's political and social development no longer lagged well behind its economic modernization, and as a result, politics and government have become less central to people's lives. The younger and better-educated people could hardly avoid dismissing with contempt or treating with patronizing indifference the ideologically rigid political views of the older Mainland generation. For them politics could never be the central purpose of life, as it was for the traditional Confucian elite. They could concentrate their energies on nonpolitical and usually highly technical pursuits. Although, at best, politics was limited to casual conversations, they more often preferred these to be apolitical, indeed antipolitical.

Finally, the most important reason for Taiwan's break with traditional Confucian views about political authority was the humiliation that the KMT experienced in its loss of China to the Communists. After such a defeat it was impossible for most Nationalist leaders to uphold the posture of arrogance associated with traditional Confucian notions of authority. The defeat made some of the old guard more stubborn in their desire to cling to total authority; but for the majority the reality principle overcame their usual Chinese tolerance for cognitive dissonance, forcing them to accept limitations on their ambitions for political authority. Out of demoralization came the wisdom of allowing the private sector more scope than was natural in Chinese political culture.

The need for greater modesty in the reach of authority was reinforced by subsequent government failures. By the 1970s it became clear that state-operated enterprises could not keep up with the private sector, but further divestiture was not easy because most of these enterprises were not likely to become profitable. Working for the government not only brought no prestige but was taken as a sign that one could not make it in the "real" world.

The government's prestige was also damaged in foreign affairs. After relying heavily upon its alliance with the United States, Taiwan leaders found themselves isolated after the American opening to Peking. Although "derecognition" did not bring disaster to the economy, it did challenge the self-confidence of a significant segment of the KMT, making the party more anxious to unite with, rather than dominate, the population.

The constructive role of failure in modifying some Confucian views about power in the Taiwan political culture has relevance for the political modernization of the People's Republic of China. There the dramatic failures of the Mao era have made Deng Xiaoping less sure that government can or should try to solve all of China's problems. While modesty has begun to have some appeal in Peking, the arrogance of authority is still strong throughout the country, and therefore what has been a floodgate in Taiwan is only a crack in the wall in China. Nevertheless, even if all the "humiliations" of one hundred years of Western "impact" on China have not undermined China's sense of being the "center of the world," and if all of Mao's blunders and self-destructive policies have not brought political humility to Peking, what happened to the KMT did modify their arrogance and produce a dramatic change in their political views. It must, in fact, have been one of the most profound psychic shocks in all the history of political cultures.[34]

To return to the comparison of Taiwan and Korea, there were basic political-economy reasons why Taiwan did not develop along the lines of South Korea, where the state dictated the creation of a *zaibatsu*-type system of economic and financial "groups." Taiwan, with a population of only 18 million, lacked the domestic markets that Korea (like Japan) had; and therefore in Taiwan nearly all enterprises had to think in terms of exports from the time of their inception. Taiwan never went through a phase of import substitution as Korea and Japan did, except in the field of banking. Consequently, the growth of the Taiwanese economy depended upon a host of entrepreneurs looking for opportunities through arrangements with foreign, particularly American, associates.

In Korea the combination of American aid and the need to reconstruct the whole country after the devastation of war generated the basis for a substantial construction industry. In addition, the need to maintain what had been emergency capacities, such as steel and cement-making, machine maintenance and building, were redirected toward more lasting enterprises, such as shipbuilding and international engineering enterprises. The transition was from a form of import substitution to exports, in rapid order.

Since Taiwan had no comparable domestic market, firms could not test their strength at home before venturing abroad. More important, innovative industries were not able to copy the Japanese and Korean practices of licensing or buying slightly dated American technologies on which to base self-generated innovations. Most licensing and sales agreements, even those concerning penultimate technologies, include clauses forbidding sales in the American and other choice markets for a set period of time. For Japanese and Korean enterprises such constraints were not obstacles because they could use the stipulated time to experiment with their own profitable home markets. Not so for the Taiwanese firms, which had to choose between producing for American distributors and going it alone—which often meant ignoring patents and producing cheap imitations.[35] Taiwan's growth thus has quite a different base from that of Korea. Because Singapore and Hong Kong also have different strategies for economic growth, it is improper to speak of the "gang of four" NICs as though they were all alike.

To summarize, Taiwan, in spite of all its lingering Confucian rhetoric, has made a greater break with Confucian attitudes toward authority than has China, Korea, or Vietnam. As the government has come to accept that it is not omnipotent, Taiwan leaders have become more like the Japanese, who long ago separated the political and economic spheres. Ironically, in Taiwan the trend is toward even more autonomy for the economy, while in Japan governmental "guidance" in economic decision-making may be increasing.

That the government in Taiwan has become more limited and the leadership more tolerant of its opposition does not mean, however, that

Taiwan has broken completely with Confucian attitudes toward authority. The Taiwan system is still basically authoritarian, and although the secret police are not so heavy-handed as they once were, they have not disbanded. For some time to come, the Taiwan authorities will respond to a crisis by using naked force, in the traditional Confucian belief that authority is its own judge of what is necessary and that it cannot be limited by law. Thus, although the society and polity have become more pluralistic, the cultural potential for authoritarian rule remains.

Yet it must also be acknowledged that of the bureaucratic Confucian societies—as distinct from the feudalistic Confucian society of Japan—Taiwan has gone the farthest in modifying basic assumptions about the omnipotence of authority. The refugee regime on the island along with its local population has also had to go through a harsh experience in learning that dependency cannot provide security and that all individuals must look out for themselves and find strength in independence. In Korea, on the contrary, bold risk-taking seems safe because others, such as the United States or Japan, can be counted on to provide security and support. In China, the political system still revolves around providing the security needs of a psychologically dependent population that values both the concept of an "iron rice bowl," that is, job security, and the traditional concept of *guanxi*, or personal connections. And in Vietnam, revolutionary fervor has been fueled by dependency, first in the form of the illusion that "we have friends everywhere in the world," and then by heavy reliance upon the Soviet Union.

Vietnam: Little Dragon, Bigger "Hegemonist"

This is not the place to recount the tortures of Vietnam in its sequence of wars, first to drive out the French, then to unify north and south in defiance of United States intervention, and finally to control Cambodia and Laos, the rest of Indochina, at the cost of border wars with China. Vietnam's commitment to warfare is, from our perspective, a function of a deeper Vietnamese cultural characteristic—their concept of power, which has been colored by their colonial experiences under both the Chinese and the French.

Only the Indians come close to the Vietnamese in the degree to which they have psychologically "identified with the aggressor" and thereby adopted the arrogance of their former colonial rulers. More than any of the other non-Chinese cultures, the Vietnamese took to the ideals of power of traditional Confucianism. In the imperial capital of Hue, after the end of direct Chinese rule, they replicated to the smallest detail the

Chinese imperial court system of an emperor ruling through a Confucian bureaucracy. And during the century of French rule, Vietnam was Paris's "proudest colonial possession."³⁶ None of the Asian colonial countries matched Vietnam in the extent to which its people assimilated the imperial European culture. Vietnamese became doctors, lawyers, mathematicians, scientists, and musicians, and these Westernized professionals practiced in France on equal terms with the French in far larger numbers than did the Indians in England or the Indonesians in Holland. In short, the Vietnamese had the human talent and the historical opportunities to be at the forefront of Asian modernization. Their cultural views about power, however, have left their country at a disadvantage in relation to both the other Confucian cultures and the Southeast Asian ASEAN countries. At the same time, the success of the Vietnamese in absorbing first the Chinese and then the French culture not only made them feel superior to all their neighbors but also produced the self-confidence and arrogance which have made it possible for them to accomplish the unbelievable on the battlefield while still stubbornly pursuing policies less modernized than those of other Asian countries.

The ability of the Vietnamese to blend the Chinese and French cultures has contributed to their propensity to make status more important than achievement. The Vietnamese use of power is like that of the traditional Balinese: they emphasize the drama of power more than its practical payoffs. Historically this has been shown in the Vietnamese dedication to victory without meaningful rewards, or at least without benefits for the vast majority of people who had made the sacrifices. In 939 A.D. after nearly a thousand years of Chinese domination, the Vietnamese finally drove out the Chinese. The result was rewards for a handful of the elite but disaster for the multitudes. Conditions of life throughout the country declined; greed and lust for power split the elite, and by 966 anarchy was all that remained of independence. Similarly, in 1975 the conquest of Saigon by Hanoi set the stage for a general decline in the Vietnamese standard of living, in the north as well as in the south, which was accelerated by Hanoi's invasion of Cambodia in 1978 and its subsequent border wars with China. The notions of the Vietnamese elite about how power should be used ensured that years of struggle and sacrifice by the obedient masses would bring them only a harsher, more austere standard of living. The Vietnamese, and their conquered neighbors in Cambodia and Laos, are the only people in Asia who have a lower standard of living in the mid-1980s than they had during the Great Depression of the 1930s.

It seems surprising, in view of the paternalistic obligations of their Confucian concepts of authority, that the Vietnamese elite can carry out policies without regard for their effect on the people. The explanation seems to lie in the cultural gap that exists between the Confucian, and Westernized, elite's concepts of power and the more popular pre-Confucian ideas of leadership and authority.

Building on the debate, first among French scholars and later among American scholars, concerning the nature of Vietnamese culture and society, more recent scholarship has found that the earlier picture of Vietnamese society tended to exaggerate the extent of Confucian influence and to underplay the durability of non-Confucian sentiments among the masses.[37] Although certain concepts in popular Vietnamese culture seem to be close to the basic Confucian views about power and authority, subtle differences exist which make them something more than vulgarizations of Chinese cultural concepts. In this mass view of authority, leaders should strive to promote *phuc duc,* a term which has no direct English equivalent but which a dictionary describes as, "Do something good and your children will benefit from it." The key point is that individual effort and achievement are important for the collectivity of the family. The family in a sense has its collective karma or fate, which can become more favorable and prosperous if each generation of leaders makes the proper effort to achieve virtue, usually by self-sacrifice and denial. Authority must thus be nurturing, and if misfortunes arise for the family it is assumed that somewhere along the line the father has failed to do the right thing. It is also assumed, however, that if the head of the family promotes *phuc duc* the rest of the family will follow suit and accumulate more *phuc duc* on their own behalf. In a peculiar way the concept of *phuc duc* resembles the idea of the Mandate of Heaven, brought down to the family level but enriched by Buddhist overtones of accumulating merit for a collective fate. As Stephen Young notes, "What we think of as Vietnamese 'family loyalty' is more the fulfilment of reciprocal obligations by those who depend on others for *phuc duc* and those who are earning *phuc duc* for the family."[38]

The popular culture also holds a distinctive concept of legitimacy called *uy tin,* which can be translated as "trustworthy authority." The emphasis is upon reliability, dependability, and a degree of moral responsibility. The essence of *uy tin,* again according to Young, is a combination of three concepts.

The first is *tai,* or "ability," with emphasis upon practical skills. Legitimacy thus calls for a degree of effectiveness which is not a part of Confucian thinking about authority. Yet it is not entirely pragmatic because the goal of authority should be to advance *duc,* or "virtue," which has a Buddhist rather than a Confucian dimension.

The second aspect of *uy tin* is *duc* itself, the concept of "virtue," which has to be understood as having that dimension of self-sacrifice and the "destruction of the ego" which is so basic to the Buddhist notion of gaining merit through the elimination of desires. People are expected to strive to gain more *duc* in life so as to have a better afterlife. One of the most effective ways of accumulating *duc* is to help others to get it. Leaders, above all, are expected to forego material advantage and strive to increase their *duc* and that of their followers. This Vietnamese concept of virtue that is basic to legitimacy has Confucian overtones in that it stresses the values of propriety and filial piety, but it also has a logic that goes beyond social ethics and incorporates divine forces. In fact, the idea of *duc* as a part of legitimacy is a blending of divine and status-based concepts of authority.

The third element in *uy tin,* which is *so,* or "fate," makes this connection to supernatural forces even clearer. The ingredient of *so* says that legitimate authority depends upon forces that lie beyond the command of any political actor, and therefore leaders themselves are victims of fate. Fate can be either kind or harsh to them, depending upon their manifestation of *phuc duc* and the degree to which they have acted for the benefit of the collectivity. But no one can be the complete master of his fate, and much that happens lies beyond explanation. Thus a leader can be seen as losing legitimacy simply because things have gone wrong for him.

These popular views of authority and power are quite different from the Confucian concepts, colored by Western, including Marxist-Leninist, thought, of the national elite. Historically, the rule of government in Vietnam was, "The reach of the Emperor's authority stops at the bamboo hedge," where village leadership took over. The French penetration of society was also limited. The Communists were only identified with the elite culture, for as Stephen Young notes, "Ho Chi Minh, recruiting since 1925, had only 5000 followers in 1945; whereas Huynh Phu So, who founded the Hoa Hao sect in 1939, had gathered nearly 2 million followers in only six years."[39] It is true that Ho had to operate clandestinely for part of that period, but the fact remains that the Communists did not find it easy to penetrate the popular political culture.

The elite and mass cultures do, however, have two traits in common. The first is a strong emphasis upon dependency and upon expecting superiors to be nurturing and generously supportive in both strength and wealth. Village leaders are called upon to be self-denying and attentive to the well-being of their "children," who see them as a source of *phuc duc.* At the national level the government of South Vietnam quickly became demoralized when it felt abandoned by the United States; and, of course, the Hanoi government, which had an exaggerated idea of the amount of support it could expect from abroad, became surprisingly dependent upon the Soviet Union. The intensity of Vietnamese nationalism in opposing French and, earlier, Chinese colonial domination led many observers to underestimate the Vietnamese craving for dependent ties with a properly nurturing superior authority. The second common trait of the two cultures is a sensitivity to status, to the point of treating it as the substance and goal of power. In Vietnamese culture the drive for achievement, which has made the individual highly successful in a wide range of pursuits, tends to become perverted, in social and political contexts, into status considerations rather than utility maximization. This propensity of the Vietnamese to emphasize the values of status—of esteem in the eyes of others, and of self-glorification—over practical payoffs and realistic judgments can be found in numerous areas of Vietnamese life whenever questions of power and hierarchy are at stake.

For example, Gerald Hickey explains that in the village of Khanh Hau each *dinh,* or communal temple dedicated to the ancestors and guardian spirits, had its cult committee, membership in which was a great honor. But the honor could carry the burden of having to accept a title, in return for which payment had to be made—even a lowly title such as Huong Hao cost 200 piasters. People would go into debt to make the necessary payments even though this brought only prestige and not the slightest material benefit.[40] Although it is not nearly so extreme as the practices of the Kwakiutl Indians of the Northwest coast of America, who vigorously dissipated their natural wealth in potlatch ceremonies, the Vietnamese culture still has a strong tendency to make sacrifices for symbolic or status objectives.[41]

This valuing of pride, with its tendency toward arrogance, is maintained among the elite in spite of the propensity among those without power to adopt a "scoffing attitude" and "clownish levity" toward the pretensions of authority.[42] The Vietnamese need to pretend to greatness in an environment where there is often little reverence for authority helps to explain their potential for fragmentation and factionalism when not bonded in a clear hierarchical structure.

Anyone claiming authority has to be highly sensitive to considerations of "face" and quick to respond to insults. To do so he must maintain distance, especially from anyone who might be disrespectful. This distancing of the leader means that power requires seclusion. Vietnamese leaders, whether emperors or cadres, have not routinely appeared in public or interacted with the crowds.

The notion that authority should be more absorbed with status than with utility has created a politics of stubborn pride which can easily be out of touch with reality. For example, at the Fourth Party Congress in

1977 the Vietnamese leaders proclaimed a five-year plan that called for $7 billion in foreign assistance. At that time Vietnamese propaganda was trumpeting the questionable slogan, "We have friends everywhere in the world," and the serious decision-makers deluded themselves into thinking that such levels of aid were conceivable. The year before, Premier Phan Van Dong had displayed a similar lack of realism on a visit to Singapore. Driving back to the airport with Premier Lee Kuan Yew, the Vietnamese was awed by the skyline of the modern city and the turnpike-style highway. He turned to the Singapore leader and said, "You are going to have to help us now! We fought to protect you from the Americans so that you could build all this." Premier Lee replied that they should not have gone to such trouble. He did not add, as he might have, that Singapore would have found it very much harder without the Americans.[43]

Another example of the Vietnamese divorcement from reality, again associated with an exaggerated sense of importance, was the Vietnamese approach during secret talks in 1978 with Richard Holbrooke, assistant secretary of state for East Asia and Pacific Affairs. Mr. Holbrooke was committed to the well-intentioned but strategically questionable policy of achieving early normalization with Hanoi, or at least of preventing relations from descending into the deep freeze, as they had done with China during the previous twenty years. Hanoi, caught up in a complex game of diplomacy in the hope that it might establish relations with Washington before normalization occurred between Washington and Peking, persisted in demanding that "in return" for establishing formal relations Washington should pay Vietnam $2 billion. This figure had been mentioned in the Paris Peace Accords of 1972, but Hanoi should have known that no United States Congress would vote such a sum after Hanoi's 1975 violation of the accords. Two days after President Carter signaled to Peking that Washington would be ready for normalization by the end of the year, Hanoi dropped its unrealistic demands; but by then it was too late.[44]

Hanoi's overblown expectations of assistance from others, a manifestation of its dependency mentality, has contributed to its increasing isolation, so that it has become ever more dependent upon its latest patron, the Soviet Union. Hanoi's troubles arise in part from a peculiar negotiating style, again an outgrowth of its particular form of dependency. Whereas the customary approach of parties to negotiations is to establish an initial position and then to work by the logic of quid pro quo toward modification and compromise, the Vietnamese go about it in exactly the opposite manner. They say at first that everything is negotiable and that they are prepared to be totally reasonable and accommodating if negotiations are established, but having said that, they become totally un-compromising. Henry Kissinger was frustrated by this Vietnamese practice of being reasonable in public and intransigent in private.[45] Later on, when Vietnamese Foreign Minister Nguyen Co Thach sought to engage the ASEAN capitals in negotiations about Kampuchea, his posture of rea-sonableness was well understood and distrusted.

That no country except the Soviet Union and Sweden was willing to trust the word of Hanoi by 1978 was not surprising to the Vietnamese, because in their political culture few people ever trusted the public pos-tures of authority. The Confucian pretension of superior morality on the part of government officials, combined with years of anticolonial struggle and reinvigorated by enthusiastic Marxist-Leninist revolutionism, has caused the Vietnamese to think about power in a convoluted, clandestine way.

Indeed, long before Hanoi's victory, the common belief in Vietnam was that nothing publicly stated could be true, and that real power was always several steps removed from public view. This quality of clandes-tineness, described by Douglas Pike,[46] produced a post-Confucian culture in which everyone was too wise to believe the authorities, even while being totally dependent upon them. No one took seriously the words of official spokesmen because everyone understood that real power does not show its hand. Hence the dilemma of the Hanoi elite during the years of warfare was whether to identify itself with enthusiastic partisans who appeared to believe the superficial rhetoric designed for the unsophisti-cated, or to disassociate themselves from the naive and adopt the more serious posture of a true source of authority. In the Vietnamese political culture it was proper for authority to conceal its hand and not to become emotionally involved in the public rhetoric of acknowledged front men, who customarily occupied the stage of politics between significant de-velopments.

Authority in Vietnam is thus committed to deceiving not only the "enemy," but also, surprisingly, the self. Ho Chi Minh used more than half a dozen pseudonyms, and it was never clear whether he was trying to confuse his "enemies" or to avoid facing up to his own identity. The style of clandestineness meant that everyone who was in on the act could aspire to heroic greatness; yet those in the know also suspected that others were engaged in pretense. Since there are no grounds for trust, and since clandestineness determines that the initial positions will be false, true compromise becomes impossible. The accusation of selling out, of allowing everything to become negotiable, is so feared that the only alternative is to prove steadfastness by becoming totally uncom-promising, even when reasonableness would be profitable.

The spirit of clandestineness breeds intrigue, convoluted calculations, and a constant suspicion that no relationship is what it appears to be. The leadership, to be competent, must be made up of a small, cell-like group of men—in the entire history of the Vietnamese Communist party only twenty-four people have been members of the Politburo. The dilemma for followers, particularly middle-level cadres and functionaries, is extremely complex: they need the protection of higher officials, but they can never be sure of the lasting power of anyone. Hence they need to profess loyalty but always to be prepared to make realignments according to the shifts of clandestine power. As Pike has noted, "No strong traitor stigma prevails in Vietnam. The majority of Vietnamese of middle age or older have been on all sides of all political issues."[47]

All of this leads to a politics of fluid factionalism, which "manifests itself in the Great Game of *bung-di* or faction bashing."[48] The Vietnamese are more realistic than the Chinese in accepting the inevitability of faction-forming. They do not pretend, as the leaders in Peking do, that factions are a troublesome, minor phenomenon, involving only a few misguided cadres. Rather, they assume that factions will emerge, and they seek only to contain the more negative consequences. The rules of *bung-di* allow the individual to seek security in return for a limited commitment of loyalty. The relationship is, however, a relatively weak patron-client tie, as compared to the dyadic relations in the other Southeast Asian cultures. Yet the impulse for forming factions is the generally recognized need for protection.

These psychological responses reinforce the traditional Vietnamese view that participation in collective endeavors is consistent with personal striving for recognition. As Douglas Pike has noted, "The bureaucrat in Vietnam is system-oriented, not program-oriented and he tends to see government chiefly as an avenue to success, a means for getting rewards from society."[49] Thus, while demanding a degree of collective loyalty, the Vietnamese still give scope to individual achievement. The individual's striving should be to gain merit through virtue, but in practical terms it also means gaining status and commanding dignity and deference from others.

Vietnamese can gain respect in the eyes of others by excelling at essentially foreign activities. At one time high status came from Chinese and later French pursuits. Indeed, much of the Vietnamese measure of greatness has involved outdoing the foreigner at his own game, often in order to gain only status and recognition, not real material advantages. The myths of Vietnam's national origins depict the first Vietnamese as performing heroic feats which awed the Chinese.[50] For example, the great legend of Vietnamese nationalism is the struggle of the Trung sisters to rid the homeland of the Chinese. But as every Vietnamese knows, this greatest victory of Vietnamese heroism produced only three years of freedom, for the Chinese were victorious again and reintroduced foreign rule for nearly a millennium. The stress was on the individual's deeds, not on collective accomplishments.

It is not surprising, then, that for all its nationalistic impulses, Vietnamese political culture is characterized by sadness, indeed deep melancholy.[51] Historically, the Vietnamese view was that authority could trust no one, that any opposition was by definition immoral and should not be tolerated; yet, at the same time, authority had only one purpose— to prove its superiority. Those in power had to demonstrate their superior status, and the rest of society had no option but to hope that the game of the elite would not be too damaging—a logic which led to both sadness and a lack of hope for progressive improvement in daily life. The prophecy made by Ho Chi Minh in 1945 that the struggle of Vietnamese nationalism would call for sacrifices that would leave the people of Vietnam worse off than before has proved to be correct.

Three Variations on a Cultural Theme

The three Confucian cultures of Korea, Taiwan, and Vietnam are modernizing along quite different lines—lines as divergent as may be found in any three Christian cultures of Europe. Although they still show certain basic Confucian traits, they have made different modifications and adjustments—exploiting different strengths of that culture to different purposes, masking the weaknesses in different ways, and allowing some scope for pre-Confucian indigenous ways. All three still share a sensitive respect for hierarchy and an appreciation for order and moral respectability, for the discipline of self-cultivation, and for achievement; and all three manifest in different ways a belief in the propriety of paternalistic authority and the legitimacy of responding dependency.

In Korea, first the mindless arrogance of the Confucianist *yangban* was humiliated by the period of Japanese rule, and then the whole society was leveled by the ravages of the Korean War. As much as elements in the society despised the development, power became associated with an authoritarian ruler, based mainly on military clout. As in a more traditional society, the state became the final arbiter of most phases of life, including the economy. Businessmen became rich, but they remained dependent upon government and hence had no voice in affairs. The state itself has remained highly dependent on foreign support. Although multinational corporations were slow to show interest in the war-devastated

Korean economy, the massive amounts of American aid turned the economy around and opened the way for a complex pattern of foreign economic relations with Korea. Foreign banks were so generous in making loans that Korea became the largest debtor country in Asia. At the same time, Korean industries in many sectors developed dependent trading ties with foreign firms, mainly American.[52]

The Korean government, for all of its legitimacy problems, was able to stifle opposition and prevent an extension of the society's power base by insisting that the national security problems posed by North Korea required firm discipline. The government could justify the credibility of the threat not only by pointing to violent activities by the Communist north but also by referring to the fact that the United States was willing to station fifty thousand of its troops in South Korea. That alone was enough to end debate as to whether the government was exaggerating the foreign threat and hence the need for solidarity.

The authorities in Taiwan went through an even more shattering experience, which damaged their sense of historic Confucian superiority over all other peoples. The Chiang Kai-shek government that retreated in defeat to the island could not act with the same Confucian arrogance that it had displayed in Nanking and Chungking. Worse still, its claim to being under imminent threat, like Korea, became increasingly hollow, especially after the United States decided that its troops were no longer essential to the security of the island.

Over a thirty-year period government officials in the ROC have accepted a decline in prestige, if not in actual importance—an entirely unConfucian pattern. Taiwanese businessmen, through their private ties with foreign enterprises, have made their own way with relatively little government help. The backwaters of the Taiwan economy are the various state-run enterprises, which the government, out of a paternalistic impulse, preserves even when they are unprofitable. (In Korea the state technocrats would have simply eliminated such drags on the economy.) Except for preserving such examples of "bureaucratic capitalism" or "Confucian socialism" and for maintaining secret police establishments, Taiwan has probably gone further than the other two states in abandoning Confucian ways—but ironically, it has been the most vigorous in its state support of the Confucian tradition. The erosion of Confucianism has taken place because the politics of status and prestige has had to give way to utilitarian values of a materialistic nature. Taiwan has become a society so energized by economics that politics has yielded up its pretensions of importance. Moreover, to the degree that the status of officialdom has been redefined, Taiwan has tended toward a pluralistic polity and away from a dutiful, disciplined Confucian society which defers to governmental authority. This happened possibly because the authorities experienced a more profound "loss of face" than any other surviving Confucian elite. The shock felt by the defeated KMT was in some respects more painful than what happened to the Japanese after World War II because there was no graceful exit of the sort provided by the benevolent American occupation of Japan.

The need for dependency in Taiwan has been channeled into economic relationships, not toward power and prestige. In this sense, Taiwan is following the lead of Japan in breaking out of the Confucian mold. It is still unlikely that Taiwan will be able to institutionalize competitive politics and carry out graceful transferals of power as Japan has done. What is keeping Taiwan from becoming a freer society, perhaps second only to Japan in East Asia, is the compromised Confucian notion of power still held by its old-guard KMT.

Whereas both Korea and Taiwan have redirected their Confucian tradition of authority and propriety toward economic development and limited political freedom, Vietnam has kept its priorities on government, albeit revolutionary government. Those who had succeeded in becoming the Vietnamese elite decided long ago that Communism was the wave of the future. Even though the market economies all around them have become more prosperous, and Communist China has chosen to join the world economy, the faith of the old men in the Hanoi Politburo has not weakened. Yet their instinct for dependency is not in decline. They still believe that their military accomplishments, which are far from insignificant, should be rewarded with more than just the immediate spoils of victory. They desperately crave recognition.

The success of North Vietnam may be explained as a function of a combination of Communist single-mindedness, Saigon demoralization over being abandoned by its protector (the United States), and the mood of fatalism in the popular Vietnamese culture. In addition, Hanoi's ambitions to rule all of Indochina can be understood in terms of the model set by the French. What is hardest to understand is the Vietnamese elite's readiness to call for ceaseless suffering by the people. The Confucian ideal of paternalistic benevolence no longer exists in the Vietnamese political culture. What does remain is the ideal of duty, of making sacrifices without asking why.

In spite of these striking variations, the three cultures still preserve, in varying degrees, a key ingredient of the Confucian political culture: they remain elitist and paternalistic, and their leaders are still convinced that they know what is best for their respective societies. In Korea and Taiwan, economic successes lend some credibility to the authoritarian pretensions, and in Vietnam revolutionary and military achievements may serve the same function of justifying paternalistic authoritarianism. It is uncertain what the popular reaction would be to economic crises in the first two states or to military and revolutionary exhaustion and disillusionment in the third. In all three states the leaders seem to have stretched to the limits their people's cultural instincts for togetherness and group solidarity. The reaction to prolonged crises might therefore be a resurgence of more private forms of solidarity.

9 Malaysia: Confrontation of Two Incompatible Cultures

THE VIETNAMESE INVASION of Cambodia in 1978 shocked the five ASEAN countries, but none more than Malaysia, whose leaders for more than a decade had been the most critical of American involvement in South Vietnam, the most inclined to think well of Hanoi's leaders, and the most anxious for peace and tranquillity throughout the region. Kuala Lumpur had been the lone advocate of making Southeast Asia a "zone of peace, freedom, and neutrality," and it had encouraged the other members of ASEAN to hold out olive branches to Hanoi after its conquest of Saigon in 1975. Malaysia's sensitivity to conflict in the region is largely a function of its being an ethnically divided country, with Muslim Malays in the majority and Confucian Chinese in the minority.

The problems of ethnic or communal relations between the Malays and the Chinese have produced a fragile polity in which the cardinal rule of governance has been to avoid controversies which might arouse passions. The Malay leaders, who as the majority community set the tone of politics, insist that nation-building can take place only in a peaceful international atmosphere in which every country is anxious to have good relations with all the others. This viewpoint is not entirely convincing, since in many ethnically divided countries the need to mobilize against a foreign foe has cemented national unity. That has been the style of Singapore, whose government has repeatedly lectured its citizens on the imperatives of unity in a dangerous international environment. The birth of Malaysia in 1963 prompted Indonesia's President Sukarno to proclaim his policy of "Confrontation," a low-level military challenge to the Malaysian states that shared the island of Borneo with Indonesia. Singapore learned from that challenge the need to maintain a strong defense, based on three years of compulsory military service. But Malaysia chose to put the conflict out of mind as soon as it ended and to seek cordial relations with Sukarno's successor.

This contrast between the behavior of Singapore and that of Malaysia tells much about the different attitudes toward power in the Confucian and Southeast Asian cultures. The Confucian spirit demands that leaders stand up for their rights and proclaim their grievances. Consider, for example, the historical stance of Chinese leaders, who bewail, almost with pride, China's mistreatment by foreigners—a tradition which is expressed in the National Humiliation Day celebrated by the Communists as a reproach to the Soviets, and in their complaints about Taiwan to the United States.[1] The Chinese value harmony and correct etiquette, but they find it exceedingly difficult to suffer perceived injustice without voicing anguish to somebody. Ideally they would like to shame the one who hurt them, but if that is impossible any bystander will do. It is not just that one can gain face by being an innocent victim, but a public scolding can also cause the misbehaving party to lose face. By contrast, the Southeast Asian style in dealing with unpleasant and even dangerous situations is one of avoidance and silence, of repressing emotions in the hope that the problem will go away if matters are smoothed over. The Malays resemble the Indonesians and Thais in eschewing harshness and seeking gentleness and refinement in human relations.

These cultural differences, which become exaggerated at the elite level because they call for contrasting authority styles, constantly surface in Malaysian politics. After the "divorce" of Singapore and Malaysia on August 6, 1965, the Singapore side of the story was presented to the world, while Kuala Lumpur remained silent. The factional politics of the Malayan Chinese Association (MCA) routinely become public feuds that are reported in the press as every actor tries to draw attention to his mistreatment, claiming that he was completely correct in his conduct and thus innocent of all wrongdoing. Relations among the Malay leaders remain unreported, by contrast, thus conveying the impression that all is harmonious, which certainly is not the case.

The Malayan defense mechanism of denial can also be seen in the tendency to make troublesome or delicate issues taboo as subjects for public discussion. For example, in what is otherwise an open and free society it is illegal to discuss publicly such matters as the position of the traditional Malay rulers or sultans, and especially their economic dealings. Even more important, after the riots of May 1969 the Malay leadership clamped a lid on discussions of race or communal relations. For Malays, talking about trouble makes matters worse.

It was in connection with those bloody riots of 1969 that William Parker discovered the striking differences between the Chinese and Malayan responses to anxiety and subsequently documented them through standardized psychological tests. He was struck by the fact that the foreign press received only the Chinese side of the story while the Malays remained tight-lipped.[2] He found that the Chinese had been quick to articulate their anxieties after the riots, passing on rumors, embellishing their accounts, and above all trying to get the ear of observers so as to proclaim their innocence and attract sympathy for what they considered to be their mistreatment. The Malays had responded only with silence, which, of course, egged on the Chinese to become more vocal in articulating their fears and their sense of injustice—a reaction which made the Malays even more withdrawn in their need to practice denial.

At a deep psychological level the extreme contrasts between the ways in which the two cultures handle anxiety are not only different but profoundly antagonistic. And even on the surface these cultures present numerous points of conflict that make Chinese and Malays scornful of each other. The Chinese are urban people, interested in money and market activities, and they are committed to self-improvement and have strong family ties. The Malays are rural, are contemptuous of merchants, prefer service careers in the army and police, are more easygoing in social relations, and are tolerant of divorce. The Chinese are at home in a "tightly structured" society; the Malays have a "loosely structured" society. With respect to religion and customs, the two rub each other the wrong way: Malays practice Islam in varying degrees but they universally abhor the pig; Chinese have vaguer religious identities and are fond of eating pork.

All of these contrasts, which are identified in standard interpretations of Malaysia's ethnic tensions,[3] would be quite enough to create problems of nation-building; but they are made far worse by the deeper psychological ways in which each community tries to cope with the tensions that exacerbate their antagonisms. Politically the situation is explosive because the concepts of power and of the proper use of authority are antithetical. Consequently, when the leaders of one community do what is expected of them in their own culture, the members of the other community are infuriated.

Dilemma of Chinese Leadership and Power

The existence of a Chinese political culture in the Malaysian context presents two basic problems that have made the creating of an integrated political community exceedingly difficult. First, although according to the Confucian culture there should be consensus and conformity, the Chinese in Malaysia are far too divided by linguistic groupings, places of family origin in China, and class interests to achieve true consensus. No Chinese leader can in practice articulate a common Chinese position. Second, the Confucian political culture does not contain any guidelines for minority leadership in a community dominated by a non-Confucian culture. The Chinese concepts of authority are entirely premised on the assumption that both the omnipotent leader and his dutiful subordinates are Chinese; that a Chinese leader should be the subordinate of a "foreigner" is culturally unthinkable. As a result, large numbers of Chinese in Malaysia feel that a truly national politics is unattainable for them and that any Chinese who acts as a leader must be an impostor if he is subservient to the Malay majority leadership. The Chinese search for security thus becomes the tribal one of opting out of the majority system and focusing on special parochial groupings. For the older generation this has meant concentrating on their respective ethnic welfare associations and even on various secret societies. For the younger people the escape has taken the form of identifying with Chinese nationalism and with Chinese Communism—of pretending either that they are only accidentally in Malaysia and really at home in China, or of thinking that they are doing China's "revolutionary" work in spreading Peking's influence.[4]

It would be hard to overemphasize the problems the Chinese have in carrying on constructive dealings with a superior authority whom they perceive as "foreign." In colonial Malaya the Chinese immigrants displayed very early an extraordinary talent for organizing themselves into tightly structured communal associations and societies. Practically all Chinese belonged to some kind of larger grouping, most of which had the potential to become effective pressure groups. Such organizations, whether a benevolent association representing different dialect communities or the various merchant guilds, could have worked to advance the interests of their memberships by approaching the governmental authorities. Yet in practice the power they were able to create out of their capacity to organize large numbers of people was used entirely to shield their membership from the rest of society.[5] They operated as protective associations, not pressure groups. Whether they were legitimate benevolent associations or illegal secret societies, their Chinese cultural attitude toward power compelled their leadership to turn inward and to seek to minimize formal contacts with a state power that was seen as "foreign."[6]

The reluctance of association leaders to engage in power deals with the authorities did not reflect a totally inward-looking mentality, because within the Chinese community there were constant feuds between not only the secret societies but also the benevolent associations. They were prepared to use power to fight each other but not to pressure non-Chinese power.[7] This did not mean, of course, that individual Chinese were hesitant to approach the British authorities if they felt it was in their interest to do so. When I arrived in Malaya in 1952 during the Emergency, I assumed that it would be a major problem for the British to get information from the clannish Chinese community. Instead I discovered that the British problem was an overload of information. Any Chinese who was having trouble with another Chinese was quick to go to the police to report that his foe was a "Communist." People routinely tried to settle their personal scores by making up stories for the police, who then had to sort out valid intelligence from such malicious reports. The situation was not surprising to the British because long before the Emergency they had had extensive experience with Chinese tattling.

The inability of Chinese to function effectively in a polity in which they are a minority and lack the basis for an easy consensus is not limited to Malaysia and the other Southeast Asian countries. Even in the United States, where there are large concentrations of Chinese, the number of Chinese politicians participating in national, state, or city politics has been very small. The leaders of Chinatowns are content to focus on their internal affairs and to avoid competing in larger arenas. By contrast, Japanese-Americans, although fewer in number, have been more outgoing and are often quite successful in politics, particularly in Hawaii, where they dominate political life even though the Chinese outnumber them.

Historically the Chinese in Malaysia have been unable, by themselves, to solve the two problems of consensus and minority leadership. A politically effective and participatory, though not revolutionary, political movement was organized only after High Commissioner Sir Henry Gurney forced the issue, following the Malayan Communist party's decision to instigate armed struggle in 1948. Gurney quietly called together the wealthiest and most Westernized Chinese, whose natural leader was the Straits-born Sir Chenlock Tan, a rubber baron who spoke only English. Gurney pointed out that unless they organized a non-Communist party the entire Chinese community would be suspected of being in sympathy with the Communists, who by going into the jungles had triggered the Emergency conflict. Thus was born the Malayian (later Malaysian) Chinese Association (MCA), which has remained the junior partner of the Malays' party, the United Malay Nationalist Organization (UMNO), the dominant force in what was called first the Alliance and later the National Front, which has controlled Malaysian politics ever since.[8] (Before independence, when the country was called Malaya, the term Malayan was used in reference to both the general society and the Malay ethnic community. When Malaya became Malaysia, the national, and multi-ethnic, term became Malaysian, while Malayan has become more specifically identified with the Malay people.)

From its inception the MCA has had frustrating problems as a political force because it has never been able to achieve the ideal of authority expected by Chinese political culture. The British in their time assumed that the wealthiest and best-educated Chinese would be the natural leaders of the Chinese community, but in Confucian culture merchants and businessmen are not looked upon as wielders of political power. Moreover, in a political climate of Communist rhetoric about class warfare and the collusion of imperialists with the "national bourgeoisie," the designated leaders of the MCA did look suspiciously like British puppets.[9]

Even after independence the MCA's problems did not disappear. The lack of any clear hierarchical structuring of power, so essential for harmony and stability among Chinese, has made the inner politics of the MCA a story of continuous feuding. The Chinese concept of power, based on an unambiguous leader or father figure, has made collegial rule impossible. Someone must dominate, and to be in second or third place is intolerable for pretenders to leadership. The top leader is forever tempted to make his competitors appear subservient, and thereby to lose face while he gains it. From the time of the leadership of Sir Chenglock Tan and Dato Sir Henry Hau Shik Lee, followed by the struggles between Dr. Lim Chong Eu and Tan Siew Sin in the 1960s, and then by those of a younger generation in the 1980s, the MCA has never been without internal tensions.[10]

The Chinese cultural norms relating to power have also confounded the MCA's external relations both with its Chinese public and its UMNO senior partner in the Alliance and National Front. Following the traditional Chinese belief that complaints should be aired and redress sought from authority figures, especially if someone feels he has been wronged, the Chinese population has incessantly demanded that the MCA leaders should voice all the grievances of the Malaysian Chinese. Yet whenever the MCA leaders do respond in ways that please their constituents, they irritate the Malays, who have the ultimate power and who find Chinese behavior unacceptable. If the MCA leaders try to change tactics and ingratiate themselves with their Malay partners, the Chinese public dismisses them as impotent or selfish politicians who have sold out to non-Chinese, that is, to inferior people.

That there is no role for minority leadership in Chinese political culture contributes to the atmosphere of grumbling among Malaysian Chinese. As long as they do not have leaders who are both Chinese and the dominant authority they will be insecure, will feel that they are being discriminated against, and will seek sympathy by expressing their anxieties. Even though the Chinese community outstrips the Malays economically, its members will go on feeling mistreated by what they perceive to be a silent, unresponsive Malaysian government.

The validity of these observations about the psychodynamics of Malaysian Chinese behavior is confirmed by the political process in Singapore. There the Chinese are in the dominant, majority position, and the consequence is a politics of consensus in which opposition as trivial as the loss of a single seat by the People's Action party (PAP), is treated as a major, and personally insulting, threat to the regime.[11] The imperatives of conformity and the belief that total emotional commitment to unity is essential for collective success reflect Singapore's Confucian attitude toward power. When Prime Minister Lee Kuan Yew called for a reassertion of Confucian values in 1983, his proclamation that his society was becoming degenerate and needed to return to basic values was the rhetoric expected of a statesman in the Confucian tradition.

During the two years (1963–1965) when Singapore was a part of Malaysia, the contradiction between Chinese and Malay political culture was dramatized. Singapore's People's Action party decided it should cross the causeway and challenge the MCA and, in effect, the Alliance. Although it pressed to be the champion of "socialism" and to seek a noncommunal approach to politics, the move was seen by others as an attempt to alter the ethnic balance of power by uniting the Singaporean and Malaysian Chinese under the PAP banner. The head of UMNO and the Alliance, Prime Minister Tengku Abdul Rahman, responded in typical Malay style by calling for a "divorce" without giving any explanation.[12]

Although Lee Kuan Yew immediately moved to make his city-state—75 percent Chinese—into a conformist, one-party system, few Singaporeans questioned the relevance of Chinese cultural norms in an island country surrounded by Islamic and Southeast Asian cultures. Dato Lee Kong Chian, the leading rubber magnate, frequently complained to visitors that the Chinese in Southeast Asia were the last, anachronistic remnants of the colonial era and should therefore adapt to the era of nationalism. He saw three possibilities for the overseas Chinese. First, he considered Lee Kuan Yew's idea that it would be possible to have a noncommunal, one-man, one-vote democracy in Malaysia-Singapore, but he believed this was doomed to failure because the norms for such a system were an artificial British import which would erode in the postcolonial era. Second, the Chinese could follow the advice of the *towkays,* or businessmen, to leave politics to others and use Chinese economic strength behind the scenes or "under the table" to protect Chinese interests—a solution Lee believed to be unacceptable because its corrupting effects would ultimately backfire against the Chinese. The third possibility would be a social contract that would include a functional division of labor, with the Chinese concentrating exclusively on economic activities and agreeing to a non-Chinese monopoly of politics and government. This was the solution Dato Lee favored because, he insisted, for more than two hundred years there had not been a respectable Chinese-run government anywhere in the world.[13]

It is true that Lee Kuan Yew's Confucian authoritarian approach to politics has alienated some of the nontechnocratic intellectuals in Singapore. Indeed, some university people in the humanities and social sciences have complained about their government much as Chinese intellectuals in Malaysia complain about theirs. Yet, these exceptions aside, what is more impressive is the degree to which the Chinese in Singapore not only accept their firmly in-control government but also are prepared to welcome its paternalism.[14]

The contrast between the positions of Chinese citizens in Malaysia and Singapore captures almost perfectly the dilemma of the Confucian tradition (Chinese version) in confronting the challenge of modernization. In Malaysia the Chinese are discontented because, as a minority group in a democratic electoral system, they must bow to a non-Chinese majority, a situation they find intolerable. Therefore they complain as openly as possible, and to the degree that the Malay majority system is democratic, this means incessant claims of mistreatment. In Singapore, where the Chinese majority controls the government, the system of authority is unambiguous: one party and one man run the entire enterprise, everyone is expected to join in the consensus, and any deviant is automatically classified as a subversive. Conformity prevails in the polity although there is grousing that the father figure, the single leader, has not done his job perfectly. Such grumblings in a Confucian culture system should not be confused with desires for significant change in the system—they only serve to make the demands for consensus more incessant.

Malayan Authority: Dignity Striving for Effectiveness

The Malay ideal of authority is totally different from the Chinese. Whether in the case of the *punghulu* (the village leader) or the sultan of an unfederated Malay state, the expectation is that the supreme figure will always rise above his immediate passions and achieve a blend of impartial detachment and self-centered arrogance. Unfortunately, while the Malays have an instinctive understanding of the finest gradations of hierarchy and so are never confused as to who outranks whom, they are less certain about how power should be used. For example, should superiors be allowed to rejoice in their good fortune, or should they act as protecting patrons?[15]

The Malay image of authority is an extraordinary blend of traditional Southeast Asian sentiments of deferential accommodation, Islamic norms of fatalistic commitment to uncompromising ideals, and British aristocratic standards of fair play (but with status barriers). Colonialism in Malaya did not produce the leveling effect it has been accused of having in other subjugated societies. Instead the British practiced indirect rule in the Unfederated States, where sultans were allowed the charade of ruling but British advisors were at the elbow of their *mentri-bazars,* or prime ministers. In the Federated States British officials acted as the supreme figures according to their notions of traditional authority. The sultans were treated with all the deference instinctive to the British, but they were spared decision-making in all but their most personal realm. This created no problems for the British because in Anglo-Saxon culture there is no sense of hypocrisy over contradictions between status and effectiveness, between ritualistically honored figureheads and their competent subordinates. The Malays, however, were confused by this separation of status and command.[16]

Did the sultans really deserve all the pomp and circumstance which the British were prepared to give them? Historically their ancestors had claimed governmental authority, but only because they were able to provide the essence of government, or as a once popular American musical comedy defined it, "security at monopolistic prices." Others might call the sultans pirates and brigands. The British gave them respectability, but not a clear definition of the purpose of their power, if their status could be called that.

Behind the facade of the several sultans and their respective realms the British created a highly centralized bureaucracy, staffed with technocrats and general administrators of high professional competence.[17] The result was what Milton Esman has called an "administrative state."[18] The Malayan Civil Service (MCS), now known as the Perkhidmatan Todbir dan Diplomatik (PTD) has been recognized since British days as an elite service that provides the true structure of the Malaysian polity. It is significant that Malaysia was spared the sort of traumatic conflict between colonial-trained administrators and nationalist politicians that weakened the Burmese, the Indonesian, and a number of African political systems. Independence came to Malaysia more gradually, and the British members of the MCS did not leave immediately after independence. Consequently Malaysian politicians learned to work with ministries staffed by technically competent Britishers who had once been their rulers, while

Malaysian administrators had the benefit of the Westminster system, in which senior administrators could show deference to their political "masters" while making sure professionally that policies and practices remained sound. This situation, in which Malay politicians worked for several years with British civil servants, provided stability and continuity for Malaysian political development.[19]

The British followed a dual policy in shaping the concepts of authority among the Malays. One line was to establish a clear sense of professional careerism for Western-educated Malays in the civil service. The other was to reinstitutionalize the traditional rulers and make their authority conform to the standards of the European aristocracy and the Indian maharajahs and nizams, even to the point of having relative rankings among the international nobility. This blending of careerism and royalty reinforced the traditional Malay appreciation of status and hierarchy. Among Malays the most natural basis for social relations was respect for social distinctions.

The Malays' concern for deference springs from their basic socialization process, which, much like the Burmese process, does not provide sustained or predictable support and affection from the parents, but which, unlike the Burmese, does stress punishment and harsh discipline.[20] This combination of casualness and off-handed treatment, interrupted occasionally by punishment, prepares the Malay for service in such disciplined, hierarchical organizations as the army, police, and the bureaucracy. The tendency is to be lax whenever possible but to accept sudden, and even arbitrary, disciplinary treatment; yet the expectation is that one will be taken care of in a paternalistic fashion. Physical courage and the ability to endure pain are culturally prized, as is the capacity to get away with things that superiors do not approve of.

The Malay ideal of authority calls for sternness, dignity, and paternalistic concern; but it is also understood that those in authority can easily become angered and do irrational things. Hence it is imperative not to provoke authority but to stay out of its way as much as possible. Rather than expecting that correct conduct will be rewarded, as in Chinese culture, Malays tend to believe that it is prudent to avoid conspicuous actions by relying upon ritualized routines. The result is a low level of trust even among high officials. Having been socialized to expect uncertainty and unpredictable treatment by superiors, Malay officials continue to believe that it is best to avoid contact with them. But there is no expectation of complete abandonment. One will always be taken care of, even though there may be some bad moments.

James C. Scott has argued that this characteristic of distrust among Malay officials stems from a culture of poverty which includes the belief that because resources are limited there is only a "fixed pie" and every-thing is part of a zero-sum relationship.[21] Milton Esman concurs in this view.[22] It is likely that Malay culture has, over time, incorporated many of the orientations common to a culture of poverty, in which the belief prevails that there is a rigidly fixed social product. Yet the attitudes of distrust and ineffectiveness are also characteristic of well-to-do Malays who have had generous support in their education and have moved into the ranks of the elite. Not many members of the MCS come from peasant backgrounds, but many belong to the aristocracy and have a casual attitude toward material things and a tolerance for conspicuous con-sumption.[23] Indeed, the Malays seem to think that the Chinese are misers and hoarders, but they believe themselves to be generous and mutually supportive.

According to both Esman and Scott, Malaysian officials regard people as self-seeking, egotistic, and opportunistic, hence needing to be checked by government and religion, and as having a low sense of efficacy and a strong sense of hierarchy—characteristics which both scholars attribute to a fixed-pie orientation. But these characteristics are also consistent with what would be expected from the Malaysian socialization practices. Malay children, even in middle-class families, are taught to have pride and to maintain their personal dignity. Their world is also filled with dangers in the form of both this-worldly enemies and otherworldly spirits. Even before formal religious training begins, the Malay child is exposed to the idea that invisible forces are constantly at work in his environ-ment.[24] Indeed, Scott and Esman completely ignore the Malay's patient expectation that something miraculous is going to happen.

The fixed-pie orientation assumes that there is little scope for change and that all is fairly rigidly set. Yet in the Malay culture people are always prepared for the unexpected. They believe that supernatural agents can create something great out of nothing, or can deflate the pompous and make them into nobodies in the wink of an eye. At the village level the *bomor,* the ritual healer, sorcerer, shaman, or medicine man is always ready to perform feats of magic. Indeed, the basis of uncertainty in all of life is that magic exists, and that the other person's magic is likely to be greater than the magic that one can call up oneself. The world is never governed by rigidly fixed social forces—someone can always produce the miraculous out of thin air. Villagers and elite alike live in a world filled with supernatural agents—there are Muslim spirits (*jin Islam*), pagan spirits (*jin kafir*), guardian spirits (*penunggu*), ancestor spirits (*datuk-datuk*), the shepherd of the black tiger (*gembala harimau purun*), the vampire cricket banshees (*pelesit*), flying ghouls (*langsuyar*), devils (*iblis, setan*), Shiva (*Hantu Raya*), and many more.[25] The extreme rhythms of a rice culture, with its alternating frantic and relaxed periods, its manic and depressive tempos, combined with a hunting culture in which the jungle can provide less than expected or more than is needed, can hardly be the basis for the static, uptight outlook of a fixed-pie mentality. Moreover, the potential for surprise—both in terms of one's own good fortune and even more likely in terms of some outside malevolent power—prepares one to be on guard at all times. But it also means that for those who are always hopeful and confident, the worst may never happen.

A point often missed by the theorists who divide the world into rural-traditional-static societies and urban-modern-dynamic societies is that rural people who live close to the land are constantly exposed to the erratic forces of nature, while urban folk have their predictable, routine habits of daily living. It is no wonder that rural people are often more religious and superstitious, for they are sure that there are magical forces in the universe, while urban people are bound by the limits of human endeavors.

The Malay concept of power, as vividly depicted by Malay novelists, is one which begins with the expectation that cause and effect are not closely governed by the rational considerations of a zero-sum world. Instead, Malay fiction is filled with the workings of supernatural forces and the whimsical surprises of a people who are still close to raw nature.[26] Malays are brought up with stories of the incredible feats of *bomors* (medicine men), whose abilities to perform the unbelievable are so widely accepted that it is commonplace to believe in the impossible. Indeed, during the years of the Emergency when the Malaysian Communist party turned to violence, the British, on the one hand, feared that the Chinese in the party might break the ethnic barrier and entice Malays with the attractions of dialectical materialism—an ultimate form of magic—and, on the other hand, appealed to *bomors* to work their powers against the Chinese in the jungle. Malay convictions of the powers of such supernatural forces were so great that even the British were affected, and their armed forces committed blunders which rank among the more ludicrous in the annals of British military history.[27]

The belief that power is essentially invisible creates great uncertainty whenever circumstances call for competition. For example, when there is an opening for the headman's role in a *kampong*, or village, the potential aspirants face a quandary. To pretend to power that one cannot command is to be a fool and the laughingstock of the community; but it would be even worse to have the right to power and fail to claim it, for that would be a violation of nature. Although Malay culture includes some of the same rhetoric about decision-making by consensus as Indonesian culture does, in actual practice power struggles and feuds have been more common. In the matrilineal states, such as Negri Sembilan, such competition was kept in check by a system of rotational headships called *giliran*.[28] In colonial days when such struggles threatened to get out of hand, British District Officers would try to resolve the problem of power by what to them was the most natural method—holding elections. These events, however, could become the source of collective embarrassment to the *kampong*. When the candidates were ordered to make speeches, their usual response was to indulge in grandiose and boastful rhetoric, which would leave the audience uneasy about whether they should laugh or be awed.

Indeed, the basic dilemma inherent in the Malay attitude toward power is that power has always been seen as on the borderline between comical pretentiousness and reverential deference. The uncertainty that surrounded traditional concepts of power, which were associated with the supernatural, could be compounded by the uncertainty regarding role relations in a "loosely structured" society. A "nobody" could suddenly be discovered to have astonishing abilities and, as if by magic, could be instantly transformed into an awesome figure. But it was also likely that the posturing wise man would have no answers and that disaster would befall those who listened to him.

The opposite of this traditional Malay tendency to see power as unexpected, whimsical, and malevolent was the British colonial tradition of treating power as the orderly, ritualized management of affairs. In planning for the time after the Japanese surrender, officials in London hoped to tidy up Malaya's government by dispensing with the sultans and establishing a Malay Union that would be a truly centralized administration. That idea immediately ran into opposition from the old Malaya hands in England and the supporters of the traditional Malay rulers. It was seen both as a breach of faith with the rulers and the Malay population (although many Malays had collaborated with the Japanese) and as a concession to the Chinese (many of whom had fought against the Japanese). When the Union plan was abandoned, the Chinese community raised complaints, but these were soon vitiated by the Communist uprising, which was recognized as primarily a Chinese affair.[29]

Paradoxically, the retention of the traditional rulers turned out to be a major safeguard for Chinese interests in post-independence Malaysia. In nine of the eleven states in the peninsula the hereditary rulers have become a force for maintaining the status quo and have not tampered with the rule of law and the constitution. Although the rulers were originally conceived of as champions of Malay interests and defenders of Islam as the state religion, they have acted as a moderating force, checking Malay radicalism which might easily have become anti-Chinese—under the guise either of anti-capitalism or of outright Malay nationalism. The sultans have enough economic interests of their own to be sympathetic toward Chinese commercial anxieties. Older Chinese, in fact, constantly warn the younger and more radical Chinese not to stir up ideas of socialism because the Malays might decide to "nationalize" private industry by expropriating Chinese interests and dividing their wealth among the Malays.

The administrative state built by the British has been modified not only by the authority of the rulers but also by the style of the Malay politicians and by friction among the Malay bureaucrats, who have "humanized" Max Weber's ideal of bureaucratic authority by tolerating a moderate degree of slothfulness and petty corruption.[30] An easy relationship between politicians and administrators is to be expected in Malaysian political culture, but special credit must be given to the personal role of Tengku Abdul Rahman in setting the style for politicians. As the first prime minister it was natural for him to be called the father of his country, but that he was popularly known as Bapa Malaysia was due to his warm, paternalistic, and accommodating style of rule.[31] The Tengku's gentleness and his deflection of abrasive issues reflected the ideal of the Malay aristocrat, refined by many years of living well in London. As Esman has noted, the Tengku believed "that living the good life is not only a virtue in itself but that 'wining, gambling, and womanizing,' horseracing, sports, and beauty contests, however offensive to intellectuals, help to keep politics in their proper pragmatic perspective."[32] In many respects he typified not just the Malay but the more general Southeast Asian ideal of leadership, in that as long as he was treated with appropriate deference he would respond with kindness and friendship. He ruled by leaving technical matters to the civil servants, by showing respect to the sultans, by acting as a wise man for the Malay masses, and by being friendly to the non-Malays. He did not attempt to blur the ethnic lines or to demand assimilation or the creation of a single Malaysian national culture. The result was what Karl von Vorys has called "democracy without consensus."[33] The Tengku expected that each community would take care of its own affairs, according to its own cultural norms, and that at the top he could preside over a "directorate" which would work out any problems of accommodation. When action was called for, it usually took the form of co-optation rather than repression. When Malay religious teachers complained that the government was more concerned with Chinese interests than with Islamic values, the Tengku responded by giving them better pay and better conditions of service. In his Malay style he tolerantly listened to their protests but was slow in acting because he understood that time was the best healer of pent-up passions.

His approach did not work, however, in the race riots of May 13, 1969, and in 1970 he stepped down. His deputy, Tungku Abdul Razak, a more abrasive man, took over and began the policy of trying to reduce the ethnic inequalities of the Malays.

Limits of Power for Change

Emergency rule continued for two years after the riots, and it conformed very much to the Malay cultural style of handling problems by avoiding them. Race relations were not to be discussed in the public press, and criticism of the authorities was not allowed. Razak's administration decided that accommodation and co-optation, especially in relation to Chinese interests, were not adequate bases for stability and, therefore, a return to rule by the Alliance Party Directorate system would have to be accompanied by an explicit policy of favoring Malays not only in the cultural and symbolic areas but in seeking greater economic equality. A New Economic Policy (NEP) was instituted which explicitly called for reducing "racial differences" by affirmative action.

The Bumiputra ("sons of the soil") policy included quotas in education, employment, and ownership, as well as a variety of subsidies, licenses, and credit schemes.[34] In some areas the plan was exceedingly ambitious, calling, for example, for Malays to have 30 percent of corporate equity ownership by 1990, although they had only 1.5 percent at the time. New universities and technical institutions for Malay students were established, and Malay became the official language of university instruction. The Chinese were denied the right to have their own Chinese university. Quotas were established for university admissions, and in the higher civil and diplomatic services a 4 to 1 ratio of Malays to non-Malays was required.

Although the Bumiputra plan soon fell behind its target goals for erasing inequalities, the Chinese increasingly felt the stings of discrimination and the Malays were frustrated when they failed to catch up with the Chinese. The plan resulted in more tension within both communities and a worsening of race relations, but there was no dramatic explosion. The Chinese had to acknowledge that the Malays possessed majority power and should not be provoked. Furthermore, the expansion of the Malaysian economy at a rate of 7 to 9 percent during the decade of the 1970s meant that the Chinese continued to hold a substantial lead over the Malays, the per capita income ratio being nearly 2 to 1.[35]

The political consequences of the NEP have, however, had significant ramifications for Malaysia's future. Chinese discontent has put great strain on the MCA, which has increasingly been charged with failing to protect Chinese interests. Two minor Chinese parties outside the Alliance have been able to win fifteen seats. Although the MCA lost only four of the seats it contested in the April 1980 general elections, it was not rewarded with additional cabinet posts beyond the four it already held. By 1983 the internal power struggle between acting president Neo Yee Pan and his chief rival, Tan Koon Swan, had reached the point at which each was trying to expel the other's faction from the party. In short, the stress of the NEP was fragmenting the Chinese community. Diffuse feelings of insecurity among the Chinese were causing them to turn inward to ever smaller and more intimate groupings for support. The idea of participating in a competitive political system which was not based on Confucian rules seemed increasingly foolish, if not dangerous. The result was a retreat into privatization, with increased concentration on professionalism and commercial enterprises.

The changes in the Malay concepts of power were also significant. In 1981 Dr. Mahathir Mohamad became prime minister, and he and his deputy, Datuk Musa Hitam, working closely in what was called the "2-M government," sought to upgrade civil service performance. Their assumption was that the failure of the Bumiputra plan was largely traceable to bureaucratic incompetence. Their slogan for the bureaucracy was "Clean, Efficient, and Trustworthy." This attack on administrative performance, even though it was done to advance Malay interests, was soon seen as a criticism of the Malay style of authority. Older officials who had known the more comfortable ways of governing under the Tengku were passed over as younger "technocratically trained" officials were pushed ahead.

Dr. Mahathir's attack on the traditional Malay style of easygoing administration was not entirely surprising because before becoming prime minister he had written a book, *The Malay Dilemma,* in which he had explicitly dealt with Malay cultural characteristics as racial traits. For example, he wrote, "It [inherent racial character] explains why the Malays are rural and economically backward, and why the non-Malays are urban and economically advanced. It is the result of the clash of racial traits. They are easy-going and tolerant. The Chinese especially are hardworking and astute in business. When the two came in contact, the result was inevitable."[36] Some Malays, especially those in the bureaucracy, reacted to Mahathir's "administrative reforms" by saying that the prime minister had gone beyond seeking equality for the Malays and was determined to "transform Malays into Chinese," which to them would be an abomination.

This suspicion got greater circulation in the fall of 1982 when Mahathir provoked a constitutional crisis by seeking to weaken the powers of the sultans, and especially those of the Yang di Pertuan Agong, or the rotating "king" elected by the sultans from their own ranks for five-year terms. Here again, paradoxically, the institutions of traditional Malay authority were seen as being supportive of Chinese interests and obstacles to the advancement of the Malays.[37] The crisis was finally resolved by reducing the sultanate's power to delay legislation, but the effect was further to erode traditional Malay authority without clearly strengthening the authority of the administration.

The objective of the 2-M government went beyond trying to raise the standard of living of rural Malays, a goal that remained elusive, and became increasingly that of making Malaysia a member of the NICs (newly industrialized countries).[38] Dr. Mahathir specifically called for the country to "look eastward," that is, toward Japan and Korea, and he talked about "Malaysia Incorporated." Ironically, the economic effects of these policies were beneficial for many Chinese enterprises and also for the new state-supported enterprises with Malay management. But the success of many of these state industries was still a matter of uncertainty in the mid-1980s.[39]

One of the responses to the stresses introduced into Malay society by the appeals of the 2-M government for a better work ethic and more diligence and productivity among Malays was a subtle backlash in the form of a strengthening of Islam in the country. Many of the programs that sought to raise the consciousness of Malays caused them to think about their ethnic identity and this led to a greater awareness of the rules of their Muslim faith. Students at the Malay University, for example, successfully demanded separate dining facilities for men and women. The increased numbers of Malays at the multiracial universities also had the effect of making Islam a more critical element in the Malay sense of identity. At these institutions the Chinese and Indians tend to concentrate on the science and engineering faculties and on economics, while the Malays gather in the humanities and history departments. In some cases the rather shrill advocacy of a purified form of Islam seems to be a kind of compensation for difficulties in competing with non-Malays in secular pursuits.

The government became aware of the danger of a fundamentalist Islamic revival, which would certainly destroy its prime objective of industrializing the country and altering the life-style of the Malays. Yet the very policies of the government in seeking rapid advancement significantly weakened the forms of authority which were the traditional models for the Malays. For many Malays the only alternative to becoming more "like Chinese" was to become more truly Muslim.

It is unlikely that the government will force matters to the point of provoking a mass movement toward Islamic fundamentalism. Most Malays are content with their more relaxed version of Islam. In all probability the government will have to try to strengthen the directorate system within the National Front by insisting that both MCA and UMNO be more accommodating toward each others' problems. The Chinese can recognize that Islamic fundamentalism is just as dangerous as Malay rioting, while UMNO leaders can see that if the MCA is further weakened by uncompromising anti-Chinese policies the constraints of the Chinese community would be weakened, which in turn could only lead to greater political instability. Everyone can therefore recognize that it is in the collective interest to make sure that the pace of economic progress is maintained and that each community continues to uphold its own sense of order. Fortunately, in their different ways both the Chinese and the Malays have a need for dependency, and hence there is a latent bias in favor of going along with their respective leadership groups. The test is whether the elites will be able to maintain their own cohesiveness.

10 Islamic Power: The Pulls of Reformism and Fundamentalism

F OR ONE HUNDRED YEARS Asia has been haunted by a series of fears of impending political explosion. Originally China as the "awakening giant" threatened to "shake the world"; next the various nationalist movements opposed colonial rule; and then came the Japanese version, "Asia for the Asiatics." In the first postwar decade the presumed frustrations of Westernized "intellectuals" made them the leading candidates for igniting political explosions. In the 1960s the "peasants" were fancied to have the intuitive cunning to "defeat the greatest power on earth" and to tilt the world balance of power by their "invincible" revolutionary power.

By the mid-1980s, in the wake of the Iranian revolution, many came to believe that the prime candidate for disrupting Asia's development was the ancient religion of Islam. Significantly, the rulers of the Islamic countries were even more nervous than the distant foreign observers about the unpredictable power of a revived faith in the Word of the Prophet. We cannot predict whether Islamic fundamentalism will derail political development in Malaysia or Indonesia or weaken further the remaining secular authority in Pakistan and Bangladesh, but we can describe the complex and often contradictory ways in which different versions of legitimate Islamic power have facilitated or impeded national development and modernization in the four major Muslim countries of Asia—Pakistan, Bangladesh, Indonesia, and Malaysia.

Historically, the earliest forms of Islamic power in Asia were those of a conquering or ruling aristocracy. In India, Islam was identified, of course, with the Mogul conquests and a tradition of imperial governance that looked to Persia and its emperors. Although Arab traders were principally responsible for spreading the Word of the Prophet to Southeast Asia, Islam as a political phenomenon was first associated with the sultans and local rulers, some of whom in time became partners of the British and Dutch in a system of indirect rule. With remarkable grace such rulers sought out their assigned niches in the hierarchies of Europe's aristocratic rankings. As individuals, the sultans, nizams, and princes took on a form of upper-class Westernization which suggested that they were "modernists," fitting comfortably into Europe's class-ridden society.

In time the ulama, or learned religious men, came to accept the partnership of local Muslim rulers and European colonial authorities. By the time Islam had reached Asia it was accepted that state power might not adhere to the laws of God as revealed in the Koran and the Hadith, the six collections of remembrances, by friends and family, of Muhammad's words. (The putting into practice of the Hadith, together with other accounts of the Prophet's deeds, constitutes the Sunna, or "beaten paths," from which comes Sunni, the name of the main branch of Islam, especially in Asia.) The fall of Baghdad to the Mongols, which ended the possibility that the caliphate could claim to trace its line back to Muhammad's rule from Medina, forced Islam to acknowledge that sacred and secular authority could not be one. It was a compromise, however, which left Islam permanently plagued with a contradiction that still bedevils its followers' understanding of power. Under Muhammad no distinction had existed between sacred and secular power, and the principles of the Koran were supposed to guide equally Muslim rulers and Muslim religious teachers. With the ending of the caliphate and the fragmentation of Muslim power, Muslim secular power and Islam as a religion acquired separate identities. The teachings of Muhammad became the ideals of behavior and not the specific goals of political power. As Edward Mortimer has noted, "By the eleventh century A.D., most of the *ulama* were teaching that obedience was an absolute duty, even to an unjust ruler, since an unjust ruler was better than none at all."[1]

This was not a satisfactory solution for a faith which in its written word clearly denied any such separation. Thus in the modern era there has been a widespread craving to recapture the purity of an "Islamic state," in which political authority would once again support the religious doctrines and rules of personal conduct laid down by Muhammad. Western colonialism, ironically, helped to bring the political and religious back together because the Muslim rulers could be seen as protectors of their fellow believers from the worst effects of rule by infidels. Although they were not always disciplined, practicing Muslims, they could at least understand what the ulama were teaching. In India, the transition from Mogul to British rule still left some Muslim rulers with a special grandeur. In Indonesia, the Dutch acknowledged the authority of the sultans and of the *priyayi* aristocracy by agreeing that Indonesian commoners should not have their Islamic faith threatened by Christian or secular educational institutions. In Malaysia, the sultans, in both the Federated and the Unfederated states, whatever their personal proclivities, were compelled by their respective British residents or advisors to see that Islamic customs were respected. The shared faith of the traditional rulers and the *kampong* farmers and fishermen, honored in British law, was also a common defense against the encroachments of the materialistic Chinese lacking any articulated religion.

Thus for a time in India, Malaysia, and Indonesia, Muslims could identify in varying degrees with the ruling authorities. Beyond whatever sense of specialness their faith gave them, Muslims could picture themselves as closer politically to the ruler of the realm than were the Hindu and Chinese "unbelievers." This was not, however, a stable or durable situation. Colonial rule brought dynamic changes, and the spread of secular ideas forced the educated Muslims to rethink their relationships with both their traditional rulers and the European colonial authorities. The first stirrings of a modernist awakening among educated Muslims in India and Indonesia in the first decade of the twentieth century was greatly accelerated by the breakup of the Ottoman Empire and the subsequent spiritual reformism that swept through much of the Middle East. In no small measure Islamic Reformism of that day, and particularly puritanical Wahhabism, was a reaction to decay in Muslim societies.[2] In India such thinkers as Sayyid Ahmad Khan, Sayyid Amir Ali, and Mohammad Iqbal sought to open Muslim minds to accepting modern (Western) knowledge as a way of strengthening the position of Muslims in a colonial society. Sayyid Ahmad Khan went so far as to argue that modern science was really the study of the laws of nature, and since nature was the work of God, which was revealed through the Word of the Prophet, therefore Islam and science were as one.

The clash between modernist reformers and the more orthodox ulama inevitably had political repercussions under Western colonialism. The reformers were inclined to see varying degrees of merit in aspects of British and Dutch rule. In particular they established the tradition that such activities as governmental administration and military life could not be guided entirely by the rules of conduct set down in the Koran. Thus they opened further the gap between the sacred and the secular; some, such as Sayyid Ahmad Khan, even went so far as to call for total loyalty to colonial rule.[3] By contrast, the orthodox Muslims were increasingly driven into the odd situation of becoming more anti-Western, hence anticolonial, but without a solid view of what nationalism should represent.

These tensions among the traditional Muslim rulers, the Westernized reformers, and the more orthodox ulama set the stage for Islam to become a force in Asian nationalism, but one that contained some very basic contradictions. The ultimate trend was toward a populist form of Islamic power, the dynamic character of which is more easily traced in Indonesia than in India, where Muslim reactions were further complicated by the existence of a Hindu majority and by the need to compete against a Hindu-dominated Congress party.

Contradictions in Islamic Nationalism

In a peculiar way Dutch colonial policies both inspired and undercut Islamic power as the key element of Indonesian nationalism, an ambivalence that was reinforced by contradictions in Indonesian society. Changes in Dutch thinking about colonial responsibility in the early 1900s brought about the abandonment of liberal, laissez-faire policies and the adoption of more paternalistic policies, which often had the contradictory effect of strengthening traditional customs while undermining traditional authority. For example, by transferring some power to Indonesians at the province or regency level, the Dutch weakened the traditional Muslim rulers and gave more prominence to Westernized Indonesians. As Harry Benda pointed out, "the *priyayi* were degraded from their previous status of nominally absolute rulers to that of mere chairmen of Regency Councils, whose members were as often as not far better educated and more adept at quasi-parliamentary debates than was the Regent."[4] Thus the movement toward granting more power to Indonesians, which accelerated with the establishment of the Volksraad or People's Council in 1918, meant a weakening of the regal ideals associated with the traditional Muslim rulers and the encouragement of more populist forms of Islamic power.

Hence, it was not surprising that the first Indonesian cultural society, Budi Utomo (the Noble Endeavor), founded in 1908 and composed of *priyayi* nobility, soon foundered, while the second party, Sarekat Islam (the Islamic League), founded in 1912 by Westernized intellectuals, flourished. The ideology of Sarekat Islam was largely defined by its Western-educated leader, Haji Umar Sayyid Tjokroaminoto, who had learned about reformist Islam in the Middle East and wanted to carry the message to the *desa,* or villages, and their religious leaders and teachers. In a matter of only seven years the movement swept the rural countryside by appealing to those with social and economic grievances and suggesting that the evils of the day could be traced to the failings of an "infidel" government.

Thus the birth of the Indonesian independence movement was wedded to the ideals of Islam. The appeal was broadly based, but, in view of the notorious inexactness of Indonesian figures, its claim in 1919 to having 2 million members should be taken with a grain of salt.[5] In fact, by the early 1920s Sarekat Islam was in dramatic decline. Its Westernized leadership was split between its reformist thinkers and a Marxist faction, which in 1920 broke away to form the Indonesian Communist party (PKI).[6] Moreover, the Dutch authorities reacted predictably to the movement's popularity; and, surprisingly, the somewhat demoralized *priyayi* staged a revival and sought to reassert their version of Islamic authority through the Budi Utomo.

Sarekat Islam was also countered by another element in Islamic politics, the Muhammadiyah, a third party that was both reformist and anti-obscurantist and that stressed secular activities for urban people. It emulated many of the activities of the Christian missions by forming youth and women's associations and establishing schools that provided secular education as well as religious training. Indeed, it was in the field of education that the differences between Sarekat Islam and Muhammadiyah became most acute and where Dutch policies exacerbated the clash. As Sarekat Islam began to lose out in the cities, it became more dependent upon the *kiyayi*, or religious teachers, at the *pesantren*, or religious schools in the villages. The Dutch authorities became increasingly critical of the questionable education provided by the *pesantren*, which often seemed to be modeled on Mr. Squeers's school in *Nicholas Nickleby*.[7] Thus in 1925 the Dutch passed the "Guru Ordinance," which required the *kiyayi* to register what they would teach, and in 1932 went further in trying to regulate the quality of such enterprises.[8] In the meantime, the Dutch subsidized the Muhammadiyah schools because they met the standards appropriate to modern life.

Relations within the Islamic community were made even more complicated when the Dutch sought to codify adat, or traditional, law, which had long been the province of the ulama. Instead of insisting upon a modern code of laws as the British did in their colonies, the Dutch believed it should be possible to standardize adat law and make it consistent, and they even established special adat law schools. But the ulama believed that the very essence of adat was that it was full of contradictions and hence only those with the wisdom that came from Islamic religious training could properly apply it. Thus the Dutch not only challenged the authority of the ulama, but they legitimized the mixing of religion and politics by their attempts to "rectify" what they saw as "abuses." A major effect of the government's actions was to politicize the ulama, who consequently formed the Nahdatal Ulama (NU) party, which became strongly orthodox and antireformist. In the meantime Muhammadiyah (and later Masjumi) became the defender of reformist Islam and the advocate for Muslims working in modern institutions.

These historical details show how Indonesian Muslims have become divided between those who accept modernist or Westernized ideas—either the aristocratic or the more technocratic version—and those who are inclined toward populism and orthodoxy. Indonesian nationalism thus became delicately balanced between a somewhat secular view of the state and a strong leaning toward fundamentalism. Those of the latter persuasion distrusted the former, for as Benda noted, they "saw in the Western-trained intelligentsia a product of a godless, materialistic West which was cunningly undermining the very basis of Indonesian identity, which to them was coterminous with Islam."[9]

In Indonesia, as in India and later in Malaya, the ideal of Islamic power became hopelessly confused. Should it be a return to the desert ways of Muhammad, a world long gone? Or should it be a Muslim response to the West, an aggressive assertion that present-day Believers should be the competitive equals of Europeans? Those tilting toward orthodoxy, that is, the more conservative, said that Muslims were special people who had their distinctive values, and hence they should not try to compare themselves with European Christians. They were like the Chinese Confucianists, who resisted all forms of Western knowledge. The modernist reformers wanted a revitalization of Islam so as to make Muslims the equals, if not the superiors, of Westerners in carrying out the burdens of being modern, rational people. They were like the Japanese Confucianists.

Dutch policies contributed to this polarization. But the Dutch also balanced their challenge to the religious leaders with support for the modernists, which in the end ensured that, when independence came in 1949, national leadership would go to those who were at home with secular ideas. Thus Sarekat Islam, in spite of having become a formal political party in 1929, quickly lost out to the Parti Nasional Indonesia (PNI) as the champion of Indonesian independence.[10]

Ironically, once Indonesia became independent, the more secular nationalist leaders were soon as distrustful of Islamic fundamentalism as the Dutch had been. They confirmed the prediction by Snouck Hurgronje, the leading Dutch authority on Indonesian Islam: "If . . . the millions of native Indonesians, whose daily labor as small peasants does not permit their spirits to rise above the level of their fields of rice, find themselves attacked by the epidemic of Pan Islamism, their compatriots, who have become our associates and equals, will themselves have the greatest interest to ward off this menacing danger."[11]

The "menace" came in the form of the Dar'ul Islam rebellion of 1948–1962 that took some 25,000 lives in West Java before its leader, S. M. Kartosoewirjo, was finally executed for treason. The rebellion began as an attack on the returning Dutch authorities after the Japanese surrender, but it continued against the new Republic of Indonesia. Thus, right from the inception of Indonesia as a state, the political class was given a warning that Islamic fundamentalism could become a dangerous force in their Muslim society. Even though Karl Jackson's research has demonstrated that whether villages supported the rebellion, opposed it, or remained neutral was less a function of religious conviction than of *bapakism* (or patron-client ties), the explosive potential of fundamentalism was an important factor.[12] Indeed, Jackson's research makes fundamentalism more threatening by suggesting that it can be quite unpredictable. He was able, through survey questionnaires, to challenge, as far as political behavior, the neat distinction, popularized by Clifford Geertz and others, between the devout, orthodox *santri* and the more syncretist, spirit-believing *abangan*.[13] The term *abangan* has been used to cover a wide range of people, from those who may be deeply religious but who adhere to a mixture of doctrine and ritual that is only partly Islamic, to people who are barely aware of any feature of Islam or even of traditional animism. (Western writers have tended to ignore the Indonesian label for the latter, *Islam statistik*, or "a Muslim for statistical purposes.") The conventional view has been that if religion intruded unduly into Indonesian politics it was likely to be the work of the *santri*, and that the *abangan* masses would be less likely to be religiously motivated. Jackson found that even fanatical behavior in presumed support of religious ideals had been carried out by superficial believers, while devout Muslims had been quite restrained. Factors other than just the intensity of belief were critical in mobilizing support for a nominally Islamic religious cause. Yet, as Jackson concedes, the movement did arise out of Islamic concepts, and therefore the authorities had a right then, as they do now, to be concerned about the potentially explosive character of Islamic fundamentalism.

Potential for Explosion

Every government in Asia with a predominantly Muslim population has made extensive concessions to that faith, yet all are sensitive to the dangers of ever greater fundamentalist demands, which, if unduly frustrated, could produce rebellions. The basis of this potential for explosion is two-fold. The first factor is the appearance of a leader who is passionately devoted to the Prophet's Message and who is ready to sacrifice himself in a Holy War, that is, to lead a jihad, particularly to overthrow an *ummat kafirun,* "rule by infidels," and to establish a true Islamic state for the *ummat Islam,* the "Moslem community." The second factor is the potential followership, usually rural people who are distressed about modern society, see it as plagued with abomination and polluted with secular vice and corruption, and who crave to recapture the communal bliss they believe once characterized Asian village life. Thus the need is for a spark and a tinderbox.

In regard to the first factor, leadership, Muhammad Ali Jinnah was the archetype of the successful, fanatical Muslim leader. Although there were other strong voices in the Muslim League, Jinnah's personal passion and unyielding willpower were probably critical in the creation of Paki-stan. Elsewhere such fanaticism for Muslim power was less successful. Kartosoewirjo failed in Indonesia. In Malaysia, Dr. Al-Hemy Barhan-uddin attempted to establish a Malay Nationalist party by appealing to Pan-Islamic values, but he failed to attract followers, partly because his effort was too obviously an attempt to incorporate Malaya into Indo-nesia.[14] In Pakistan, Abul A'la Maududi, the founder, before independ-ence, of the Jamat'e Islami, a fundamentalist Islamic party, was able in 1953 to mobilize passionate mob violence over the Ahmadis issue. In Bangladesh the student leader Ghulam Azam stirred up considerable popular agitation with his language movement when he demanded that Bengali be accepted as the equal of Urdu as an official language in what was then East Pakistan. (Ironically, Ghulam Azam opposed the inde-pendence of Bangladesh on the grounds that it would weaken the "unity of Islam.")

The contradiction, inherent in the Islamic concept of power, between autocratic, absolutist ideals and a sense of democratic community has produced a vexingly ambiguous picture of what a good leader should be like. The image of the Prophet and of those who spread the Word of Allah by the sword suggests that the deeds of the individual should command admiration and respect; yet the culture also accentuates the communal values of a brotherhood in which no one person's views should be imposed arbitrarily. The standards of personal conduct set by the Koran and the Hadith are severe in the extreme, and much is forbidden—declared to be *haram,* "tabooed." Hence he who is seen as exemplary is likely to command instant deference. At the same time, however, im-mediate access to Paradise is given to one who sacrifices his life for the brotherhood, for *ummat Islam.*

The collectivist ideals of the Islamic "brotherhood," which compel both reformists and orthodox to value a sense of togetherness, produces an inescapable tension for those who would stand out as leaders. The hesitation of religious leaders to come forward into political roles and their compulsive, driven style after doing so suggest that they have a sense of inner turmoil, resembling guilt feelings. To be individualistic in a group-oriented culture is difficult enough, but when this individualism, as a style of leadership, is associated with Westernized roles which might corrupt Muslim life, it is far worse. Thus while Islam seems to encourage the ideal of the upright person, willing to sacrifice for the community, it is ambivalent toward the religious leader who also acts as an individualistic political leader.

In Islam religious leaders are not priests who may intervene between the believer and the divine, but rather they are teachers whose task it is to instruct, to clarify doctrine, and to preserve the purity of rituals. The relationship between teacher and student can be of a binding nature, calling for total obedience and lifelong loyalty. The ties, however, are not the same as in the Chinese *guanxi,* the Japanese *on-giri,* or even the Indonesian *bapakism,* in that there is nothing of the nature of a quid pro quo. Instead of a sense of real reciprocity, there is only obligation and duty. But even that is not standardized, since there are no set rules of obligation. The teacher, if he sees fit, can call for support from his pupils. Their response may also be somewhat uncertain, for time may have weakened the ties with him, especially for those who have gone on to other activities. Yet if enough teachers are stirred up over an issue, their appeals can produce a broad mobilization of passion and action. The power of the ulama and the *kiyayis* can at any moment move into the secular domain because the Koran does not recognize a sharp divide between the sacred and the secular. Hence, again, an explosion can come if religious teachers are inspired to collective action.

The second factor that causes governments to worry about fundamentalist reactions is the "combustible" component of followership—of a Muslim public that has become frustrated and feels threatened by modernization developments. As with the leadership factor, popular reactions are hard to predict because Muslim behavior tends to be polarized. Much of the time there is a fatalistic acceptance of whatever happens—it is "Allah's will," "Allah will provide," and all the variations of the common Arabic phrase, *inshallah* ("if God wills"). The Asian cultures express something more than "Middle Eastern passivity": Malaysians and Indonesians, in particular, embrace the non-Islamic ideal of tranquillity and avoid agitating the inner psychic state of others. But this apparent state of calm can be suddenly broken by collective rage, as when racial riots erupted in Kuala Lumpur in 1969, and when Pakistani mobs burned down the American Embassy in Islamabad in 1979 because they had heard false rumors that the United States had had something to do with an attack on the Grand Mosque in Mecca.

The potential for otherwise peaceful and disciplined Believers to become violent results in no small measure from the sharp line drawn by Islam between good and evil, between purity and pollution, between virtuous and abominable behavior. Muslim standards of personal conduct seem so unattainable to the common people that they are driven to compensate for personal failings by expressing righteous indignation toward superiors who appear to them to be violating the spirit of Islam.

Modernization, with its secular values and urban life-styles, can easily provoke such rage. The understandable insecurities that often accompany rapid social change can readily cause Muslims to romanticize their earlier traditional order and to see all that is occurring about them as a demonic threat to their desires for spiritual purity.[15] The evils of the modern world are especially troublesome because they are so readily identified with the Christian West. The more the processes of economic and social change pull Malays from their *kampongs* and Indonesians from their *desas,* the more the urban populations in those countries will contain people who at a moment's notice can shed their inherent timidity and burst into rage.

Significantly, in both Malaysia and Indonesia it is university students, not the older generation, who have demanded stricter "Islamic" rules. Traditionally Malay women had neither worn veils nor worried about allowing their hair to be seen, but in the early 1980s university students on Malaysian campuses began to demand separate dining facilities and even to agitate for partitions in classrooms to separate men and women. Neither university administrators nor government ministries have been sure how to handle such religiously inspired demands. To be totally unsympathetic could provoke mass action and expose the authorities to the charge that they are hostile to Islam and champions of modern Western values; yet to give in too easily could open the way to escalating demands which could be endless because it is not clear what Islam requires in the running of a modern institution.

This unanswerable question concerning what the standards of an Islamic society should be creates persisting problems for those Asian governments that have Muslim populations. It is a question which will continue to surface even after the threat of explosive behavior has been successfully managed. This problem has been particularly acute for Pakistan (and Bangladesh), which was to have been the perfect "Islamic state."

What Is an Islamic State? What Is a Muslim?

From the time the British overthrew the Moguls, the messianic ideal of an Islamic state began to possess the public mind of the Muslims of the subcontinent. Paradoxically, it was the Westernized elite who became the captives of such an idealistic objective, while the traditionalist ulama initially opposed the idea of a separate Pakistan.[16] The Westernized Muslim elite were driven to the idea of separation from Hindu India because they could foresee that in a united, post-British India they would be hopelessly outnumbered in national politics by the Hindus, and therefore at best they could only be provincial figures. This seems to have been the logic which changed Jinnah from an early exponent of a united India to a dogmatic fighter for a separate Islamic state.[17] Jinnah himself had some doubts about the ideal of an Islamic state, for he said that in Pakistan "there would be no discrimination between one community and another," and that one could "belong to any religion or creed—that has nothing to do with the business of the State."[18]

Pakistan was founded on Islamic ideals, but it was not clear in 1947, or thirty-five years later, what those ideals were. Jinnah died less than a year after he had achieved his goal: a "Muslim state." Yet, as Aziz Ahmad has noted, those who founded Pakistan were ambivalent about what the essence of an Islamic state was, for "after the creation of Pakistan, its ruling elite was content to see that Pakistan had an external Islamic personality, but that the government was run on lines as close to British Indian secular principles as possible."[19]

Jinnah's successor, Liyaqat Ali Khan, was immediately confronted with the logical and spiritual contradictions which have darkened the idealism that was supposed to be Pakistan's special merit. During his brief premiership from 1947 to 1951, when he was assassinated, he was frantically trying, with one hand, to push aside the rising tide of the conservative ulama's enthusiasm for their newly discovered vision of a truly Islamic state, and, with the other, to give Pakistan all of the British secular standards of government which he knew India was trying to realize under Nehru's rule.[20]

The ulama insisted, for example, that in an Islamic state only Muslims should be allowed to hold office because public life and private life should be one and the same. But more pragmatic minds recognized that the logical result of such religious norms would be that in a non-Muslim state such as India no Muslim could hold public office. This would put "Islamic" Pakistan in the intolerable position of opposing the political accomplishments of Muslims in every other country.

Simultaneously, the Kashmir conflict with India unexpectedly challenged the ideals of Islamic power in Pakistan. The Pakistan government, wishing to avoid a total war with India over Kashmir, had taken the qualified position that the fighting was a jihad for only the local Muslims in the provinces of Kashmir. The religious thinker Maulana Abul A'la Maududi immediately embarrassed officialdom by saying that they could not have it both ways: either Pakistan as a true Muslim state should be the protector and carry out the obligations of a Holy War, a jihad, or the issue of Kashmir was not a matter of Pakistani state pride. For such annoying reasoning Maududi was arrested.

Yet the Pakistani authorities remained the prisoners of their almost ridiculous contradictions. The most modernized Muslims had championed the ideal of an Islamic state in the belief that it could come closer to the British style of democracy than Hindu India. But they were challenged constantly by orthodox and fundamentalist Muslims who had opposed the idea of Pakistan as an inappropriate mixing of religion and politics, but who insisted that once the Islamic state had been established it should be true to the Faith.

In 1953 the ambiguities of Pakistan as an Islamic state were exposed in a crisis over a sect known as the Ahmadiya, whose claim to be Muslims offended the more orthodox but whose most distinguished member was needed by the state-building elite. The originator of the sect was Mirza Ghulam Ahmad, who claimed that he had received a revelation from God—thereby suggesting that Muhammad's was not the final revelation—which made all of his followers apostate in the eyes of orthodox Muslims. What brought the crisis to a head was that one of the members of the Ahmadiya was Sir Muhammad Zafullah Khan, Pakistan's brilliant foreign minister, who was skillfully elevating the country's prestige internationally. The religious leaders took it out on the ordinary members of the sect, and for a time the government tried to look the other way as mobs killed them off. Finally, however, near-anarchy swept Lahore, the capital of the Punjab, and the government had to act against the Islamic fundamentalists.

Pakistan then, as it was to do on an almost permanent basis, escaped into martial law. An extraordinary court of inquiry was established under the chief justice of the supreme court, Muhammad Munir. The Munir Report was a most revealing document, for while it found that the Ahmadiya sect was not Muslim, it also conclusively demonstrated that the most learned of the ulama could not agree on what a Muslim was. As a liberal-minded, British-trained jurist, Munir did not flinch at exposing the fact that, although people might proclaim Pakistan an Islamic state, there was no way of legally establishing what made anyone a Muslim. On this point the leading ulama passionately disagreed with one another—much as Israeli thinkers might disagree about who is a Jew.

The Pakistani elite had been hoisted with their own petard. Believing that they could create a modern nation-state according to British democratic and administrative principles, which would also be consistent with the ideals of an Islamic state, the modernist pragmatic leadership increasingly learned that what defined Islam could be both broad and ambiguous. They also learned another painful truth: "Islamic democracy" could not be an inspired reproduction of Western one-man, one-vote democracy. Because populism belonged to the fundamentalists, "power to the people" would mean either rule by reactionary orthodoxy or ethnic fragmentation into the historically divided communities that made up the provinces of Pakistan.

A stark dilemma has confronted all the rulers of Pakistan since Ayub Khan, that is, since 1958: the justification of Pakistani nationalism has been the ideal of an Islamic state, an absolutely essential basis of legitimacy in order to overcome all the ethnic divisions that compartmentalize the population; yet the very ideal of an Islamic society is more divisive than it is unifying because there can be no agreement as to what a Muslim is.

The short-term escape from this dilemma has been the expedient of martial law. In a peculiar way Muslim ideals of power and authority find martial law and military rule very attractive. The principle of strict, harsh discipline coincides with some aspects of Islamic justice. Also, the combination of the rigorous self-control of the soldier and the austerity of barracks life comes close to providing, in modern times, an elite culture that captures elements of what Muhammad's government in the desert idealized. Thus, although President Zulfikar Ali Bhutto and his Pakistan People's party (PPP) could mount a significant populist appeal for "Islamic socialism," he was vulnerable because he was perceived as a soft, civilian leader. It was easy for people to suspect that behind his glib rhetoric there was probably a corrupt heart, capable of plotting the murder of his enemies. So, in 1977 when Bhutto's electoral victory over the more conservative Pakistan National Alliance (PNA) produced a springtime of violence and disorder, General Muhammad Zia-ul Haq had no problem in taking control as the martial-law administrator.

The execution of Bhutto in April 1979 may have shown the firmness of Zia's rule, but it did not help to resolve the basic dilemma concerning the essence of Pakistan's "Islamic" nationalism. Each experience with popular elections, even when the winner espoused "Islamic socialism," only strengthened the voices of the fundamentalists and weakened those of the more pragmatic modernists. President Zia's martial-law administration could only slow down the pace at which orthodox ideas became government practices. In March 1981 Zia introduced his own version of an Islamic state when he promulgated a Provisional Constitutional Order which was, in its own words, designed "to hasten the process of Islamization of the society in Pakistan."[21] Some punishments decreed in the Koran were legalized—eighty lashes for drinking alcoholic beverages, stoning to death for adultery, and amputation of the right hand for theft—but there had to be four witnesses to the act of adultery and there were eleven restrictions on deciding when amputation was possible. The High Court could declare any law invalid if it ran counter to the spirit of the Koran and the Sunna. A tax on capital and savings to help the poor was introduced, and first steps were taken toward interest-free banking.[22] Government officials were expected to promote an "Islamic" style in all their activities.

In short, Zia was steadily pushed to make more and more concessions to the fundamentalists, even while he strove to protect the essence of a modern state administration. The ideal of one-man, one-vote democracy, which had been the goal of the Westernized elite involved in the founding of Pakistan, had consistently produced an attempt to resurrect the system of government of the seventh century caliphate. The public was very strongly influenced by the orthodox ulama. What had seemed to be the straightforward and honorable goal of making Pakistan a truly Islamic state based on nationalism defined in terms of the Muslim identity had become a complex set of trade-offs which was producing a situation that was satisfactory neither to the orthodox nor to the modernists who wanted to get on with the tasks of nation-building and economic development.

Islamic Power as Personal Virtue

Wilfred Cantwell Smith has written, "The fundamental *malaise* of modern Islam is a sense that something has gone wrong with Islamic history. The fundamental problem of modern Muslims is how to rehabilitate that history."[23] In Pakistan, Bangladesh, Indonesia, and Malaysia, the modernists, on the one hand, feel that Islam has become decadent, largely because of the obscurantist and narrow-minded views of the ulama and the *kiyayi*. The orthodox, on the other hand, see only contamination and compromise that has threatened the purity of the faith. Throughout the four main Muslim nations of Asia there is still a feeling that there is and should be an *umma*, a Muslim community, and that the powers of government should be guided by the principles laid down by the Koran and the Hadith. At the same time there is simply no agreement as to what a Muslim is and what constitutes an Islamic state, or even a state whose policies are consistent with Muslim values.

At least five different types of people have, in very different ways, claimed to represent Islamic ideals of authority. First came the traditional sultans and hereditary rulers. Coming second, the modernist, Westernized elite have accepted secular norms for government and believed that their countries should be "Islamic" in much the same way as European countries are Christian. Third, the potentially explosive fundamentalists have reacted to modernization as a threat; they are generally lower-middle-class, are urbanized, and have some modern education. Finally, the fourth type, the traditional ulama, who would be happy to focus on religion and ignore politics, can be distinguished from the fifth type, the orthodox Muslims who demand strict adherence to all the rules of personal behavior of the Hadith—rules that cover even the trivial aspects of daily living, such as how to brush one's teeth or which shoe to tie first.

These, of course, are only the ideal types; in reality the differences are multiplied many times over. Thus the idea that there should be a common "Islamic community" of like-minded thinkers has become a source of frustration for all Muslims who want to use political power to achieve that dream. As elsewhere in the Muslim world, the response in the four Asian Islamic countries has been to seek clarity and agreement by going back to the sacred texts and finding words that might produce consensus. This effort, however, has only created more controversy and division.

As long as the search is confined to the realm of doctrine and texts—according to the "teacher, learned-man" tradition of Islam—there is little prospect that the goal of conformity and consensus will be realized. Muslims expect the answer to their problem to be theological, for it is manifest to them that what makes them different and special is their faith. They are not divided, as Jews can be, over whether their distinction lies in blood lines and ethnic identities or in religious practices and beliefs. For Muslims there is only religious identity; but there are also tremendous differences in practices and in doctrinal interpretations.

From a political perspective it may seem as though the more modernist and Westernized elites have been put on the defensive in recent years by the threat of fundamentalist explosions. But this may not be the main trend of their history. What has happened in Pakistan and Bangladesh, and has raised anxiety in Indonesia and Malaysia, is that the establishment of state power, which glorifies the ideal of an Islamic state, has stirred up orthodox thinkers who had long been absorbed in nonpolitical concerns. Many of these people have unrealistic expectations about the ability of governmental policies to change social practices. They have even less appreciation of what is essential for the maintenance of a political system.

If we approach this Islamic problem from the standpoint of the role of power in political cultures rather than theologically, we find far more agreement among Asian Muslims. In all four cultures Muslims share the idea that personal virtue should be translatable into community power. The good should rule. Moreover, if the total community is made up of "good people," collective power will be enhanced. Moderates and fundamentalists may disagree as to what constitutes a "good" person, but they agree that personal qualities are, and should be, decisive in affecting public events. They all seem to want to recapture the conviction that the whole cosmic order is held in place by leaders and followers adhering to rigorous norms of personal behavior. The vivid division between good and bad in Muslim thinking is no doubt associated with their keen recognition of the power of Satan to lead people away from Allah's commandments by tempting them into personal immorality.

Thus power in Islamic political cultures is still highly personalized. Leaders are still judged in personal terms: sometimes their failings are criticized, sometimes they are overlooked and excused. Yet, because of the basic Islamic ambivalence about the authority of the "brotherhood," the traditional Muslim leader is also expected to reflect in his personality the essential values of the community.

The leader is supposed to approximate *hasunat jamiu' khisalihi,* "the condensed essence of all beauty in his character." The Islamic concept of beauty is a blend of *jalal,* manliness, or better still, majesty, and *jamal,* softness, quietness, and subtlety, which can be seen as elegance. The Muslim ideal is one of masculine assertion held in check by extreme restraint, so that the leader always speaks in a soft, low voice, and never engages in laughter. A smile is quite enough. The Muslim hero is one "whose glance is enough to change the fate of the world"; authority lies in the power of his eyes, in the way he looks at others.

The Islamic concept of the beauty of the leader includes also the notion of virtue, which should go beyond just *hadd,* "limited," that is, limited to the letter of the law, and encompass *taqva,* the spirit of the law, that is, being truly God-fearing and manifesting the culture of the Koran. The leader should be so advanced in *taqva* that every aspect of his personal and public life can pass the closest scrutiny.

Finally, the leader's quality of beauty must include *baraka,* the quality of blessedness, which should be so bountiful that he can share his divine blessing with others. Those who accept him will hope to be rewarded with divine blessings in their turn.

The Islamic ideal leader is therefore a man who is not perfect—only Muhammad achieved perfection—but whose divinely inspired quality of blessedness can bring blessings on his followers when, as brothers, all strive to perfect their ways and obey the obligations required by membership in the Islamic community, the *umma*. In practical political terms this means that loyalty is a supreme value—leader and followers are bound together in a compact that is a part of Allah's will for an orderly social world of Believers. Treachery, while always possible because of the imperfection of man, is a supreme evil, for it involves breaking a pact with a God-ordained brotherhood. Thus, all of the theological reasoning or doctrinal disputation about rituals, power, and authority in Muslim cultures ultimately comes down to direct personal ties between teacher and student, leader and follower.

11 The Substance of Asian Power: Formal Structures and Informal Relations

IN HIS BRILLIANT and at times both hilarious and profound account of the downfall of Emperor Haile Selassie, Ryszard Kapuscinski, in purported interviews with former servants, flunkies, and ministers, quotes one of these as saying: "It's so very difficult to establish where the borderline runs between true power that subdues everything, power that creates the world or destroys it—where the borderline is between living power, great, even terrifying, and the appearances of power, the empty pantomime of ruling, being one's own dummy, only playing the role, not seeing the world, not hearing it, merely looking into oneself." For His Benevolent Majesty, His Most Distinguished Majesty, the form of power had become so divorced from the substance of power that, as Courtier C explained, "His Venerable Majesty wanted to rule over everything. Even if it was a rebellion, he wanted to rule over the rebellion, to command a mutiny, even if it was directed against his own reign."[1] In the end His Most Extraordinary Majesty, left with only an octogenarian servant, was unable to understand that, although he could go through exactly the same motions, adhere to the same rituals, and utter the same phrases as when he had been the King of Kings, he was nevertheless completely impotent: his power had evaporated.

What happened to Haile Selassie, and has happened to a lesser degree to many Asian rulers, reaffirms the generally forgotten fact that the great illusion of politics is that power presumably flows downward from the ruler through the elite to the masses, whereas in actual fact the process is precisely the reverse. For although it may seem to go against the laws of nature, power can only flow upward. Commitments must come from those below. The magic of power is ultimately in the eyes of the beholder. Where power resides at any moment is determined by what goes on in the minds of those below. It cannot be merely willed by those above.

Indeed, it is precisely their awareness that power must ultimately flow upward, through channels built by networks of loyalty and obeisance, and also by ambition and opportunism, that has caused numerous Asian rulers to distrust the vaguer ties of civilian hierarchies and to turn to the more disciplined commitments of the military ethic, thereby opting for army rule. Yet, power even under military rule depends upon the subordinate's willingness to obey. Every soldier knows that if he should withdraw support and ignore orders there would be others ready to obey and therefore to punish him.[2]

Asian rulers understandably prefer the illusion that power in its most natural form flows downward from on high and that nobody should question that fact. Those at the pinnacle want to be confident that below them are layers of human relationships in which each subordinate is alert to the wishes of his superiors and eager to translate their desires into action, much as the mute conductor of an orchestra can bring forth desired sounds from each player. In actual practice, of course, rulers must bluff and pretend that it is they alone who are making the music.

The two concepts of legitimacy and institutionalization, so central to theorizing about political development, refer to precisely this illusion about the source of power. Legitimacy is achieved when those who are channels for the upward flow of power bow to the presumption of the higher-ups that it is their wishes which determine the course of action. The terms for the acceptance of the illusion differ, of course, from culture to culture.

Institutionalization occurs when power relationships have become so regularized as to transform these dynamic processes into structures, which are, in fact, the routinized interactions of designated superiors and assigned subordinates whose relationships have fallen into the worn grooves of habit. Processes become structures when habit constricts random outcomes of power relationships within predictable molds. Expectations about how others will behave have become so standardized that they create the myth of "offices" and "posts" as being no more than depersonalized forms of power. With institutionalization people have come to accept structures, which are really no more than patterns of behavior, as historically given realities, as part of their natural social and political environment.

These general observations are basic for an understanding of the formation of state power in Asian societies. Since all of the Asian nations have adopted state institutions modeled in varying degrees upon Western forms, the process of creating the illusion of a downward flow of power has been facilitated by the idea that current rulers have captured the magic of Western political power, even though the ultimate test is still the willingness of the people to make commitments of loyalty upward. The particular forms of government were, of course, introduced by colonial officials or by Asian reformers and revolutionaries. The transformation of such suggested forms of government into more enduring structures did, however, require those below to acknowledge their acceptance of the institutional arrangements as being at least tolerable. In time the structures of state authority have become the inheritance of the various nations; Asians have grown up with the state as though it were a normal part of their world, like their other social institutions. Thus most are routinely socialized to accept without question the sovereignty of their governments; but, of course, others are socialized to oppose what exists, and still others develop their own ideas about the structures of government.

The actual operation of state power, how power is used—at times in the making and implementing of decisions, at times in essentially affective, ceremonial, or deferential ways—depends upon the character of the power relationships that relate to the structures of government. Are those at the top able to tap the energies that flow up from the commitments of subordinates? How do those elements in society that have their own sets of cohesive relationships relate to the official government? Who is constrained, and to what degree, by the rules of legitimacy that ensure that those in presumably important offices are not engaged in mere charades? What is the accepted scope of governmental power, and what determines the changing of the boundary limits? These questions suggest that in the different Asian cultures the flow of power relationships gives vitality to the formal structures of state authority.

To uncover the actual flow of power it is necessary to look through the formal arrangements of authority to the dynamics of the informal relationships, which generate the substance of power that is ultimately decisive in determining political developments. Rulers can pretend, as Haile Selassie did, that all that shapes society stems from the magic of one man, that the formal lines of constituted authority are all that matter. Yet the reality is that formal structures are given vitality largely through informal relationships, which usually are highly personalized, and make up the substance of real power in the society. In most Asian societies these relations are not broadly based within the general society; rather, they are limited to associations among those who have been recruited to the ranks of officialdom. A gap usually exists between those who have become a part of the elite culture and those who are a passive part of the mass culture. But until the pretensions of sovereign authority are supported at the local level by direct superior-subordinate relationships, there can be no structure of national power.

In the key countries of Asia the formal claims to sovereign power are either being reinforced and given substance by the dynamics of personalized relationships, or they are being countered and turned into charades of power by the dyadic relationships that constitute the real power in all of these cultures.

Japan: Sensitive Relationships, Rigid Structures

Again Japan provides a vivid baseline for constructive comparisons. The distinctiveness of the substance of power in Japanese political culture lies in the combination of two factors: first, the extraordinary sensitivity of those involved in the flow of power upward and their delicate empathy in superior-subordinate relationships; second, an astonishing rigidity in the formal structures of power. In the human relationships which provide the dynamics of power, a constant process of adjustment and accommodation occurs as all parties respond to their readings of the feelings of others; yet at the same time the Japanese seem helpless when it comes to making changes in whatever they take to be fundamental arrangements. Japanese politicians, who can be acutely sensitive to the concrete wishes of their constituencies, become immobilized in trying to deal with such abstract or generalized issues as the appropriate size of the defense budget, import liberalization, or the constitutional renunciation of armed forces.

The human relationships in Japan which are the most critical for the operation of power are of two opposite types. Those most basic to the flow of decision-making tend to be marked by behavior that is highly sensitive to nuances, quick to respond to subtle hints, and loaded with empathy. In these relationships the Japanese seem to have delicate nerve-endings and instantaneous reflexes. But there is another category of Japanese behavior in which all actions and responses are guided by inflexible rituals and uncompromising rules of conduct. Rigidity occurs whenever behavior fits into established conventions. In all cultures some activities become routine and ritualized, but in Japan the carrying out of conventions is generally more disciplined. Consequently, whenever Japanese patterns of behavior become standardized enough for processes to become institutionalized, the resulting institutions tend to become exceedingly rigid structures. Even patterns of relationship which are never formally institutionalized in a legal sense can become as rigid and firmly entrenched as the formal rules and institutions of the West. For example, what started out as informal paternalistic understandings in Japanese industrial relations have become, without legalistic regulations, rigid rules of job security, in which a tacit trade-off was made between lifetime employment and total loyalty to the company, including the acceptance of company unions as proper defenders of workers' rights. Similarly, the initially informal linkages between the huge manufacturing concerns and the countless small, traditional establishments have become the solid bonds that have integrated Japan's "dual economy." Within the governmental realm it is impossible to understand the workings of the Japanese style of "administrative guidance" without an appreciation of the ways in which informal relationships can, without legal sanctions, become as firmly established as constitutional institutions in the West. Japanese officials will claim, for example, that Japan's capital markets are completely open to the world; but the persistence of low interest rates—in spite of higher government deficits than those in the United States—and the continued low value of the yen make it obvious that constraints exist that are keeping Japanese savings (among the highest in the world) from flowing to more profitable markets. This can only happen because "guidance" in Japan is as powerful as law is elsewhere, if not more powerful.

Because political power in Japan is systematically built up from below through solid ties of relationships, leaders have a clear sense of the reality of the power that they can command in any situation. In contrast to the other Confucian cultures, factions (habatsus) can be acknowledged in Japan, for their personal ties of loyalty are openly honored. In return, leaders have to manifest their sense of indebtedness to those who are their supporters. By openly admitting their mutual dependency, the paternalistic leader and his dutiful followers are able to escape the complications which inhibit the effectiveness of, say, Chinese leaders. In Japan, the ideals of loyalty and competence fit together so naturally that the Japanese have been spared any form of the "red or expert" problem— the problem of deciding the relative importance of ideological commitment or loyalty, on the one hand, and competence or technical skills, on the other, which has bedeviled the Chinese Communists. The Chinese, starting with the "self-strengtheners" at the end of the nineteenth century and continuing through the Kuomintang, have persistently believed in an inescapable polarization between loyalty to basic values and competence in Westernized skills. The roots of this dichotomy can be found in neo-Confucianism and the distinction between ch'i, or the material aspect of things, and li, or the universal ideal of the thing. It was further elaborated in the distinction between *t'i,* or the superior Chinese cultural values, and *yung,* or the Western applied technology of lesser value. At the same time, however, the Chinese became concerned about such a possible contrast because their concept of power left no room for any separation between competence and ultimate authority—he who is in charge should be omnicompetent and not dependent upon more skillful subordinates. By contrast, a Japanese authority figure can be manifestly dependent upon the skills of subordinates without threatening his own legitimacy.

Instead of showing the aloofness of Chinese authority, Japanese leaders are expected to be sensitive to the feelings of subordinates, for everyone should be understanding of the needs of others. Takie Sugiyama Lebra insists, "For the Japanese, empathy *(omoiyari)* ranks high among the virtues considered indispensable for one to be really human, morally mature, and deserving of respect. I am tempted to call Japanese culture an *'omoiyari'* culture . . . The ideal in *omoiyari* is for Ego to enter into Alter's *kokoro,* 'heart,' and to absorb all information about Alter's feelings without being told verbally."[3]

The importance of empathy is accentuated by two other related Japanese qualities, that of feeling highly vulnerable, especially if not supported by a group, and that of having strong obligations of reciprocity. The Japanese psychiatrist Takeo Doi has characterized the Japanese as being almost obsessed with feelings of "helplessness" and vulnerability. These feelings are due partly to Japan's frequent and devastating natural calamities, but they are also rooted in a socialization process that stresses the rewards for competence and the horrors of failure, to the point that shame can readily result in suicide. The nearly universal awareness of how vulnerable people can feel opens the way for extensive mutual byplay and manipulation by both superiors and subordinates. These go well beyond the obvious possibilities of superiors using subtle intimidation or, better still, nurturing acts to govern the behavior of subordinates. They also include the propensity of subordinates to play the role of supplicants and humble themselves in order to shame their superiors into granting favors.

To understand the structure of Japanese power relationships it is important to appreciate that the ties of reciprocity created by the burden of *on* (moral indebtedness) and *giri* (the constraints a debtor feels toward a creditor) are not just social conventions. They involve powerful feelings of what can only be called guilt—feelings which give great intensity to the relationship. Evidence of such a feeling of guilt can be seen in the Japanese practice of saying, "I am sorry," when trying to say, "Thank you" with true sincerity. As Doi has observed, the commonly used word *sumanai* expresses both gratitude and apologies.[4] To forget a favor, to be *on-shirazu* ("unaware of *on*"), is truly unforgivable.[5] The highest form of guilt for Japanese does not consist in violating any generalized rules of conduct but in hurting someone else by failing to meet that person's expectations of what one's behavior should be. As Robert Christopher has observed, "When her children misbehave or disappoint her in any way, the typical Japanese mother does not get angry and shout. She forgives—and by making her children feel guilty about letting her down gains the upper hand."[6]

The combination of building guilt feelings in terms of reciprocity relations and exacting shame for failure to conform does not seem to encourage rebelliousness. A 1980 survey revealed that 70 percent of Japanese high school students felt that their parents treated them with "warmth" and a genuine effort at "understanding," and 35 percent of the boys and 51 percent of the girls confessed that they wanted "to go on being a child."[7] The Japanese socialization process seems to produce a high degree of sensitivity toward the feelings of others, without bitterness toward the authority figures who have instilled the feelings of guilt about insensitivity. Consequently, in later life Japanese subordinates typically manifest no resentment toward their superiors, whose every wish they rush to satisfy.

Thus, the reciprocity sentiments which form the dynamic basis of Japanese paternalistic power relationships are far more intense and binding than the comparable patron-client relationships in the other Asian cultures. Moreover, the Japanese relationships tend to be more finely calibrated than the *guanxi* ties of China or the patron-client bonds of the South and Southeast Asian cultures, all of which makes for flexibility and even subtlety in the substantive nature of Japanese power.

Yet at the same time the universal imperatives of conformity, when combined with the sensitivity of authority to the feelings of others, produce a rigidity in the forms which institutions take. Japanese prime ministers seem to have little ambition to leave their mark by changing the structural forms of government and administration. Conformity prevails where situations are established and public; nuances and subtlety exist only in immediate personal relationships. Fortunately for Japanese policymaking, it is the latter qualities which are critical for directing the uses of power.

The striking rigidity of the Japanese with respect to institutional forms and structural arrangements, in spite of their dexterity in direct power relationships, illuminates one of the great mysteries concerning the achievement potential of the Confucian cultures. In case after case people socialized in a Confucian culture—Vietnamese, Chinese, Koreans, and indeed Japanese—are able to blossom and become successful in the more open atmosphere of, say, American society, while at home the demands of conformity stifle their innovative and achievement drives. The very qualities which have made the Japanese so effective in tapping the energies of subordinates—that is, younger and more educated people—also work to inhibit creativity. Superiors and subordinates in Japan have to operate with such tender concern for each other's feelings that neither can strive for individual recognition. The ambitious subordinate, who dedicates himself to the collectivity and to supporting his paternalistic superior, cannot endeavor to go very much beyond the confines set by the conformity standards of the existing institutional arrangements.

The rigidity of structures is not, however, something that is imposed on subordinate and superior alike, as some kind of absolute principle or set of regulations; rather, it arises because both agree that their needs for each other are so critical that neither wants to test the boundaries of their structural ties. Each finds it more comfortable to accept the discipline of custom and the constraints of established manners. The reward for accepting the constraints of collective conformity—that is, for accepting the given institutional framework—is the opportunity to manipulate the richly complex relationship between superior and inferior, to resolve the feelings of guilt and gratitude in the delicate exchanges of *on* and *giri,* by more than repaying the kindness of a superior through compulsively delicate service. Thus, again, the "informal" cues of authority are translated into inexorable laws by "inferiors," as, for example, in the control of economic affairs through "administrative guidance" even while the Japanese government professes to be innocent of intervention.

The strong *on-giri* ties between superiors and subordinates help to eliminate from Japanese politics the moral ambiguity that bedevils American leaders as to whether they should expose and dismiss the loyal subordinate who has misbehaved—as a stern Puritan father would do—or whether they should try to cover up his misdeeds and only reprimand him privately—as a protective, understanding father would do. In Japan, the unambiguous norm is loyalty. Former prime minister Tanaka's power did not decline after he was convicted of accepting a bribe from the Lockheed Corporation: the members of his faction have proudly stood by him, and he has justified what he did on the grounds that he used the money to help those who were dependent upon him.[8]

This is the picture of the Japanese power structure when all is going well. But there is another side, which appears when the structural constraints of conformity are destroyed—when the Japanese are outside their own environment, traveling abroad or conquering a foreign land. Under these conditions the "sword" replaces the "chrysanthemum," decorum evaporates, and behavior may become astoundingly rude and even vicious.[9]

It is not surprising, therefore, that Japan has been successful in the disciplined roles of economic achievement but less effective in world politics and diplomacy. The Japanese have not been able to generate power in international relations mainly because their ways of creating effective power depend so heavily upon having sensitive "subordinates" who are ready to respond instinctively to the subtle cues of their "leaders." They have been caught between undue modesty and unappreciated arrogance in their self-created dilemma. Toward their Asian, and especially Southeast Asian, neighbors they have tried to mute their accomplishments with a humble and even apologetic posture—the posture which in Japanese culture is effective in tapping the guilt of subordinates and creating respect, but provokes the opposite reaction in other cultures where people find pleasure in humiliating the humble. In relations with the more powerful in world politics, the deference of the Japanese often suggests that they are not willing to pull their own weight but prefer to depend upon the generosity of others. Frustrated in both contexts, their response has been one of arrogance, of openly flaunting their normally restrained sense of superiority over all foreigners—a response which is usually counterproductive. Hence their dilemmas in dealing with insensitive foreigners and in managing unaccustomed contexts. But within the comfortable framework of their own institutions their human basis for power relationships continues to produce an extraordinarily stable structure of power.

China: More Brittle Relations, Less Lasting Institutions

The structural basis of power in Chinese political culture is the direct opposite of the Japanese basis. The institutional forms in China have tended to be decreed from above, not built up from a solid base below. Consequently leaders are never sure of how much support—that is, real power, not the pretensions of power—they can command. Within established institutional frameworks individuals will turn in all directions—toward their immediate superior colleagues or even to subordinates—to find personal ties of security, *guanxi,* or connections. Whether the pattern of such networks adds up to power for the institution or becomes an inhibiting force is almost a matter of chance. But, again in contrast to the Japanese, Chinese leaders can make institutional changes almost by whim. Under the Communists, constitutions have come and gone in a most offhand fashion, ministries are added and subtracted as though built of cards, and grand objectives that supposedly commit over one billion people to specific goals are proclaimed by a single leader with minimal consultation.

In part, of course, the problem is one of size. It is simply impossible for a Chinese leader to have a solid base of power, built on specific human ties, that would flow upward from the general population to the ultimate centers of power, as is possible in Japan.

In China a wide divide has always existed between formal government, emanating from the imperial or national capital, and the private governance that rules the daily lives of people through family institutions, clan associations, secret societies, trade and professional organizations, and a variety of *hui-guan,* or co-provincial clubs. Historically, imperial power was not erected upon the bases of these private organizations of power, although they were tolerated, indeed exploited, as surrogates for maintaining order and extracting resources for the state. The relationship between local power and central power in China was entirely different from that in Japan, where local lords competed with one another and the strongest daimyo, through conquests and alliances, became the shogun. National and local power in China had very separate domains and quite different pretensions. Since the center was not built upon the sum total of effective blocs of local power, the highest forms of authority could always be exposed as having more pretense than substance. When the Chinese Communists fought their way to power during and after the Japanese occupation, they succeeded in mobilizing a rural base and hence established structures of power that were intimately rooted in Chinese village life—much like the road to power of the first emperors of many Chinese imperial dynasties. But once established in the Forbidden City in Peking, the Communists made it clear that they were adherents of Chinese political culture, and for them power would properly emanate from the Center, the *chung-yang;* and in a few years they had re-established the traditional Chinese division between centralized power and local concerns. Society no longer gave direct support to state authority, and questions were repeatedly raised about the source of the Center's supreme authority.

In addition, in the institutions of the central government a lack of fit has been evident between the formal arrangements and the informal power relationships among officials. Whether in the case of the Manchus, the Kuomintang, or the Communists, Chinese officials have rarely been united in a common loyalty to their particular organization. Rather, in any hierarchical structure there have been separate clusterings of people with different in-group and out-group feelings. Because these cleavages of trust and distrust are not always manifest, outsiders may think that they are only marginal, but not Chinese who tend to believe that the special ties of *guanxi* are always at work.

Moreover, since the Chinese seem to assume that the locus of power is external to themselves, they normally suspect that others, who are almost by definition their "enemies," have stronger *guanxi* ties, and hence they fear that the reality of *guanxi* in their culture is working against their own interests.[10] Consequently most Chinese feel that it is entirely natural to decry the existence of *guanxi* in their society, even as they personally try to exploit whatever *guanxi* they may have.

The Chinese seem to have an instinctive sense that there is something inherently sordid in the relationships that are essential to the building of informal power structures. This view is in sharp contrast to that of the Japanese, who find dignity in the bonds of loyalty that are basic to personalized power.

Indeed, both the rationale and the dynamics of *guanxi* are quite different from those of the *on-giri* reciprocity relationships. *Guanxi* does not call for the sensitivity or empathetic feeling that is central to *on-giri* relations, and it is not solidified by the Japanese blend of shame and guilt. The basis of *guanxi* is not deeply internalized sensitivities and compulsions. *Guanxi* relationships can, however, be greatly strengthened by *ganqing*, which Bruce Jacobs rightly says has no English equivalent since it does not exactly mean "sentiments," "feelings," or "emotion," but is nevertheless the "affective component" of *guanxi*.[11] If the *ganqing* is "good" then the *guanxi* will be "close." *Ganqing* is neither friendship nor moral obligation.[12] It is the quality of a relationship that is premised to a substantial degree on common interests. Chinese negotiators, for example, are always anxious to establish a basis of "friendship" or "general principles" at the start of negotiations; but they have in mind not the sentiments that Westerners associate with friendship, but the feeling of *ganqing* which will make it possible, subsequently, to exploit a dependent relationship and seek the payoffs of *guanxi*.[13]

The guiding principles of *guanxi* lie not so much in the psychological realm as in objective factors and conventions of behavior. The inner responses are limited to trying to read the expectations of others in specific situations and calculating appropriate responses. Among Chinese it is expected that people who share a common background will instinctively be mutually supportive: people who are from the same place— village, province, or region—or who attended the same school, or, better yet, were classmates, or who served in the same organizations are expected to be available to help one another. Thus it is presumed that objective information about the backgrounds of leaders should provide solid guidance as to whether particular figures do or do not have *guanxi*.

Nevertheless, there is no guarantee that in any particular situation the individuals involved will recognize that they should be bound by *guanxi* obligations. In contrast to the intense interaction of reciprocal obligation and indebtedness in the *on-giri* ties, which makes the participants certain of their relationship, a Chinese is often uncertain as to whether another will respond positively to the evoking of *guanxi*. There is always the possibility that the other party will "look the other way." This element of uncertainty allows the *guanxi* networks to remain latent and passive, needing to be triggered into actual power constellations by some initiative, usually by an official who feels insecure. Thus, while objective factors are presumed to be the basis of *guanxi* relationships, the actual operation of *guanxi* as a power factor can be quite subtle and thus may seem to be devious, if not conspiratorial.

Chinese tend to speak of *guanxi* almost as though it were an objective thing. They will ask whether specific people do or do not have *guanxi*. Furthermore, they will treat the knowledge of its existence as a factor that can properly influence the calculations of even those who are not directly involved. As I have noted elsewhere, "If X inquires of Y whether A and B have *guanxi* and it is established that they do and that Y has a relationship with B, then it can be assumed that X should be able to establish a claim with A."[14] In this situation B and Y are likely to be willing channels of influence because it will put them in the envied Chinese position of being middlemen.

That middlemen have well institutionalized roles in bringing together parties in what are called *guanxi* ties shows that such ties are not based on internalized sentiments but on socially understood behavior that is judged to be mutually beneficial. Middlemen can reduce uncertainty, clarify the respective rewards and advantages, and thus put the relationship on an objective basis, thereby reducing the importance of the emotional dimension.

Guanxi also differs from the *on-giri* ties, and from patron-client relationships, in that it presumes a degree of equality because the parties share some common quality. Although *guanxi* does usually bridge class or status differences, it is not seen as explicitly a superior-subordinate relationship. Indeed, since it is assumed to be premised upon a shared particularism—a common place of origin, a blood relationship, a shared experience in schooling or in career advancement—there is at least a pretense of equality. That one is seeking a favor of another is treated as only an accident of circumstance. Should the situation change at some future time, then presumably the quest for favors could go the other way.

Moreover, since the Chinese relationship is not based on feelings of obligations for specific indebtedness, the quid-pro-quo calculus is not so systematic as that of the Japanese, or of the Southeast Asian patron-client ties. In a *guanxi* relationship one party can repeatedly press for favors, or, as the Chinese express it, *la guanxi*, that is, "pull *guanxi*." Since the core element of *guanxi* is not reciprocity but a particularism, and since *guanxi* can quite properly be used for material advantage, a party seeking benefits can repeatedly ask for favors from the more advantaged party without making any explicit sacrifices in return. It is only necessary for the party seeking the favor to appeal to established rules of propriety and to try to shame the other into acting for him. Indeed, according to Chinese social logic, a person seeking further favors from a patron can argue that the benefits already received have strengthened their *ganqing* and hence even more benefits can be legitimately expected in the next round. In the relationship between Peking and Washington, for example, the Chinese authorities frequently seek to "shame" American administrations in regard to living up to the "spirit" of general agreements, and they declare that relations can "improve" only if the Americans do what the Chinese believe to be right—but they give no indication as to what benefits Washington might expect from the promised "improvement," no hint of a real quid pro quo.

Those who are in superior positions in China may find the demands of *guanxi* annoying. Aloofness is the obvious answer, which the benefit-seeker must try to overcome with a blend of flattery and appeals to propriety. Fear of losing face, of being "shameless," is thus a prime force behind the maintenance of *guanxi* ties, a fact that decreases the potential of the relationship to produce a solid basis of power. The most immediate reward for the one bestowing a benefit in a *guanxi* relationship is the psychic satisfaction of gaining face through the flattery and subservient behavior of the soliciting party. In the longer run, however, there can be substantial material payoffs from retaining the loyalty of those one has helped. Within government, for example, senior officials who have helped subordinates to get *guanxi* ties can be confident that these subordinates will cover up for them and not expose their use of office for personal benefit.

In Chinese political culture there have always been ambivalent attitudes about *guanxi* because of its tendency to compromise impersonal relations and weaken the building blocks of formal power in governmental institutions. High officials in Confucian as well as Communist times have decried the existence of *guanxi,* saying that it undermines the upright administration of government, but at the same time officials persist in making use of *guanxi,* with the justification that government should be by men and not by impersonal laws. Both the Nationalists and the Communists have denounced the relationship as a feudal remnant, thus making it more tacit and subtle, and hence less predictable, but not causing it to disappear.

Indeed, the persistence of *guanxi* is explained in part by the uncertainties created by the public doctrine that only formal regulations can guide governmental behavior. This doctrine is a source of anxiety because officials can easily convince themselves that others are quietly violating the formal rules and hence gaining an unfair advantage. The idea that everyone else is scrupulously observing the general regulations is simply too implausible for most Chinese to believe. Their own insecurities convince them that they cannot find justice without the benefit of some particularistic support. Therefore, the more that *guanxi* is attacked, the more people "seek" *guanxi—jao guanxi,* as the Chinese call it.

This propensity in modern China to denounce publicly the core relationship in the building of informal power tends to give a conspiratorial aspect to the dynamics of Chinese politics. The more the public authorities proclaim that government should and does operate in response to ideologically decreed norms, the more people are driven to the secret manipulations of informal power relationships. In most situations, whether in the party, the bureaucracy, or in nongovernmental institutions such as schools and factories, too many people are waiting in line for advancement and too few openings exist for the formal procedures to do the job of selection. Therefore everyone must prudently seek *guanxi* ties.

Moreover, within the bureaucracy the formal regulations tend to be overly constrictive, producing cumbersome procedures and little effective action. Communication, to say nothing of coordination, among offices and bureaus tends to be slow. Hence the informal structures of power built through the *guanxi* networks often serve as the most effective way of getting the state's business done. Michel Oksenberg holds that *guanxi* seems to be an important factor "in making the rigid bureaucratic edifice work."[15]

Since the *guanxi* system is not based on the reciprocity of explicitly acknowledged quids pro quo, it is not surprising that Chinese politics is not based upon an openly acknowledged system of patronage, as is the case with politics in Japan, India, and most of Southeast Asia, including especially the Philippines. In China it is, of course, known that people use "the back door"—children of high cadres have special benefits, and the elevation of one high official is usually followed by promotions for his associates. Yet there is a certain vagueness as to what can be expected. This is due, in spite of the very materialistic character of *guanxi,* to the tendency to obscure the distribution of patronage by stressing the vaguer, but grander, principles of loyalty and reliability.

As I have observed elsewhere, "the virtue of loyalty unquestionably enjoys a loftier position in the Chinese political system than it does in liberal Western politics . . . where loyalty is a value to be balanced with effectiveness, honesty, farsightedness, the appearance of high moral purpose, personal charisma, and a host of other values."[16] In the West, and especially in America, loyalty is either an absolute value ("My party right or wrong"), or it amounts to remembering the favors one has received. In China, by contrast, loyalty means sticking by a relationship even when the bonds are harmful, because to break the ties would be to cause greater damage. One person supports another through thick and thin since to do otherwise might cause great mischief and chaos, which would be self-destructive.

The concept of loyalty and reliability that underpins *guanxi* is thus one in which the parties are not necessarily working to advance each other's interests in terms of exchange of favors, but in which they are usually trying to avoid a worse situation, which would arise if *guanxi* were disregarded. Superiors and subordinates are thus caught in a deterrence relationship in which "mutually assured destruction" would result if either broke the bond of loyalty. A subordinate cannot hope to advance himself by exposing the failings of his superior because such an act of disloyalty would make him appear unreliable to other potential superiors.[17] A superior needs to develop the reputation of being a reliable protector of his subordinates if he is to attract an expanding network of *guanxi* ties, which in turn would give him a broader base of power from which to move upward.

These general features of the *guanxi* system make it clear that the Chinese structures of informal power lack the coherence and dynamic effectiveness of the Japanese pattern. The relationships basic to informal Chinese power can at times facilitate bureaucratic performance, but in the main they operate to provide security for superiors and subordinates. Informal power thus tends to mask the failings of both high and low officials and to protect their positions. The effect is to substantially separate the announced purposes of government from the realities of governmental power, which in turn creates problems of policy implementation.

This arrangement can sometimes produce a comfortable relationship between formal authority and informal power, especially since the Chinese cultural tolerance for cognitive dissonance allows for large amounts of what might be called hypocrisy. More often, however, the result is considerable tension.

The first reason for this tension is the sharpness with which Chinese tend to react when they feel they have been mistreated; and if policy implementation is not absorbing energies, there are many opportunities to complain about real or fancied slights and injustices. In short, when informal power relationships check the performance of formal institutions, those involved become anxious and tend to react to stress in much the same way as the Chinese do in Malaysia.

The second reason for tension, which is closely related to the first, is the Chinese tendency to treat the failures of formal institutions as symptoms of faulty and unworthy authority, deserving of angry rebuke. The propensity of Chinese to express hostility over the inadequacies of their leaders can be traced to the severe demands of filial piety in their socialization experiences. Young Chinese are obligated to display total submission to parental authority; above all, they cannot give vent to the natural hostility of a son toward a father. This need to suppress aggression at an early and critical stage of development is reinforced by the subsequent use of shaming in training. The result is a marked inclination to suppress emotions, to adhere to conventional rules of behavior, and to be passive toward authority. Yet, when authority conspicuously fails, outbursts of aggression can suddenly be legitimized. The attack on the surrogate authority of government can be extremely bitter because the psychic cost of suppressing aggression against parental authority has been so great. Thus anger plays a major role in the attitude of Chinese toward authority that has failed to live up to their exceedingly high expectations.[18]

There is obviously a crucial difference between the Japanese and the Chinese in regard to the character and functions of the strongest emotions in the operation of power relationships. The Japanese have intense feelings of guilt and obligation, which give great weight to the bonds of mutual obligation; thus these feelings play a constructive role in building informal power and in ensuring that the power thus created can be channeled to support formal institutions. The strongest Chinese sentiments tend to be produced by frustration over the failings of authority, which, as can be seen from the violence of the Red Guards during the Cultural Revolution, can be exceedingly destructive. In Chinese political culture, therefore, it can be very difficult to sustain commitments to constructive power relationships, and it is very easy for destructive impulses to come to the surface.

This potential for explosive reaction to any sign of a breaking of faith by the authorities helps to explain why the reform programs of Deng

Xiaoping must proceed with great caution whenever they touch on dependency feelings. Thus China faces the persisting problem of what to
do about all the subsidies that are distorting its economy and limiting
the resources available for new investments to replenish its out-of-date
capital stock.

Southeast Asia: Fixed Relationships, Unstable Institutions

The bureaucratic legacy of the traditional monarchy in Thailand and the
legacies of the colonial administrations in Burma and Indonesia have left
those countries with the structures of so-called bureaucratic polities. By
contrast, in the Philippines the Americans encouraged participatory democracy and electoral politics rather than public administration. As a
consequence of these two very different patterns of development, the
basic motivations in the use of patron-client ties have also differed. In
the case of Burma, Indonesia, and Thailand the early implantation, by
rather arbitrary means, of clearly defined authority structures meant that
the power relationships tended to be among people who were thinking
largely in terms of careers in government. Their patron-client relationships were mainly directed toward the search for security, and they regarded the structures of government as ladders for advancement to secure
niches where they would have protecting superiors and deferential subordinates. By contrast, among the Filipinos personal ties were more directly linked to a process through which people outside of administrative
office could gain the influence necessary to extract resources from the
government. The style was pork-barrel politics, in which government was
seen as having resources which were always available to those with influence.

In Burma the attempt to wed a system of electoral politics, based on
party loyalties, to the colonial-established bureaucratic polity created
tremendous tensions between the nationalist politicians and the British-
trained administrators. In part, the politicians wanted to shoulder aside
the administrators and gain job security for themselves, usually in the
management of newly established state enterprises. But in addition the
politicians clashed with the more procedurally oriented administrators
because they wanted direct access to governmental resources (the pork
barrel).

The same kinds of tensions emerged in Indonesia between the civilian
politicians and the administrators.[19] Significantly, after the fall of Sukarno
the military rulers in the New Order found it easier to work smoothly
with the administrative bureaucracy than had the civilian politicians. Not

only did the two hierarchies understand each other, but the military appreciated the value of technical skills, and hence they were far more ready to utilize technocrats than the civilian politicians had been.

Similarly, in the complex alliances between civilian politicians, military officers, and bureaucratic administrators in the Thai governmental system, the role of the military hierarchy was to modify the clash between politicians seeking to tap the resources of government and administrators anxious to protect their domains.

The character of politics in all four countries has changed as a result of the greater expectations made possible by economic growth. In the Philippines all the leading political figures came traditionally from the wealthy landed families, and therefore, although they were frequently not above seeking some personal benefits, their prime interest in getting access to government funds was to make distributions to their followers, thereby cementing their party organizations. Even before the regime of martial law began in 1972 a noticeable change occurred as the stakes became greater, the benefits of access grew significantly larger, and people of higher status began seeking the favors that went with victory.

Under President Marcos the need to use patronage for electoral purposes disappeared and, increasingly, government resources were transferred to immediate friends, producing a politics of cronyism. Marcos shamelessly sponsored a form of "crony capitalism" in which his personal friends were encouraged to establish companies that would be given easy access to foreign loans guaranteed by the government, as well as generous government contracts. The result was not capitalistic development but a serious drain on the Philippine economy and a massive foreign debt. Finally, when the International Monetary Fund (IMF) exerted decisive pressures, Marcos had to turn his back on some of his friends. Roberto Benedicto, Marcos's fraternity brother, whose National Sugar Trading Corporation (Nasutra) had been given a total monopoly of one of the country's biggest dollar earners, had to comply with the World Bank's insistence that the Philippines return to free trade in sugar. Rodolfo Cuenca, a golfing partner of Marcos, was allowed to build up the Construction and Development Corporation (CDCP) to become a huge but inefficient contractor on the basis of deals with the state. Herminio Disini, husband of a first cousin of Imelda Marcos, was helped to make his Herdis Group into a $1 billion conglomerate of some thirty companies before the government stopped bailing him out, a decision which left him with only one company. Ricardo Silverio lost much of his corporate empire when Marcos could no longer compel the Philippine National Bank to extend him credits. In spite of the country's foreign exchange crisis, Marcos has been able to protect some of his cronies: Eduardo

Cojuangco still has a monopoly over the lucrative cocoanut trade; and the Romualdez family empire, directed by Benjamin Romualdez, brother of Mrs. Marcos and Philippine ambassador to Washington, remains strong.[20] Thus, in spite of the problems of the Philippine economy, Marcos has dramatically elevated the financial payoffs for supporting the government and has given a new dimension to the concept of the pork barrel.

The trend in the other three countries has also been toward escalation. Initially, the Indonesian, Thai, and Burmese bureaucrats of high status might have augmented their low incomes by exacting petty payments for providing the expected services, but eventually those with influence demanded greater rewards. In Indonesia a combination of two factors has accelerated the process. First, most of the businessmen who have needed licenses are Chinese, and Indonesian officials have had no trouble in convincing themselves that, when squeezed, Chinese have an almost infinite capacity to pay. Second, the quasi-socialist ideology of the independence movement has led officials to extol the merits of state-run enterprises, which also happen to give them excellent opportunities to "transfer" wealth from the "public sector" to their own "private sector."

Indeed, in all four countries the rewards for having the right patron-client connections have risen dramatically since the immediate post-independence era. Not only can fortunes be made from such contacts, but it is almost impossible to become rich without having personal ties in the political arena. The ethics that governed mutual support activities and provided sensitivity toward those in need in cultures of scarcity can take on quite a different significance when resources become more bountiful. The bonds of dependency are not necessarily broken, but they can be used to stimulate greed-inspired conspiracy.

In the Philippines, for example, politics continues to be largely an upper-class pursuit among members of the established families, but change has been taking place—quickened by the debasing effects of martial law—so that the level of gentility has declined and some newer, and more crassly ambitious, elements have joined the game. Yet personal relationships, including obligations and resentments that are passed down from the older generations, continue to play a major role. For example, former Senator Salvador Laurel, who as president of the United Democratic Opposition (UNIDO) led the dramatic challenge to President Marcos in the 1984 national assembly election, is the son of José P. Laurel, the puppet president under the Japanese occupation, who on two occasions saved Marcos, then an anti-Japanese guerrilla, from the Japanese police. Even before that, when Marcos was accused of murdering a political rival of his father in 1940, José Laurel was the presiding judge of the supreme court which acquitted him. Then, in 1964, after Marcos had failed to get the Liberalista party nomination for the presidency, the Laurels helped him switch parties and gain the presidency in the following election. The Laurels only broke with Marcos in 1980 after he had rejected one of their relatives as the electoral candidate of his Movement for a New Society (KBL).[21]

Another example of family-based Philippine politics, as well as the ability of the Filipinos to adapt to changing circumstances, is the relationship between Lorenzo Tanada and the Aquino family. A former student of Felix Frankfurter, Tanada led the prosecution of the Filipino collaborators with the Japanese, who included not only José Laurel but also the father of Benigno ("Ninoy") Aquino. Yet after Ninoy's assassination, Tanada joined Ninoy's brother Agapito ("Butz") Aquino in leading the movement to boycott the 1984 elections for the national assembly.[22]

Family and personal relationships continue to play a significant role at the pinnacle of Philippine politics. Benigno Aquino, Jr., was the scion of one of the wealthiest landowning families in Tarlac province—they started and long dominated the Philippine tobacco industry—and his wife, Corazón, came from an even wealthier family, the Cojuangco clan. Yet the head of that clan, Eduardo Cojuangco, was an early supporter of Marcos, and he backed Marcos's KBL in the elections fought over the memory of Ninoy.[23] Furthermore, Ninoy was a personal friend of Imelda's and had dated her before she married Marcos.[24] In no other political elite in Asia do personal and family relationships play such a prominent role as they do in the Philippines—nor is there one in which love can so readily turn to hate.

That people know each other so well has produced a degree of civility, but not much predictability, in Philippine politics. Although a Filipino learns early to establish a network of supporting friendships, and everyone is tolerant of the need for others to establish their particular bonds, there seems to be little jealousy about crosscutting ties and thus putting family members in different political camps with different patrons. It has often been suggested that a Philippine family will place members of its clan in different parties, so that it will always have someone on the winning side; but this is probably not the usual case, if only because clans are not organized for such strategic maneuvering.

In the Philippines with its faltering aristocratic politics, public life is characterized by increasing brutality and violence. In the 1950s most of it stemmed from excessive enthusiasm at election time, but recently it has been of a more calculating nature. During the 1960s leaders turned with greater frequency to hiring goons, as they are called in Manila, to intimidate, first of all, followers suspected of disloyalty, and then followers of opponents. The rising level of violence meant that bodyguards became necessary, and soon those hired began to take prophylactic action and strike first against suspected enemies.[25]

It is clear that in the Philippines extensive reliance upon informal power arrangements has not been adequate to make up for the inadequacies of the formal power structure. Although the country has sought to follow the South Korean and Indonesian example of calling upon technocrats to design development policies, governmental authority remains weak and is constantly being undermined by the erratic workings of the loose patron-client system. The failure of the formal institutions of government to control informal power relationships has heightened the tendency toward cynicism. Everyone assumes that others are exploiting the possibilities of government for their own private advantage.

In the other three countries, the bureaucratic polities of Southeast Asia—Indonesia, Burma, and Thailand—Indonesia can be regarded as the model polity because it lies between the two extremes of Burma and Thailand.

In contrast to the Philippines, Indonesia has a more disciplined system of dependency relationships which is reinforced by a more solidly structured formal system of governmental authority. The result, however, is little more than an illusion of an orderly power structure, for the way in which patron-client ties operate tends to produce unexpected patterns of decision-making. Structurally the Indonesian elite is organized in what appears to be a well-defined hierarchy in which each participant has a vivid sense of who his superiors and his subordinates are. The gradations are not so vividly defined or so explicitly articulated as in Thailand, but the system that centers in Jakarta is far more stable, and the relative status of officials more ordered and lasting, than in the Philippines. Indonesian officials can strive to put into practice far more subtle ploys and tactics than can Filipino politicians, but there is still less craft in Jakarta politics than in the more delicately coordinated Bangkok game. While one can imagine in Bangkok a variety of finely calculated coup d'etat maneuvers in which substantial change occurs without anyone being hurt, in Jakarta one would expect a bloodbath to follow any coup d'etat attempt.

Before the establishment of the New Order under General Suharto there was considerable confusion among the Indonesian elite. In the first year after independence it was a problem to sort out the civilian politicians, who had distributed themselves among a variety of parties but avoided determining relative power rankings by the simple tactic of not holding popular elections. It became increasingly apparent that even the artful Indonesians would not be able to operate an orderly parliamentary system without elections, and therefore the stage was set for President Sukarno to try to command state power by manipulating relations among a triad of hierarchical power structures: his Nationalist party, the Communist party, and the army. Gradually it became apparent that for all of Sukarno's "charismatic" goings-on, the people were seeing him less as a forceful ruler and more as a pretender to power. The declining illusion of Sukarno's power was one important factor in the decision of the Communists to attempt their ill-fated coup.

With the New Order under General Suharto a new triad was created as the basic framework for Indonesian politics: the army as the key element, a rejuvenated civil bureaucracy, and an "official," functionally based "political party" called Golkar. Suharto displayed surprising, and extraordinary, political genius when he decided that the strongest based political structure would be a coalition of a large number of occupationally, professionally, and socially defined subgroups, each hierarchically organized according to *bapakism*. This was precisely what the Dutch had discovered much earlier. Golkar insists that it is not really a political party but a higher order of popular participation. To ensure the electoral success of Golkar, General Suharto executed the clever ploy of insisting that the two religious parties should merge into the Muslim United Development party (PPP) and that the secular opposition parties should become the Indonesian Democratic party (PDI), a requirement which forced people without *bapak* ties to work together. As a consequence they could only engage in unseemly feuding, proving to everyone that they lacked the coherence necessary for ruling the country.

The combination of Golkar, the army, and the bureaucracy would appear to be a well-ordered structure of power for governing. Indeed, the orderly hierarchical character of the Indonesian polity suggests that there should be no structural excuse for confusion in policymaking. Yet the appearance of a coherent polity is deceptive. First of all, the illusion of coherence stems from the fact that the Indonesian Armed Forces (ABRI) dominates the government; and, since armies are supposed to have clear lines of command and control, there should be no uncertainty as to who has responsibility for particular decisions. In the past, before the New Order, this was not the case because the military was politicized: there were numerous factions among the officers, which in turn were tied to different civilian politicians.[26] With the New Order, ABRI has become professionalized, and as an institution it no longer engages in national policy outside of the military domain—except, of course, to give unqualified support to the government. Decisions in the defense field are made at monthly *rapat pimpinan* (leadership meetings). The Department of Defense and Security (HANKAM), which is the ultimate authority for ABRI, does have to make decisions in assigning military officers to civilian jobs, but once the assignments are made HANKAM no longer controls day-to-day activities. Indeed, because of criticism by civilian bureaucrats of the *karyawan* system whereby military officers are used in civilian jobs, ABRI through HANKAM has leaned over backward to appear not to be managing political decision-making.[27]

This is not to say that military officers in civilian roles have not engaged in political maneuvering, for, of course, they have. Furthermore, President Suharto has surrounded himself with advisors from the officer class. Even his former religious guide was a military man, Major General Sujono Humardhani, who is said to have had such a close spiritual union with him that "a prayer by Sujono on behalf of the president fully substitutes for a prayer by Suharto himself."[28] The main point, however, is that the illusion of an orderly structure, to which the military contributes, is also due to the civilian bureaucracy's remarkable freedom from power struggles. The Indonesians are proud that they do not have a system of checks and balances. Indeed, the various ministries, bureaus, and offices of the Indonesian bureaucratic polity are not independently institutionalized, and thus they do not consistently champion their legally defined interests and responsibilities. Ironically, one of the few articles of the 1945 constitution which Indonesians have faithfully upheld is the one decreeing that the government will have a "distribution of powers" and not be a system of "checks and balances," which would produce unseemly adversary relationships. The different bureaus and ministries have almost no stomach for infighting, and leading bureaucrats tend to give one another considerable room for maneuver.[29] Unexpected reversals of decisions do not occur in Indonesia because the jurisdiction of one part of the government overlaps that of another. Indonesia does not have a politics of legalism.[30]

In other words, the apparently neat structure of power in Indonesia is not based on legalistic specifications of responsibilities or precise definitions of each post or office. Instead, the Indonesian pyramid of power seems orderly because it is composed of tiers of personally related groups that tend to array themselves as hierarchical offices because Indonesians invariably define their personal relationships in hierarchical terms. Any two Indonesian officials meeting for the first time instinctively recognize who is the superior and who the inferior. Since the culture is, to all intents and purposes, devoid of peer relationships among equals, each such official is either the superior or the inferior of the other.

This propensity, when translated into organizational terms, means that the Indonesian bureaucratic polity can be envisaged as a multitude of

quasi-independent clusterings of officials who loyally support their respective leading figures, and since the leaders all have a keen sense of
their relative status the apparent result is an orderly bureaucracy. To
understand Indonesian decision-making, however, one must realize that
the scrupulous displays of deference by inferiors to superiors do not mean
that superiors can always command inferiors. Although everyone rec-
ognizes his relative place in the total scheme of things, a superior is not
always entitled to interfere with developments within the entourage of
inferiors. Subordination to the leaders calls for deference, not obedience.

The obligations of obedience lie almost entirely within the component
clusterings. The Indonesian phenomenon of *bapakism*—consisting of a
father figure, the *bapak,* and a circle of loyal followers called *anak buah,*
or children—is the cohesive glue which holds together the most intimate
groupings in the bureaucracy. The *bapak–anak buah* relationship is pervasive in giving structure to what are formally designated as bureaus or
offices. It also may be a factor in linking together different principal
figures along lines which may or may not follow the formal hierarchy of
the bureaucracy.

Bapakism is often confused with another Indonesian cultural trait, the
extraordinary ability to sense and manifest status differences. Although
the two may coincide in a particular relationship, this is not always the
case. Individuals without the bond of *bapakism* can recognize each other
as superior and inferior, but such a relationship is devoid of power or
influence.[31] Thus, structurally, the Indonesian bureaucracy, in spite of its
hierarchical appearance, is not one in which information and command
flow smoothly and coherently between superior and subordinate offices.
Rather, most offices, and even most officials at the same level, are often
quite autonomous, acknowledging their superiors but not necessarily
behaving as dutiful subordinates. Therefore people who appear to have
enough status to know what is likely to take place may not be well
informed about a colleague's domain. The informal pattern of relationships may not coincide with the formal hierarchy of power. Since officials
appreciate the importance of upholding their own status as well as that
of others, there is little need or desire to become knowledgeable about
the affairs of others. It is enough for all to pretend to knowledgeability,
with little expectation that they will ever be challenged.

To understand why Indonesian officials prefer the passive nature of
status to the active dimensions of command it is necessary first to note
the burdens that decision-makers are expected to assume, especially in
contrast to the comforts of dependency that subordinates have. This
apparent reversal of preferred positions can be appreciated after a closer
look at some key features of *bapakism*.

It is true that in the *bapak–anak buah* relationship there are certain elements which come close to the Western concept of power. For example, the obligations of the *anak buah* or followers are almost limitless, and thus they can be expected to do whatever their *bapak* bids them to do. Yet the central thrust in the relationship is not one of command or control. Indeed, the Western practice of characterizing *bapakism* as a patron-client relationship exaggerates the suggested advantages of being the superior and grossly understates his defenselessness against accumulating unlimited subordinates, who claim the right of favors and protection from him. Indeed, if the Indonesian term *bapak* is translated as "fatherism," it comes closer to the mark by accentuating the notion that the role of fathers is to look after every need of their children without complaint.

In the bureaucracy, the burdens of being *bapaks* cause high officials to play their cards very close to their chests. Superiors cannot be entirely candid in communicating with subordinates, for that would open the way to being used by an ever-expanding circle of dependents. Each principal official is already surrounded by more dependent officeholders than are needed for any practical purposes of government. Since the superior officials can usually appreciate one another's problems, there is a general tendency to "go easy" with one another. In a sense, everyone keeps his distance, to avoid causing trouble or being troubled. Rarely does one try to find out what may be on the minds of others, but instead, one puts a positive gloss on what the others are doing, almost as though that would bring about good relations with everyone.

In this seemingly eccentric way Indonesians transform the bureaucratic game into one of protecting the status of the others, rather than expanding one's own jurisdictional powers. Hence, even where jurisdictions may overlap—in the economic decision-making realm, for example, where the respective domains of the economic czar, Widjojo, and the minister of industry, Abdul Rauf Suduh, are not clearly differentiated—there is no need for tension because each appreciates the burdens of the other.

The process of creating a *bapak–anak buah* relationship can often be slow, with one party, usually the inferior, repeatedly extending favors to another in a superior position, and thereby building a fund of indebtedness which at a much later date he can tap for a return favor. The arithmetic of indebtedness does not call for a quick return of a favor for one given. On the contrary, the logic of creating a permanent bond of reciprocal ties demands that favors should not be so readily balanced as to allow for a situation in which obligations are canceled out, thereby causing the relationship to erode.

One of the consequences of the subtle linkages between interpersonal actions and the interpretations of those actions is that a premium is placed on avoiding direct statements and on speaking elliptically. It is well known that Javanese enjoy the use of symbolism and the caricatures in the *wayang* shadow plays, but their officials have a special appreciation of subtlety for many reasons, not the least of which is the tradition in decision-making of *mufaket* (the need for unanimous consent of all involved) through a process of *musyawarak* (intensive deliberations). Presumably, all who are in any way involved are expected to contribute their views, and decisions may not be made until everyone is in agreement. In practice, however, there is usually a strange inverse ratio between status and degree of articulation, as the principal figures hold back while subordinates vigorously expound their views and "consensus" is at last declared on the basis of the judgment of the principals. Everyone seems to understand that the opinions of subordinates are irrelevant exaggerations, useful only for filling in time, while superiors must be more judicious in expressing their ideas. This is not just because deliberateness is associated with wisdom in Javanese culture, but also because the fewer words that are said, the less likely they are to complicate personal relations with other notables. Even high officials practice among themselves the Javanese art of *etak-etak*, that is, telling a person what he wants to hear.

The result is that much of the communication in any inner circle of decision-makers takes the form of tacit understandings in which much is left unsaid. Blunt language and clear expression of views are assumed to be likely causes of embarrassment for others, if not for one's self. This Javanese fondness for indirect communication is of course another obvious source of misunderstanding about Indonesian decision-making.

Another reason for failure in communication among Indonesians is their extreme sensitivity about upsetting one another emotionally. Among Javanese, in particular, there exists a cultural imperative to achieve and maintain a state of *halus*, which means to have tranquillity in one's inner life, to be refined and subtle in one's social relations, to be imperturbable, and thus to be truly civilized. One should also go to great lengths to avoid being *kasar*, which means to be crude, rude, and emotional.

Because all decisions must be based on *musyawarak* and everyone must strive for the state of *halus*, nothing can be said that might agitate others. The Javanese believes that is it better to tell another what will please him than to aggravate him with the truth. The result is the Javanese art of indirectness, which is calculated to ensure that one neither provokes another nor reveals one's own feelings. The more elite the circle, the more masterful people are in disguising their own feelings and soothing the feelings of others.

This hypersensitivity reflects a profound anxiety about aggression in Javanese culture. The longing for tranquillity is reinforced by the universal belief that people generally have only a tenuous grip on their emotions, and if that grip slips there is no telling what damage might be done—hence the Malay-Javanese concept of running amok. Since there is a cultural consensus that aroused people can be dangerous, everything must be done to avoid provocation in social situations.

The concern about aggression is related to what has been described as "the peculiar cultural trait in the greater part of Indonesian society which rejects—even abhors—motivation by personal ambitions, leading to the suppression or explicit denial of any personal interests or motives."[32] It is not just that anyone who displays inordinate ambition would be instantly identified as dangerous by others and thus quickly isolated and in time destroyed, but that Javanese are quite literally frightened by any hint of their own ambitions. One should not be overly motivated, for that would be *kasar*. In Indonesian bureaucratic politics there is thus no category of the young supporter who is both loyal and ambitious, for such a person would be too threatening to superiors. Instead the category is loyal and obedient, for even youthful participants are expected to be unmotivated by ambition.

These psychological factors contribute to a bias in Indonesian politics against action and toward passivity. In Indonesian officialdom it is widely believed that inexperienced people can propose courses of action but that only the wise are able to imagine all the reasons for not acting. Those with a compulsion for action are seen as irredeemable underlings destined never to rise to high office, while those given to reflection and calculation are considered to have a promising future.

This means that status in the bureaucracy belongs to planners, not to implementers, and that more careful attention is given to the planning process than to the execution of programs. It is assumed that planning on paper calls for great skill and conscientious effort, while anyone can try to carry out the plans because nothing will be accomplished anyway.[33]

The stress on planning rather than action is related to another striking feature of the Indonesian decision-making process, which is that the ratio of speculation and rumor to hard evidence is higher in Jakarta than in most other political systems. Indonesians, who have a thirst for gossip, find genuine entertainment in talking about the activities of important figures. The elite, however, have an instinct for secrecy, for they feel that there is safety in silence. The authorities are quick to censor the flow of information to the public, which therefore must generate its own version of what is going on in officialdom. In addition, lower officials often react to the need for inhibition in their deliberations with the principal figures by talking surprisingly freely outside the councils of decision-making. What they say, however, may not be factual. Many observers would agree with Ulf Sundhaussen's statement that Indonesian politics has "always had an element of untruthfulness, lack of factual evidence, willful distortion, plotting, double-dealing, and groundless insinuation in it."[34]

Although superiors use great care when speaking directly to another leader, even the highest Indonesian officials may evidence a spirit of wild abandon when they are speaking from a public platform. Public speeches in Indonesia do not usually reflect the caution one would expect of those who are speaking for the record. Instead, Indonesians seem to treat public addresses as essentially theater, and hence their rhetoric is inspired by drama and make-believe rather than by any strict attention to detail. This practice presents few problems for the Indonesians, for they attach little importance to pointing out inconsistencies, contradictions, or even falsehoods in the statements of others.

Although the use of damaging rumors was far greater during the Sukarno era than it is in the mid-1980s, gossip is still used by government officials to challenge one another. The flow of rumors is spurred not only by the delights of malice but also by the low regard which most Indonesians have for precision. Not many people would stop a rumor merely because they deemed it implausible; instead, no matter how unlikely the report might be, they would pass it on because of their delight in fantasy.

This problem is heightened by the fact that Indonesians see no sharp divide between the world of myth and mysticism, on the one hand, and the mundane world, on the other. The supernatural and the natural are easily blended, particularly since in explaining cause and effect Indonesians will pick and choose factors from either world to account for whatever has happened. An impressive number of high Indonesian officials and politicians, starting with the president and including even many Socialists, are mystics. In other cultures political figures are often strongly religious, but in most cultures it is assumed that divine intervention in public affairs is exceedingly rare if not completely implausible. Among Indonesians, however, there are few who will not claim that either they themselves or a trusted acquaintance has had some experience with the supernatural.[35]

All of these considerations help to explain the erratic nature of Indonesian decision-making. The formal structures of government seem tidy, the people understand hierarchy and are inclined to be deferential to superiors; but the informal relationships of superiors and subordinates do not necessarily conform to the organization tables of the formal structures. Those who are in responsible positions in the government have to relate with great sensitivity to the informal associations beneath them.

Therefore they frequently have to balance off important subordinates, allowing each of them to go ahead with his respective policy preference, sought by his following, even though this may result in contradictions and the appearance of confusion.

The examples of such contradictory policy initiatives are legion, not only under Sukarno, who relished playing off subordinates against one another, but also under Suharto, who has preferred orderly chains of command but has wanted them all to come under his authority. In 1984, for example, Suharto's trusted advisor General Benny Murdani was sent to Hanoi in the hope of establishing better relations with Vietnam, even while Foreign Minister Mochtiar, as chairman of the ASEAN foreign ministers' conference, was defending the isolation of Vietnam. Such apparent irregularities in policymaking reflect the nature of informal power in Indonesian politics and explain why the system of patron-client relations, although it can give the appearance of order to the formal government, cannot ensure the smooth functioning of government. The rules that govern the operation of the formal structures of government are not abstract general laws and regulations, but they usually reflect the influence of the informal power relationships.

The South Asian Subcontinent: Dual Systems of Power

It is in the South Asian subcontinent that the contrast between formal structures of state power and informal patterns of power relationships is most vivid and most explicitly acknowledged. This is not only because the extended period of British rule created strongly established norms as to how both the administrative and judicial authorities should operate, but also because the well-developed nationalist movement that opposed British rule established comparably strong traditions for mobilizing power in the society to challenge or influence formal governmental authority.

In India, in particular, the traditions of the Indian Civil Service (ICS), which are still carried on in the Indian Administrative Service (IAS), built a remarkably unambiguous model for what institutional authority should be. Power seemed to flow downward from the British Raj, but it was not divorced from locally based power. First there were the princes and the traditional rulers, and then throughout British India the zamindars, large landlords who functioned as tax collectors. But power was also being built upward, starting with the founding of the Congress party in 1885 and of the Muslim League in 1906. As nationalist political parties they mobilized first the Westernized professional elites, then the emerging middle class, and finally rural notables and the wide range of followers of Mahatma Gandhi.

With independence, the Congress party and the government administration had a relatively easy time fitting together their different power structures. In short order they squeezed out the intermediate level of rulers of the princely states and the zamindars.[36] To replace the previous contention between nationalistic politicians and law-and-order administrators, a different bifurcation soon evolved, one between the central authorities—both party leaders and administrators, located in New Delhi—and the local power figures in the districts, who controlled both the local party organizations and the local administrations. Myron Weiner, in referring to this division in Indian power, speaks of dual political cultures, an elite and a mass political culture, neither of which could be classed as traditional and each of which has some qualities inappropriate for furthering modernization.[37]

The elite culture, especially under prime ministers Jawaharlal Nehru and Lal Bahadur Shastri, was in comfortable command of the centralized structure of authority, which they used to generate elaborate five-year plans and to attract attention on the international stage—but with a somewhat limited effect. At the level of the mass culture, party politicians, especially those of the Congress party, were busy cementing personalized relations with leading elements in the general public. In the rural areas these relationships were mainly with two categories of people: first, those with economic power, which in agricultural settings usually meant the landowners; second, the spokesmen for the dominant castes and also, wherever they were strong, the leaders of the scheduled castes (the untouchables), the tribes, Muslims, and other "minority" groups.

Power at the national level pretended to be responding only to inspired ideologies about planned economic growth and liberal democratic ideals. At the local level, power was seen in much more pragmatic terms: it was openly based on exchange relationships in which citizens sought favors from politicians in return for contributions and promises to mobilize votes at election time.

The two cultures might have drifted apart in their separate dynamic ways had it not been for the integrating obligations that flowed from the logic of periodic national elections. Those in command of the elite power structures might have found themselves presiding over only the pretensions of power, as Haile Selassie eventually did, had it not been for their absolute dependence upon the local politicians who could mobilize the votes at each election. The local politicians in their turn were dependent upon the chief ministers at the state level and cabinet ministers at the center, who could command the bureaucrats to provide the services that they had promised to deliver as favors in return for local support. Although the center had its problems in consummating its announced ambitions, the linkage between the two cultures, built upon a solid base of patronage, provided the elements for a workable democracy.

The realities of power for the multitudes of Indians were only marginally touched by the matters that bulked large in the rhetoric of the national leaders. The local government they knew had real power because they constantly had to seek favors from local politicians who were in a position to "expedite" the issuing of licenses, to "facilitate" administrative decisions, and to "resolve" legal tangles.[38] The power of local politicians extended both into the community and above the ranks of the locally assigned administrators. With his contacts with higher ranking politicians at the state and national level, the local politician could influence the promotions of bureaucrats and call for their transfer to less desirable places if they failed to deliver the services requested by his clients. The fact that the ideology of the government was "socialist" in the sense of wanting the state to have a hand in as many activities as possible naturally increased the politician's power. Because businessmen, for example, could do very little without government permits and official contracts, they had to become regular visitors to the offices of the politicians.

For a time this arrangement of power relationships appeared to be giving India far more stability than had been expected by observers whose attention was focused on the country's ethnic, linguistic, and caste differences.[39] At the local level, factions among the Congress politicians tended often to cut across caste, tribe, or religious lines, thereby reducing ethnic cleavages. At the same time, however, struggles among the politicians took place with increasing frequency. Local politicians were on to such a good thing that they could not help attracting competitors. The central authorities under Nehru and Shastri did not choose to make selections among the local politicians, but rather left it to the politicians to fight it out among themselves at the village and *taluka* level, and then to compete again for membership on the district Congress committees and finally for places on the state or *pradesh* committee. Losers at one level could try their luck at the next. As Myron Weiner has noted, "Out of this process—inchoate, interminable, and opportunistic—emerged men who knew how to build coalitions within the party, influence the local bureaucracy, use the patronage of the state to maximize their support, and bargain with the central authorities for resources."[40]

This building of power upward gradually upset the balance of the Indian system. Effective power brokers at the state level became a threat to the central authority, especially after Mrs. Gandhi became prime minister. Nehru's daughter saw these figures as personal threats, and responded by trying to increase the central power by "ruling through ordinances, by frequent and arbitrary imposition of President's Rule over the state governments, by direct control of local party decisions on such matters as distribution of tickets to contested elections for the state legislative assemblies as well as Parliament, by creation of new centralized institutions of police and intelligence, and by other means."[41] These other means included establishing a dynastic order by granting extraordinary power to her son Sanjay.

The emergence of increasingly strong power brokers at the state level also altered relations at the local level. The ascetic tradition of Congress politicians, which was personified by Mahatma Gandhi but was also a part of the older tradition of the Hindu guru style of leadership, steadily eroded, particularly as some economic growth took place and businessmen could become more generous. Congress politicians looked away from those who might deliver the vote and became more enamored of those who could pay well for services rendered. In the rural areas the ties between local notables and politicians were weakened, particularly after the central authorities initiated further attempts at land reforms which would have damaged the interests of the descendants of the "former great *zamindaris* and *talukdars* who [had] managed to hold on to extensive landholdings during the post-*zamindari* abolition years."[42]

In this developing situation several key elements of Indian society that had contributed to stability became restless and assertive. Various "minorities," ranging from landless workers to lower-caste peoples, who felt they could no longer count on Congress politicians for help since the latter were concentrating on those who were better off, became increasingly prone to violence. Landed proprietors were having more trouble with their laborers, and the politicians no longer acted as pacifying agents. Local politicians, in fact, turned increasingly to criminal elements and thugs in order to intimidate their critics. Local notables found it difficult to decide whom to work with in order to advance their own interests. Some turned to their own thugs and strong men, while others sought ties with other political parties and even with politicians at the state and national level. Opportunism prevailed as people were obliged to make quick changes in their loyalties if they were to keep up with the rapid shifts in power relationships.

In short, the once strong personal ties at the local level which had provided stabilizing power were collapsing, and hence the entire Congress organization began to disintegrate. Mrs. Gandhi's response was to use central authority in ways which bypassed the lower-level politicians of her party. At first she did this by using populist tactics which attacked both "big business"—which had always supported the Congress party—and her own party bosses. The result was that in 1969 the Congress bosses sought to take the party away from Mrs. Gandhi, calling it Congress (O), the "O" being for "organization," a reference to those who had been state-level power brokers. Tensions mounted in India as power became increasingly fragmented, and violence steadily rose. Finally in 1975, Mrs. Gandhi declared an "emergency" and democratic politics ceased. Thereafter the party withered, and local power figures had no real contacts with the top. In 1977 she terminated the emergency and allowed elections, which brought to power India's first non-Congress government under the Janata party.

During the next three years power became further fragmented as factionalism at the top prevented Janata from giving India coherent rule. Janata consisted of six major groupings and a number of prima donnas who could not work together.[43] The party could neither build up power from below nor assert effective authority from above, particularly since its prime minister, Morarji Desai, who was over eighty, was unpopular with the rank and file and indecisive in policy matters. Most of his limited energies were spent struggling against Charan Singh, the second most powerful figure in the party.

In defeat, Congress's strains became greater, and in 1978 the split in the party became official when Congress (O) was matched by Congress (I), for Indira, an organization that was loyal only to Mrs. Gandhi and her son Sanjay. As the Janata party dissipated its power through ineffectualness in policy matters, insensitivity to patronage obligations, and indulgence in personal spitefulness at the top, and as Congress (O) became a collection of over-the-hill strong men who had no power of patronage, Mrs. Gandhi, as the heir to Nehru and the apparent tutor of a dynastic successor, made a remarkable comeback by winning the 1980 election. As Myron Weiner, reflecting shared insights with Paul Brass, has noted, there was a paradox in her reconstruction of power: "In her person she represented both authority and a concern for the underdog. It is these perceived attitudes that enabled her and her party to win support from the very rich and from the very poor, from Brahmins and ex-untouchables, from well-to-do businessmen and government bureaucrats, from tribal agricultural laborers and Muslim weavers."[44]

The return to power of Mrs. Gandhi in popular elections, in spite of her tainted record of earlier autocratic rule during the emergency of 1975–1977, might have appeared on the surface to be a return to Indian democracy under the aegis of the Congress party. But in fact it was not a restoration of the past because Congress (I) could not be compared with the Congress party of her father. That once formidable organization, whose power had been built up from below through the efforts of hard-working local politicians seeking patronage and providing services and whose top leadership at least had had visions of grand, if unconsummated, policies, no longer existed.[45]

Upon returning to office in 1980 Mrs. Gandhi instinctively reverted to the style of rule she had followed in the years leading up to the emergency. Using the authority and resources of the center, she "toppled" opposition governments by rewarding state ministers who came over to her side, but she was slow to respond to the needs of influential people at the local level who had once been the essence of Congress power. Paul Brass has vividly described the plight of the son and sole heir of the former Rajah of Mankapur in Gonda district of Uttar Pradesh. Anand Singh over the years had delivered the vote of the district Congress party, but he found in 1981 that he could not acquire for his constituency one of the four fertilizer plants to be allocated to U.P.[46] Technical studies based on data fed into a computer had selected other sites. Eventually, he was able to arrange a meeting with the prime minister, who promised him that Gonda would get a $300 million French-built telecommunications factory. But again the data fed to the computer by technocrats in New Delhi said no, at which Anand reportedly told the industry minister that the computer might be used to "fetch the votes the next time." Ultimately Mrs. Gandhi did overrule the ministry, and Anand Singh got the factory; but this exercise demonstrates how power has been centralized and how local leaders have to go to the top to get the political returns which once came from operating through the hierarchy of the Congress party. Under Nehru the competition would have taken place within the party organization, so that all the political considerations involving rewards and punishments would have been established before the technical variables were reviewed. After the 1980 election Mrs. Gandhi herself, and her other, surviving son, Rajiv, personally made most of the decisions that affected life at the district level.

As a result, power in India has recently been seen as decidedly more centralized and also more out of touch with local problems. Since the upward flow of power has been diffused, those at the center must act in more authoritarian ways and rely increasingly upon the coercive capabilities of the state apparatus. With the erosion of the structures of localized power, people have turned more often to violence to achieve the objectives they once sought through political ties and associations.

The government itself no longer has the networks of power relationships that linked administrative officials to the Congress politicians and also to key elements in the public. These were the relationships which provided channels for bargaining and for working out accommodations that prevented problems from becoming so explosive as to disrupt the social order. For example, the tragedy of having to order the army to storm the Sikhs' Golden Temple in June 1984 might never have happened if Mrs. Gandhi had been willing to negotiate with the moderates and meet some of the Sikh demands.[47] At one time, when the Congress party was a vital force, it could have routinely accommodated the range of issues posed by the moderates, thereby isolating the militant, terrorist Sikhs; but without the substantive power relationships, especially at the local level, which the party once provided, Mrs. Gandhi was forced into personal confrontation. She had to project the appearance of strength precisely because, in her need to rely almost entirely upon formal power structures, she was slipping toward Haile Selassie's problem with power.

Fortunately for India, however, her British heritage of a strong state structure combined with the ideals of democracy worked to compensate for the withering of the once impressive process of building power upward from concrete personal relationships. Thus, even though there have been signs of anarchy in different parts of the country, the tradition of a strong administrative structure of power has masked the decline of organized political power in India.

The vulnerability of the formal structures of power, unsupported by an upward flow of power, has been heightened by the traditional propensity of Indian bureaucrats to practice in their own domains all the forms of compromise and accommodation which make decisive policy programs impossible. Thus the Indian government can readily strike the posture of initiating grand policies, all the way from advancing socialism to liberalizing the economy; but in the end the instinct for caution, the hesitation at consummation, means that policies are invariably compromised. As for Indian "socialism," former Ambassador John Kenneth Galbraith accurately described it as "post-office socialism"; and as for the more recent claim that the economy would be less restricted, few businessmen in Bombay or Calcutta really believe that they can operate without personal ties with key government officials.

The essence of the play of power in India is that the dichotomy between formal, legalistic power, on the one hand, and personal, human-relations power, on the other, continues to exist, but the points of reinforcement and contradiction have shifted. A fundamental change has taken place as ordinary people throughout the country seek security and benefits from groups and associations with little or no access to government or the elite political culture, while Mrs. Gandhi's and Rajiv Gandhi's government has increasingly responded to particularistic relationships, the kind of relationships which were once dominant only at the mass culture level. The weakening of the Congress party has produced highly personal politics at the center, to the point that Mrs. Gandhi's private relationship with her widowed daughter-in-law, Maneka, could become a serious matter in national politics. Mrs. Gandhi seemed to trust no one except her son Rajiv, whom she successfully groomed for dynastic succession— but without the support of the powerful politicians who once controlled the Congress party and picked successors. In achieving her near monopoly of authority at the center, Mrs. Gandhi accelerated the fundamental change in Indian politics which brought about an elevation of state power and the decline of New Delhi's authority. At the local level, competition among aspiring Congress politicians no longer determines who will be able to compel the government to provide benefits to a chosen group; rather, key local figures may now have the personal connections necessary to call upon the coercive powers of the police.[48]

Thus the contradictory changes that have resulted from the decline of the Congress party have caused power at both the central and local levels in India to become more dependent upon naked coercion. Indian journalists and intellectuals, because of their earlier criticism of the crass patronage practices of the politicians, have been slow to appreciate the significance of the decline of the local Congress party organizations. Some of the intellectuals, for example, Rajni Kotari, have sought to fill the void at the local level with direct action on the part of the common people, through a form of anti-politics populism.

After Mrs. Gandhi's assassination on October 31, 1984, Indians did not publicly question the legitimacy of her wish that her son Rajiv should succeed her, and his readiness to call for prompt national elections was welcomed. What remained obscure was whether the untried leader would follow in the mode of his mother or that of his grandfather. Would he choose to control all patronage from the center, or would he allow leaders to emerge again at the state level?

Although Indian democracy is in trouble because of the decline of power that is built up from below, the advantages that India still has become clear when it is compared with Pakistan and Bangladesh, countries which shared India's tutelage under the British but which have found democracy elusive and have therefore been under military rule for most of their post-independence existence. The reason why India and the Muslim states have developed so differently is not hard to find: the tension in Islam between authoritarian rule and democracy has favored authoritarianism, largely because in the original Pakistan, before the separation of Bangladesh, it was impossible to build up effective power from below and hence the formal structures of the state became the critical source of power for the society.

Before independence the Muslim League was a more elitist party than India's Congress party, and, more important, its electoral strength was "in Hindu majority provinces and not in the areas that subsequently became Pakistan."[49] Moreover, those who took the greatest interest in establishing Pakistan and who after independence became the national elite were the *muhajirs,* or immigrants from Hindu India. Because they obviously did not have strong local ties, they were not able to build up locally based power, as Congress could do in India.

The state structure that Pakistan inherited lacked the institutional strength of the Indian administration system. Of the 549 Indians in the Indian Civil Service only 101 were Muslims, and of these 95 opted to go to Pakistan.[50] Sensitivity over their comparatively weak government compelled Pakistan's leaders to demand more authoritarian powers and to distrust the mobilizing of local power. Indeed, it was precisely the fear of regionally based local power, in the form of the rise of the Awami League in East Pakistan, that triggered the civil war which resulted in the birth of Bangladesh. In Pakistan, anxiety that ethnic differences would produce local power bases became the prime justification for military rule. In Bangladesh, the destruction of the popular Awami League came at the hands of its own leaders, including the country's first civilian president, Mujibur Rahman; but this only set the stage for the military to take over to "protect national integration."

The military rulers in Pakistan have found themselves in a no-win situation when they have tried to gain popular favor by supporting "Islamic" policies and practices; whatever they do, it is never enough to satisfy the fundamentalists, who will only be content with total power for themselves, nor is it pleasing to the more secular middle classes. Although President Zia has pushed an Islamization program, which includes a penal code that adheres to the dictates of the Koran, as well as certain economic institutions, such as interest-free banking, he has not been able to win true popularity.

Hence Pakistan's rulers may face the revelation that, for all of their autocratic pretensions, their command of real political power borders on illusion.[51] The contrasts between Pakistan and India illuminate the importance of personalized relationships in the creation of effective power in all of those Asian cultures that have paternalistic patterns of authority.

12 Paternalistic Authority and the Triumph of Dependency

O NE OF THE TROUBLESOME PROBLEMS of political science as a field of study, and, indeed, of the social sciences in general, is that the attempt to achieve generalizable concepts often generates a terminology that obscures the very phenomenon being analyzed. In dealing with the problems of power and political modernization, we are quick to speak about "legitimacy" and "institutionalization" as though they are matters about which we have real knowledge. Yet these are the very subjects that need to be examined under our "microscopes." To say that political modernization calls for the "institutionalization of new forms of legitimacy" is no more than a tautology, if we do not first determine what is involved when people's actions become "institutionalized" and what conscious and unconscious states of mind are associated with all that "legitimacy" entails—the notion of social contracts, moral or legal compacts, collective feelings about propriety and exemplary conduct, or perhaps only the sense of the natural inevitability of hierarchy in social life and the idea that rank should have its privileges.

Our examination of the sentiments that lie behind such obscuring terms in Asian cultures has uncovered many examples of what Westerners would think of as contradictions. For example, it is conventional in the West to conceive of "power" as the distinctive attribute of an elite, the stick that superiors hold over the general public, while "legitimacy" is usually thought of as residing in the public as a check on their rulers, and hence legitimacy is seen as flowing upward from the masses.[1]

In Asia, power and legitimacy operate in exactly the opposite manner. Power usually flows upward in that it depends critically upon the compliance of subordinates and is not produced out of thin air by the commands and posturing of superiors, whereas legitimacy has been generally defined in Asia by those with the greatest pretensions of power. In Confucian cultures it was the scholar-officials who worked out the rules of propriety lying behind legitimacy. In Southeast Asia and in India the rulers and the high-caste priests decreed what kings and princes should do to preserve the cosmic order and perform as proper rulers. With the coming of modernization the elites in the various countries have been trying to establish new rules of legitimacy, although their capability to do so has been limited by the predispositions of the masses.

Of course, there must be reciprocal responses in the creation of both power and legitimacy, for both are two-way streets. In return for the assurance of deference which flows upward from subordinates, the leaders must act out the roles expected of the powerful; and in response to the definition of legitimacy by the leaders there must be general acquiescence.

Revival of Paternalistic Power

The key problem of political modernization in Asia is the question of how these reciprocal relationships should be played out in changing circumstances. What do leaders have to do in order to mobilize the substance of real power from below? And what will make the masses in general, and subordinate officials in particular, respond positively to the elite's redefinition of legitimacy?[2]

In the post-World War II environment, when most Asian countries found themselves facing an unexpected crisis of legitimacy, there was considerable reluctance to yield up power to the new nationalist leaders. Nationalism seemed to contain the essence of legitimacy, but it soon proved to be lacking in endurance because it was defined as little more than anticolonialism. Once the Western powers left Asia, the legitimacy inherent in the anticolonial movements gradually evaporated, and leaders were confronted with the need to find new terms for their legitimacy. Some, of course, hoped they could recapture the past by announcing that the American "imperialists" were about to penetrate their lands.

Paradoxically, in Japan the American occupation, as a form of colonial rule, made it easier to establish a new legitimacy, one based on democratic ideals. The extraordinary success of the occupation can be seen in the nearly total compliance of Japanese governments with the norms introduced by the Americans. In China the new legitimacy was also in some degree a foreign import: Marxism-Leninism was of course a Western ideology, and in the 1950s the Soviet model became the norm of legitimacy in practical matters.

The instinctive response of most Asian leaders, including the Chinese, to their crisis of legitimacy was to try to manufacture new ideologies. To gain power from their people, as well as support from their bureaucratic subordinates, leaders sought to generate new belief systems, a practice which has been extensively studied.[3] Eventually these attempts faltered, producing, more often than not, cynicism rather than enduring commitments.

The success of grand ideologies depends in the last analysis upon their ability to speak to very basic psychological needs. If their messages do not resonate with what people intuitively feel to be the truth—that is, if they do not tap powerful sentiments and dimensions of the unconscious emotions of a people shaped by the culture's socialization processes—then the people will feel that they are listening to "false prophets."[4] In Southeast Asia, particularly in Burma and Indonesia, the first generation of leaders had some limited success in generating acceptance for their ideological formulations, but in time their appeals lost conviction. U Nu's attempt to blend Buddhism and "socialism" inspired a few people, angered more, and produced mainly a consensus of cynicism. Sukarno's efforts held the country together by sparking national pride, but they accomplished little else; few tears were shed when he was pushed aside.

Ideology in China and India worked in different ways, with different immediate consequences, but the long-run effects have been surprisingly similar. In China, Maoism was used to mobilize, on a grand scale, a huge population that performed a few useful, but many pointless, deeds. It can be argued that during Mao's reign the top decision-makers were less captured by the passions of the ideology than was the Chinese public. Hence decisions in China were often made by clear heads, while impassioned subordinates and the mass public responded by mindlessly accepting the regime's legitimacy and pledging disciplined obeisance without asking for concrete benefits in return. By contrast, in India the secular socialism that was Nehru's ideology never succeeded in stirring up the Indian masses, although it did briefly resonate with the ascetic ideals of a first generation of Congress politicians. Instead, ideology in India operated mainly to addle the thinking of the top decision-makers, to the point that they ensnarled the Indian economy in red tape and, paradoxically, created quite unintentionally a substantial "black economy," which has become a massive private sector wholly unregulated by the government.[5]

In both India and Burma an awareness that the "new" versions of "socialism" lacked the earlier appeal of anticolonialism inspired the leaders to use the bogey of impending penetration by malevolent foreign powers to incite nationalistic fervor. To make an ideological virtue of Burma's "neutralism," first U Nu and then Ne Win had to raise the specter that the superpowers would attempt to exterminate Burma's independence unless they were vigilant. Eventually, however, even the common man in Burma began to wonder whether his country's real problem was not that the outside world was unaware of Burma's existence.

The spokesmen for public opinion in India were less sophisticated. Whenever Mrs. Gandhi, aware of the limited appeals of her father's ideology, sought to stimulate paranoia over foreign penetration in India, as she did especially before elections, Indian journalists were quick to embellish official "hints" with wild speculations—as when they proposed that the CIA was behind the Sikh militants in Amristar and therefore the government was justified in storming the Golden Temple in June 1984. Indians in general, and Indian intellectuals in particular, are so narcissistic that they are completely unaware that Washington's own problems have allowed little time for concern about India.

For two decades China seemed to be the one exception to the rule that in Asia power flows upward, for Maoism as an ideology very nearly succeeded in legitimizing a new form of authority. Until they overplayed their hand in the excesses of the Cultural Revolution, Mao Zedong and his ideological colleagues seemed to have hit upon a belief system that struck a positive chord in the psyche of the Chinese and thereby was able to inspire them to extraordinary sacrifices.

Two aspects of Mao's essential message sprang from a common psychological source. At one level he spoke to a belief in the inherent goodness and greatness of the Chinese people; he certified their craving for dignity; he blessed their sense of pride; and in his preaching of puritanical virtues he reassured the enthusiasts that they deserved their sense of righteousness. On another level he justified hatred and depicted enemies against whom uninhibited aggression could be channeled. Mao's own borderline personality, shaped by an indulgent, loving mother who had had to "abandon" him when his siblings arrived, made him acutely sensitive to the longings of a generation of Chinese who felt that their inherent worth had never been properly appreciated by the "authorities"—the very ones they had tried to impress. The Chinese people's nurturance of narcissism had primed them to proclaim their virtuousness, as in the Cultural Revolution, and to explode in rage at the faltering of authority—the perfect psychological combination for the ideological mix that Mao and his companions had brewed.[6] The result for a few years was one of the greatest outpourings of human energy and of collective self-sacrifice in the history of the world.

But in the end the Chinese need to give vent to aggression, to allow hatred to reign, became self-defeating, and the final outburst—the Cultural Revolution—left the Chinese public exhausted, numb, and even confused as to who should be hated. Mao's heirs have found the question of ideology the most perplexing part of his legacy. The backlash against the years of mindless devotion to Mao Zedong Thought has been so strong that Deng Xiaoping and his associates have had to move cautiously to prevent Chinese Communism from being engulfed in cynicism.

Mao's successors have used the same approach as the other Asian leaders who have had to assume authority in the wake of collapsed ideologies. They have had to proclaim the virtues of "pragmatism" and technological progress, as though pragmatism did not have its own array of biases. True, in comparison with the intense ideological passions of the Mao era, Deng Xiaoping and his associates may seem to be mere "pragmatists," but in reality there is no such thing as pure pragmatism. Any group of individuals who can successfully commingle as a coherent political leadership must have a solid body of shared sentiments and common outlooks to ensure not only their own unity but also the harmony of their spontaneous actions.

What happened in China after Mao's death is much the same as what occurred in the other Asian countries: a reversion to traditional cultural norms about power and legitimacy, with modifications appropriate to the quest for political modernization and economic development.[7] More specifically, in nearly all of Asia paternalistic forms of authority have been reasserted, coupled with the open acknowledgment that people need and welcome dependency relationships. The sense of awkwardness comes when these must operate in the context of state institutions.

There was nothing particularly deterministic about these changes. It was merely that throughout the continent attitudes about authority and power that had been learned in the family became more salient as other concepts of authority lost ground. In other words, primary socialization experiences became increasingly dominant as secondary forms of political socialization were compromised with the weakening of the ideological bases of legitimacy. Because family practices have been among the slowest of all Asian social institutions to change, traditional cultural ideas about authority have persisted with remarkable continuity.

The durability of the family is not surprising. Even in Western culture, as Edward Shorter has shown, the family became stronger during the earliest phases of modernization. In Europe during the Middle Ages the family was completely integrated into the community; and because there were no sharp boundaries between basic social institutions, the family did not stand out as a particularly noteworthy institution. In Shorter's analogy, the traditional Western family was like a ship so securely tied to a dock that it was one with the dock; but when modernization came, the ties were broken and the ship was set afloat; thus the modern family became a distinctive, private institution, built upon strong personal sentiments. In the West it was the family members "who severed the cables by gleefully reaching down and sawing through them so that the solitary voyage could commence."[8]

The Asian family was probably stronger historically than the Western family, and certainly it has remained a strong refuge in an otherwise rapidly changing social scene. In Japan, the most industrially advanced and most urbanized society in Asia, husbands still want to return every night to traditional households after a totally modernized workday, and they expect their wives to bring up the children in the old-fashioned ways. In India even the most Westernized intellectuals continue to favor arranged marriages, and they expect their wives not only to dress in traditional costumes but also to adhere to traditional religious values. In Indonesia and Thailand, one of the difficulties in competing with Chinese businessmen is that the traditional cultures make such heavy family demands on the heads of households that they cannot concentrate on other concerns.

There are, of course, strains on the family in Asia, especially as young women from the countryside find employment in the cities and are less inclined to marry and return to life on the farm. In general, however, the authority of the family, and of lineage, remains strong, and Asians continue to be socialized into accepting the obligations of deference toward paternal authority and sacrificing individual interests for the collectivity.

Thus paternalistic power has survived in Asia in spite of changes in other aspects of the society and economy. Indeed, the personal insecurity aroused by rapid change in the more successfully developing countries seems to have provoked an almost frantic search for new forms of dependency, especially among the newly urbanized elements.[9] In Jakarta and Manila, in Seoul and Taipei, opposition leaders have been repeatedly disappointed when people who seemed to have much to complain about have sought out personal accommodation with the authorities. Authoritarian regimes are not just tolerated; they are able to command surprisingly broad support. Even more revealing is the unquestioning support of the Chinese people for the system that created the horrors of the Cultural Revolution and that has only marginally improved their standard of living. The attraction of paternalism and the compulsion of dependency are powerful forces in Asian cultures.

Psychodynamics of Dependency

In every Asian culture the basic strength of informal power is the bonding quality of personal reciprocal relationships between superiors and subordinates. The amazing strength of those relationships can be seen not only in the intense feelings of obligation and indebtedness which they evoke, but also in their tendency to endure even when they cause annoyance and trouble—as when subordinates manipulate superiors. The model for all relationships is the family, and therefore the sentiments at the heart of power in the various Asian countries reflect the family values of the individual cultures.

Thus the cornerstone of power-building in the Asian cultures is loyalty to a collectivity. Out of the need to belong, to submerge one's self in a group identity, is power formed in Asian political cultures. The sense of security which the family can provide becomes the ideal to be recaptured in new bonding relationships. Loyalty to a collectivity can offer the exhilaration or thrill of being on a "team."

This strong sense of family in Asian cultures, this sense of being group-oriented, is understood. What is less understood is the reason why the demands of conformity to the group do not seem stifling. How is it possible to keep in check the oedipal reaction and to give so little direct challenge to father figures? Why is the spirit of revolt not stronger and the search for individual autonomy not more intense? Why is discipline so easily accepted? Why is there no chafing to overthrow authority and be "free"? Why is the desire for change only a wish for a purer, more virtuous authority that will be stronger and less "corrupt"?

The dominant pattern in Asian cultures is a surprisingly muted oedipal reaction, combined with a much stronger narcissistic response. Compared with all that comes afterwards, the first years of life in most Asian households are a time of singular warmth and security when the infant, particularly the male child, is the center of attention. Nurturance is unstintingly given, and even as the child gains his separate identity he can still sense that he is special, that his inherent goodness should make him omnipotent and in total command of his environment. When he learns later that virtue and correct behavior provide access to forces that lie outside of himself, that one can be in tune with the Tao, he is only being formally taught what he has known instinctively from early childhood.[10] Of course, the oedipal response must also be there. But in most Asian cultures the stern and overpowering demands of filial piety, of awe for the father, are so great and so uncompromising that the reaction has to be repressed, and thereafter the idea can only be restored to consciousness through such defense mechanisms as negation.[11] When Asians say how much they revere their fathers, they are really saying how much they fear them. When on occasion they give vent to anger at surrogate authority figures and become consumed with hatred, they at last are expressing what has been repressed.

The repression of aggression against paternal authority is reinforced in most Asian cultures by an early awareness that behind the actual father stands a line of ancestors who are now frightening spirits, demanding conformity. The awareness that one is a link in a long biological chain, and that one will be succeeded by a line of descendants, makes the mere idea of revolt troublesome. The child is taught that everything has its place, even the child. Thus when outbursts of anger do occur, they are truly explosive because they are to some degree attacks upon the self.

Most of the time, however, the comforts of narcissism prevail, and they make the idea of dependency appealing. In most Asian cultures the demands of morality are not the commandments of a stern authority that become the constraints of the superego and hence are laden with aggression as the ego feels it is being repressed and contained. Rather, morality is the expression of the superior virtues of an inherently admirable and praiseworthy self—a self that is safe from shame and worthy of respect, hence properly immune to criticism. In Western cultures the restraints of morality are felt to be external impositions against which the self naturally wants to rebel. Hence, once the individual is compelled to accept the rules of morality, he wishes to generalize them and therefore to insist that everyone else should also be forced to comply. "If I have to accept the rules, then others should also have to do the same, or it will not be fair." Such is the reasoning of not just the Western puritan but of most put-upon American teenagers. In the West the demand for fairness thus becomes a solace for having to yield to an imposed superego. Morality is a follow-up of the oedipal experience. In Asian cultures morality is related to the spirit of narcissism, to the pleasure of asserting one's natural goodness, and of expecting to be applauded for being exemplary.[12]

This contrast is exaggerated in public life. In the West one must be careful about preaching to others, for unless one is a legitimate surrogate "father" and qualified to reinforce the superego, it can mean picking a fight. Morality and aggression are too often the opposite sides of the same coin. Indian and Chinese leaders, on the contrary, seem to be blind to the idea that they might be causing annoyance, indeed provoking hostility, by lecturing to others on how they should conduct their affairs. Among Indians such behavior is usually taken as an act of pure narcissism, of self-righteousness, and there is little expectation that anything will be accomplished by sermonizing, except possibly to prove one's own superiority. The Chinese, who seem to believe that they can achieve their objectives by shaming another—as one shames a child to make him behave properly—have few inhibitions in telling others, especially those whom they call friends, how they have misbehaved. They cannot understand why Westerners might find this irritating, because in their own minds they are acting as proper, nurturing parents, anxious to guide the child in the right way. The Japanese, who are models of disciplined behavior but who also reflect their Confucian heritage, are surprisingly blind to the possibility that they could be acting aggressively by using moral criticism—as, for example, when they assumed that as "junior partners" of the United States they could freely criticize American policies without incurring resentment.[13]

Moreover, in Asian cultures feelings about the inherent goodness of the self tend to reinforce the security of dependency. Most Asians feel that they will be accepted and looked after by the collectivity if they behave in the expected ways. The ideal position for the individual in his relationships with authority is much like the situation a child might wish to have within the family. The citizen is inclined to picture himself as always the innocent party. He finds modest satisfaction in detecting faults in his leaders, for to do so inflates his own self-esteem; but there is a limit to such self-gratification because he also needs to believe in the ultimate benevolence of public authority—much as children draw back from their fantasy wishes that their parents will disappear, while at the same time clinging to their need to believe that their parents will be all-protecting.[14]

Dependency, based on a sense that doing right should guarantee security, also calls for some tolerance of the authority's failings. Asians may sound as though they are critical of their leaders and may even be deeply cynical about them, but at the same time they put up with harsh authoritarian rule because they are slow to revolt. Complaining in the hope of shaming, yes; but actual rebellion, not often. Although they can have profoundly ambivalent feelings toward authority—much as children have toward parental authority—in acting them out they are prepared—just as children are—to accept considerable mistreatment by authority.[15]

Paternalistic authority cannot be held to rigorous standards of performance. Indeed, the greater the moral sense of superiority of the subjects of such authority, the more they will find satisfaction in grumbling about, but ultimately enduring, mistreatment. Here is a distinctively Asian phenomenon—the acceptance of apparently authoritarian rule long after a population seems to have reached a stage beyond either needing disciplining or being willing to tolerate such controls. In the West, when people reached the standard of living of those in East Asia today, they

usually insisted upon having greater freedom. The Asian ideal of paternalistic authority makes authoritarian rule more endurable.

On Paternalistic Authority

Convention holds that paternalistic authority can survive only in small
arenas, such as tribes, feudal fiefdoms, outlaw bands like the Mafia,
family enterprises, or companies operating in backward environments.
The imperatives of successful organizational management supposedly
preclude the continuation of paternalistic practices. Max Weber declared
that patrimonial authority, his version of what we are calling paternalistic
authority, was historically superseded by three more profound forms of
authority—traditional, charismatic, and rational-legal.[16] Yet in Asian
political cultures the establishment of the nation-state as the basic framework of politics and government has not weakened, and indeed in many
cases has strengthened, the ideals of paternalistic authority.

Probably the cardinal feature of Asian paternalistic power is an overriding concern for unity, for holding the national community together.
Paternalistic authority, especially in the Confucian cultures, can demand
conformity on the basis that everyone should be willing to make sacrifices
for the collective good. In terms of political development the demand for
unity and conformity has been translated into unquestioning patriotism.
Chinese intellectuals stifle criticism because of their anxiety about attacking surrogate "father" figures. In Japan the commitment to the nation
and to one's own personal community is just as deep; without being told
to do so, Japanese instinctively buy domestic, not foreign goods, and
thus make marketing difficult for foreign competitors. Japanese bureaucrats do not need the guidance of official policies to favor the Japanese
over the foreigner, the *gaijin*.

In the immediate postwar years it was assumed that Asian nationalism
was largely a reaction to colonialism and the Western impact, which to
a degree it was. Since then it has become clear that the intensity of
xenophobia is more closely correlated with the strength of paternalistic
styles of authority. The more the culture conceives of authority as being
a nurturing force for a "family" collectivity, the sharper the sense of
boundary between its members and foreigners. Distrust of the foreigner
has resulted not so much from bad experiences with outsiders as from a
deeply felt need to repay paternalistic authority and maintain the cohesion
of the collectivity.

These powerful sentiments of patriotism are clearly a function of political authority, for without strong paternalistic leaders neither ethnic, linguistic, nor religious communities can easily become effective political forces. Indeed, one of the most significant factors shaping Asian political development is the contradiction between the leader's call for unity and conformity, on the one hand, and the restless search of followers for particularistic ties, on the other. Only the topmost leaders can expect to command conformity and collective loyalty. Those below usually find it hard to create lesser communities, unless they have the benefits of geography and a definite territory, as with the linguistic states in India—which in a sense are embryonic nations with the cohesion of national identity. Unity and conformity are readily realized only at the basic level of the family, the village, and other face-to-face groupings. In general the maintenance of unity is limited to those groups or collectivities which face manifest external challenges. When such external threats do not exist, people are usually absorbed in seeking out special advantages and establishing particularistic ties, rather than voluntarily uniting to create power which might challenge the supreme paternalistic authority.

Thus although strong appeals can be made to national unity, there is no national establishment outside of government which can give the society and polity a greater sense of cohesion. In Korea there is a strong sense of national identity, but no real national establishment. In the Philippines there is no effective power structure that can discipline Marcos; the wealthy landlords and industrialists are much too active in seeking out "crony" deals to unite even for their own collective economic interests. The same is true in Indonesia and Thailand, where enterprises have to make their own separate arrangements with the bureaucratic polity. In India and Pakistan the national governments can easily "divide and conquer" the private sector, which cannot speak with a common voice.

Paternalistic authority thus must be coupled with feelings of dependency which can evoke a spirit of communality at two different levels of the society: first, at the most basic level of social institutions—in the family, the village, the company, the *danwei*—and, second, at the national level. In between, particularisms tend to take over and everyone has his or her separate line of trust and distrust, reciprocity and avoidance. Only in Japan, where power is explicitly built up from below, are there strong regional associations or national federations which are neither an adjunct of government nor a product of governmental prodding. But even in Japan the combination of paternalism and dependency has precluded the creation of large-scale corporatist institutions, like those in Latin America and southern Europe.[17]

The reason why strong "establishment" institutions have not emerged under Asian paternalistic authority is clear: with paternalism, adversary relations are an abomination. In no Asian culture but India is public confrontation seemly. In China the contending of factions is a sordid matter, not a respectable political practice. In Southeast Asian cultures those who would challenge the supreme authority are by definition insurgents, people unwilling to play by the rules of the game, that is, the rules defined by the rulers. The ideal of Asian paternalistic authority is order; and even in India, where a generation of nationalists made sport of the British stress on "law and order," the current theme of legitimacy has become the imperative of order.

The expectation that authority should produce tidiness and order also justifies the practices of obtrusive authority. It is accepted that the state can and should probe into the recesses of society. In return anyone with a problem can appeal to officialdom. Although the ideals of Amnesty International in exposing torture and civil rights violations are widely understood in Asia, there is little appreciation of the Western ideal that people should have both the right to privacy and protection from the curiosity of the community and the prying of officials.

Not only is paternalistic authority not rigorously codified, but it usually operates through pliable institutions which can be bent to the convenience of the power holders. Thus in China nobody finds it anomalous when Deng Xiaoping asserts that China is moving toward a modern legal system, even though he himself continues to act as a strong man, above the law, and to make most of the key decisions without the constitutional authority to do so. In Korea every president who has been in office for any length of time has introduced his own new constitution. Only in India and Japan does the commitment to elections compel leaders to respect the preservation of institutional arrangements.

The weakness of institutional constraints in several Asian paternalistic polities contributes to a tendency toward gerontocracy. The absence of fixed terms of office, a cultural respect for age, and a disinclination to abandon a good thing help to account for the fact that those at the top levels of the Asian ruling classes are dramatically older than their Western counterparts.

Paternalistic power is softened by the belief that it is responsive to human sentiments. Its exponents are usually considered to be guided by high ideals and moral principles, but they may also, of course, be charged with personal corruption and greed. Indeed, the most common public issue in the politics of most Asian countries is that of corruption. If it is not the leader himself who is suspect, it may be his wife or family, as has been the case in Indonesia, Korea, and the Philippines.

Paternalistic authority's greatest vulnerability is the generally awkward, and at times indelicate, question of succession. The trappings of such authority suggest immortality. No wonder the Chinese emperors and Southeast Asian god-kings publicized their desire to find the elixir of life, for they must have been convinced that they were indispensable. Even in modern times the attraction of dynastic succession has persisted, whether in Hindu India with the Nehru-Gandhi dynasty, or in Confucian Taiwan, or, most surprisingly, in Communist North Korea. The inherently personal, and nonlegalistic, character of paternalistic authority makes the question of what comes after the current leader a major one in all Asian countries, except in the case of the strongly institutionalized systems of Japan, India, and possibly Malaysia. Everywhere else in Asia it is not clear what will happen when the current leader dies. In China, Deng Xiaoping hopes that his wishes, in the form of complex policies, will become routinized, rather than that legal succession procedures will become institutionalized. In Southeast Asia, it is disturbing to consider what will happen after Marcos, after Suharto, after Ne Win. In India, the dynastic transition has taken place, but it has put into power an untested leader.

These are some of the negative features of Asian paternalism. There are, however, some positive elements, which, when combined with the strong sentiments of patriotism and group loyalty, can make paternalistic authority an effective force for political development. First, and most important, is the possibility for great flexibility in policies. Leaders can change direction without fear of losing their constituents' support. Loyalty to the leader is usually tied to the need of belonging and of finding group identity through participation rather than to enthusiasm for particular policy objectives. As long as patronage requirements are met, the followers are likely to be tolerant of their leader's choice of strategy and tactics. Sometimes this freedom has been poorly used by Asian leaders, as was true of Mao Zedong and Mrs. Gandhi at many points in their careers; but at other times it has made possible bold and imaginative policies, as in the case of Lee Kwan Yew, Suharto, and Park Chung Hee, at several junctures in their rule.

Except for the Chinese expectation that their leaders should be omnipotent, the ideal of paternalistic authority has not been opposed to the utilization of technocratic advisors and other types of specialists. In South and Southeast Asia the traditional view that kings could properly turn to astrologers for advice in decision-making without threatening their divine image has a counterpart as modern economists and engineers become members of the ruler's outer circle. Indeed, paternalistic authority can have a great advantage in that it avoids a basic dilemma of political development that appears under more legalistic forms of authority. This dilemma is that legitimacy based on legal principles invariably calls for continuity, routinization, and a general standardization of most forms of governmental activity, whereas the successful use of knowledge usually calls for adaptation, accommodation to changing circumstances, and experimentation. Legal authority, which calls for orderly procedures and predictability, thus can clash with the best ways to utilize technology. This is particularly the case when rational-legal authority is weakly institutionalized and frequent changes must be made for technical reasons. Such a need for frequent change may be seen as vacillation and thus may undermine popular confidence in the steadiness of state authority. Paternalistic authority can rise above this dilemma, for it does not have to feel constrained by consistency. Indeed, the very proof of the power of personalized authority is often the ability of a leader to change his mind and still demand respect.

Although paternalistic authority usually has a way of avoiding accountability, it also can heighten peoples's sensitivities concerning whom they should turn to if they want to get something done. The well-institutionalized, rational-legal bureaucratic state often seems too impersonal to be approachable. Thus people who have innovative ideas often do not know how to get them implemented; and there is, furthermore, a general presumption that the "specialists" in government know more than the outside amateurs. With paternalistic authority, however, it is easy for outsiders to imagine that responsible people would wish to have help with their problems. Not only do the "suggestion boxes" in Japanese factories elicit nearly ten times as many voluntary proposals as do similar boxes in American factories, but Japanese citizens with ideas tend to seek out the appropriate action points in the government in order to present their suggestions directly. They do not waste their time with the meaningless, but possibly ego-gratifying, practice of Americans who believe they have accomplished something by writing a letter to the editor. Under paternalistic authority it is possible to have empathy for leaders who have problems and also to believe that those in positions of responsibility have the freedom to respond to good ideas rather than being prisoners of regulations and established procedures.

The autonomy of leadership in policymaking can also be translated into longer time perspectives in policy practices. Spared the constraints imposed by set terms of office, leaders who are secure in their paternalistic authority can engage in long-range planning. The advantages of this practice can be seen in the way in which the successfully industrializing East Asian countries have worked out their economic development programs.

The pluses and minuses of paternalistic authority cannot be summed up in general terms because the decisive factors are the personalities of the individual leaders and the particular characteristics of the respective cultures. We would only suggest that development is possible under paternalistic authority and that successful modernization will not necessarily weaken Asian forms of paternalistic power. These kinds of authority are consistent with the operations of modern nation-state institutions. This is particularly true because the sentiment complementary to paternalism is dependency, which can be a positive force for development.

The Positive Face of Dependency

In Western thinking, from moral philosophy to modern psychology, the emphasis has been on the virtues of independence and autonomy, the assumed prerequisites for self-realization and healthy, complete personal development. Dependency is thought to have only negative qualities. At best, it is associated with immaturity and a phase of childhood which needs to be outgrown if effective, creative development is to be realized. At worst, dependency is a sign of a permanent liability, of distorted growth, and of inevitable weakness. Yet in the Asian cultures examined in this study, dependency is thought of in a positive way. Moreover, in those cultures people conceive of power in a way that makes dependency a constructive force in national political development.

It is true that some Asians, particularly among the urban, educated youth, have found their traditional group-oriented norms constricting, and therefore they have been as determined as Westerners to achieve personal independence and a greater sense of individualism. In the main, however, the psychology of dependency remains strong; and it is being channeled in ways that contribute to modernization, but a form of modernization which will be significantly different from that produced by Western individualism.

The most constructive aspect of the psychology of dependency is its potential for building cooperation and strong bonds for teamwork. Acceptance of conformity and commitment to the group make it easy to suppress egotistical assertiveness and to work smoothly with others. As society, with modernization, becomes more complex and collective enterprise more critical, such team endeavors become increasingly important. If the proper style of leadership is provided, cultures which stress dependency can be remarkably effective.

A key qualification is sympathetic, supportive leadership. If this element is missing, the psychology of dependency will cause people to feel mistreated, and there will be endless bickering and complaining within the organization or group. Formal rules ensuring equal treatment are not enough—as they might be with more individualistic personalities—because the dependent personality has to be treated in a special, particularistic way in order to satisfy its narcissistic needs. When the leadership fails to be appropriately nurturing, the level of anxiety will rise and group tensions will develop instead of teamwork.

At the same time, leadership can be stern and authoritarian. Because, in return for their cooperation, psychologically dependent people must be sure that the group they have identified with will have durability, they look for a lasting authority. This is why they are inclined to seek out strong authority figures as their leaders.

To the Western mind, individualism is essential for aggressive, creative behavior; dependency, which is seen as stifling and immature, is regarded as an obstacle to modernization.[18] Yet the experiences of both private companies and public institutions not only in Japan but in most Asian countries indicate that people who are secure in their immediate settings, and who have supportive superiors, can be boldly aggressive and creative in their risk-taking. Moreover, such risk-taking is usually not a matter of gratifying personal pride but of accomplishing something exceptional for the collectivity.

In terms of formal theory this suggests that Asian modes of dependency produce people who have a strong appreciation for the value of collective goods, who feel that it is right to expend effort and resources not only for the maximization of private and personal values but also for the general betterment. In theory this should be the case, but in actual practice there has not been any marked tendency to appreciate the value of collective goods anywhere in Asia, and especially not in Japan. The well-to-do have generally not displayed much altruism, and expenditure for public goods by government lags behind growth in GNP. In Japan, investments in roads, sewers, and environmental matters remain far below Western investments at comparable levels of development.

One answer to this paradox is that the prime thrust of dependency is to seek immediate benefits for the self in return for loyalty to the group, and that a willingness to sacrifice for the collectivity can only come with more private affluence and greater personal security. Maybe in time the readiness to contribute to expenditures for public goods will increase. In the meantime, however, the impetus behind building grand public structures comes primarily from paternalistic leaders with personal pride and a desire for national greatness.

This explanation of the collective goods paradox is consistent with the expectation on the part of the dependent personality that in return for concrete, materialistic rewards—that is, the substance of nurturance—one owes positive sentiments of loyalty and obedience. Asians may be slow to support collective goods, but they will not hesitate to make great, even ultimate, sacrifices for their particular group. In short, nationalism is a powerful sentiment in Asia, one that Westerners simply cannot comprehend.

In the West, the values of individualism and self-realization must compete with collective loyalties, trade-offs must be made, and the virtues of altruism must be weighed against personal benefits.[19] In Asian cultures the logic of dependency reduces the perception of such conflicts and opens the way for extraordinary commitments to nationalism.

Solidarity in a Competitive World

The combination of paternalism and dependency which seems to be the strongest common element in the diverse attitudes toward power which are shaping the political development of Asia has contributed to a vivid sense of Asian nationalism in which a sharp divide exists between the national community and "foreigners." The intensity of nationalism is used to justify suppressing almost any form of dissent or domestic opposition. The unity which Deng Xiaoping's regime demands in order to achieve the Four Modernizations in China is only a few degrees less intense than the ideological conformity of Mao's China. The tenacity of Vietnamese nationalism has forced a whole population to regard extraordinary sacrifices as normal and natural. In prosperous Singapore the idea that serious opposition to the government could bring ruin is not seriously challenged. Even in India, where democracy has been institutionalized, Mrs. Gandhi's party routinely suggested that disturbances which challenged the government had been instigated by foreigners.

This in-group feeling is so strong that whenever significant opposition elements want to challenge the existing authorities legitimately, they seek dependency under what they hope will be a sympathetic paternalistic authority. Thus opposition leaders in Korea and the Philippines routinely try to shame the United States into helping their causes. The concept of power modeled on family relationships does encourage the idea that those who are perceived as strong, as "father figures," can be influenced and even manipulated by moral persuasion and by shaming. In Asian politics this practice has been universal: Nehru preached to the West about the moral superiority of the "nonaligned," and Peking has a way of saying that Washington is not abiding by "agreed principles" on the Taiwan issue. The psychology of dependency is so strong that Asians have little awareness that such conduct might be counterproductive. Some of the opposition leaders in the Philippines are frustrated because their barely masked dependency appeals, which sound like harping criticism of Washington, seem to turn off American officials.

The problem of tolerating an opposition is a serious problem in the political development of Asia. The psychology of the political cultures that develop strong state authorities produces a profound distrust of criticism of authority and of domestic competition. Through the 1970s and early 1980s the concept of power in most of Asia led to increasingly firm state institutions, and in many cases it caused strong state authority to direct the private sector toward rapid economic growth. And even where impressive growth did not take place, as in South Asia, the role of the state has been strong.

The question for the future is whether ideas about power will evolve that result in more room for domestic competition and less need for the sovereign authority to be seen as all-powerful and all-wise. On the one hand, the example of Japan, and now possibly of Taiwan, does suggest that gradual but successful progress can be made in combining strong state authority with tolerance for political competition. On the other hand, in India the attitudes toward power which allowed for the development of democratic practices seem to be changing toward more authoritarian views.

Whatever the direction of change, it is certain that the politics and government in the various countries will continue to reflect the distinctive evolution of each in combining past and present attitudes about power. Moreover, even though the Asian countries see more and more that state power can be rationally employed to carry through policies for modernizing their societies, they will continue to hold to their traditional view of power as associated with dignity, with status, and even with a sense of being a part of the cosmic order. Therefore, a continuing source of Western misunderstanding of Asia is likely to be the mistaken assumption that Asian leaders and followers are operating under Western concepts of the nature of power and the purposes of public policy.

Without doubt, Asian leaders in the years ahead will increasingly follow the international practices of statesmen and will therefore employ a political vocabulary suggesting that they intend to use power to implement articulated policies and programs. Confusion will almost certainly arise when Westerners fail to appreciate that often this rhetoric is less a policy commitment than an assertion of status—that it is either a way of seeking moral respectability or just a ritual act designed to reassure the faithful that their leader is cognizant of the trendy developments in modernization. Already there is considerable uncertainty as to how seriously one should take apparent policy statements by almost any of the

Asian leaders. Are all of the policies promised by Deng Xiaoping and his presumed successors really going to be carried out? Or are some statements intended only to reassure followers and demoralize opponents? Which ones are going to become administrative programs, and which are made only to serve the purpose of "politics"? Who really believes that the government of India is about to implement all of the statements of its ministers or even of its prime minister? How seriously should one take the pledges of Japanese prime ministers to foreign leaders about changes in Japanese governmental practices?

The question is not whether the gap between words and deeds is greater with Asian politicians than among politicians in general; the point is rather that Asian cultural attitudes about the nature and proper uses of power will at times confound Western observers who take a narrow view of the purposes of power and believe that it should be mainly the servant of calculated policies.[20] In no political culture does the ability to articulate an apparently calculated policy necessarily signal a commitment to implement that policy; but in some political cultures—and in most Asian ones—there are more reasons for a gap between words and deeds because the motivations for the use of power are different.

The fact that Asians do not agree with Westerners in emphasizing the prominence of policy in the overall functioning of political power does not mean that the governments of Asia will have no meaningful policy programs or that they will not move steadily ahead in modernization. It should be remembered that no Western country modernized through the implementation of policy programs. Power in the West was seen in utilitarian terms quite early, but largely as a way of realizing the interests of particular elements. The idea that power could be the means for total national development only came with the Russian Revolution, the New Deal, and the Keynesian movement that culminated in the Marshall Plan.

In Asia, as in the West, politics will continue to be a combination of applying state authority to grand purposes and of scheming to take advantage of some people and to nurture and support others. The style of politics, however, will definitely not be like that of the West. The difference between the Western ideal of a chief executive—tough, capable, on top of everything, holding on until someone can "beat him out"—and that of the Asian leader—nurturing, protecting, but also self-centered and prideful—ensures that the Asian states will not follow any standard Western model of statehood.

As we indicated at the beginning of this book, the underlying fact which justifies our speaking of Asia as a single entity is the shared goal of their diverse cultures to achieve modernization. At one time their model of wealth and power was Western industrialization. Now, however, the late-developing societies have the Asian examples of Japan and the "gang of four" (Korea, Taiwan, Hong Kong, Singapore). These models offer a larger role for state authority than do Western societies, and therefore they are likely to be more attractive to other Asians whose cultures revere authority. The Western idea that power should be checked is still seen as dangerous in cultures where the imagined horrors of "primitive power" lie ahead if authority is weakened.

The modernization of Asia is thus going to emphasize state authority. This does not mean that there will be a single, common pattern for the entire continent; for even though Asians exalt the ideal of authority, their cultural understanding of power is extremely diverse. Indeed, because they give so much importance to these culturally determined views of power, some of the Asian states will have continuing problems with modernization, for it is no easy feat to achieve the complex relationships required in a modern, technological society while paying homage to authority. China will have to find a balance between centralized and decentralized authority. In Southeast Asia the various bureaucratic pol-ities will have to achieve working relationships between informal patron-client ties and the formal operations of government, relationships which will go beyond providing mere stability. In India the politics of patronage must find some limits so that the state does not incessantly hamper economic initiative. Pakistan and Bangladesh will need to resolve the question of the proper allocation of authority between Islamic values and modern governmental practices.

In none of the Asian countries will the solution come easily. Yet in every one the answer will have to be found in the domain of politics; for politics is the interplay of power and values, and the problem of mod-ernization in Asia is precisely the question of what should be done about power.

What Prospect for Democracy?

If Asian concepts of power are beginning to work in support of strong national economic development, will this in turn lead to the advancement of democracy in the region? The conclusion which follows from our analysis of paternalistic authority is that the prospects for democracy, as understood in the West, are not good. At the same time, Asians are not insensitive to the value the world places on democracy. Historically in nearly all the Asian countries the vision of modernization as economic development and national strength was combined with an awareness that there should be progress toward some form of democracy. The Western impact on Asia was not just a diffusion of technology; it also included the spread of democratic ideals.

To this day Indian democracy rests heavily upon memories of what the British taught. Thus, for Indians the idea of democracy is intimately related to the concepts of "fair play" and the "rules of the game." The traditional Indian belief in amoral political leadership has had to contend with the British ideas about "following the rules." The difficulty of combining the two has fueled the growth of Indian cynicism.

Elsewhere in Asia, any thrust for democracy that exists tends to result from the desire to appear respectable in Western eyes. Consequently Asians often confuse the achievement of democracy with the attainment of favorable recognition in the West. Progress in areas in which the West has excelled is taken to be the equivalent of progress toward international respectability and thus to be the equivalent of democracy. In Singapore, the government takes offense at any suggestion that democracy is limited, for the authorities believe that their extraordinary achievements and the intellectual brilliance and ingenuity of their policies make them exemplary democratic rulers.

Among the Chinese, commitment to the higher goals of the Four Modernizations is taken to mean that somehow democratic respectability is being advanced, and that it is bad form for foreigners to criticize the country's lack of a domestic legal system capable of protecting the individual. In Taiwan the same belief that commitment to exalted goals is the equal of democratic advancement has taken the form of assuming that dedicated anti-Communism makes a country a part of the "free world" and thus a democracy. In fact, in Taiwan the traditional Chinese view that it is unseemly for authority to be criticized has caused people to mask the extent to which the society has become pluralistic and to play down the diversity of opinions.

In the Philippines, people have been confused about what to take as the appropriate standard for democracy. They still tend to look to the United States for guidance, but they have been receiving contradictory signals ever since Marcos introduced martial law. This problem results only partly from the perception that the American government has supported the Marcos administration. The enthusiasm of the American public for China and the generous American praise for the Deng Xiaoping administration, when compared to American criticism of the Philippines, are perplexing, because it is obvious that there is more democracy in the Philippines than in China.

A clue to the continuing difficulty of advancing democracy in Asia can be found in the development of Japanese democracy. Unquestionably

Japan has all the institutional arrangements associated with a healthy democracy—a free press, legal protection of the individual, and all kinds of opposition parties. Yet the country is thought of as having only a "one-and-a-half party" system. The interplay of paternalistic authority and dependency means that as long as the leaders are seen as "understanding" the people's needs, then the public ought to respond by being equally "understanding" of their leaders. Inhibitions about adversarial relationships determine that in election campaigns there are no sharp attacks on personality and no serious discussion of issues—the candidates can only humbly beg for votes.

Distaste for open criticism of authority, fear of upsetting the unity of the community, and knowledge that any violation of the community's rules of propriety will lead to ostracism, all combine to limit the appeal of Western democracy. As a result, the development of more open and enlightened politics in Asia is likely to produce a much more contained form of popular participation in public life. At best it is likely to be a form of democracy which is blended with much that Westerners might regard as authoritarian.

Asian prospects for modernization with or without effective democracy rest very much upon the potential inherent in paternalistic power. Yet the risks are also great, because whenever paternalistic power falters there can be strong emotional reactions on the part of dependent followers and the general public. The result can be cynicism and a privatizing of interests. At worst there can be explosions of rage against failed authority, as in China's Cultural Revolution.

Enduring Importance of Culture

Our argument that the traditions of paternalistic authority in Asia will produce forms of modernized societies different from those known in the West might seem to go against the theory that modernization evolves a distinctive culture and that "modern" people shed their traditional ways in order to adopt a uniform personality. If it is true that the structural changes that come with the spread of literacy, dissemination by the mass media, increased education and urbanization, and the learning of the routines of factory labor tend to obliterate ancient ways of thought, then will Asians not in time become indistinguishable from Westerners? Certainly the evidence from sociological studies, beginning with the work of Daniel Lerner and culminating with that of Alex Inkeles, suggests that there is indeed a modern personality type.[21] Moreover, it is generally true that any culture able to sustain modern institutions, such as the factories

Inkeles studied, must have people who share such "modern" attitudes as getting to work on time and faithfully doing their assigned jobs. Therefore scales that measure such attitudes would probably not register much difference from culture to culture.

The degree to which cultures converge during the process of modernization is significant since they are all participating in the spread of a world culture based on advanced technology. Yet political cultures will always have a strongly parochial dimension because every political system is anchored in its distinctive history, and the central political values of loyalty and patriotism and the phenomenon of national identity mean that differences are certain to persist, and possibly even to increase with modernization. Proof of this fact can be found in the Western experience. Although all West European countries have "modern" societies composed of "modern" people, the political cultures of the individual countries remain profoundly different, at least in regard to their attitudes toward power and authority.

Another possible challenge to our emphasis upon the cultural basis of Asian paternalistic authority patterns is the structural argument that in the contemporary world late-industrializing countries must have strong, authoritarian state institutions if they are to speed up their modernization. This is a case that is not only popular with some Third World politicians but also with many scholars, including most notably Alexander Gerschenkron.[22] Thus our finding that Asian countries have a propensity for paternalistic authority patterns may be more a function of their being late-developing countries than a carry-over of traditional attitudes about power and authority.

Most people would agree that no Asian country is likely to modernize successfully if it is ruled by a weak and inefficient government. But it should not therefore be concluded that all countries with strong authoritarian governments can realize rapid development. Indeed, the case that the late-developing countries need strong state structures was first popularized in the late 1930s as a rationalization for the adoption of fascism by Germany, Italy, and Japan. Then after World War II it was thought that Stalin's Russia provided a universal model for rapid industrial development. Many of those who accepted this view either felt that the late-developing states could not afford the "luxury" of democracy or believed that the democracies were on the decline and the technocratic-managerial state was the wave of the future. This was not just Soviet propaganda; it was also the view of many Western intellectuals who held that history was on the side of state planning of basic economic activities. Therefore it is no wonder that many of the Third World leaders were tempted by the "Soviet model." In the 1960s, in fact, it was widely believed that democratic India was severely handicapped in its competition with totalitarian China.

In time, however, events revealed that "strong states" could bring more problems than solutions. The simplistic conclusion would be that effective development calls for a greater appreciation of market forces than was popular among Gerschenkron's generation of economists. The record of development in Asia shows that while effective governmental authority is necessary, strong state authority is not enough, for it is essential to take into account the more complex question of how political authority can facilitate rapid economic growth. Most Asian leaders, of course, are happy to use the argument of having to "catch up" with the advanced nations in order to justify their predisposition toward authoritarian rule.

Our review of Asian countries suggests that for historical reasons some cultures are more likely than others to appreciate the complex and subtle relationships between political authority and economic development. The effort of a state to influence economic development can be as much a liability as an asset, as the first twenty years of Chinese Communist rule have shown. Strong state authority can be as great an obstacle to development as weak state authority. Our comparison of policy choices in Korea and Taiwan revealed that finely tuned differences can exist in the way "strong states" influence economic policies.

Our final conclusion is that the modernization of Asia will produce systems that are even more varied than those in the West, but that at the same time the shared characteristics of these different Asian polities will set them apart from the modern cultures of the West.

The tragedy of the late-developing societies is that they have too often allowed themselves to be caught up with the insoluble, and in the end totally irrelevant, question of whether they are becoming "too Westernized" in their progress toward modernization, that is, too enthusiastic in emulating the West and hence forgetful of their own cultural heritage. The verdict of history will certainly be that the issue so posed is a conundrum of the mind and the psyche, a matter that cannot stand up to the light of rigorous analysis.

Asians are going to produce their own versions of modernization, which will have their own particular strengths and weaknesses. The West should no more stand in awe of future Asian strengths than Asians should stand in awe of earlier Western strengths. The different Asian systems may escape some of the problems that have bedeviled modern Western societies, but they will certainly have their own peculiar problems and their own modernization dilemmas.

An immediate, major problem for the late-developing Asian societies is the lack of well-established models for their forms of political modernization. Some of the Southeast Asian leaders have talked of the need to "look to the East," that is, toward Japan, Korea, and Taiwan, rather than to the West. Yet Japanese culture is far too distinctive to provide a ready model for others. As for the more recently industrializing states of Korea, Taiwan, and Singapore, they are still in a state of political transition with unresolved problems of legitimacy and succession, and therefore they are not the best models for other states.

In time, however, a variety of modernized Asian states will emerge. Then, as now, Asian success should not be measured against parochial Western standards, but against more universal models that will overarch the enduring gulfs between the world's great civilizations.

Notes

Index

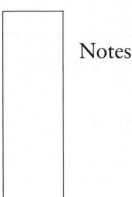

Notes

1. Asia and Theories of Development

1. I first used the concept of world culture to signify the core intellectual and affective aspects of the more diffuse concept of modernization, in *Politics, Personality, and Nation Building* (New Haven: Yale University Press, 1962), pp. 10–15.

2. A classic study which treats Latin America as having distinct cultures is Hubert Herring, *A History of Latin America: From the Beginnings to the Present* (New York: Alfred A. Knopf, 1968). A more recent social science argument that favors cultural uniqueness over dependency is Howard J. Wiarda, *Corporatism and National Development in Latin America* (Boulder, Colo.: Westview Press, 1981).

3. Chinese reactions to the challenge of the West are well summarized in the documents translated in Ssu-yu Teng and John K. Fairbank, *China's Response to the West* (Cambridge, Mass.: Harvard University Press, 1954).

4. *Far Eastern Economic Review,* December 10–16, 1982, pp. 67–68.

5. A description of Chinese policies as being strongly oriented toward the world economy is to be found in A. Doak Barnett, *China's Economy in Global Perspective* (Washington: Brookings Institution, 1980).

6. William Watts, *Americans Look at Asia: A Need for Understanding* (Washington: Potomac Associates, 1980).

7. Myron Weiner, "Political Science and South Asian Studies," in Lucian W. Pye, ed., *Political Science and Area Studies: Rivals or Partners?* (Bloomington: Indiana University Press, 1975), p. 137.

8. Montesquieu, *The Spirit of the Laws* (London: Hafner, 1962).

9. Adam Smith, *Wealth of Nations* (New York: Modern Library, 1937), p. 789; John S. Mill, *A System of Logic* (London: Longmans, 1961).

10. Karl A. Wittfogel, *Oriental Despotism* (New Haven: Yale University Press, 1957).

11. Marx's use of the word "Asiatic" rather than the currently popular "Asian"

should not be taken as pejorative but rather as testimony that over time the implications of terms can be reversed. Before the emergence of India as a spokesman for Asia the word Asian was understood, especially in East Asia, as a pejorative term having effete overtones, while Asiatic had manly and even heroic dimensions. The Japanese rallying cry for military expansion was "Asia for the Asiatics," and Western companies on the China coast, not wishing to offend the Chinese, included the word Asiatic in their titles. It was the Indians who insisted that Asiatic, with barbarian overtones, was demeaning, while Asian was complimentary. Today in East Asia, and particularly in Korea, Asiatic is becoming increasingly popular.

12. For an excellent discussion of Marx's changing concept of the "Asiatic mode of production," see Perry Anderson, *Lineages of the Absolutist State* (London: New Left Review, 1974), pp. 462–549.

13. Dependency theorists, while generally professing to be Marxists, violate the spirit and letter of Marx, even of Lenin, when they deny the possibility of capitalism emerging in the "periphery" areas in conjunction with the spread of capital from the "metropole," and when they refuse to acknowledge the "progressive" aspects of such capitalistic development. A masterful review of the extent to which the Marxian dependency theorists of the *Monthly Review* school have sought to refute the classical Marxist-Leninist theory of imperialism is Albert Szymanski, *The Logic of Imperialism* (New York: Praeger, 1981). Paul Baran, as a "father" of the dependencia school, initiated the deviation from Marxism by stressing the conflict of interests between the "mature" capitalists and capitalists in the "periphery" (*La Economía Política del Crecimiento*, Mexico City: FCE, 1969). Gunder Frank in his various writings, but especially in *Capitalism and Underdevelopment in Latin America* (New York: Monthly Review Press, 1967), carried the split further from classical Marxism by arguing that only by a revolutionary break in the metropole-satellite network of the world capitalist economy could there be an end to "underdevelopment" of the periphery countries. Theotonio Dos Santos carried the break even further by arguing that it is hopeless for a dependent economy to "expand through self-impulsion" since it is completely at the mercy of "world capitalism" ("The Structure of Dependence," *American Economic Review*, 60, no. 2, 1970, 231–236).

Fernando Henrique Cardoso in his extensive writings on dependency has retreated from the idea that Latin American countries are totally impotent in the face of the industrial world, but he does not hold out much hope for their economic development because not only their entrepreneurs but also their intellectuals are dependent upon what takes place at the "center." For excellent reviews of the dependency school see Gabriel Palma, "Dependency: A Formal Theory of Underdevelopment or a Methodology for the Analysis of Concrete Situations of Underdevelopment," *World Development*, 6 (1978), 881–924; and J. Samuel Valenzuela and Arturo Valenzuela, "Modernization and Dependency," *Comparative Politics*, 10 (July 1978), 535–557.

By the mid-1980s empirical research in Latin America had eroded confidence in the relevance of dependency theory. The ideologically committed continued to hold to a romantic view of socialism, and to reify to the point of caricature the "world capitalist system," as they blamed outsiders for all of Latin America's problems. Fortunately, the obligation to face the facts of that continent's economic and political development has operated not only to puncture the sillier versions of the theory but also to depoliticize to some degree scholarly work on development problems.

14. Louis Hartz, *The Liberal Tradition in America* (New York: Harcourt, Brace and World, 1955).

15. For a criticism of some scholars' failures to treat earlier work in comparative politics accurately, see Gabriel A. Almond, "Corporatism, Pluralism, and Professional Memory," *World Politics*, 45 (January 1983), 245–260.

In the 1970s the work on political development was further victimized by the perverse use of one of the most pernicious concepts ever imported into the social sciences, that of "paradigm." As used by some social scientists "paradigm" became a way of politicizing research and of dismissing the actual diversities and rich subtleties of intellectual creativity. By crudely dividing scholarship into only gross categories, based usually on ideological considerations, evaluation of individual merit was replaced by simpleminded labeling. It is usually safe to assume that people who are quick to use the word paradigm lack sophistication in understanding the creative process in the social sciences.

16. The well-established correlation between exercises in systematic, causal theory-building and trite findings made questionable the criticisms by Robert T. Holt and John E. Turner of work of the Committee on Comparative Politics of the Social Science Research Council, in their "Crises and Sequences in Collective Theory Development," *American Political Science Review*, 69 (September 1975), 979–994.

17. My study of Burma *(Politics, Personality, and Nation Building)*, done in 1958, was undertaken precisely because, though Burma was a country that had all the objective conditions for progress, it was already predictable that it would have great troubles, both politically and economically. Everett E. Hagen's *On the Theory of Social Change* (Homewood, Ill.: Dorsey Press, 1962) pointed out further limitations to economic development in much of the Third World. Fred Riggs's study of Thailand, which introduced into the literature the concept of "bureaucratic polity" and set the stage for his concept of "prismatic" societies, points more to difficulties than to easy progress: *Thailand: The Modernization of a Bureaucratic Polity* (Honolulu: East-West Center Press, 1966). Much the same picture emerges from a reading of Myron Weiner's *Party Politics in India* (Princeton: Princeton University Press, 1957). Indeed, except for those who naively believed that independence from colonial domination would resolve all problems, most work based on fieldwork in Asia tended to identify problems and obstacles to progress. With respect to Africa—prior to the Congo crises and the beginning of military coups—there was more unwarranted optimism, especially among defenders of the proposition that one-party rule on that continent was somehow consistent with democratic government.

18. Compare Samuel Huntington's "The Change to Change: Modernization, Development and Politics," *Comparative Politics*, 3 (April 1971), 283–322, with, for example, Huntington and Joan M. Nelson, *No Easy Choice: Political Par-*

ticipation in Developing Countries (Cambridge, Mass.: Harvard University Press, 1976).

19. Gabriel A. Almond and James Coleman, eds., *The Politics of Developing Areas* (Princeton: Princeton University Press, 1960), pp. 20–25.

20. David Gellner, "Max Weber: Capitalism and the Religion of India," *Sociology*, 16, no. 4 (1982), 526–543.

21. Nathan Leites, "Psycho-Cultural Hypotheses about Political Acts," *World Politics*, 1 (October 1948), 107.

22. The extraordinary need of some scholars to believe that the world is ruled by reason and deliberate judgments, not passions and predilections, has contributed to an odd development in comparative politics. Although most scholars know enough about American politics to appreciate the importance of personality and power, they will describe esoteric systems, such as the Chinese, as revolving around rational "debates" over policy preferences. Some have even gone so far as to play down the madness of the Cultural Revolution and to suggest that it involved, not power struggles, but policy options.

23. In retrospect it is surprising that there were not more systematic studies comparing India and China. In part the problem was that China scholars as area specialists worked very much in isolation from the field of comparative politics and sought to stress the uniqueness of Mao's revolution. Only after the changes accompanying the death of Mao and the rise of Deng Xiaoping were Chinese events and practices treated in the same developmental context as those of the non-Communist world.

24. Aidan Foster-Carter sought in 1976 to suggest that development theory was outmoded and due to be replaced by the more radical dependency paradigm: "From Rostow to Gunder Frank: Conflicting Paradigms in the Analysis of Underdevelopment," *World Development*, 4 (March 1976), 167–180. In making his case, Foster-Carter seems to have recognized how shaky and vulnerable the dependency "paradigm" was, for he concluded that "if events in China and Cuba were to prove as disappointing as most neo-Marxists now think the USSR to be, yet another paradigm would arise—probably a very pessimistic one" (p. 177). So far, although there has been no sign of a new "paradigm," his prediction about the decline in popularity of dependency theory has proved true, but for reasons which go well beyond China's and Cuba's desires to escape from "autonomy" and benefit from a share in the "world economy."

25. Harry Eckstein, "The Idea of Political Development: From Dignity to Efficiency," *World Politics*, 34 (July 1982), 451–486.

26. Lloyd I. Rudolph and Susanne Hoeber Rudolph have, for example, gone so far as to argue that all bureaucracies have forms of patrimonialism, citing as examples those who have attached their careers to Robert McNamara: "Authority and Power in Bureaucratic and Patrimonial Administration: A Revisionist Interpretation of Weber on Bureaucracy," *World Politics*, 31 (January 1979), 195–227. Robin Theobald, in the spirit of Eckstein's demand for greater care with concepts, has sought to restore the more limited and precise meaning Weber gave to that concept, in "Patrimonialism," *World Politics*, 24 (July 1982), 548–559.

27. Lucian Pye, "Culture and Political Science: Problems in the Evalution of the Concept of Political Culture," *Social Science Quarterly*, September 1972, pp. 285–296.

28. Chalmers Johnson, "What's Wrong With Chinese Political Studies?" *Issues and Studies*, 18 (June 1982), 19.

29. Only in the last phase of the work of the Committee on Comparative Politics of the Social Science Research Council was some success achieved in collaborating with historians. The effort at that time was to determine if it might be possible to discuss patterns of sequential change and thus to identify typologies of history, an ambitious goal that would have gone beyond Eckstein's call for a more linear treatment of history. This attempt to work with historians resulted in: Charles Tilly, ed., *The Formation of National States in Western Europe* (Princeton: Princeton University Press, 1975); and Raymond Grew, ed., *Crises of Political Development in Europe and the United States* (Princeton: Princeton University Press, 1978).

30. Gabriel A. Almond, "Comparative Political Systems," *Journal of Politics*, 18, no. 3 (1956), 392–422. I can testify that concern about power was not entirely absent at the beginning of work on political development. In 1953, shortly after I had returned from fieldwork in Malaya, I was invited by the Committee on Political Behavior to attend a Sunday meeting at the SSRC headquarters at 230 Park Avenue to give my firsthand views on the prospects of research work in the developing countries. The meeting was successful in that it led directly to the establishment of the Committee on Comparative Politics, but I ran into some problems in my presentation. I had decided to advocate a program of research which would try to go beyond the fragile formal institutions and nationalist ideologies and focus on the behavior of power groups, and to ask why such comparable groups as Westernized elites, bureaucrats, landowners, military, and trade unions act similarly or dissimilarly in different countries. My problem was that Robert Dahl kept pestering me to explain how I would know who had power—a question that mystified me until his book *Who Governs?* was published.

The initial phase of the Committee's work did deal with group analysis, and the results were the classic studies of interest groups by Joseph LaPalombara on Italy and Myron Weiner on India, and of bureaucracies by Fred Riggs on Thailand. It soon became apparent, however, that unless there was a way of looking at total systems it would be hard to make the research cumulative. Hence the adoption of structural-functionalism.

31. Charles E. Merriam, *Political Power: Its Composition and Incidence* (New York: McGraw-Hill, 1934). Bertrand Russell, *Power: A New Social Analysis* (New York: Norton, 1938). Harold D. Lasswell, *Politics: Who Gets What, When, How?* (New York: McGraw-Hill, 1936); Harold D. Lasswell and Abraham Kaplan, *Power and Society* (New Haven: Yale University Press, 1950). The leading examples in international relations would be Nicholas J. Spykman, *The Geography of Peace* (New York: Harcourt, 1944); and Harold and Margaret Sprout, *Foundations of International Politics* (Princeton: Van Nostrand, 1962).

32. Robert Dahl, *Who Governs?* (New Haven: Yale University Press, 1961).

33. Floyd Hunter, *Community Power Structure* (Chapel Hill: University of North Carolina Press, 1953). Not surprisingly, differences in grappling with such a complex and unexpectedly elusive concept as power can easily lead to ideological clashes among academics.

34. Susan L. Shirk, *Competitive Comrades* (Berkeley: University of California Press, 1982).

35. In a brilliant analysis J. P. Nettle has distinguished two general types of modernizing traditional societies. The first, which is like most of the Asian societies, and also like such historical European countries as Britain, he calls "elitist" systems, in which authority is associated with particular individuals or a ruling class. The other type he calls "constitutional" systems, in which authority at a very early stage is legalistically defined and prescribed, institutions and not individuals have powers and responsibilities, and authority can be divided and checked, as it was from the beginning of the political development of the United States. See his *Political Mobilization: A Sociological Analysis of Methods and Concepts* (New York: Basic Books, 1967).

In elitist systems it is accepted that the entire political process will adhere to informal practices and operate in a latent manner, with key actors working behind the scenes. Institutions in elitist systems are highly expendable. Leaders tend to "capture" whatever institutions exist and bend them to their own purposes. Thus institutional changes are easy, but there may be little turnover of elites.

36. In social psychology there has been considerable interest in the question of whether children do or do not generalize from their experiences with parental authority to other forms of authority. The evidence is somewhat inconclusive but seems to suggest that children make the jump from parents to teachers rather easily but not so to peer group leadership. See James Alston Davies, "Does Authority Generalize? Locus of Control Perceptions in Anglo-American and Mexican-American Adolescents," *Political Psychology*, 4, no. 1 (1983), 101–120.

37. It is peculiar that the field of business and industrial management, which incorporates so much of psychology, is insensitive to the limits to copying culturally determined practices. The question of the legitimacy of teaching management seems to get confused with the question whether it is possible for people consciously to change their basic styles of behavior. A not untypical example of the idea that managers should be able in different situations to choose rationally different styles of leadership, and hence overcome the limits of personality, is Robert Tannenbaum and Warren H. Schmidt, "How To Choose a Leadership Pattern," *Harvard Business Review*, 36, no. 2 (1958), 95–101.

38. The distinction between Western individualism and Asian group consciousness has been a dominant theme in Sir George Sansom's interpretation of Japan, John K. Fairbank's descriptions of China, Louis Dumont's work on India, and the work of such general theorists as Michael Polyani, Sir Thomas Maine, and of course both Max Weber and Karl Marx.

39. A telling example of this contrast occurred in the summer of 1983 when Congressman Stephen Solarz visited Taiwan and made statements about the importance of human rights in a way that would seem unexceptionable to most Americans, but that triggered the anger of the mayor of Tainan City. Su Nan-cheng,

who is a Taiwanese, not a member of the Kuomintang, and the winner of the Magsaysay Award for civic leadership, exploded at what he saw as American hypocrisy: "Everybody knows that the test of human rights is whether a government makes its citizens feel secure. Therefore, if people are afraid to ride the subways at night, do not dare to roam freely in Central Park in the moonlight, and feel they must lock up their apartment as though it were a jail, they have been denied the most basic of human rights by their government."

Evidence that such attitudes run deeper than mere ideological disagreements was provided in the same summer, when the Peking government initiated a campaign of rounding up what they called "the dregs of society" and publicly executing hundreds if not thousands of "criminals" who had not been given even the pretense of a formal trial. The only explanation offered by the Chinese authorities for such actions was that "the social order" was being "threatened by a rising wave of crime."

40. Mary Douglas and Aaron Wildawsky have tellingly made the point that modern man, seduced by the abilities of science and technology to reduce the scope for chance, has become as expectant of certainties as traditional man, who knew that nothing could be accidental and that what happened on the hunt, a drought, or somebody's death had to be caused by someone violating the laws of pollution or by leaders not behaving correctly. See their *Risk and Culture* (Berkeley: University of California Press, 1982).

41. Significantly Gabriel A. Almond, writing in the spirit of the 1950s and early 1960s, pointed the study of political development toward the goal of "probabilistic theory-building." Almond and James S. Coleman, eds., *The Politics of the Developing Areas* (Princeton: Princeton University Press, 1960), pp. 58–64. It was therefore not strange that his harshest critics were those who wanted a more absolute concept of theory, such as Holt and Turner, in "Collective Theory Development," and a variety of Marxists.

42. Claude Lévi-Strauss, "Social Structure," in A. L. Kroeber, ed., *Anthropology Today* (Chicago: University of Chicago Press, 1953), pp. 538–542, cited in Robert R. Jay, *Javanese Villagers* (Cambridge, Mass.: MIT Press, 1969), pp. xii–xiii.

2. The Evolution of Asian Concepts of Power

1. One of the handicaps of the social sciences is that, for reasons too complicated to explain here, it has become conventional to presume that a generalization could be completely dismissed if a single exception was found. Imagine where medicine would be if physicians followed the same perverse concept of science! They would long ago have thrown out the germ theory because of documented cases of people being exposed to purportedly communicable diseases and not coming down with the illness. We would even be unsure where babies come from because cases have been recorded of sex without progeny. In medicine—and we hope in social science as it becomes more mature—the demolishing of a theory calls for more than just one incidence of noncompliance because in matters dealing with human affairs we can usually specify only the *necessary* conditions (sex for procreation) but not the *sufficient* ones (sex for conception).

2. Carl J. Friedrich brought considerable clarity to the concepts of legitimacy and authority in political science by making legitimacy unambiguously a legalistic term and authority a term to describe the taming of crude, physical force, but with a moral dimension added. Carl J. Friedrich, *Man and His Government* (New York: McGraw-Hill, 1963).

3. In contrast to Aristotle, Augustine, and Locke, who on different bases had essentially single sources for legitimacy, Max Weber was "the first to discover the universal applicability of the notion of legitimacy." Wolf Stenberger, "Legitimacy," in *International Encyclopedia of the Social Sciences* (New York: Macmillan, 1968), vol. 9. Weber's distinctions, however, were limited to his well-known typology of "traditional," "charismatic," and "rational-legal." We shall be concerned with considerably more refined distinctions.

4. David McClelland the psychologist, at the second meeting of the Joint Harvard-MIT Seminar on Political Development in 1963, in responding to my presentation on the role of tradition, noted that political science as the study of government should properly begin with an analysis of the arrangements man has made to handle the absolutely basic human phenomenon of aggression. How a society, on a collective basis, manages to repress, divert, channel, and generally control aggression thus becomes the most fundamental question of the discipline.

5. Samuel P. Huntington has argued the case that with advanced political development comes an overloading of the political system as more demands are made than can possibly be satisfied. Hence the presumably powerful modern governments are nearly as impotent as the governments of developing countries which lack adequate authority to provide the necessary order for effective development. See in particular his analysis in *American Politics: The Promise of Disharmony* (Cambridge, Mass.: Harvard University Press, 1981).

For a profound yet energetic demonstration that in the West the concept of "progress" preceded the rise of nationalism and technological progress, see Robert Nisbet, *History of the Idea of Progress* (New York: Basic Books, 1980).

6. Many views about the origins of the state can be found in the West, and no doubt the Age of Absolutism which preceded the Enlightenment caused such writers as Locke and Mill to take as given a prior state structure before speaking of limiting the power of government. Yet even so, it is noteworthy that the dangers of revived anarchy or of governmental ineffectuality were largely ignored. These problems are illuminated in Quentin Skinner, *Foundation of Modern Political Thought* (Cambridge: Cambridge University Press, 1978).

7. Barbara Tuchman, *A Distant Mirror* (New York: Random House, 1978).

8. Samuel P. Huntington, *Political Order in Changing Societies* (New Haven: Yale University Press, 1968), pp. 100–102.

9. Joseph R. Strayer has made the point that understanding the Middle Ages is important for understanding the modernization of Europe; see his *On the Medieval Origins of the Modern State* (Princeton: Princeton University Press, 1970).

Another profound, historically oriented study on the origins of the modern state is Reinhard Bendix, *Kings or People: Power and the Mandate to Rule* (Berkeley: University of California Press, 1978). Bendix follows in the tradition of Max Weber, but he employs a more subtle and complex view of the nature of authority and hence pioneers in the direction which our study seeks to follow.

10. Keith Thomas, "The United Kingdom," in Raymond Grew, ed., *Crises of Political Development in Europe and the United States* (Princeton: Princeton University Press, 1978), chap. 2.

11. Harry J. Benda, "The Structure of Southeast Asian History," in Robert O. Tilman, ed., *Man, State, and Society in Contemporary Southeast Asia* (New York: Praeger, 1969).

12. See Benoy Kumar Sarkar, *The Political Institutions and Theories of the Hindus* (Leipzig: Market and Pettera, 1922); K. P. Jayaswal, *Hindu Polity: A Constitutional History of India in Hindu Times* (Bangalore: Bangalore Printing and Publishing Co., 1955); D. Mackenzie Brown, "Traditional Concepts of Indian Leadership," in Richard L. Park and Irene Tinker, eds., *Leadership and Political Institutions in India* (Princeton: Princeton University Press, 1959).

13. The Hindu texts are quoted in John W. Spellman, *Political Theory of Ancient India: A Study of Kingship from Earliest Times to Circa A.D. 300* (London: Oxford University Press, 1964), pp. 4, 6.

14. H. V. Hudson, *The Great Divide: Britain-India-Pakistan* (New York: Atheneum, 1971); V. P. Menon, *The Transfer of Power in India* (Princeton: Princeton University Press, 1957).

15. George Sansom, in his *History of Japan, 1334–1615* (Stanford: Stanford University Press, 1961) details the story of Japan's factional strife better than most historians.

16. For example, in their classic and exhaustive modern analysis of the concept of power, Harold D. Lasswell and Abraham Kaplan overlook completely the basic Chinese notion that power is related to chance and also good fortune in the sequencing of events. See their *Power and Society: A Framework for Political Inquiry* (New Haven: Yale University Press, 1950).

17. The relationship of power and responsibility, according to Western cultural perceptions, was central to the writings of Hobbes and Weber. It is also a major concern of those who believe that Western democracies have been "overloaded" by more popular "demands" than states have the capabilities to satisfy. See Michel Crozier, Samuel P. Huntington, and Joji Watanuki, *The Crisis of Democracy* (New York: New York University Press, 1975).

18. Jonathan D. Spence has demonstrated that Chinese emperors were obligated to carry out very precise ceremonies but that they were never sure what consequences would flow from their actions. See his *Emperor of China: Self-Portrait of K'ang-hsi* (London: Jonathan Cape, 1974).

19. Marcel Granet, *The Religion of the Chinese People,* trans. and ed. Maurice Freedman (New York: Harper and Row, 1975).

20. Although peasants in China did travel to the magistrate's yamen to protest the effects of announced policies, they also acted in the same manner in seeking help for matters entirely unrelated to a rational notion of the limits of public

policy. See William T. deBary, *Self and Society in Ming Thought* (New York: Columbia University Press, 1970). In Southeast Asian cultures there tended to be a more intimate relationship between rulers and subjects, and consequently people were inclined to take any and all personal problems to their superiors. L. Cadière, "La famille et la religion au Viêt-Nam," *France-Asie*, 13 (1958), 260–271; Jasper Ingersoll, "Fatalism in Village Thailand," *Anthropological Quarterly*, 39 (July 1966), 200–225; Lucian Hanks, "Merit and Power in the Thai Social Order," *American Anthropologist*, 64, no. 6 (1962), 1247–61.

21. This dilemma underlies Arthur F. Wright's introduction to the volume he edited, *The Confucian Persuasion* (Stanford: Stanford University Press, 1966).

22. The Chinese ambivalence about the efficacy of moral example as compared with that of painful punishment is well illustrated in Derk Bodde and Clarence Morris, *Law in Imperial China Exemplified by 190 Ch'ing Dynasty Cases* (Cambridge, Mass.: Harvard University Press, 1967).

23. Wright, *Confucian Persuasion*, pp. 6–7.

24. Ibid., p. 11.

25. Susan Shirk, *Competitive Comrades* (Berkeley: University of California Press, 1982).

26. Ray Huang, *1587: A Year of No Significance* (New Haven: Yale University Press, 1981).

27. Clifford Geertz, *Nigara: The Theater State in Nineteenth-Century Bali* (Princeton: Princeton University Press, 1980).

28. See Benedict O. Anderson, "The Idea of Princes in Javanese Culture," in Claire Holt, ed., *Culture and Politics in Indonesia* (Ithaca: Cornell University Press, 1972); Robert Heine-Geldern, *Conceptions of State and Kingship in Southeast Asia*, Data Paper no. 18 (Ithaca: Cornell University Southeast Asia Program, 1956).

29. For the details of early Southeast Asian warfare see Brian Harrison, *Southeast Asia: A Short History* (London: Macmillan, 1954), and D. G. E. Hale, *A History of Southeast Asia* (New York: St. Martin's Press, 1955).

30. See in particular the contribution of Samuel E. Finer, Gabriel Ardant, and Rudolf Braun, in Charles Tilly, ed., *The Formation of Nation States in Western Europe* (Princeton: Princeton University Press, 1975).

31. The Asian view of "corruption," as contrasted with the Western legalistic view, is illustrated by the easy way in which the Japanese political system responded to former Prime Minister Tanaka's conviction for accepting a large cash bribe, which he presumably dispensed to supporters, and the American revulsion toward President Nixon for covering up for his supporters.

32. The classic interpretation of China's intellectual reaction to the West is Joseph R. Levenson, *Confucian China and Its Modern Fate*, 3 vols. (Berkeley: University of California Press, 1958, 1964, and 1968).

33. For a discussion of the *t'i-yung* formula as related to the dichotomy between *li*, ideal form or theory, and *ch'i*, mutable matter or data, see my "Description, Analysis, and Sensitivity to Change," in Austin Ranney, ed., *Political Science and Public Policy* (Chicago: Markham, 1968), pp. 239–261.

3. East Asia

1. Gunnar Myrdal, *Asian Drama,* 3 vols. (New York: Twentieth Century Fund, 1968).

2. See, for example, Roy Hofheinz and Kent E. Calder, *The East Asia Edge* (New York: Basic Books, 1982).

3. In Benjamin Schwartz's careful analysis of Western and Confucian thought he notes "that the heart of Chinese religion is the idea of filial piety," and that Yen Fu equated the Confucian ideal of filial piety with Christianity in the West: "All action [presumably moral action] derives its origin here [in filial piety]. Extending it to the service of the lord, it becomes the virtue of loyalty. When applied to an elder brother it is fraternal piety. In its farthest extension it even determines the Chinese attitude of reverence toward Heaven." *In Search of Wealth and Power: Yen Fu and the West* (Cambridge, Mass.: Harvard University Press, 1964), pp. 38–39.

4. For the concept of "virtuocracy" see Susan Shirk, *Competitive Comrades* (Berkeley: University of California Press, 1982).

5. The contradictory themes of Korean culture have been well documented by Vincent Brandt in *A Korean Village* (Cambridge, Mass.: Harvard University Press, 1972), and in "Sociocultural Aspects of Political Participation in Rural Korea," *Journal of Korean Studies,* 1 (1979), 205–224.

6. On the pervasive sense of melancholy in Vietnamese culture, see Nathan Leites, "The Viet Cong Style of Politics," RAND Corporation Memorandum RM-5487, May 1969.

7. Max Weber, *The Religion of China,* trans. Hans H. Gerth (New York: Free Press, 1951). Thomas Metzger, *Escape from Predicament* (New York: Columbia University Press, 1977). Paul Hiniker, "Chinese Reactions to Forced Compliance: Dissonance Reduction and National Character," *Journal of Social Psychology,* 77 (1969), 157–176.

8. Joseph Needham, *Science and Civilization in China,* 5 vols. (Cambridge: Cambridge University Press, 1954–1983); and Mark Elvin, *The Pattern of the Chinese Past* (Stanford: Stanford University Press, 1973).

9. For a succinct statement of the Chinese values of harmony and stability, see Arthur F. Wright, "Struggle or Harmony: Symbol of Competing Values in Modern China," *World Politics,* 6 (October 1953), 31–34.

10. On the problems that Chinese governments have had with the idea that racially non-Chinese might not properly be considered to be Chinese citizens, see June Dreyer, *China's Forty Millions* (Cambridge, Mass.: Harvard University Press, 1976); and Stephen Fitzgerald, *China and the Overseas Chinese* (Cambridge: Cambridge University Press, 1972).

11. Lucian W. Pye, "The International Position of Hong Kong," *China Quarterly,* 95 (September 1983), 456–468.

12. The cautiousness of Japanese authority and the brusqueness of Chinese authority highlight a fundamental difference in the way the two cultures have interpreted a basic Confucian theme, that of harmony or concord. The Chinese version of *ho* emphasizes the differences in social roles and makes it clear that

real harmony requires that those who command should command, and those who are to obey should obey. By contrast, the Japanese concept of *wa* holds that harmony can only exist when differences are smoothed over. "Harmony consists in not making distinctions; if a distinction between good and bad can be made, than *wa* does not exist." Ono Seiichiro, *Nihon hori no jikaku teki tenkai* (Self-conscious development of Japanese philosophy of law) (Tokyo: Yuhikaku, 1942), p. 300, cited in Kawashima Takeyoshi, "The Status of the Individual in the Notion of Law, Right, and Social Order in Japan," in Charles A. Moore, ed., *The Japanese Mind* (Honolulu: East-West Center Press, 1967), p. 264.

13. Cornelius Osgood, *The Koreans and Their Culture* (New York: Ronald Press, 1951); Choi Jai-senk, "Family Systems," in Chun Shin-yong, ed., *Korean Society* (Seoul: International Cultural Foundation, 1976), pp. 18–33.

14. I have developed the argument about China's basic "authority crisis" in *The Spirit of Chinese Politics* (Cambridge, Mass.: MIT Press, 1968).

15. The standard relationships in both the traditional and the more modern Chinese family have been well described in Marion Levy, *The Family Revolution in Modern China* (Cambridge, Mass.: Harvard University Press, 1949); and C. K. Yang, *The Chinese Family in the Communist Revolution* (Cambridge, Mass.: MIT Press, 1959).

16. Choi Syn-duk, "Social Change and the Korean Family," *Korean Journal,* 15 (November 1975), 4–13; Lee Hyo-chia, "The Changing Family in Korea," *Journal of Social Sciences and Humanities,* 29 (December 1968), 87–99.

17. For a full discussion of the *gosenzo,* see Jiro Kamishima, *Modernization of Japan and General Theory of Politics* (Tokyo: privately printed, n.d.).

18. Ibid., p. 30.

19. Choi, "Social Change and the Korean Family," p. 10.

20. One of the explanations for the disproportionate number of Peking operas dealing with nomads, who otherwise did not bulk large in the Chinese imagination, was that such themes permitted the dramatic blending of political stratagems and the calculations regarding marriage arrangements.

21. In developing the concept of ideal-type analysis, Weber was seeking to break out of the Germanic tradition of *Geisteswissenschaften* or *Kulturwissenschaften,* in which the study of cultures had to be treated in "historical" terms which presupposed that all sequences and developments had to be unique because the "facts" were always unique. Weber's notion of ideal types, which combined normative imperatives with patterns of social action, established categories, and hence frames of reference, that permitted comparison and thus the identification of general causal factors. Anthropology also broke out of the shackles of having to see each culture as unique when it adopted the analogous concept of "model personality." For an introduction to these methodological problems, see Talcott Parsons, "Weber's Methodology of Social Science," in A. M. Henderson and Talcott Parsons, trans., *Max Weber: The Theory of Social and Economic Organization* (New York: Oxford University Press, 1947), pp. 8–29; *Max Weber on the Methodology of the Social Sciences,* trans. and ed. H. A. Finch and E. Shik (Glencoe, Ill.: Free Press, 1949).

22. I have developed these themes of Chinese political culture in some detail in *The Spirit of Chinese Politics*.

23. Kamishima, "Modernization of Japan," p. 90.

24. For a discussion of the relationship between physical exertion and Chinese political behavior, see my *Spirit of Chinese Politics,* chap. 8.

25. This is a frequent theme in classic Chinese novels, such as the *Dream of the Red Chamber.*

26. Richard Solomon, *Mao's Revolution and the Chinese Political Culture* (Berkeley: University of California Press, 1971).

27. The connection between Japanese views and the Protestant ethic has been documented in Robert Bellah, *Tokugawa Religion* (Glencoe, Ill.: Free Press, 1957). The relationship between spiritual discipline and ostentation in Japanese culture is of course too complex to be summarized in a few words. Historically the Japanese merchant class, the *chonin,* avoided conspicuous display of wealth for other reasons, including the desire not to provoke the envy of the samurai, who could put them to the sword with no questions asked. Yet the samurai, especially during the era of Tokugawa peace, sought in Edo to prove the greatness of their respective lords, or daimyos, by not flinching when paying for the entertainment of others—a tradition which Japanese on expense accounts emulate to this day. Spending for the enjoyment of others is not treated the same as conspicuous consumption for one's own pleasure. Here disciplined conformity and a suggestion of frugality are still prized.

28. Alexander Woodside, *Vietnam and the Chinese Model* (Cambridge, Mass.: Harvard University Press, 1971).

29. Samuel L. Popkin, *The Rational Peasant: The Political Economy of Rural Society in Vietnam* (Berkeley: University of California Press, 1979), p. 87.

30. The tension between Confucianism and the various religions was a central dynamic force in all four of the Confucian countries. In China it produced an elite which was not without religious sensibilities but which strove to separate ethics from otherworldly concerns. In Vietnam, the Confucian elite absorbed the Buddhist movement. In Korea, by contrast, the Confucian rulers sought to disparage Buddhism, causing it to become a disdained heterodoxy, appropriate only for the lower classes. In Japan, Confucianism and Buddhism were more completely blended, and both were accepted as expressions of Chinese culture; hence the Japanese subsequently found it easy to utilize religion for political purposes.

31. During the years of debate over the American involvement in Vietnam an attempt was made, in certain quarters, to romanticize precolonial Vietnamese society and to suggest that only with the arrival of the Westerners had harmony been destroyed at the village level. This was the view of Frances Fitzgerald, as reported in her popular *Fire in the Lake* (Boston: Atlantic-Little, Brown, 1972), which was based on the essays of Paul Mus and John McAlister. Samuel L. Popkin, after reviewing all the scholarly writings of both the French and the Vietnamese, concluded that the traditional Vietnamese village was as riven with animosities as traditional villages usually are. Popkin, *Rational Peasant.*

32. For an excellent review of the *yangban* class, see Cornelius Osgood, *The Koreans and Their Culture* (New York: Ronald Press, 1951), pp. 133–152.

33. Ibid., p. 141.

34. On the examination system and the social backgrounds of the Yi dynasty elites, see Kim Yong-mo, "The Traditional Elite," in Chun Shin-yong, ed., *Korean Society* (Seoul: International Cultural Foundation, 1976), pp. 75–102.

35. Young-Sop Ahn has provided me with translations of excerpts from Woo-Keun Han, *Han Kuk Sa* (The History of Korea) (Seoul, 1970).

36. Gregory Henderson, *Korea: The Politics of the Vortex* (Cambridge, Mass.: Harvard Unniversity Press, 1968), chap. 2.

37. The gap between the Confucian sense of the private ethics of rulers and their public roles and the Western sense of the same distinction was dramatized by the Asian puzzlement over Watergate—with the Chinese taking moral pride in not abandoning their "friend" for what they saw as a trivial matter—and the Japanese response to Tanaka's Lockheed scandal—with the Americans unable to understand how a former prime minister who had been convicted of bribery could continue to be the most powerful politician in the country.

38. Wang Fu (ca. 100–150) wrote a remarkable essay, translated by Lily Hwa in Patricia Buckley Ebrey, ed., *Chinese Civilization and Society: A Source-book* (New York: Free Press, 1981), pp. 30–32, which recounts how imperial criticism of a high official could cause his retainers and followers to abandon him, and how a lonely scholar-official, seen as poor and without prospects, would be despised by everyone.

39. Quoted in T'ung-tsu Ch'u, *Local Government in China under the Ch'ing* (Stanford: Stanford University Press, 1962), p. 173.

40. Ibid., p. 169. In some cases guild associations did have access to political authority; in particular, merchants engaged in the salt business could demand dealings with officials because of government policies to monopolize salt.

41. For a comparison of the politics of merchants in China and Japan, in which the paradox is noted that the more ascriptive Japanese feudal system compelled the *chonin* class to specialize and hence excel, while the more mobile Chinese society allowed merchants (or certainly their sons) to become officials and hence the Chinese merchant class remained weak, see Marion J. Levy, Jr., "Some Aspects of Individualism and the Problems of Modernization in China and Japan," in Simon S. Kuznets, Wilbert E. Moore, and Joseph J. Spengler, *Economic Growth: Brazil, India, Japan* (Durham: University of North Carolina Press, 1955), pp. 496–536.

4. Southeast Asia

1. As the anthropologist Cora Du Bois once testified: "There is probably no other area of the world so richly endowed with diverse cultural strains." *Social Forces in Southeast Asia* (Minneapolis: University of Minnesota Press, 1949), p. 27.

2. Rupert Emerson was one of the earliest scholars to be intrigued by the use of Western values in the articulation of anticolonial versions of nationalism. *From Empire to Nation* (Cambridge, Mass.: Harvard University Press, 1960), chaps. 1 and 2.

3. Josef Silverstein, *Burmese Politics: A Dilemma of National Unity* (New Brunswick: Rutgers University Press, 1980).

4. Willard Hanna, *Bung Karno's Indonesia* (New York: American Universities Field Staff, 1967).

5. Charles Donald Cowan, *Nineteenth Century Malaya: The Origins of British Political Control* (London: Oxford University Press, 1961); and Rupert Emerson, *Malaysia: A Study in Direct and Indirect Rule* (New York: Macmillan, 1937).

6. The classic study of the economic effects of various patterns of colonial rule is J. S. Furnivall, *Colonial Policy and Practice* (Cambridge: Cambridge University Press, 1948). The later edition (New York: New York University Press, 1956) will be cited in this chapter.

7. For a personalized view of what foreign rule was like in the colonial days, see such firsthand accounts as: Mi Mi Khaing, *Burmese Family* (Calcutta: Longmans, Green, 1946); U Ba U, *My Burma: The Autobiography of a President* (New York: Taplinger, 1958); Ba Maw, *Breakthrough in Burma* (New Haven: Yale University Press, 1968).

8. Robert A. Scalapino, *Asia and the Road Ahead* (Berkeley: University of California Press, 1975), p. 18.

9. The clash between politicians and administrators is a central theme in my study of Burmese politics, *Politics, Personality, and Nation Building* (New Haven: Yale University Press, 1962).

10. One of the best studies of the emergence of nationalist leaders under the conditions of Japanese occupation during World War II is Harry J. Benda, *The Crescent and the Rising Sun* (The Hague: Van Hoeve, 1958).

11. The legitimacy problem of the Confucian cultures resulted, in part, from their demand that rulers behave as exemplary models for their subjects, while in the Southeast Asian cultures there were no such constraints. There leaders were expected to be freed from the restrictions that ordinary people had to live with, and thus the very eccentricities of leaders could point to their legitimacy.

12. For a comparison between Burma and Thailand that stops short of cultural and psychological analysis, but which says that such factors are decisive for explaining the differences, see Fred W. Riggs, *Thailand: The Modernization of a Bureaucratic Polity* (Honolulu: East-West Center Press, 1966), chap. 1.

13. Kenneth P. Landon, *Siam in Transition* (Chicago: University of Chicago Press, 1939); and David A. Wilson, *Politics in Thailand* (Ithaca: Cornell University Press, 1962).

14. Furnivall, *Colonial Policy and Practice*, cited in Riggs, *Thailand*, pp. 29–30.

15. Maung Maung, *Burma in the Family of Nations* (Amsterdam: Djambatan, 1956), p. 29.

16. John F. Cady, *A History of Modern Burma* (Ithaca: Cornell University Press, 1958), pp. 3–38.

17. Maung Maung, *Burma,* p. 34.

18. D. G. E. Hall, *A History of South-East Asia* (New York: St. Martin's Press, 1956), pp. 519–520, quoted in Riggs, *Thailand,* p. 24.

19. For a description of the organization and practices of the Burmese monarchy, see E. C. V. Foucar, *They Reigned at Mandalay* (London: Dobson, 1946); R. F. Johnston, *From Pagan to Mandalay* (London: John Murray, 1908); and Maung Maung, *Burma,* chap. 1.

20. G. E. Harvey, *History of Burma from the Earliest Times to 1824* (London: Longmans, Green, 1925), p. 329.

21. Riggs, *Thailand,* p. 35.

22. Philip Woodruff, *The Man Who Ruled India* (New York: St. Martin's Press, 1954), II, 120–122; Maurice Collis, *The Great Stone Image* (New York: Alfred A. Knopf, 1943); and Robert Heine-Geldern, *Conceptions of State and Kingship in Southeast Asia,* Data Paper no. 18 (Ithaca: Cornell University Southeast Asia Program, 1956).

23. Mary R. Haas, "The Declining Descent Rule for Rank in Thailand," *American Anthropologist,* 53 (October-December 1951), 585–587.

24. Lucien Hanks and Herbert P. Phillips, "A Young Thai from the Countryside: A Psychological Analysis," in Bert Kaplan, ed., *Studying Personality Crossculturally* (New York: Harper, 1961), quoted in David A. Wilson, "The Military in Thai Politics," in Robert O. Tilman, ed., *Man, State, and Society in Contemporary Southeast Asia* (New York: Praeger, 1969), p. 334.

25. Manning Nash, *The Golden Road to Modernization* (New York: John Wiley & Sons, 1965), p. 1.

26. Maurice S. Collis, *Last and First in Burma* (London: Faber & Faber, 1956).

27. Josef Silverstein, *Burmese Politics: A Dilemma of National Unity* (New Brunswick: Rutgers University Press, 1980), chaps. 2 and 3.

28. I have treated these problems of trust in Burmese political culture in *Politics, Personality and Nation Building: Burma's Search for Identity* (New Haven: Yale University Press, 1962).

29. U Nu, "Leftist Unity Program," in Roger Smith, ed., *Southeast Asia: Documents of Political Development and Change* (Ithaca: Cornell University Press, 1974).

30. In the 1950s while doing fieldwork in Burma, I repeatedly confronted the unbridgeable gap between American and Burmese concepts of power and decision-making. During working hours I was harangued by exasperated Burmese officials who complained that the American advisors they had hired, at what were to them astronomical salaries, to solve their country's problems only presented them with seemingly endless alternatives and options, and therefore more problems than they had known they had. The last thing Burmese officials wanted was to have more choices; they simply wanted problems to go away. In the evening, after work, I would hear the American advisors complaining about the refusal of Burmese officials to make decisions. They apparently would not play

the part of power holders, as conceived by Americans. Occasionally an American advisor, almost as if confessing a sin, would report that he had, shock of shocks, made a decision for the Burmese government. For him this was a violation of the ethics which separates advisors from power holders. Yet for the Burmese it must have seemed as though that advisor had at last done something to earn his living. Personally, I found it impossible to explain either culture to the other.

31. Nash, *Golden Road,* pp. 76–77.

32. Ibid., p. 77.

33. Maung Maung Gyi, *Burmese Political Values: The Socio-Political Roots of Authoritarianism* (New York: Praeger, 1983).

34. For an analysis of the concept of *ahnadeh,* see Hazel Hitson, "Family Patterns and Paranoidal Personality Structure in Boston and Burma" (Ph.D. diss., Radcliffe College, 1959), chap. 2.

35. George Orwell in *Burmese Days* captures these Burmese sentiments in his descriptions of the convoluted calculations of the less than admirable, but always aspiring, U Po Kyin, particularly in his skillful feuding with the Indian, Dr. Veraswami.

36. Lucien Hanks, "Entourage and Circle in Burma," *Bennington Review,* Summer 1968.

37. Hitson, "Family Patterns," chap. 2.

38. Heine-Geldern, *Conceptions of State and Kingship;* H. G. Quaritch Wales, *Ancient Siamese Government and Administration* (London: Bernard Quaritch, 1934).

39. John F. Cady, *Thailand, Burma, Laos, and Cambodia* (Englewood Cliffs, N.J.: Prentice-Hall, 1966), p. 80.

40. Walter F. Vella, *The Impact of the West on Government in Thailand* (Berkeley: University of California Press, 1955); Abbot L. Moffat, *Mongkut: The King of Siam* (Ithaca: Cornell University Press, 1961), pp. 9–22.

41. Cady, *Thailand, Burma, Laos, and Cambodia,* p. 127.

42. The Siamese traditionally had a strictly hierarchical status system called *sakdina,* which involved numerical grading on a scale that went from the king to the meanest slave. Riggs, *Thailand,* p. 73. A Thai official visiting America once explained to me that after he had returned from studying in England he belonged to an "informal" group of other returned students who met regularly and that he "ranked 18th in the group of 33." There are not many cultures in which people would have such a vivid sense of everyone's position in power relationships.

43. Herbert Rubin, "Will and Awe: Illustrations of Thai Villagers' Dependency upon Officials," *Journal of Asian Studies,* 32 (May 1972), 425–495.

44. Although Rubin's "Will and Awe" describes *krengjie* as "awe," many Thais would insist that it is closer to the notion of considerateness; hence equals can "*krengjie* each other," and a good superior can "*krengjie* his subordinates" when, for example, he refrains from making inconvenient demands on them, such as imposing on them during their off-duty hours. Using the word in this broader sense of displaying good manners in a considerate way, the Thais still feel that only they have a natural feeling for "making *krengjie,*" and they will

insist that Sino-Thais, for example, "can't do *krengjie*." Indeed, some Thais claim that it is easy for them to recognize Sino-Thais precisely because they "can't do *krengjie*." At the same time, Thais are sometimes astonished, and thrilled, when they come across an American who "can do *krengjie*."

45. After the initial dramatic coup of 1932, which ended the absolute monarchy and brought in a constitutional monarchy, the Thais became increasingly skilled at performing bloodless coups. During a sequence of six coups there was only one fatality, and that involved a soldier who got carried away with the excitement of it all and fell out of his truck.

46. For example, none of the junior officers involved in a very serious 1981 coup attempt was punished. When an American, in the presence of a Thai official, asked a South Korean what would have happened in the same situation in his country, that follower of a sterner form of paternalism known as Confucianism, immediately replied, "They would have been shot in half an hour." When the Thai was asked to explain the difference, he could only come up with, "It doesn't snow very much in Bangkok."

47. Lucien Hanks, "Merit and Power in the Thai Social Order," *American Anthropologist*, 64 (1962), 1247–61.

48. The pioneering work on the political and economic effects of Dutch colonial rule is J. C. van Leur, *Indonesian Trade and Society: Essays in Asian Social and Economic History* (The Hague: Van Hoeve, 1955). The classic work, which compares Dutch rule in Indonesia with British rule in Burma, and which has been an inspiration for much of the work of those interested in a "moral economy" approach to peasant behavior is Furnivall, *Colonial Policy and Practice.*

49. For the degree to which the leaders of Indonesian independence movements were dependent upon Western ideas, see George McT. Kahin, *Nationalism and Revolution in Indonesia* (Ithaca: Cornell University Press, 1952); and Robert van Niel, *The Emergence of the Modern Indonesian Elite* (Chicago: Quadrangle Books, 1960). For an empirically based study of the first and second generation of Indonesian leaders, see Donald K. Emerson, *Indonesia's Elite* (Ithaca: Cornell University Press, 1976).

50. Karl D. Jackson, *Traditional Authority, Islam, and Rebellion: A Study of Indonesian Political Behavior* (Berkeley: University of California Press, 1980), p. xix.

51. The most detailed recounting of the politics of "musical chairs" among the Indonesian politicians, who were concentrated in Jakarta and increasingly lost touch with the Indonesian masses, is Herbert Feith, *The Decline of Constitutional Democracy in Indonesia* (Ithaca: Cornell University Press, 1962).

52. Although almost all Asian cultures, and especially those of Southeast Asia, praise the ideal of consensus, the Indonesians are the ones who carry it to an extreme at the village level. Indeed, in Indonesian villages the process of arriving at consensus is wonderful to watch: young hotbloods will expound their views with dramatic passion, the middle-aged will strive to hit the right note so as to suggest wisdom, and then, without the slightest hint that cloture might be

at hand, an elder will calmly define what the consensus is and deliberations will cease.

53. For discussions of symbolism in Indonesian politics see Benedict R. O'G. Anderson, "Cartoons and Monuments: The Evolution of Political Communication under the New Order," in Karl D. Jackson and Lucian W. Pye, eds., *Political Power and Communication in Indonesia* (Berkeley: University of California Press, 1978), pp. 282–321; and Anderson's *Mythology and the Tolerance of the Javanese,* Cornell Modern Indonesia Project Monograph Series (Ithaca, 1965).

54. *Sukarno: An Autobiography,* as told to Cindy Adams (Indianapolis: Bobbs-Merrill, 1968), p. 45.

55. "From the Natives' Point of View: On the Nature of Anthropological Understanding," *Bulletin of the American Academy of the Arts and Sciences,* 28 (October 1974), 26–45.

56. Ibid. For an excellent report that captures the style of Sukarno's leadership, see Willard Hanna, *Bung Karno's Indonesia* (New York: American Universities Field Staff, 1961).

57. The most detailed study of the military's style in politics and of Suharto's relations with his officers is Ulf Sundhaussen, *The Road to Power: Indonesian Military Politics, 1945–1967* (Kuala Lumpur: Oxford University Press, 1982). A less detailed but balanced study is Guy Pauker, "The Role of the Military in Indonesian Politics," in J. J. Johnson, ed., *The Role of the Military in Underdeveloped Countries* (Princeton: Princeton University Press, 1962).

58. Karl D. Jackson, "Bureaucratic Polity," in Jackson and Pye, *Political Power and Communication in Indonesia,* chap. 1.

59. I learned how *anak buahs* build up credit with their *bapaks* during an interview with an Indonesian professor who had also had periods of government service. He suddenly became quite depressed and said I had no appreciation of how traditional Indonesian society was. I suggested that tradition could be turned to the purposes of modernization, as was being done in Japan. He threw up his arms and said I was the typical, incorrigible American optimist who could always find a silver lining in every cloud. Then he said, "You think it only involves superiors and subordinates using different forms of address and nobody wanting to get their hands dirty. Let me tell you what a deferential society really is. It is a society in which you have more money in your bank account at the end of the month than at the beginning, and there is no quid pro quo, for that would make it a materialistic society." This, no doubt, helps to explain why tradition is so slow to change in Indonesia. He was telling me that people simply make "gifts" to high officials with the expectation that in time reciprocity will take place.

60. Benedict R. O'G. Anderson, "The Idea of Power in Javanese Culture," in Claire Holt, Benedict Anderson, and Joseph Siegel, eds., *Culture and Politics in Indonesia* (Ithaca: Cornell University Press, 1972).

61. For a firsthand account of prewar Philippine politics by an advisor to Quezon and Osmeña, see David Bernstein, *The Philippine Story* (New York: Farrar, Straus, 1947). For an account of the American administration written by

a former governor-general, see Cameron W. Forbes, *The Philippine Islands* (Cambridge, Mass.: Harvard University Press, 1945).

62. A detailed biography is Carlos Quirino, *Magsaysay of the Philippines* (Quezon City: Phoenix Press, 1958).

63. For a study of the Philippine style of bargaining as the basis of early Philippine democracy, see Jean Grossholtz, "The Bargaining Process and Democratic Development: A Study of Philippine Politics" (Ph.D. diss., M.I.T., 1961).

64. Mary R. Hollensteiner, *The Dynamics of Power in a Philippine Muncipality* (Quezon City: University of the Philippines Community Development Research Council, 1961); and Remigio E. Agpalo, *The Political Elite and the People: A Study of Politics in Occidental Mindoro* (Manila: University of the Philippines Press, 1972).

65. Jean Grossholtz, *Politics in the Philippines* (Boston: Little, Brown, 1964), p. 166.

66. Elipidio Quirino, "Memoirs," *New York Times Magazine*, January 27, 1957, pp. 25–26, quoted in Grossholtz, *Politics in the Philippines*, p. 167.

67. George M. Guthrie, *The Psychology of Modernization in the Rural Philippines* (Manila: Ateneo de Manila, 1971), pp. 44–52.

68. John L. Phelan, *Hispanization of the Philippines* (Madison: University of Wisconsin Press, 1959).

69. Carl Landé, *Leaders, Factions and Parties: The Structure of Philippine Politics*, Yale University Southeast Asia Monograph Series (New Haven, 1965).

70. Carl Landé, "Networks and Groups in Southeast Asia: Some Observations on the Group Theory of Politics," *American Political Science Review*, 67, no. 1 (1973), 103–127.

71. Albert Ravenholt, "The Peso Price of Politics," American Universities Field Staff Report, May 1958.

72. The Dutch persistence in helping to maintain the distinction explains one of the anomalies of Indonesian statistics. According to the standard treaties signed with the various sultans in order to establish the various forms of indirect rule, the Dutch promised that they would not interfere with the Islamic religious beliefs of the people, which was taken to mean that secular education would be restricted. Yet, as members of the elite, the *prijaiji* were assumed capable of getting the necessary modern education without disturbing their religious convictions. Hence classrooms were estabished for *prijaiji* children; and in time, to help fill the rooms and to make the teachers' efforts worthwhile, non-*prijaiji* were allowed to sit in and even to take examinations. Form had to be preserved, however, and therefore in the official statistics only *prijaiji* were counted as students. In the meantime, Indonesia gradually got enough "graduates" to create a problem of unemployed "intellectuals."

73. Frank J. Moore, *Thailand: Its People, Its Society, Its Culture* (New Haven: Human Relations Area File Press, 1974), pp. 139, 145.

74. Hildred Geertz, *The Javanese Family* (Glencoe, Ill.: Free Press, 1961), pp. 91, 102–103, 105.

75. Most anthropologists reporting on Burmese family life describe emotional vacillations, unpredictable behavior, and eventual anxieties over superior-

subordinate relations. Hazel Hitson found that Burmese family culture trained people to direct their aggressions outward in a paranoidal style, and hence the high incidence of sudden violence in the society. Lucien M. Hanks, in "The Quest for Individual Autonomy in the Burmese Personality," *Psychiatry*, 12, no. 3 (1949), 285–300, concluded that the sharp break between the indulgence of the first year and the stern disciplining of the monastery schools left Burmese males distrustful of all superiors in later life. Geoffrey Gorer, in his "Burmese Personality," New York Institute of Inter-Cultural Studies Report, 1943, hypothesizes that the emotional instabilities of the early socialization process leave Burmese males insecure and anxious to attract attention to themselves but fearful of any serious tests of efficacy. Sen Tu, in "Ideology and Personality in Burmese Society," mimeographed (Harvard University, 1955), goes even further and suggests that the intimacy between the child and the mother and the fear of an unpredictably stern and distant father results in a tendency to handle the oedipal problem by identifying passively with the mother and thereby seeing the father to be a seductive rather than a destructive threat. For more on these and other interpretations, see my *Politics, Personality, and Nation Building,* chap. 13.

76. For a discussion of Burmese beliefs about the behavior of *nat* spirits, see H. Fielding Hall, *The Soul of a People* (London: Macmillan, 1898), chap. 20; James G. Scott [Shwoy Yae, pseud.], *The Burman: His Life and Notions* (London: Macmillan, 1910), chap. 22; Melford E. Spiro, *Buddhism and Society: A Great Tradition and Its Burmese Vicissitudes* (New York: Harper and Row, 1920), chap. 6.

77. Compare the discussion of propitiating spirits in Spiro, *Buddhism and Society,* chap. 6, with that in Moore, *Thailand,* pp. 143–148.

78. On the effects of the blending of Islam and animistic beliefs that can lead to such contradictory feelings, see Clifford Geertz, *The Religion of Java* (Glencoe: Free Press, 1960).

79. Moore, *Thailand,* p. 200.

80. Charles Murray, *A Behavioral Study of Rural Modernization* (New York: Praeger, 1977).

81. On the Burmese hatred of government, see Maung Maung Gyi, *Burmese Political Values,* p. 154–176.

82. Jackson, *Traditional Authority,* chap. 8.

83. Robert R. Jay, *Javanese Villagers* (Cambridge, Mass.: MIT Press, 1969), pp. 201–206.

5. The South Asian Subcontinent

1. Myron Weiner, "Ancient Indian Political Theory and Contemporary Indian Politics," in S. N. Eisenstadt, Reuven Kahane, and David Shulman, eds., *Orthodoxy, Heterodoxy, and Dissent in India* (Berlin: Mouton, 1984), pp. 111–129.

2. Max F. Millikan and Walt W. Rostow, *A Proposal* (Boston: Little, Brown, 1960).

3. Not all observers were optimistic about India's prospects, especially not those who focused on India's communal, language, and caste problems. See, in particular, Selig Harrison, *India: The Most Dangerous Decade* (Princeton: Princeton University Press, 1960).

4. Without getting into the controversial issue of when and how caste distinctions evolved in Indian history, we can note that in the ancient India of Manu there was apparently an undifferentiated religious-political society in which the authority of kings and priests was united. See Bhaskar Anand Saletore, *Ancient Indian Political Thought and Institutions* (London: Asia Publishing House, 1963), chap. 2. In the age of the Satapatha Brahmana came the separation of kings, as Kshatrivas, and priests, as Brahmans. The fact that in Southeast Asia the reference to Indian thought is in terms of respect for the laws of Manu suggests that the identification with India goes back to a pre-caste era. This would be plausible except for the fact that the Burmese, Thai, and Khmer kings liked to surround themselves with Brahman astrologers, who rejoiced in the doctrines of caste and did not accept the ideas that they might be coequal with Kshatrivas.

5. *Manusmriti*, X, 97, as quoted in Sarvepalli Rodharkrishnan and Charles A. Moore, eds., *A Source Book in Indian Philosophy* (Princeton: Princeton University Press, 1957), p. 184.

6. Louis Dumont, *Homo Hierarchicus: The Caste System and Its Implications* (Chicago: University of Chicago Press, 1970), pp. 77–78.

7. For a penetrating analysis of the need of people to establish distinctions according to rules of purity and contamination, see Mary Douglas, *Implicit Meanings* (London: Routledge and Kegan Paul, 1975), chaps. 3, 10, and 14.

8. *Manusmriti*, XI, 62, quoted in Rodharkrishnan and Moore, *Source Book,* p. 186.

9. *Manusmriti*, VII, 3, quoted in Georg Buhler, *Sacred Books of the East* (London: Oxford University Press, 1886), XXV, 218.

10. Saletore, *Ancient Indian Political Thought,* chap. 4.

11. Ibid., chap. 5.

12. Originally the word *danda* meant the staff used to ward off demons, which was given to a youth upon attaining manhood and which he was expected to use as a weapon or as an implement to herd cattle. In time it came to mean the ruler's power to coerce through punishment.

13. *Manusmriti*, VII, 18, quoted in Saletore, *Ancient Indian Political Thought,* p. 219.

14. Ashis Nandy, *At the Edge of Psychology* (Bombay: Oxford University Press, 1980).

15. Dumont, *Homo Hierarchicus,* pp. 77–78.

16. Quoted in John W. Spellman, *Political Theory of Ancient India* (Oxford: Clarendon, 1964), p. 38.

17. Saletore, *Ancient Indian Political Thought,* pt. II.

18. Kautilya, *The Arthasastra,* quoted ibid., bk. III, chap. 7, p. 165.

19. Saletore, *Ancient Indian Political Thought,* pp. 307–309.

20. Spellman, *Political Theory of Ancient India,* p. 40.

21. Arthur L. Basham, *The Wonder That Was India* (London; Sidgwick and Jackson, 1959), p. 86.

22. Nandy, *At the Edge of Psychology,* pp. 50–51.

23. For a discussion of the psychodynamics of "identification with the aggressor" as a dimension of the colonial experience, see Everett E. Hagen, *On the Theory of Social Change* (Homewood, Ill.: Dorsey Press, 1962), pp. 417–418.

24. Nandy, *At the Edge of Psychology,* pp. 60–62, 70–93 (quotation from 61). In a penetrating analysis, Nandy demonstrates that it was psychologically "natural" that Gandhi's assassin should have been an orthodox Hindu who could see that the Mahatma was doing more to violate the essential character of Hinduism than even the British had.

25. Harold D. Lasswell has suggested that American politicians tend to have basically insecure personalities and hence a need to compensate. *Psychopathology and Politics* (Chicago: University of Chicago Press, 1930). Garry Wills is convinced that American politicians lack the imagination to be anything but completely absorbed with themselves: "Politicians make good company for a while, just as children do—their self-enjoyment is contagious. But they soon exhaust their favorite subject, themselves. The idea that a politician might be interested in something else is so refreshing that some people have made the mistake of hoping to find out something new or interesting about modern art from Nelson Rockefeller, about opera from Lowell Weicker, about Teilhard de Chardin from Jerry Brown. One soon enough finds out that Nelson Rockefeller was only equipped to tell you that Nelson Rockefeller was interested in modern art, or Weicker that Weicker liked opera and so on. There is a kind of noble discipline in politicians, in persons prepared to devote a lifetime to discourse on a single subject, over and over, with anyone who will listen, anywhere. It inspires a goofy awe, this sight of them ringing a single bell all their lives, hammering at their own heads." Wills, *Lead Time* (New York: Doubleday, 1983), p. 42.

26. The way in which the Hindu concept of "duty" hinders Indian bureaucratic performance is well documented in Stanley Heginbotham, "Patterns and Sources of Indian Bureaucratic Behavior: Organizational Pressures and the Ethics of Duty in a Tamil Nadu Development Program" (Ph.D. diss., M.I.T., 1970). In an investigation of administrative practices in Mysore state it was found that it normally takes 272.2 days for a file to be processed in the secretariat. Another study discovered that of 7,157 petitions handled at the state capital 6,111 could have been dealt with by lower levels of government. Myron Weiner, "India: Two Political Cultures," in Lucian W. Pye and Sidney Verba, eds., *Political Culture and Political Development* (Princeton: Princeton University Press, 1965), pp. 220–221.

27. The story of Dr. Aziz's enthusiastic planning for the picnic with Miss Quested and his faulty execution of the enterprise, as told in E. M. Forster's *Passage to India,* captures the essence of this aspect of Indian character.

28. An extreme example of such Indian self-criticism would be Nirad C.

Chaudhuri, *A Continent of Circe* (New York: Oxford University Press, 1966). Other examples are to be found, on almost any day, in the editorial pages of India's leading newspapers.

29. Myron Weiner, *Party Building in a New Nation* (Chicago: University of Chicago Press, 1967), p. 173.

30. Ved Mehta, "Letter from New Delhi," *New Yorker,* May 16, 1983, p. 88.

31. For basic accounts of child rearing in India, see Aiken D. Ross, *The Hindu Family in Its Urban Setting* (Toronto: University of Toronto Press, 1961); K. M. Kapadia, *Marriage and Family in India* (London: Oxford University Press, 1955); T. N. Madan, *Family and Kinship* (Bombay: Asia Publishing House, 1965).

32. Nandy, *At the Edge of Psychology,* p. 14.

33. On the dynamics of secondary narcissism, see Sigmund Freud, *Three Essays on the Theory of Sexuality* (1905), "On Narcissism: An Introduction" (1914), and *Group Psychology and the Analysis of the Ego* (1921). See also Otto Fenichel, *The Psychoanalytic Theory of Neurosis* (New York: W. W. Norton, 1945); and J. Laplanche and J.-B. Pontalis, *The Language of Psychoanalysis* (New York: W. W. Norton, 1973).

34. On Hindu passivity and narcissism, see Philip Spratt, *Hindu Culture and Personality* (Bombay: Manaktalar, 1966).

35. On the contaminating and frighteningly impure qualities of women in Hindu culture, see G. Morris Carstairs, *The Twice Born* (London: Hogarth Press, 1957), chaps. 4, 5, 9. As Carstairs observes (pp. 156–157): "Ideally, woman is regarded as a wholly devoted, self-forgetful mother, or as a dutifully subservient wife, who is ready to worship her husband as her lord. In fact, however, women are regarded with an alternation of desire and revulsion. Sexual love is considered the keenest pleasure known to the senses: but it is felt to be destructive to a man's physical and spiritual well-being. Women are powerful, demanding, seductive—and ultimately destructive. On the plane of creative phantasy, everyone worships the Mataji, the Goddess, who is a protective mother to those who prostrate themselves before her in abject supplication, but who is depicted also as a sort of demon, with gnashing teeth, who stands on top of her male adversary, cuts off his head and drinks his blood. This demon-goddess has the same appearance as a witch—and that brings her nearer home, because any woman whose demands one has refused is liable to be feared as a witch who may exact terrible reprisals."

36. Nandy, *At the Edge of Psychology,* p. 9.

37. Carstairs, *The Twice Born,* pp. 65, 74.

38. Nandy, *At the Edge of Psychology,* p. 9.

39. Indian difficulties with sex are too widely known to need documentation. They begin to be apparent with the obvious boy-girl problems of adolescence and the near absence of any acceptable forms of courting. These are followed by manifest anxieties about potency, which turn into fears about the presumed weakening effects of intercourse. Finally, there is the escape into celibacy of either

the yogi or holy man or the husband who retreats into what he describes as a search for purity.

40. Edward Shils, *The Intellectuals and the Powers and Other Essays* (Chicago: University of Chicago Press, 1972), chaps. 18 and 19.

41. Dhirendra Narain, *Hindu Character,* University of Bombay, Publications, Sociology Series no. 8 (Bombay, 1957), pp. 57–58.

42. Ibid., p. 92.

43. Peter Hardy, "Islam and Muslims in South Asia," in Raphael Israeli, *The Crescent in the East* (London: Curzon Press, 1982), p. 36.

44. Percival Spear, *India, Pakistan, and the West* (New York: Oxford University Press, 1967), p. 66.

45. Jan Morris with Simon Winchester, *Stones of Empire: The Buildings of the Raj* (London: Oxford University Press, 1983).

46. For these concepts of Islam I am indebted to Ahmed Rehman.

6. The Riddle of Japan

1. The literature on the Meiji Restoration and the initial modernization of Japan has become voluminous as historians have examined in greater depth both the thought and actions of the individual Japanese leaders and the developments preceding modernization. Some historians, such as John W. Hall, have argued that Japanese society was on the road to modernization even before the Tokugawa period. Yet the early classic studies still provide some of the best overview interpretations of the end of Tokugawa feudalism and the Meiji Restoration. These include George Sansom, *The Western World and Japan* (New York: Alfred A. Knopf, 1950); Chitoshi Yanaga, *Japan since Perry* (New York: McGraw-Hill, 1949). In terms of political and economic pressures, the classic is still E. Herbert Norman, *Japan's Emergence as a Modern State* (New York: JPR, 1940).

2. On the indebtedness of the daimyos see Norman, *Japan's Emergence,* chaps. 1 and 3.

3. See Ronald P. Dore, "The Legacy of Tokugawa Education," in Marius B. Jansen, ed., *Changing Japanese Attitudes toward Modernization* (Princeton: Princeton University Press, 1968), pp. 99–132.

4. The institutionalization of the *buraku,* or hamlet, leadership and the mura, or village, leadership under their own types of headmen, which prevented penetration by samurai seeking leadership positions, is described in Kurt Steiner, "Popular Participation and Political Development in Japan: The Rural Level," in Robert E. Ward, ed., *Political Development in Modern Japan* (Princeton: Princeton University Press, 1968), pp. 213–242; and in Erwin H. Johnson, "Status Changes in Hamlet Structure Accompanying Modernization," in Ronald P. Dore, ed., *Aspects of Social Change in Modern Japan* (Princeton: Princeton University Press, 1967), pp. 153–184.

5. Sidney DeVere Brown, "Okubo Toshimichi and the First Home Ministry

Bureaucracy, 1873–1878," in Bernard S. Silberman and H. D. Harootunian, eds., *Modern Japanese Leadership* (Tucson: University of Arizona Press, 1966), pp. 195–223.

6. Marius S. Jansen, "Changing Japanese Attitudes toward Modernization," in his edited volume bearing the same title, p. 51.

7. Albert M. Craig, "Fukuzawa Yukichi: The Philosophical Foundation of Meiji Nationalism," in Ward, *Political Development in Modern Japan*, p. 102.

8. Dore, "Legacy of Tokugawa Education," p. 119.

9. On the advancement of the genro, the elder statesmen who were to exert the guiding influence on Japanese decision-making, see Roger Hackett, "Political Modernization and the Meiji Genro," in Ward, *Political Development in Modern Japan*, pp. 70–71.

10. Harry D. Harootunian, "Social Values and Leadership in Late Tokugawa Thought," in Silberman and Harootunian, *Modern Japanese Leadership*, p. 110.

11. Ryusaku Tsunoda, William Theodore de Bary, and Donald Keene, eds., *Sources of Japanese Tradition* (New York: Columbia University Press, 1958), p. 644.

12. Harootunian, "Social Values and Leadership," in Silberman and Harootunian, *Modern Japanese Leadership*, pp. 83 (quotation), 85.

13. Craig, "Fukuzawa Yukichi," in Ward, *Political Development in Modern Japan*, p. 107.

14. Gerald L. Curtis, *Election Campaigning Japanese Style* (New York: Columbia University Press, 1971).

15. Ibid., p. 38.

16. Joji Watanuki, "Patterns of Politics in Present-Day Japan," in Seymour M. Lipset and Stein Rokkan, eds., *Party Systems and Voter Alignments: Cross-National Perceptions* (New York: Basic Books, 1967), p. 462, cited in Curtis, *Election Campaigning*, pp. 90–91.

17. Curtis, *Election Campaigning*, p. 250.

18. Richard J. Samuels, *The Politics of Regional Policy in Japan: Localities Incorporated?* (Princeton: Princeton University Press, 1983).

19. Bradley M. Richardson, *The Political Culture of Japan* (Berkeley: University of California Press, 1974), is a gold mine of survey information about Japanese attitudes.

20. On the Japanese press, see Young C. Kim, *Japanese Journalists and Their World* (Charlottesville: University Press of Virginia, 1981). For an analysis of the belief that real power should be invisible, which the Japanese maintain by pretending not to see the actions of power—much as they ignore the presence of the puppeteer openly pulling strings or of stagehands visibly changing sets at the Kabuki—see Richard J. Samuels, "Power behind the Throne," in Terry MacDougall, ed., *Political Leadership in Contemporary Japan*, University of Michigan East Asia Monographs (Ann Arbor, 1982).

21. Chie Nakane, *Japanese Society* (Berkeley: University of California Press, 1970).

22. I have it on good authority that, in the Japanese academic world, status is more tied to institutional identification than to independent achievement, so

that a nonproductive faculty member of a prestigious university can pose as the smug superior of a creative professor at a less prestigious school. In fact, a faculty member at, say, Tokyo University may never have had anything published, for recruitment is based on undergraduate performance, which obviates even the need to write a doctoral thesis.

23. Masao Maruyama, *Thought and Behavior in Modern Japanese Politics* (London: Oxford University Press, 1963).

24. Seizaburō Satō, Shumpei Kumon, Yasusuke Murakami, "Analysis of Japan's Modernization," *Japan Echo,* 3, no. 2 (1976).

25. Lewis Austin, *Saints and Samurai* (New Haven: Yale University Press, 1975), pp. 9–12.

26. George DeVos, "Role Narcissism and the Etiology of Japanese Suicide," in his *Socialization for Achievement: Essays in the Cultural Psychology of the Japanese* (Berkeley: University of California Press, 1973).

27. Takeo L. Doi, "Amae: A Key Concept for Understanding Japanese Personality Structure," in Richard K. Beardsley and R. J. Smith, eds., *Japanese Culture: Its Development and Characteristics* (Chicago: University of Chicago Press, 1962). Robert C. Christopher, a longtime resident of Japan, notes that Japan's matriarchal socialization process has left the Japanese male extremely vulnerable to guilt feelings for not reciprocating kindness from superiors. The Japanese child thus seems to Westerners to be unduly pampered. The geishas and bar hostesses play the role of building up the male ego, much as the mothers once did. The effect of this maternalistic dimension of authority is to make the Japanese highly sensitive to the emotional dynamics in power relationships. See Christopher, *The Japanese Mind* (New York: Linden Press; Simon and Schuster, 1983).

28. Takie Sugiyama Lebra, *Japanese Patterns of Behavior* (Honolulu: University Press of Hawaii; East-West Center, 1976), pp. 54–57.

29. Austin, *Saints and Samurai,* p. 128.

30. An excellent description of *ringi* is in Kiyoaki Tsuji, "Decision-Making in the Japanese Government: A Study of *Ringisei,*" in Ward, *Political Development in Modern Japan,* pp. 457–574.

31. Robert A. Scalapino and Junnosuke Masumi, *Parties and Politics in Contemporary Japan* (Berkeley: University of California Press, 1962), p. 83.

32. In 1972 when the polling for the post of chairmanship of the LDP was televised, I observed a dramatic demonstration of the supreme skill of master Japanese politicians in controlling any hint of emotion for fear of offending. In a live broadcast the Japanese public saw all the LDP party leaders march across a platform in a theater, and then, after a proper bowing, deposit their ballots in a large box. As they moved forward they made a great display of showing one another how they had marked their ballots, thus certifying their factional loyalties. As the ballots were counted, the camera moved back and forth between Mr. Kakuei Tanaka and Mr. Takeo Fukuda, the two leading contenders, who were sitting in the same row, about ten seats apart. Each man sat bolt upright, hands on knees, staring straight ahead, not moving a muscle. Finally a very elderly gentleman read out the results, and the camera revealed that both candidates

were still in their frozen positions, and that the room was remarkably quiet. The old man then called for "three banzais" for party unity, and only after the shouting did the winner, Mr. Tanaka, break into a slight smile. When I asked Japanese friends to explain such impassive behavior—commenting that in American politics the winner would have instantly expressed his pleasure by smiling and waving to his cheering followers, and the loser would have had to congratulate the victor with a handshake—I was told that such behavior would not be possible in Japan because the winner would hurt the feelings of the loser by celebrating before him and the loser would not be acting with creditable sincerity if he warmly congratulated the winner. Hence it was better for nobody to show any feelings whatsoever.

33. Bradley M. Richardson and Scott C. Flanagan, *Politics in Japan* (Boston: Little, Brown, 1984), chap. 8.

34. Ibid.

35. The great extent to which the Diet is dominated by ex-bureaucrats and the reluctance of politicians to amend the legislative proposals of the bureaucracy have led T. J. Pempel to see Japanese politics as being highly bureaucratized. See his "Bureaucratization of Policymaking in Postwar Japan," *American Journal of Political Science,* 18 (1974), 647–664. Others see decision-making in the Diet in far more dynamic terms, including a constructive role for the opposition. See Shigeo Misawa, "An Outline of the Policy-Making Process in Japan," in Hiroshi Itoh, *Japanese Politics: An Inside View* (Ithaca: Cornell University Press, 1973), pp. 12–48. For discussion of this "debate," see Richardson and Flanagan, *Politics in Japan,* chap. 8.

36. On the "helplessness" of Japanese politicians in the face of the "patriotism" of the young army officers at the time of the Mukden incident, see W. G. Beasley, *The Modern History of Japan* (New York: Praeger, 1963), chap. 13; and Gordon Mark Berger, *Parties out of Power in Japan, 1931–1941* (Princeton: Princeton University Press, 1977), chap. 3.

37. Herbert Feis, *The Road to Pearl Harbor* (Princeton: Princeton University Press, 1950); Nobutake Ike, ed., *Japan's Decision for War: Records of the 1941 Policy Conference* (Stanford: Stanford University Press, 1967); Robert J. C. Butow, *Japan's Decision to Surrender* (Stanford: Stanford University Press, 1959); Toshikazu Kase, *Journey to the Missouri* (New Haven: Yale University Press, 1950); and William Craig, *The Fall of Japan* (New York: Dial Press, 1967).

38. Gordon W. Prange, *At Dawn We Slept: The Untold Story of Pearl Harbor* (New York: McGraw-Hill, 1981).

39. See David Apter and Nagayo Sawa, *Against the State: Politics and Social Protest in Japan* (Cambridge, Mass.: Harvard University Press, 1984).

40. John Creighton Campbell, *Contemporary Japanese Budget Politics* (Berkeley: University of California Press, 1977).

41. Ronald Dore, *British Factory—Japanese Factory* (Berkeley: University of California Press, 1973).

42. For a firsthand account of Japanese auto workers who accept without complaint what American workers would consider to be inhumane "exploitation," see the report of a journalist who spent six months as an ordinary worker

in a Toyota factory: Satoshi Kamata, *Japan in the Passing Lane* (New York: Pantheon Books, 1982). In Ronald Dore's introduction to this work he stresses that the attitudes of the Japanese workers, rather than just management techniques, account for the docile, cooperative spirit in an otherwise very harsh work place.

43. Although some Japanese Socialist leaders have been extremely doctrinaire, most Socialist Diet members are as tied to personal networks as are the LDP members. The main difference is that their power bases tend to be in the trade unions. In recent years this has created problems for certain Socialists because the trend has been for unions to become "company unions," so that shop stewards are often foremen. Consequently, some Socialist politicians have closer ties to management in large enterprises than do those LDP members whose clients are still rural people.

44. Joseph Schumpeter, *Capitalism, Socialism, and Democracy* (New York: Simon and Schuster, 1942); Daniel Bell, *The Cultural Contradiction of Capitalism* (New York: Basic Books, 1976).

7. China

1. Studies of local government in China, both past and present, tend to tell little about local practices. They consist essentially of another approach to understanding national politics and government, because the main focus of local government in China has been its relation to the central authorities. On the Ch'ing dynasty see Ch'u T'ung-tsu, *Local Government in China under the Ch'ing* (Cambridge, Mass.: Harvard University Press, 1962); John Watt, *The District Magistrate in Late Imperial China* (New York: Columbia University Press, 1972). On more modern times, see Ezra Vogel, *Canton under Communism* (Cambridge, Mass.: Harvard University Press, 1969); and Lynn T. White III, *Careers in Shanghai* (Berkeley: University of California Press, 1978).

2. In my *Dynamics of Chinese Politics* (Cambridge, Mass.: OG&H, 1981), chap. 5, I have analyzed the paradox that, although geographical considerations can provide a strong basis for factional groupings in Chinese politics because of the personal trust shared by people of the same locality, such factions rarely push for policies which would favor their geographic interests.

3. For a study of the way in which Mao's pressures for provincial autarky, especially in grain production, led to the ironic outcome of increasing inequalities and making China even more dependent upon imported grain, see Nicholas R. Lardy, *Agriculture in China's Modern Economic Development* (Cambridge: Cambridge University Press, 1983); and his "Consumption and Living Standards in China, 1978–1982," *China Quarterly*, 100 (December 1984).

4. The ideals of leadership in Communist China are described in John W. Lewis, *Leadership in Communist China* (Ithaca: Cornell University Press, 1963). The practices in coping with leadership are analyzed by Michel Oksenberg, in "Getting Ahead and Along in Communist China: The Ladder of Success on the Eve of the Cultural Revolution," in John Wilson Lewis, ed., *Party Leadership*

and Revolutionary Power in China (Cambridge: Cambridge University Press, 1970). For a compilation of statements demonstrating the extreme lengths to which the Chinese will go in glorifying their heroes, see George Urban, ed., *The Miracles of Chairman Mao* (London: Tena Stacey, 1971).

5. In spite of decades of Communism and its doctrines of international proletarianism, Beijing authorities continue to operate on the basis of racial trust, as seen in the way in which they favor working with overseas Chinese in their efforts to bring in outside technologies. Chinese officials seem to see nothing anomalous in honoring and relying upon visiting Chinese ethnics who have left China because of Communism, even though their actions may cause bitterness among those who stayed behind and suffered under the Anti-Rightist campaign and the Cultural Revolution.

6. The word pathological is not extreme, for the Chinese authorities still make major efforts to deny the existence of any form of factionalism in their country. For example, American researchers working on Chinese village life have been explicitly prohibited from exploring factionalism or kinship conflicts. And of course the Chinese continue to deny the existence of any factional strife in their elite politics.

On the intensity of the Chinese desire for harmony, see Derk Bodde, "Harmony and Conflict in Chinese Philosophy," in Arthur F. Wright, ed., *Studies in Chinese Thought* (Chicago: University of Chicago Press, 1953). On the Chinese fear of disorder, or *luan,* see Richard Solomon, *Mao's Revolution and the Chinese Political Culture* (Berkeley: University of California Press, 1971).

7. On the importance of ideology see Chalmers Johnson, ed., *Ideology and Politics in Contemporary China* (Seattle: University of Washington Press, 1973).

8. The problems the Chinese have with aggression have been explored in some detail in my *Spirit of Chinese Politics* (Cambridge, Mass.: M.I.T. Press, 1968).

9. For a discussion of the issues of "altruism" and "interests" in Chinese thought, see Lu-tao Sophia Wang, "Journalists and the Transformation of Modern Chinese Political Culture" (Ph.D. diss., M.I.T., 1984).

10. Translated by Lily Hwa, in Patricia Buckley Ebrey, ed., *Chinese Civilization and Society* (New York: Free Press, 1981), pp. 124–125.

11. John H. Fincher, *Chinese Democracy: The Self-Government Movement in Local, Provincial, and National Politics, 1905–1914* (New York: St. Martin's Press, 1981).

12. Socialization within the Chinese family system, with its stress on filial piety and correct moral behavior, helps to explain the Chinese tendency to think of revolution not as rebellion but as pointing to the decadence of the older generations and the virtues of youth—the central theme of "revolution" from the May Fourth generation to the Cultural Revolution. I have analyzed the psychodynamics of this phenomenon in my *Spirit of Chinese Politics.*

13. On the psychological aspects of factionalism in Chinese politics see my *Dynamics of Chinese Politics.*

14. The identification and analysis of the emergence of such local-interest articulation by cadres has been greatly advanced by the work of Dorothy J.

Salinger, in "Politics in Yunnan Province in the Decade of Disorder: Elite Factional Strategies and Center-Local Relations, 1967–1980," *China Quarterly,* 96 (December 1983), 628–662; and in "The Fifth National People's Congress and the Process of Policymaking: Reform, Readjustment, and the Opposition," *Issues and Studies,* 18 (August 1982), 63–106.

15. Andrew Nathan, *Peking Politics* (Berkeley: University of California Press, 1976).

16. Benjamin Schwartz, *In Search of Wealth and Power* (Cambridge, Mass.: Harvard University Press, 1964).

17. John K. Fairbank, in his review of Eugene Lubot's *Liberalism in an Illiberal Age,* in *China Quarterly,* 96 (December 1983), 739.

18. Jonathan D. Spence, *The Gate of Heavenly Peace* (New York: Viking Press, 1981). The earlier period is also well covered by Eugene Lubot, "New Cultural Liberals in Republican China, 1919–1937," in his *Liberalism in an Illiberal Age* (Westport, Conn.: Greenwood Press, 1982); Joseph R. Levenson, *Liang Ch'i-ch'ao and the Mind of Modern China* (Berkeley: University of California Press, 1953); William Ayers, *Chang Chih-tung and Educational Reform in China* (Cambridge: Harvard University Press, 1971); and Y. C. Wang, *Chinese Intellectuals and the West* (Chapel Hill: University of North Carolina Press, 1971).

19. Merle Goldman, *Literary Dissent in Communist China* (New York: Atheneum, 1971), and *China's Intellectuals: Advice and Dissent* (Cambridge, Mass.: Harvard University Press, 1982). See also Theodore H. F. Chen, *Thought Reform of the Chinese Intellectuals* (Hong Kong: Hong Kong University Press, 1960); Roderick MacFarquhar, *The Hundred Flowers Campaign and the Chinese Intellectuals* (1960; reprint ed., New York: Octagon, 1973).

20. The phenomenon of Democracy Wall in the winter of 1978–79 was a moving event for champions of liberty, but it did not involve China's leading intellectuals. See, for example, John Fraser, *The Chinese: Portrait of a People* (New York: Summit Books, 1980). Moreover, after Deng Xiaoping closed down the wall the intellectuals were quick to explain that the "goals of the Four Modernizations" required that all concentration be given to development and that talk of freedom should not be allowed to cause diversions. The attitude of Chinese intellectuals was illustrated by the leading woman novelist, Ding Ling, during her visit to America in 1981. Ding Ling was first "sent down" to the countryside in 1957 during the Anti-Rightist campaign, which was in part the handiwork of Deng Xiaoping. She was to spend the next twenty-one years living as a peasant. After the "fall of the Gang of Four" she was moved to the main political prison near Peking for three years of solitary confinement before her case was reviewed and she received her final release. The only political moral that Ding Ling was apparently able to draw from all of this was that her treatment was entirely the fault of the Gang of Four, and she further told her American audiences that "everything should be devoted to the revolution, regardless of the sacrifices," implying that everyone should support the Chinese regime without reservation. As for her own experiences, the worst part was having to "feed chickens early every morning and again in the evening." Solitary confinement

was better, because she had regular meals, no work, and could read Marx, Lenin, Stalin, and Mao all day. She did not believe that any of her experiences provided material for her writing, and therefore she planned after returning to China to write a novel about the evils of the Shanghai bourgeoisie during the 1920s and 1930s. Her peculiarly Chinese concept of patriotism made any more timely subject unthinkable.

21. David Bonavia, "The Scholars' Lot Today: Life among the Ruins," *Far Eastern Economic Review*, February 9, 1984, pp. 34–35.

22. This case and numerous others are reported in Amanda Bennett, "China's Scholars' Learning Stints Abroad Earn Few Gold Stars Back Home," *Asian Wall Street Journal*, July 9, 1984, p. 1.

23. Ross Terrill's *White-Boned Demon: A Biography of Madam Mao Zedong* (New York: William Morrow, 1984) documents vividly how in the 1930s the awakened generations' absorption with the theater led them, as they broke from the constraints of arranged marriages, to take up "love" as a way of dramatizing the self, without any of the deeper levels of affection usually associated with love. Romance for Jiang Qing, Mao Zedong, and other "liberated" young Chinese of that period meant playing to a gallery and acting out roles, not responding to deeper sentiments.

24. The ease with which Chinese can strike the pose of the heroic, or respond with awe to those who do, can be seen in numerous practices. In the 1930s, and still today in both the PRC and Taiwan, Chinese, whether in the military or as middle-school students, seemingly cannot "run laps" in physical education without making the exercise into a grand and noble endeavor in which they are transported from mere running to performing acts of bravery in front of an audience.

25. The type of propaganda designed to build morale among Japanese troops during the Pacific War would have seemed subversive had it not been for their concept of identifying self-sacrifice with patriotism. One film that was widely shown to troops in the China theater and the South Pacific dwelt on the tragic experiences of a company of Japanese soldiers. The parents of one were killed in a bombing attack on Tokyo, another wasn't getting any letters from his wife because she had taken another man, and a third soldier heard that one of his children had died because his wife couldn't find a doctor. But they all kept on soldiering in the endless China campaign, and in the last scene they marched off into the setting sun on another all-night patrol. This film supposedly firmed up Japanese morale, but it plunged the American intelligence officers who viewed a captured version into a state of depression.

26. The degree to which Indians automatically think of India as one of "the developing nations" was shown by an experience I had at an international conference. As I was giving a paper on an aspect of development, the Indian discussant assumed that I was speaking only about India, even though I had not mentioned India in the text.

27. *Asian Wall Street Journal*, July 9, 1984, p. 12.

28. See Lucian W. Pye and Nathan Leites, "Nuances in Chinese Political Culture," *Asian Survey*, 22 (December 1982), 1147–65.

29. The Chinese had a tradition of popularized histories called *yeh shih* ("wild histories"), which blended gossip, rumor, and speculation about the private activities of public figures. See Fox Butterfield's review of Ross Terrill's *White-Boned Demon* in the *New York Times Book Review,* March 4, 1984.

30. For a discussion of the role of deception in Chinese political culture, see Pye and Leites, "Nuances in Chinese Political Culture."

31. Because the Chinese press has only these two versions of politics, some Western analysts have concluded that in Chinese Communist politics factionalism exists only when there is public evidence of contention, as during the Cultural Revolution and the struggle against the Gang of Four, and that when the surface of Chinese politics is serene, factions or groupings do not exist. A little reflection should make it obvious that intense factional groupings cannot be formed instantaneously, and that under the cloak of conformity there must be clusterings of individuals with channels of trust and barriers of suspicion which eventually will develop into factions.

32. R. G. H. Siu, seeking to teach Americans some Asian insights about power, stresses the critical role of timing and "maneuvering and striking." He uses such axioms as, "The battle for power is simultaneously fought on a wide variety of platforms . . . Coil yourself omnidirectionally . . . There is an optimal time and place to attack or defend . . . Waiting for the propitious moment without giving oneself away manifests the courage of confidence. Be observant of the cyclic patterns. Be decisive at the turning points . . . Mix blame with pain in your punishments." *The Craft of Power* (New York: Quill, 1984), p. 21.

33. For evidence of the high expectation in Chinese culture that the locus of power is always external in the technical psychological sense, see my *Dynamics of Chinese Politics,* pp. 90–93.

34. This sense that "history" as it unfolded in the West can and will be repeated in China, because Confucianism bears similarities to Greek thought and therefore "modernization" will inevitably come to China, was expounded in some detail by the Chinese participants at the International Conference on the Problems of Modernization in Asia, Asiatic Research Center, Korea University. See in particular the papers by Professors Carsun Chang and Tang Chu-I in the *Report of the Conference,* June 28–July 7, 1965.

35. Mao's view was the opposite of the belief of Lenin and his followers that the great weakness in Russian national character was a propensity for enthusiastic displays of sentiment, which led to no significant accomplishments; hence the early Bolshevik code about controlling one's emotions and being fully disciplined. See Nathan Leites, *The Spirit of Bolshevism* (Glencoe, Ill.: Free Press, 1983), chap. 5.

36. The Chinese cultural problem of repressed aggression, and its diffuse manifestations in hostility, is a central point in my *Spirit of Chinese Politics.*

37. These excerpts from the "eternal monologues" which educated Russians engage in during their loved "bibulous bonhomie 'evenings'," are from Edward L. Keenan's "Russian History and Soviet Politics," *Problems of Communism,* 33 (January-February 1984), 64.

38. "Wounded Literature" collections include: Helen F. Siu and Zelda Stern,

eds., *Mao's Harvest* (New York: Oxford University Press, 1983); Perry Link, ed., *Stubborn Weeds* (Bloomington: University of Indiana Press, 1979); and Perry Link, ed., *Roses and Thorns: The Second Blooming of the Hundred Flowers in Chinese Fiction* (Berkeley: University of California Press, 1984).

39. So much has been written on the Chinese bureaucracy that it is difficult to single out any study for special recognition, but the following rank among the best: Henry Harding, *Organizing China* (Stanford: Stanford University Press, 1981); A. Doak Barnett, *Cadres, Bureaucracy, and Political Power in Communist China* (New York: Columbia University Press, 1967); Parris Chang, *Power and Policy in China* (University Park: Pennsylvania State University Press, 1975); Stuart R. Schram, ed., *Authority, Participation, and Cultural Change in China* (Cambridge: Cambridge University Press, 1973); and Franz Schurmann, *Ideology and Organization in Communist China* (Berkeley: University of California Press, 1969).

40. Richard Baum, "Science and Culture in Contemporary China: The Roots of Retarded Modernization," *Asian Survey*, 22 (December 1982), 1167.

41. Zhao Ziyang, "Report on the Work of the Government," *Beijing Review*, July 4, 1983, p. xvi.

8. Korea, Taiwan, and Vietnam

1. Gregory Henderson, *Korea: The Politics of the Vortex* (Cambridge, Mass.: Harvard University Press, 1968).

2. Harold C. Hinton, *Korea under New Leadership: The Fifth Republic* (New York: Praeger, 1983), p. 24.

3. Quoted in Donald M. Seekins, "The Society and the Environment," in Frederica M. Bunge, ed., *South Korea: A Country Study*, The American University Foreign Area Studies (Washington, D.C., 1982), p. 69.

4. Psychological anxieties over isolation have been identified as a major explanation for the phenomenal rise of Christianity among urban Koreans, who have found city life lonely and unsettling and are anxious to find communities of fellowship. Current projections suggest that by the 1990s there will be more Christians than Buddhists in Korea, making it second in Asia to the Philippines as a Christian country. See Vincent S. R. Brandt, "Stratification, Integration, and Challenges to Authority in Contemporary South Korea," Department of State, External Research Document, August 31, 1983.

5. The combination of boldness and assertiveness was a conspicuous feature of the faction-ridden history of the Korean Communist movement during the pre-independence period. The story of these conflicts is recorded in Robert A. Scalapino and Chong-sik Lee, *Communism in Korea*, 2 vols. (Berkeley: University of California Press, 1972), vol. I.

6. Martha Wolfenstein, *Disaster: A Psychological Essay* (Glencoe: Free Press, 1957).

7. Stephen L. Keller, "Uprooting and Social Change: The Role of Refugees in Development" (Ph.D. diss., M.I.T., 1970).

8. Stephen Haggard and Tun-jen Cheng, "State Strategies, Local and Foreign Capital in the Gang of Four" (Paper delivered at the Annual Meeting of the American Political Science Association, Chicago, September 1983), pp. 6–7.

9. On the American occupation, see in particular, E. Grant Meade, *American Military Government in Korea* (New York: King's Crown Press, 1951); Sungjoo Han, *The Failure of Democracy in Korea* (Berkeley: University of California Press, 1974).

10. Stephen Haggard and Chung-in Moon, "The South Korean State in the International Economy: Liberal, Dependent, or Mercantile," in John Ruggie, ed., *The Antinomies of Interdependence* (New York: Columbia University Press, 1983), pp. 143–144.

11. Hinton, *Korea under New Leadership*, p. 29.

12. Haggard and Moon, "South Korean State," p. 151.

13. Chalmers Johnson, "Political Institutions and Economic Performance: A Comparative Analysis of Government-Business Relations in Japan, South Korea, and Taiwan," Project on Development, Stability, and Security in the Pacific-Asian Region, University of California, Berkeley, 1983.

14. See Edward S. Mason, et al., *The Economics and Social Modernization of the Republic of Korea* (Cambridge, Mass.: Harvard University Press, 1980); and Leroy P. Jones and Sakong Il, *Government, Business, and Entrepreneurship in Economic Development* (Cambridge, Mass.: Harvard University Press, 1980).

15. Probably the most successful practitioner of this form of political tutelage was Kemal Ataturk, whose competitive spirit was exhilarated by the idea of ordering some of his brightest ministers to form two separate parties and to take each other on, with no holds barred. In designing his replica of a competitive democratic system, Ataturk even went so far as to order the creation of a secret, underground, Communist party whose scheming activities in supposed support of Marxism-Leninism completely addled the Comintern agents assigned to organize Turks for Marxism-Leninism. See Dankwart Rustow, "The Near East," in Gabriel A. Almond and James S. Coleman, eds., *The Politics of the Developing Areas* (Princeton: Princeton University Press, 1960), chap. 4.

16. How a reportedly "government-kept" opposition leader, in order to show his "independence," may feel compelled to attack his country while abroad (with the government, of course, understanding the charade), was shown by the address of Yoo Chi-song, president of the Democratic Korea party, entitled "Legitimacy of Political Regimes and a Perspective on Democracy in Korea," given at the East-West Center, Honolulu, June 22, 1981. Probably no American politician has ever been so anti-American before a foreign audience as Mr. Yoo was anti-Korean—indeed, it is hard to imagine any politician making such strident attacks upon the legitimacy of the system of which he is a part. In his language and his unwillingness to make concessions, Mr. Yoo's speech resembled the rhetoric associated with, say, South African exiles. Yet in the Korean context his performance was apparently dismissed as no more than an effort to pose as an "independent" politician.

17. Studies which testify to the lack of a strong "establishment" to support the government include: David Steinberg, *Korea: Nexus of East Asia* (New York:

American-Asian Educational Exchange, 1968); Sungjoo Han, *The Failure of Democracy in South Korea* (Berkeley: University of California Press, 1974); David Rees, *Crisis and Continuity in South Korea,* Conflict Studies no. 128 (London: Institute for the Study of Conflict, 1981).

18. Cynics note that the first ten minutes of the nine o'clock news are routinely devoted to Chun Doo Hwan's activities, and therefore the news begins at 9:10. Distinguished guests at the Blue House have been astonished by the president's practice of seating himself for dinner at a separate table, a stage higher than the main table, surrounded by a wall of flowers, which further distances him even from powerful U.S. senators and ambassadors. In a further effort to prove his legitimate superiority over all others, his meal is served on a golden plate.

19. *Far Eastern Economic Review,* October 21, 1983.

20. For an excellent report on the movement, which emphasizes its successes in raising rural income, see In-Joung Whang, *Management of Rural Change in Korea: The Saemaul Undong* (Seoul: Seoul National University Press, 1981).

21. For a discussion of the efforts of North Korea to capture the banner of Korean nationalism, see Scalapino and Lee, *Communism in Korea,* II, 870–873. For the argument of South Korean intellectuals that their government is less legitimately nationalistic than that of the North, see Henderson, *Korea: Politics of the Vortex,* chap. 8.

22. On the politics of Korean students, see Thomas W. Robinson, "South Korean Political Development in the 1980s," Department of State, External Research Reports, 1983.

23. Philip Kuznets, "The South Korean Model of Political and Economic Development: Economic Aspects," Department of State, External Research contract 1724–32012, August 25, 1983.

24. Ibid.

25. Eric A. Nordlinger, *On the Autonomy of the Democratic State* (Cambridge, Mass.: Harvard University Press, 1982).

26. Personal communication from Vincent S. R. Brandt.

27. For an eyewitness report of the killing of thousands of Taiwanese by KMT forces, see George H. Kerr, *Formosa Betrayed* (Boston: Houghton Mifflin, 1965). See also Douglas Mendel, *The Politics of Formosan Nationalism* (Berkeley: University of California Press, 1970).

28. T. H. Shen, ed., *Agriculture's Place in the Strategy of Development: The Taiwan Experience* (Taipei: Joint Commission on Rural Reconstruction, 1974).

29. On Taiwan's land reform and early economic development, see Niel H. Jacoby, *U.S. Aid to Taiwan: A Study of Foreign Aid, Self-Help, and Development* (New York: Praeger, 1966); Ch'en Ch'eng, *Land Reform in Taiwan* (Taipei: China Publishing Co., 1961); Shirley W. Y. Kuo, Gustav Ranis, and John C. H. Fei, *The Taiwan Success Story* (Boulder, Colo.: Westview Press, 1981); Karl T. Wright, *Taiwan's Postwar Agricultural Development,* Michigan State University Agricultural Economic Report no. 19 (East Lansing, 1965).

30. Martin M. C. Yang, *Socio-Economic Results of Land Reform in Taiwan* (Honolulu: University Press of Hawaii; East-West Center, 1970); Ralph N. Clough, *Island China* (Cambridge, Mass.: Harvard University Press, 1978), chap. 3.

31. Interviews with Taiwan industrialists, summer 1983.

32. While dining with K'ang Ning-hsiang, a leading *dang-wai* figure, and Antonio Chiang, editor of *The Eighties,* a magazine which through censorship has had several reincarnations, I was asked as a political scientist how one created a real political party. I replied by saying that there are many kinds of political parties, and then went on to describe the Democratic party of Massachusetts as a collection of potentates, each a guardian of his own turf, with none of the principals willing to talk to one another. The more I described the relations among the leaders of the state that has the closest thing to a one-party system in the United States, the more gleeful the Taiwanese politician became, for he was convinced that I was talking about the *dang-wai.*

33. In discussions with such authorities on ethnicity as Walter Connor and Myron Weiner, I have not been able to identify another case in which political cleavages are sharper than social and personal divides. That Taiwan is the exceptional case in this respect may help to explain why politics has such a low degree of saliency there.

34. In political science so much attention has been focused on how people get power that responses to the loss of power have hardly been studied at all. The loss of empire has certainly had interesting, but different, consequences for British and French politics. Japan's defeat by the United States in World War II has had a profound effect on its political culture; unquestionably, the Japanese redirected their psychic energies to the economic realm as they sought to regain greatness. The shock for the KMT was far worse. They thought they had just won a great war that had lasted from 1937 to 1945—far longer than America was strained by Vietnam—but then came defeat by the Chinese Communists. History provides two ideal-type models for responding to such traumatic defeats: the Spanish, who have found it hard to forget that they were once great, and the Swedes, who pretend that they were never the scourge of northern Europe. Although the current generation of KMT leaders seem to incline toward the Swedish example, they may end up overplaying that reaction. Given their moralistic Confucian instincts, they are likely to be more sensitive than most people to the fact that the Swedes have compensated psychologically for their loss of power by becoming more moralistically arrogant than other Europeans. If that were to happen to the Taiwan leadership, they would be truly unbearable, because they started from higher moral ground than the Swedes did.

35. Paradoxically, the limited domestic market which drove Taiwan into export-led growth also encouraged "independence" with respect to technological developments. Taiwanese entrepreneurs could not follow the Korean and postwar Japanese practices of paying for licenses for new technologies because they lacked the cushion of a domestic market and felt they could not afford to forego competing in the lucrative American and European markets, as is required by the marketing limitations of most licensing agreements. Hence the proclivity of the Taiwanese to "copy," "steal," or otherwise treat casually the proprietary rights of others. This propensity also has a deep cultural basis, as witness the efforts of the Chinese Communists to engage in "reverse engineering" and to expect to receive technology transfers at minimal cost.

36. Joseph Buttinger, *A Dragon Defiant: A Short History of Vietnam* (New York: Praeger, 1972), p. ix.

37. This research, which traces peasant behavior back to pre-Confucian traditions, includes the following studies: Samuel L. Popkin, *The Rational Peasant* (Berkeley: University of California Press, 1979); John K. Whitmore, "The Development of Government in Fifteenth Century Vietnam" (Ph.D. diss., Cornell University, 1968); Stephen B. Young, "Unpopular Socialism in United Vietnam," *Orbis*, Summer 1977.

38. Young, "Unpopular Socialism in United Vietnam," p. 229.

39. Ibid., p. 227.

40. Gerald Hickey, *Village in Vietnam* (New Haven: Yale University Press, 1964), chap. 8.

41. Ruth Benedict, *Patterns of Culture* (Boston: Houghton Mifflin, 1934), chap. 6.

42. Paul Mus, Foreword to Hickey, *Village in Vietnam*, p. xxii.

43. Personal conversations with Prime Minister Lee.

44. For details of the complex politics of Hanoi, Peking, Washington, Moscow, and ASEAN, see my "China Factor in Southeast Asia," in Richard H. Solomon, ed., *The China Factor* (Englewood Cliffs: Prentice-Hall, 1981), chap. 8.

45. Henry Kissinger, *Years of Upheaval* (Boston: Little, Brown, 1982), chap. 2.

46. Douglas Pike, *War, Peace, and the Viet Cong* (Cambridge, Mass.: MIT Press, 1969), chap. 2; and his book-length manuscript, "Operational Code of the Vietnamese."

47. Douglas Pike, "Political Institutionalization in Vietnam" (Paper delivered at the Conference on Development, Stability, and Security in the Pacific-Asian Region, University of California, Berkeley, March 20, 1984), p. 6.

48. Ibid., p. 14.

49. Pike, *War, Peace, and the Viet Cong*, p. 62.

50. Buttinger, *A Dragon Defiant*, pp. 26–27.

51. Nathan Leites, "The Viet Cong Style of Politics," RAND Corporation Memorandum RM-5487, May 1969, p. 186.

52. Haggard and Moon, "South Korean State," pp. 147–174.

9. Malaysia

1. I examine in detail the psychodynamics of this Chinese belief that it is acceptable to discuss publicly the way in which one has been taken advantage of by others, and the lack of any sense that such conduct might underline one's own impotence, in *Spirit of Chinese Politics*, pp. 72–77 and 147–150.

2. William C. Parker, Jr., "Repression-Sensitization Tendencies among Urban Chinese and Malays in Malaysia," *The Mankind Quarterly*, 24 (Fall 1983); and his "Cultures in Stress: The Malaysian Crisis of 1969 and Its Cultural Roots" (Ph.D. diss., M.I.T., 1979).

3. Although nearly all studies of Malaysia deal with the ethnic conflicts, the more outstanding works are Milton J. Esman, *Administration and Development in Malaysia* (Ithaca: Cornell University Press, 1972); Walker Connor, "Ethnology and the Peace of Southeast Asia," *World Politics,* 22 (October 1969), 52–86; and Donald L. Horowitz, *Ethnic Groups in Conflict* (Berkeley: University of California Press, 1985), esp. chap. 16.

4. Until the follies of the Cultural Revolution were publicized in the overseas Chinese communities of Southeast Asia, many young Chinese in Malaysia believed that they could become a part of the tide of the future by supporting Maoist ideology, even going to the extreme of joining the Peking-oriented Malaysian Communist party. But when the image of successful revolutionary China collapsed, the young Malaysian Chinese were put in a state of disarray, especially after the Deng Xiaoping regime, in order to help in bailing out the Chinese economy, began courting the prosperous "bourgeois" overseas Chinese—the very people the young Chinese thought they ought to hate.

5. On the organization of the Chinese community in prewar Malaysia, see Victor Purcell, *The Chinese in Southeast Asia* (London: Oxford University Press, 1951); Purcell, *The Chinese in Malaya* (London: Oxford University Press, 1948); and Norton Ginsburg and Chester F. Roberts, Jr., *Malaya* (Seattle: University of Washington Press, 1958).

6. In the early days of colonial rule the British instituted the practice of appointing headmen, or "Capitans," as they were called, in order to communicate with the Malay, Chinese, and Tamil communities. In time, however, the British were shocked to discover that their Chinese "Capitans" were almost without exception the leaders of the secret societies the British were trying to suppress. Leon Comber, *Chinese Secret Societies in Malaya* (Locust Valley, N.Y.: J. J. Augustin, 1959), p. 65. Under the Dangerous Societies Suppression Ordinance of 1869, the commissioner of police was called upon to register and regulate the Chinese secret societies. Rather than trying to eliminate the societies, the police sought their cooperation in helping to keep crime in check in the Chinese communities. That was the beginning of a long friend-and-foe relationship between the police and the societies. Ibid., chap. 10.

7. Significantly, in prewar Malaya and Singapore violent riots frequently occurred, but almost without exception they were not race riots but conflicts within the Chinese community. K. J. Ratnam, *Communalism and the Political Process in Malaya* (Kuala Lumpur: University of Malaya Press, 1965), chap. 1; Comber, *Chinese Secret Societies,* chaps. 6 and 16.

8. Lennox A. Mills, *Malaya: A Political and Economic Appraisal* (Minneapolis: University of Minnesota Press, 1958), pp. 72–74.

9. Ratnam, *Communalism and the Political Process.*

10. The Chinese notion that institutions should "belong" to the top figure, with little room for other notables, is not limited to political organizations. I have been told that when Nanyang University was being set up as a "Chinese" university in Singapore, thousands of Chinese were asked to make contributions. The decision about the principal funds was made, however, at a meeting where the wealthiest *towkays,* or businessmen, were gathered, in which the bidding

went around the room with each one stating the sum he could put up. The "winner" was Tan Lark Sye, who subsequently was acknowledged to be the patron of Nanyang. Thereafter the "losers," in their humiliation, only needed to make modest token contributions. One of these losers was Lien Ying-chow, who later sought revenge by pressing the Singapore government to replace Nanyang University with his Amoy association's school, Ngee Ann, as the principal Chinese university.

11. *Far Eastern Economic Review*, November 6, 1981, pp. 10–12.

12. On the initial negotiations concerning the merger of Singapore and Malaya to form Malaysia, see Willard A. Hanna, *The Formation of Malaysia* (New York: American Universities Field Staff, 1964). On the split, see R. S. Milne, *Government and Politics in Malaysia* (Boston: Houghton Mifflin, 1967), chap. 12.

13. Dato Lee was expressing these views in the mid-1960s, and he died before either Lee Kuan Yew's Singapore administration or Chiang Ching-kuo's Taiwan administration was fully institutionalized. But in view of his British standards of good government, probably nothing that has happened since his death would have altered his judgment that Chinese culture is not consistent with managing an effective and just government.

14. For a report that does not minimize the authoritarian dimensions of the Singapore success story, see T. J. S. George, *Lee Kuan Yew's Singapore* (London: Andre Deutsch, 1973), esp. chaps. 6 and 7.

15. For an account of Malaysian mixed sentiments about leadership styles, see the sympathetic biography of Tengku Abdul Rahman by Harry Miller: *Prince and Premier* (London: George G. Harrap, 1959).

16. The classic study of "direct" and "indirect" rule in the "federated" and "unfederated" states of prewar Malaya is still Rupert Emerson, *Malaya: A Study of Direct and Indirect Rule* (New York: Macmillan, 1937).

17. S. W. Jones, *Public Administration in Malaya* (London: Royal Institute of International Affairs, 1953).

18. Milton J. Esman, *Administration and Development in Malaysia* (Ithaca: Cornell University Press, 1972).

19. Mills, *Malaya: A Political and Economic Appraisal*, chap. 5.

20. See H. M. B. Murphy, "Cultural Factors in the Mental Health of Malaysian Students," in *The Student and Mental Health* (Princeton: Princeton University Press, 1956); and James C. Scott, *Political Ideology in Malaysia* (New Haven: Yale University Press, 1968), pp. 154–158.

21. Scott, *Political Ideology*, pt. II.

22. Esman, *Administration and Development in Malaysia*, chap. 4.

23. Miller, *Prince and Premier*, chaps. 1, 2.

24. M. G. Swift, *Malay Peasant Society in Jelebu*, London School of Economics Monographs on Social Anthropology, no. 29 (London: Athlone Press, 1965).

25. Harry Aveling, in his introduction to Shahnon Ahmad, *Srengenge* (Kuala Lumpur: Heinemann Books, 1973), p. ix.

26. A strong taste for the mystical is helpful in appreciating the kinds of

stories that Malays find most entertaining. See, for example, Ahmad's *Srengenge*. On traditional Malay beliefs, see L. Richmond Wheeler, *The Modern Malay* (London: George Allen & Unwin, 1928), chap. 5.

27. Enough time has passed so that it should not be too humiliating to recount two examples of how Malay belief in magic infected British military discipline and produced comical decisions. When the plane carrying a British general crashed in a thunderstorm in the Pahang mountains and aerial reconnaissance could not find the spot, a mystic on the other side of the peninsula in Malacca informed the British that she had had a vision of the place where the brigadier was pinned down in the wreckage. The British, in their desperation, set up wireless contact between her house and two companies of Seaforth Highlanders, so that she could tell them the exact point at which they should leave the main highway and strike off into the jungle. From 300 miles away she gave them precise instructions, such as "You are coming to a large tree, turn left and 200 yards further on you will cross a brook." After she had led them some six hours into the jungle, she suddenly announced that her vision had mysteriously evaporated. Shamefacedly the British troops had to work their way back over the dense terrain. On another occasion a *bomor* in Selangor approached the British forces and informed them that the Malay Communist guerrilla commander (less than 2 percent of the MCP were non-Chinese) whom they were trying to catch was in fact another *bomor,* and that whenever the British closed in on him he would turn into a fox and disappear. The friendly *bomor* claimed, however, that because his magic was greater than that of the "evil Communist's" the British could apprehend him if they would surround a particular two-square-mile area with a ring of soldiers and then fly him (the good *bomor*) over the area in a plane from which he would sprinkle his superior magic water. He asked that they should reward him with only $500 Malay. The British went along with the scheme, and the troops were instructed to seize any escaping rabbit, for that was what the bad *bomor* would be turned into by the good *bomor.* When, after a two-day stakeout, a rabbit had not appeared, the exercise ended; but one week later, to the puzzlement of the British, the Malay guerrilla leader surrendered. The British predicament became even more awkward when the *bomor* asked for his promised reward.

28. Ginsburg and Roberts, *Malaya,* p. 220.

29. On the Malay Union see Victor Purcell, *Malaya: Communist or Free?* (Stanford: Stanford University Press, 1954), pp. 50–58.

30. Esman, *Administration and Development in Malaysia,* chap. 4.

31. Sir Gerald Templer's design for making Malaya a nation was based on the premise that some ambitious Malay would get the idea that he could achieve immortality by becoming the "father of the nation." He knew that he could not select the candidate, for that would compromise the man's legitimacy. I have reported Templer's explanation of his plans, as he gave them to me in confidence, in "Five Years to Freedom: Sir Gerald Templer's Part in Building a Nation," *The Round Table,* 278 (April 1980), 149–153.

32. Esman, *Administration and Development in Malaysia,* p. 36.

33. Karl von Vorys, *Democracy without Consensus: Communalism and Political Stability in Malaysia* (Princeton: Princeton University Press, 1975).

34. For details of the NEP see Esman, *Administration and Development in Malaysia;* and Robert Klitgaard and Ruth Katz, "Overcoming Ethnic Inequalities: Lessons from Malaysia," *Journal of Policy Analysis and Management,* 2, no. 3 (1983), 333–349.

35. For detailed analysis of comparative incomes after the NEP was initiated, see Klitgaard and Katz, "Overcoming Ethnic Inequalities"; and Michael W. Kusnic and Julie Da Vanzo, *Income Inequalty and the Definition of Income: The Case of Malaysia* (Santa Monica: RAND Corporation, 1980).

36. *The Malay Dilemma,* p. 85, quoted in Klitgaard and Katz, "Overcoming Ethnic Inequalities," p. 339.

37. On the status of the sultans and their relations with non-Malay economic interests, see Vincent W. Lowe, "Sovereignty and Politics in a Multi-Racial Society: The Sultanate in Malaysia" (Ph.D. diss., M.I.T., 1979).

38. For the characterization and evaluation of the "2-M government" I have benefited from Zakaria Haji Ahmed, "Evolutionary Change and Political Systems Development: The Malaysian Case" (Paper presented at the Conference on Development, Stability, and Security in the Pacific-Asian Region, University of California, Berkeley, March 17–21, 1984).

39. For early evaluations of Malaysia's plan to learn from the Japanese experience with economic development, see "Malaysia Looks East" and "Learning from Japan," *Asiaweek,* November 5, 1982, pp. 29–37; Kua Kia Soong, "Look East, but Watch for Blemishes," *Far Eastern Economic Review,* March 31, 1983; and Raphael Pura, "Malaysia's Vague Campaign to Learn from Japan," *Asian Wall Street Journal,* July 13, 1982.

10. Islamic Power

1. Edward Mortimer, *Faith and Power: The Politics of Islam* (New York: Random House, 1982), p. 37.

2. For what is still the classic study of Islamic Reformism, see H. A. R. Gibb, *Mohammedanism: A Historical Survey* (London: Oxford University Press, 1953).

3. For the details of Sayyid Ahmad Khan's thoughts about science and historiography, and the impact of the Aligarh movement in encouraging loyalty to the British empire and separatism from the Hindus, see Aziz Ahmad, *Islamic Modernism in India and Pakistan* (London: Oxford University Press, 1967), chap. 2.

4. Harry J. Benda, *The Crescent and the Rising Sun* (The Hague: Van Hoeve, 1958), p. 37.

5. Ibid., p. 42.

6. The best account of the leadership problems of Sarekat Islam is Robert van Niel, *The Emergence of the Modern Indonesian Elite* (Chicago: University of Chicago Press, 1960).

7. To this day *pesantren* frequently provide an income for *kiyayi,* who in

return give little or no education but demand total loyalty from their students. The idea that such schools are similar to the one run by Mr. Squeers is to be found in V. S. Naipaul, *Among the Believers: An Islamic Journey* (New York: Random House, 1981), p. 335.

8. Benda, *Crescent and the Rising Sun,* p. 74.

9. Ibid., p. 59.

10. Herbert Feith, "Indonesia," in George McT. Kahin, ed., *Governments and Politics of Southeast Asia* (Ithaca: Cornell University Press, 1964), p. 194.

11. Quoted in George McT. Kahin, *Nationalism and Revolution in Indonesia* (Ithaca: Cornell University Press, 1952), p. 48.

12. The outstanding political-behavior study of rural reactions to the Dar'ul Islam rebellion is Karl D. Jackson, *Traditional Authority, Islam, and Rebellion* (Berkeley: University of California Press, 1980).

13. Clifford Geertz, *The Religion of Java* (New York: Basic Books, 1960); and Robert R. Jay, *Religion and Politics in Rural Central Java,* Yale University Southeast Asia Studies Monograph Series (New Haven, 1963).

14. K. J. Ratnam, *Communalism and the Political Process in Malaya* (Kuala Lumpur: Oxford University Press, 1965), p. 228; Norton Ginsburg and Chester F. Roberts, *Malaya* (Seattle: University of Washington Press, 1958), pp. 463–464.

15. Again, the novelist-turned-reporter, V. S. Naipaul, perfectly captures the insecurities among young Malays and Indonesians who idealize their village traditions and feel a need to cluster together in the cities with other orthodox Muslims.

16. Ahmad, *Islamic Modernism,* p. 237.

17. Stanley Wolpert, *Jinnah of Pakistan* (New York: Oxford University Press, 1984).

18. Quoted in Mortimer, *Faith and Power,* p. 208.

19. Ahmad, *Islamic Modernism,* p. 237.

20. Leonard Binder, *Religion and Politics in Pakistan* (Berkeley: University of California Press, 1961).

21. Quoted in Mortimer, *Faith and Power,* p. 224.

22. To achieve the Islamic ideal of banning fixed interest, the Habib banks are to pay "profits" and charge "losses" on deposits that will fluctuate with their investments. See David K. Willis's five-part series on Islam in *Christian Science Monitor,* July 23–27, 1984, especially July 27.

23. Quoted in Ahmad, *Islamic Modernism,* p. 260.

11. The Substance of Asian Power

1. Ryszard Kapuscinski, *The Emperor: Downfall of an Autocrat* (New York: Harcourt Brace Jovanovich, 1983), pp. 145, 134.

2. Surprisingly, this dimension of the "prisoner's dilemma" has not been studied by formal theorists. If game theory were applied to loyalty situations, it

would certainly enrich our understanding of power—possibly in ways more illuminating than when it is applied to the understanding of strategy problems.

3. Takie Sugiyama Lebra, *Japanese Patterns of Behavior* (Honolulu: University Press of Hawaii; East-West Center, 1976), p. 38.

4. Takeo L. Doi, "Amae: A Key Concept for Understanding Japanese Personality Structure," in Richard K. Beardsley and R. J. Smith, eds., *Japanese Culture: Its Development and Characteristics* (Chicago: University of Chicago Press, 1962), p. 26.

5. Lebra, *Japanese Patterns of Behavior*, p. 92.

6. Robert C. Christopher, *The Japanese Mind* (New York: Simon and Schuster, 1983), p. 71.

7. Ibid., p. 72.

8. As Samuel P. Huntington has argued, the American political "creed" is based upon contradictions. Therefore it is not surprising that American politicians are constantly caught in "damned if you do and damned if you don't" situations. Whereas the tendency in other cultures, such as the Japanese, is for leaders to press for the clarification of norms so as to reduce dilemmas based on ambiguities, the American political culture cannot escape its internal tension. Huntington, *The American Political Creed* (Cambridge, Mass.: Harvard University Press, 1983). The American public seems to enjoy the merriment of seeing its leaders caught up in such dilemmas—and the more trivial the material problem, the greater the potential for blowing up the issue and causing pain.

9. The importance of the contextual basis of relationships helps to explain the striking contrast between how Japanese scholars characterize one of their own and how he is seen by foreign scholars. He may indeed be two different men, depending upon whom he is dealing with.

10. For discussions of *guanxi* and factions in Chinese politics, see Andrew J. Nathan, *Peking Politics, 1918–1922* (Berkeley: University of California Press, 1976), chap. 2, and his "A Factionalism Model of CCP," *China Quarterly*, 53 (January-March 1973), 34–66; Jurgen Domes, *The International Politics of China, 1949–1972* (London: C. Hurst, 1973); Alan P. L. Liu, *Political Culture and Group Conflict in Communist China* (Santa Barbara: ABC-Clio Press, 1976); Michel Oksenberg, "Getting Ahead and Along in Communist China: The Ladder of Success on the Eve of the Cultural Revolution," in John W. Lewis, ed., *Party, Leadership, and Revolutionary Power in China* (Cambridge: Cambridge University Press, 1970); and Frederick Teiwes, *Politics and Purges in China* (White Plains, N.Y.: M. E. Sharp, 1979).

11. J. Bruce Jacobs, "A Preliminary Model of Particularistic Ties in Chinese Political Alliances," *China Quarterly*, 78 (June 1979), 237–273.

12. Morton H. Fried, *Fabric of Chinese Society* (New York: Praeger, 1953; reprint, New York: Octagon Books, 1969), p. 226.

13. Lucian W. Pye, *Chinese Commercial Negotiating Style* (Cambridge, Mass.: O.G. & H., 1982).

14. Pye, *Dynamics of Chinese Politics*, p. 141.

15. "The Exit Pattern from Chinese Politics and Its Implications," *China Quarterly*, 67 (September 1976), 502.

16. Pye, *Dynamics of Chinese Politics*, p. 259.

17. According to the rules of Chinese politics, subordinates are only expected to recount the faults of their superiors *after* the downfall of such leaders. After they have been discredited, there is ample opportunity for former subordinates to recount the failings of their bosses; that the subordinates have remained quiet for years is, in the Chinese way of thinking, not a reason for criticizing them. By attacking their fallen leader, former subordinates are merely trying to protect themselves, not necessarily to advance themselves with a new combination of powerful figures. In this respect Chinese behavior is quite different from that of American former officials, who in their published memoirs expose the weaknesses of their former patrons.

18. I have discussed in some detail the role of hostility and anger in Chinese political culture, and how these passions seem to be related to the repression of aggression starting with the demands of filial piety, in my *Spirit of Chinese Politics,* and also in my *Authority Crisis in Chinese Politics* (Chicago: University of Chicago Center for Policy Study, 1967).

19. Donald Emerson, *Indonesia's Elite* (Ithaca: Cornell University Press, 1976).

20. The details of "crony capitalism" have been reported by Emilia Tagaza in the *Christian Science Monitor,* June 22, 1984, p. 9.

21. Paul Quinn-Judge, "Philippines' Laurel: The Opposition's Traditional Politician," *Christian Science Monitor,* April 30, 1984, p. 12.

22. Ibid.

23. Tom Ashbrook, "Aquino's Widow Becomes Symbol for Opposition," *Boston Globe,* May 27, 1984, p. 12; and Quinn-Judge, "Philippines' Laurel."

24. While Ninoy was in exile in America, Imelda met him on several occasions—once to entice him to return to the Philippines as Marcos's prime minister, and once to bribe him not to return. At the end of one of the meetings Ninoy told Imelda that his passport was about to expire—he needed one in order to travel to the Middle East to encourage conservative governments to replace Libya in funding Muslim activities in Mindanao—to which she replied that she would take care of it for him. When he told me that that was the last he had seen of the passport, I said, "Ninoy, you were taken." He immediately decried such an inference, saying that Imelda never would have done such a thing to him and therefore it must have been the timid bureaucrats in the foreign office.

Ninoy's relations with Marcos were also complex and personal. Although Marcos had jailed Ninoy for seven years and seven months, Ninoy felt no personal vengeance but continued to think of him as a fraternity brother who had been badly misguided. One of Ninoy's frustrations during his exile in Cambridge was that Marcos would telephone him from Manila, make an authoritative statement, and then hang up before Ninoy could get in a word. One of the factors which contributed to Aquino's fateful decision to return to Manila was his belief (charmingly naive, in my view) that if the authorities arrested him, Marcos would have to visit him in prison, and there he would have the half hour or so that he believed was all he needed to talk Marcos into restoring democratic institutions.

25. Discussing in Cambridge his planned return to the Philippines, Ninoy once remarked that in his country it took only $100 to hire someone to kill an

enemy, $50 down and $50 afterwards. He was fully aware of the dangers in store for him when he returned—except for the possibility of the army using its own men, a violation of norms which he could not have anticipated.

26. Guy Pauker, "The Role of the Military in Indonesia," in John J. Johnson, ed., *The Role of the Military in Underdeveloped Countries* (Princeton: Princeton University Press, 1962).

27. Ulf Sundhaussen, *The Road to Power: Indonesian Military Politics, 1945–67* (Kuala Lumpur: Oxford University Press, 1982), chap. 6. See also Hamish McDonald, *Suharto's Indonesia* (Honolulu: University Press of Hawaii, 1981).

28. Ulf Sundhaussen, "The Military: Structure, Procedures, and Effects on Indonesian Society," in Karl D. Jackson and Lucian W. Pye, eds., *Political Power and Communications in Indonesia* (Berkeley: University of California Press, 1978), p. 77.

29. Gary E. Hanson, "Bureaucratic Linkages and Policy Making in Indonesia—BIMAS Revisited," in Jackson and Pye, *Political Power*, pp. 322–342.

30. Herbert Feith, *The Decline of Constitutional Democracy in Indonesia* (Ithaca: Cornell University Press, 1962).

31. Ann Willner, "The Neo-Traditional Accommodation to Political Independence: The Case of Indonesia," in Lucian W. Pye, ed., *Cases in Comparative Politics: Asia* (Boston: Little, Brown, 1970).

32. Sundhaussen, *Road to Power,* p. 258.

33. Gary E. Hanson, "Bureaucratic Linkages and Policy Making in Indonesia," in Anne Booth and Peter McCawley, eds., *The Indonesian Economy during the Soeharto Era* (Kuala Lumpur: Oxford University Press, 1982).

34. Sundhaussen, *Road to Power,* p. 195.

35. Benedict Anderson, *Tolerance and the Mythology of the Javanese,* Cornell Modern Indonesia Project Monograph Series (Ithaca, 1965); James T. Siegel, "Images and Odors in Javanese Practices Surrounding Death," *Indonesia,* 36 (October 1983), 1–14; James J. Fox, ed., *The Flow of Life: Essays on Eastern Indonesia* (Cambridge, Mass.: Harvard University Press, 1980).

36. The process of absorbing the princely states has been described in V. P. Menon, *The Story of the Integration of the Indian States* (London: Orient, Longmans, 1956). On the emerging rural power structures after the abolition of the zamindars, *jagirdars, watandars,* and *talukdars* in the early 1950s, see the papers in Richard L. Park and Irene Tinker, eds., *Leadership and Political Institutions in India* (Princeton: Princeton University Press, 1959).

37. Myron Weiner, "India: Two Political Cultures," in Lucian W. Pye and Sidney Verba, *Political Culture and Political Development* (Princeton: Princeton University Press, 1965), pp. 199–244.

38. The best analysis of the operation of the Congress party at the local level is Myron Weiner, *Party Building in a New Nation: The Indian Congress* (Chicago: University of Chicago Press, 1967). The way in which pressure groups sought benefits from both politicians and administrators is described in Weiner's *Politics of Scarcity: Public Pressure and Political Response in India* (Chicago: University of Chicago Press, 1961).

39. The most forcefully argued case for the impending disintegration of India

was Selig S. Harrison, *India: The Most Dangerous Decades* (Princeton: Princeton University Press, 1960).

40. Myron Weiner, *India at the Polls* (Washington: American Enterprise Institute, 1983), p. 4.

41. Paul Brass, "National Power and Local Politics in India: A Twenty-Year Perspective," *Modern Asian Studies*, 18, pt. I (February 1984), 92–122.

42. Ibid., p. 93.

43. Weiner, *India at the Polls*, pp. 9–12.

44. Ibid., p. 136.

45. On the de-institutionalization of the Congress party, see James Manor, "The Dynamics of Political Integration and Disintegration," in A. J. Wilson and Dennis Dalton, eds., *The States of South Asia: Problems of National Integration* (London: C. Hurst, 1983), pp. 89–110.

46. Brass, "National Power and Local Politics in India," pp. 95–99.

47. *The Economist* (London), June 9, 1984.

48. Brass, "National Power and Local Politics in India," pp. 112–116.

49. Myron Weiner, "Institution Building in South Asia: British Tutelage Regimes and Their Future Potential" (Paper mimeographed for Project on Development, Stability, and Security in the Pacific-Asian Region, November 1983), p. 13.

50. Ibid., p. 9.

51. The novel *Shame* (New York: Alfred A. Knopf, 1983) by Salman Rushdie is unquestionably one of the most devastating (and also penetrating) criticisms of Pakistani pretensions to power.

12. Paternalistic Authority and the Triumph of Dependency

1. Although the West during the Middle Ages had the idea that legitimacy came from divine sanctions—Henry IV declared that "Jesus Christ our Lord called us to the throne," and Charlemagne declared that he had been "crowned by God"—it had been believed as early as Aristotle that the authority of the polis came from the citizens. The Roman Empire introduced the idea that legitimacy was derived from the laws, which was the starting point of Max Weber's analysis of "rational-legal" authority. Carl Schmitt, however, made a distinction between legality and legitimacy by noting that laws might be passed but be illegitimate if they failed the test of public acceptance. For the classic statement that legitimacy comes from the people and not from above, see Charles H. McIlwain, *Constitutionalism: Ancient and Modern* (Ithaca: Cornell University Press, 1940; rev. ed., 1947); and Carl J. Friedrich, *Man and His Government* (New York: McGraw-Hill, 1963).

2. David Apter has written about the efforts to create new myths of legitimacy in developing countries; see in particular his "Political Religion in the New States," in Clifford Geertz, ed., *Old Societies and New States* (New York: Free Press, 1963).

3. Clifford Geertz, as an anthropologist, took the lead in suggesting that the creation of ideologies in new states could serve the function which culture did in integrating traditional political systems. See particularly his essays "Ideology as a Cultural System," "After the Revolution," "The Fate of Nationalism in the New States," and "The Integrative Revolution: Primordial Sentiments and Civil Politics in the New States," in his *Interpretations of Culture* (New York: Basic Books, 1973).

4. The idea that ideologies which are capable of shaping history are manifestations of the deep psychological experiences of their innovators was advanced first by Erik H. Erikson, *Young Man Luther: A Study in Psychoanalysis and History* (New York: W. W. Norton, 1958).

5. Indian policymakers have consistently acted in ways which have left their country with the worst of both worlds—that of central planning and that of market allocations. The best analysis of this situation is still Jagdish Bhagwati and Podma Desai, *India: Planning for Industrialization* (New York: Oxford University Press, 1970).

6. On the borderline personality type, see Donald B. Rinsley, *Borderline and Other Self Disorders* (New York: Jason Aronson, 1982). For an account of Mao's psychological development that points out symptoms of a borderline personality, see my *Mao Tse-tung: The Man in the Leader* (New York: Basic Books, 1976).

7. One of the earliest observers to note this phenomenon of traditionalist sentiments was Ann Wilner, "The Neotraditional Accommodation to Political Independence: The Case of Indonesia," in Lucian W. Pye, ed., *Cases in Comparative Politics: Asia* (Boston: Little, Brown, 1970).

8. Edward Shorter, *The Making of the Modern Family* (New York: Basic Books, 1975), p. 4 (quotation).

9. For a general review of urbanization processes, see the UNESCO study: Sidney Goldstein and David F. Sly, eds., *Patterns of Urbanization: Comparative Country Studies* (Dolhain, Belgium: Ordina Edition, n.d.).

10. On the nature of secondary narcissism, see Otto Fenichel, *The Psychoanalytical Theory of Neurosis* (New York: W. W. Norton, 1945); and Sigmund Freud, "On Narcissism: An Introduction," in *Collected Papers*, ed. Ernest Jones, trans. Joan Riviere (New York: Basic Books, 1959), IV, 30–59.

11. For an explanation of the ways in which "separation" and the Oedipus complex can be accompanied by repression and denial and can only be brought back into consciousness by the defense mechanism of negation, see Anika Lemaire, *Jacques Lacan* (London: Routledge and Kegan Paul, 1977), p. 75 and chap. 7.

12. Freud, in both *Beyond the Pleasure Principle* (1920) and *Civilization and Its Discontents* (1930), demonstrated his belief that the imposition of the superego by moral authorities, parents, or society tended to repress the id and create aggressive feelings in the form of frustrations. For an analysis of the relationship between the origin of the superego and the attitudes toward the moralizing institutions of society, see Franz Alexander, "Psychoanalysis and Social Disor-

ganization," in his *Scope of Psychoanalysis: Selected Papers of Franz Alexander* (New York: Basic Books, 1961).

13. One of the best reviews of changing Japanese attitudes toward the United States in the postwar years was written by the staff of the Asahi Shimbun: *The Pacific Rivals: A Japanese View of Japanese-American Relations* (New York and Tokyo: Weatherhill; Asahi, 1972).

14. The ambivalence of children in wanting to see adults ("giants") harmed although they know that they need strong parents is charmingly analyzed through the study of fairy tales in Bruno Bettelheim's *Uses of Enchantment* (New York: Random House, 1975).

15. Widespread criticism of authority, especially by intellectuals, in Korea, Taiwan, Singapore, and the Philippines is matched by only modest and disorganized opposition movements, which must be explained in part by the repressive tactics of the respective regimes. All the suffering in China, especially during and after the Cultural Revolution, has not produced a significant dissident movement, even among those who have left the country.

16. Max Weber's analysis of patrimonialism is to be found in his *Theory of Social and Economic Organization* (New York: Oxford University Press, 1947), pp. 341–363. For further discussion of patrimonial authority see S. N. Eisenstadt, *Political Sociology* (New York: Basic Books, 1970), pp. 138–145; and Lloyd and Susanne Rudolph, "Authority and Power in Bureaucratic and Patrimonial Administration," *World Politics,* 24 (July 1982), 548–559.

17. Richard Samuels has explored the question whether the concept of corporatism, developed by Philippe C. Schmitter among others, is applicable to pressure groups in Japan, and he has concluded that significant differences exist; see his *Politics of Regional Policy in Japan* (Princeton: Princeton University Press, 1983), chap. 6.

18. For the most forceful statement of the incompatibility of dependency with the innovative spirit that is essential for modernization, see Everett E. Hagen, *On the Theory of Social Change: How Economic Growth Begins* (Homewood, Ill.: Dorsey Press, 1962).

19. On the problem of rationality when caught between immediate advantages and the apparent "irrationalities of contributing to the public good," see Thomas Schelling, *Choice and Consequences* (Cambridge, Mass.: Harvard University Press, 1984).

20. Significantly, there is a direct relationship between the depth of scholarly knowledge about the operation of the Asian political systems and the degree of scholarly understanding that policies are not the prime concern of Asian politicians. Scholars working on India who write about the politics of that country give only passing attention to policy protestations, since it took just one five-year plan to illuminate Indian political priorities. By contrast, scholars working on the more secretive Chinese political system tend to use policy pronouncements as guidelines for their analysis, even though over the decades the Chinese have manifestly used power for politics more than for policy implementation.

21. Daniel Lerner, *The Passing of Traditional Society* (New York: Free Press

of Glencoe, 1958); and Alex Inkeles, *Exploring Individual Modernity* (New York: Columbia University Press, 1983).

22. Gerschenkron's original statement is to be found in his *Bread and Democracy in Germany* (Berkeley: University of California Press, 1943; reprint ed., New York: Howard Fertig, 1966). The thesis is elaborated in his *Economic Backwardness in Historical Perspective* (Cambridge, Mass.: Harvard University Press, 1962), and in his *Continuity in History, and Other Essays* (Cambridge, Mass.: Harvard University Press, 1968).

Index